RIGHT WORDS

RIGHT WORDS

A Guide to English Usage in Australia

STEPHEN MURRAY-SMITH

Viking
Penguin Books Australia Ltd,
487 Maroondah Highway, P.O. Box 257
Ringwood, Victoria 3134, Australia
Penguin Books Ltd,
Harmondsworth, Middlesex, England
Penguin Books,
40 West 23rd Street, New York, N.Y. 10010, U.S.A.
Penguin Books (Canada) Limited,
2801 John Street, Markham, Ontario, Canada L3R 1B4
Penguin Books (N.Z.) Ltd,
182-190 Wairau Road, Auckland 10, New Zealand

First published 1987 by Viking
Reprinted 1987
2nd edition 1989

Typeset in 90% Times Roman by Leader Composition Pty Ltd
Made and printed in Australia by Australian Print Group, Maryborough, Victoria

Murray-Smith, Stephen, 1922–88.
Right words.

ISBN 0670 82825 4.

1. English language – Australia – Usage. 2. English
language – Australia – Errors of usage. I. Title.

428.1'0994

Words without thoughts never to heaven go.
Hamlet, III. iii. 78

Words are the daughters of earth.
Samuel Johnson

To talk about words is to talk about life, and to talk about life is to risk inanity, error and offence.

D. J. Enright

Literature being personal, and men various ... man's use or defiance of the dictionary depends for its justification on nothing but his success: ... since it takes all kinds to make a world, or a literature, his success will probably depend on the occasion.

Arthur Quiller-Couch

For last year's words belong to last year's language
And next year's words await another voice.
T. S. Eliot

It's *ow* and *garn* that keep her in place.
Professor Higgins, in *My Fair Lady*

Then said they unto him, Say now Shibboleth; and he said Sibboleth: for he could not frame to pronounce it right. Then they took him, and slew him at the passages of Jordan ...

Judges, xii. 6

I think of it as it should have been, with its prolixities docked, its dullnesses enlivened, its fads eliminated, its truths multiplied.
H. W. Fowler

Introduction to Second Edition

Since the publication of *Right Words* a little over a year ago letters discussing the book and its entries, and offering suggestions and support, have arrived in almost every post. Obviously there are a lot of Australians interested in, and worried about, their language.

These hundreds of correspondents have greatly helped in the expansion — over three hundred new entries — and the revision of the book for the second edition. I would like especially to acknowledge the help of John Bangsund, Bruce Cameron, David Castle, Dudley Clarke, Gabriel Crowley, Rob Darby, Beatrice Davis, Hume and Gwen Dow, David Ferber, Brian Gallwey, R. G. Gillis, David Glover, John Herovim, Ken Inglis, Stuart McIntosh, Lilith Norman, John Playford, Dennis Pryor, Mary Scouller, Clement Semmler, Geoffrey Serle, Sir Robert Southey, Helen Williams and Keith Windschuttle.

Stephen Murray-Smith

Introduction

"Language is not an intellectual construct," writes Anthony Burgess, "but the property of the people. Nobody is better than anyone else at it."

"You are told by experts," Dorothy Green has written, "that language has to change. To which the only retort is that it does not necessarily change for the better and there is no reason it should change overnight because some illiterate ass has a microphone in front of his mouth."

Both Anthony Burgess and Dorothy Green are right. Language belongs to us all, and we speak that language as we please. In speaking as we wish, we help to create the new language that is always being born out of the old. Still, if you call a cabbage a clock people will have difficulty in understanding what you mean. It is worth trying to reach at least temporary agreements about the way we use words.

If we may speak as we wish then we may also think as we wish. Everyone has views on the way language should be used. We may differ as to whether the evening meal is to be called *dinner* or *tea*, or as to whether we should say *aitch* or *haitch*, but we all have an opinion on the matter. Sensible people will accept the views of another only if they concede the competence of that other and if they consider those views coherent and reasonable.

Some modern theorists of language consider it to be something that 'just happens', believe the only justification for *any* use of language is that it *is* so being used. We don't agree. We believe, with George Orwell, that language is not only a natural growth but also something we shape for our own purposes. Every time someone urges the rest of us to abandon the word *nigger* or adopt the word *Ms* they are admitting this. People have always argued about language; these debates have in many cases changed the way language is used. We are not suggesting that you can drive the word *defeatism* out of the language by declaring it a non-word, as the French Academy is said to have done (it does not appear in my French dictionary), but we are saying that the way words are used depends on some kind of agreement between past and present. This book is an attempt to draft some agreements or, if you like, to "distinguish between mutations and excrescences", as Herman Wouk puts it.

At the risk of laboring the point, we believe that English is an infinitely flexible language, that much of its strength has come from varieties of use that are 'demotic', or 'vulgar', or 'non-received', whatever that last may mean. We also believe that the language loses as well as gains by attempts to impose or suggest rules. At the same time it is no use pretending, as dictionaries too often pretend, that words themselves, and the way words are used, have no values apart from their intrinsic meaning. Not only are there gradations in the acceptance of words and phrases within all social groups and by all individuals, but many people seek information on such gradations — what is 'right' and what is 'wrong' — from dictionaries and other texts. This makes some students of language uneasy; it introduces the concept of 'privilege'. But that concept is there at all times and in all languages; to evade it because it offends against some canon of hyperdemocracy is no service to the language or its users. The best that we can hope for is that such matters will not be ignored, but will be handled with reasonable sensitivity and liberality by those who write about language, or define or collect it.

Right Words has a number of aims. We seek to set out some helpful rules in the speaking and writing of English. We wish to discuss words in an interesting way, so that some of the subtlety and immanent power of words can be glimpsed. We wish to illuminate common solecisms and confusions, so that they may be avoided. We wish to encourage debate rather than to end it, and we try to avoid being too prescriptive. Above all we wish, where appropriate and possible, to apply an *Australian* understanding to words.

For we believe it is time for a specifically *Australian* guide to the use of our language. Studies in the Australian language and in Australian literature are reaching some sophistication. There is a greater awareness than there ever has been of our own contribution to the English language. There are certainly more people in Australia than ever before anxious to use the spoken and the written word in the service of their own careers. It is ridiculous that we should have to remain dependent on guides to the use of the English language which do not approach that language through two hundred years of cultural adaptation.

But how distinct as a variety of English is the Australian language? Does it diverge from 'standard' English (whatever that may be) by only a few home-grown words and a distinct accent? Does it still adhere, in other words, to some kind of 'mother-tongue' norm? Or is it, as H. L. Mencken tried to assert American English was, a legitimate, independent growth flourishing on its own ground? Or is it, as David Maurer has suggested American English is, a conglomerate of the languages of specialised subcultures within the whole community?

Australian English has not had the long history of American English, nor its rich speech-communities. For imperial reasons it has remained in much closer contact with the 'steadying' influence of English English. Our institutions, especially our educational institutions, were based on English and Scottish models. Our literate immigrants of the nineteenth century and after were predominantly British. Our books and magazines today, when foreign, are largely British. Neither social nor geographic mobility has been as marked as in the United States. In cadence, stress, even in grammar there are signs that we are following the American path towards greater independence, but that independence can — fortunately — never be fully achieved so long as English remains an international language. We remain, however, very much closer to the fount than does American English. Despite American intrusions in vocabulary and phrasing, and sometimes in spelling, the resistance of Australian English to American penetration is more surprising than its acceptance of it.

So we stand somewhere between the two great streams of English, the British and the American, and rather closer to the British. We dip our buckets into both rivers. We are fortunate to be part of the same language stock, and to be able to do so. We are also fortunate in having a lively, effective language that, especially in informal discourse, is recognisably our own. We have the best of all worlds.

This book recognises our right to pick and choose to suit ourselves, sometimes plumping for a rationality which overthrows the British tradition, sometimes for a traditionalism which rejects the American.

Right Words has had many predecessors more distinguished than itself. All who have worked in the field must first bow before H. W. Fowler's *A Dictionary of Modern English Usage* (1926) and its revision by Sir Ernest Gowers (1965). I am a writer, a teacher and a literary editor, not a grammarian or academic student of English; but I should not have attempted the level of grammatical discussion in Fowler and Gowers even had I been capable of so doing. Fowler and Gowers were writing for a wide stratum of educated speakers of English, in Britain and elsewhere. Any similar enterprise in Australia must recognise that here such an audience is much smaller. In attempting to arouse interest in the nuances of language, we have further to go.

We all use the language as best we can, in haste, harassed, beset, with multiple demands on our powers of expression even at the one time. No-one can possibly always be a paragon of good language. If everyone tried to be, it would make communication all but impossible and would bode ill for the health of the language. I therefore apologise to those whose names have been quoted as offenders in entries herein. We are all sinners, we are all outrageously ignorant of things we should know. There is no intention to point the finger at real people in any punitive way. Names are mentioned solely because they make the examples more immediate. None of us would wish to have our hurried daily writing, let alone our speech, analysed for infelicity. Who would escape whipping?

Right Words is in no sense a definitive work. It seeks merely to contribute to discussion on the way we use English in Australia. For the most part, of course, we use English in Australia very much as English is used elsewhere. Where there are important differences, these will be the concern of the folklorist, the collector of colloquialisms, the specialist dictionary-maker and the phonetician. This book, however, is directed to those using the English language in Australia, rather than to those studying it. There are many omissions, many debatable points, no doubt some errors. Comments and suggestions of all kinds are welcomed, and should be sent to me at P.O. Box 249, Mt Eliza, Victoria, 3930.

They will be made use of in subsequent editions of this book.

Many friends and colleagues have made suggestions. I owe special gratitude to Arthur Phillips who, before his death in 1985, and despite infirmity, laboriously annotated a number of my slips with a crisp clarity of comment that belied his advanced age and rouses regret that, despite his immense experience in teaching and criticism, he never wrote this book himself. I have gained from his support, his mockery, his wisdom and his wit.

Others who have patiently responded to queries or who have made valuable suggestions include Janet Mackenzie, Wendy Sutherland, John Curtain, Stuart Macintyre, Geoffrey Leeper, Dennis Pryor, Alison Patrick, Rhys Jones, George Russell, Ian Mair and Kenneth Gott. Jilea Carney, of the Australian Broadcasting Corporation's Standing Committee on Spoken English, kindly supplied me with the minutes and memoranda of that body.

Stephen Murray-Smith

Classified Guide

The majority of entries in *Right Words* discuss individual words and phrases. There are, however, a number of entries on more general topics. These include:

Grammatical terms and concerns

adjectives
adverbs
apostrophes
can/could
case
clause
collective nouns
conjunctions
determiners
double negative
double possessives
hanging participles
interjections
may/might
modifiers
mood
nouns
noun to verb: is change decay?
number

participles
parts of speech
passive voice
phrase
the possessive and the 's' sound
predicate
prepositions
prepositions at the end
pronouns
shall/will
should/would
tense
that/which/who/whose
thee/thine/thou
the subjunctive: is it still alive?
to gerund or not to gerund
verbs
verbs: the old declensions
who/whom

Spelling

-able/-ible
-æ-
apostrophes
doubling up
ei and ie
-er/-or
-ey/-y
footie/footy
in-/un-

-ise/-ize
-lyse/-lyze
-œ-
-or/-our
plurals
plurals of -f and -fe
plurals of -o
the silent 'e'
spelling reform in Australia

apostrophes

full stops

brackets

hyphens

colons

oblique stroke

commas

question marks

dashes

quote/unquote

dots

semi-colons

exclamation marks

paragraphs

Pronunciation

Aboriginal names

oo or yoo?

accent

place names

aitch/haitch

pronunciation in Australia

dance/darnce

General topics

abbreviations

moribund metaphors and similes

academic English

the Mr/Mrs/Ms problem

apartment/condominium/flat

numbers

book titles

offensive intruders

bourgeois

perpetual calendar

bully words

Pidgin

capitals

pleonasms

clichés

political terminology in Australia

educational nomenclature

poseur words and phrases

euphemisms

puffery

the female critique

referencing

foreign words and phrases

regionalism in Australian language

geographical names

slang

indicator words

spelling reform in Australia

jargon

suburban nomenclature

lost singulars

tautology

metaphor

titles

metaphorical mischief

the wandering what

misquotations

working class

Pronunciation, Cross-reference and Style

Pronunciations, where given here, are expressed in 'common sense' terms, often by suggesting a rhyme with another word. No attempt has been made at consistency in this, nor has a phonetic pronunciation system been adopted. Exact pronunciation guides are available in every standard dictionary, and this book does not set out to be a dictionary.

What has been aimed at is an unambiguous guide to *approximate* pronunciation where it is felt an entry requires such guidance. Similarly, stress or accent has only been indicated where it was felt desirable to do so, and then by the use of capital letters. YOUR-annis, for example, is given as the (approximate) pronunciation of *uranous*. The capital letters represent the accent on this word.

Cross-references are indicated by the use of bold type, thus: **hanging participles.** Where a word or phrase in an entry appears in this form, there is a separate entry on it.

The 'style' adopted by the publishers of this book accepts the recommendations of the author in regard to spelling, punctuation and other matters.

A

A.

1. The story, quite unashamedly stolen from Fritz Spiegl of the *Listener* magazine, is that Winston Churchill was visiting the Archbishop of Canterbury at Lambeth Palace. The Archbishop was complaining of the upkeep of the Palace: "We have forty-two bedrooms." "How very inconvenient," Churchill is said to have replied, "especially when one reflects that you have only thirty-nine Articles."

Spiegl used this excellent story to introduce a complaint about the disappearance of the article (*a, an, the*) in much modern writing and speaking. To put the matter in Australian terms, the complaint is that, instead of *the Premier of Victoria, John Cain* we hear or read *Premier of Victoria John Cain*. Instead of *Jasper Quill, the Clerk of Courts and Coroner at Tumbarumba, said,* we are likely to hear *Tumbarumba Clerk of Courts and Coroner Jasper Quill said* . . . Instead of *Karl Marx, bearded and burly, and an inveterate bookworm, was usually to be seen at the British Museum Reading Room,* we get *Bearded, burly bookworm Karl Marx (48) was usually to be seen* . . . and so on.

It saves space and is legitimate in what was termed *telegraphese* (presumably, these days, *teleprinterese*), but it is inelegant and is not how people talk to each other.

2. The letter *a* is pronounced like *a* (that is, like *hay* without the *h*). It is not pronounced *ee*, although Australian Broadcasting Corporation announcers, referring to the EBC, apparently believe it is.

a/an. As in *a historian, an historian*. See **an historian, an hotel?**

abalone. Critics of American cultural imperialism will of course refer to this useful shellfish by the traditional Australian name of *mutton-fish*.

Abandon hope all ye who enter here. This is frequently said to be the warning to those approaching Dante's Inferno. Not quite. *Lasciate ogni speranza, voi che entrate* means *All hope abandon, ye who enter here.*

abbreviations. We are used to indicating words that are normally abbreviated in writing by placing a full stop after the abbreviation, thus:

> The baboons, hyenas etc. then boarded Noah's Ark.
> The St. Kilda tram leaves from Swanston Street.
> The motion was passed *nem. con.,* after a lot of discussion.

1

There is now an increasing tendency to omit the full stop *when an abbreviation ends with the same letter as the full word does.* Thus such words as Saint, Doctor, Street and Road are abbreviated as *St, Dr, St* and *Rd*, without any stops.

Other abbreviations retain the full stop: *Rev.* for the Reverend, for instance, and *Cres.* for Crescent.

It should also be noted that in one or two cases it is becoming more common to drop the full stop in any case. Thus *per cent.*, short for *per centum*, is now very often written or printed simply as *per cent,* and the word *ibid.*, used in scholarly publications (meaning *in the same place,* an abbreviation of *ibidem*) is now frequently printed as *ibid*, without a full stop after it.

Such simplifications are to be welcomed.

See also **metric abbreviations.**

abdomen. The preferred pronunciation of this word is with the stress on the first syllable, but the alternative pronunciation is with the stress on the second.

In the adjective *abdominal* the stress has to go on the second syllable.

abeyance. See **in abeyance.**

abide.
1. In the sense of *stay* ("Abide with me") the past tense of *to abide* is *abode: She abode with her grandmother.*
2. In the sense of *standing by an undertaking* the past tense is *abided: He was known as a man who abided by his promises.*

abjure/adjure. Both these are verbs.

Abjure means to *renounce or repudiate.* Persons taking on a new nationality are sometimes required to *abjure* their old one. The Vicar of Bray, in the famous old song, tells how he

almost every day abjured
The Pope and the Pretender.

Adjure means *to solemnly charge or bind someone with a responsibility: He adjured me, in the event of his death, to look after his wife and children.*

-able/-ible.
1. How do we know when adjectives should be formed in *-able*, and when they should be formed in *-ible*? Is it *destructible* or *destructable, forcible* or *forceable, refusible* or *refusable*? (The answers here are *destructible, forcible* and *refusable*.)

The answer is that there are no rules which will help us much, unless we know Latin, and even that will not be of great use.

The two solutions to this problem are (a) familiarity, and (b) a dictionary. To assist with (a), we print the following examples:

ABLE

actionable	forgettable	peaceable
adorable	forgivable	personable
advisable	immovable	preferable
agreeable	immutable	probable
amenable	impassable	provable
amiable	impenetrable	rat(e)able
analysable	impressionable	reasonable
arguable	improvable	regrettable
believable	inalienable	removable
blam(e)able	incalculable	sal(e)able
changeable	inconceivable	serviceable
chargeable	incurable	tam(e)able
comfortable	indispensable	teachable
conceivable	inestimable	tenable
conversable	inflatable	tolerable
debatable	inviolable	translatable
definable	irreconcilable	treasonable
delineable	lik(e)able	tun(e)able
demonstrable	lovable	uncontrollable
detestable	malleable	undeniable
dissolvable	manageable	unendurable
drinkable	movable	ungovernable
dutiable	nam(e)able	unmistakable
eatable	notable	unpronounceable
endorsable	noticeable	unquenchable
excisable	palatable	unshak(e)able

IBLE

accessible	edible	indefensible
adducible	eligible	indelible
admissible	expressible	indestructible
audible	fallible	inexhaustible
avertible	feasible	inflexible
collapsible	fencible	intangible
comprehensible	flexible	irascible
compressible	forcible	irresistible
contemptible	gullible	legible
controvertible	impressible	negligible
credible	incomprehensible	ostensible
deducible	incorruptible	perceptible
discernible	incredible	permissible
divisible	indefeasible	persuasible

3

plausible	responsible	susceptible
reducible	reversible	tangible
reprehensible	submersible	transmissible
repressible	suggestible	vendible
resistible	suppressible	visible

2. There is sometimes a problem as to whether or not to drop an -*e* before adding -*able*. The general rule here is that the -*e* is dropped before -*able except when it is necessary to retain the -e to prevent a change in the sound of the word.*

Thus we drop the -*e* in such words as *conceivable* and *debatable*, but retain it with *changeable* and *peaceable* because otherwise we would end up with *changable* (which could be pronounced with the *chang-* rhyming with *hang*) or *peacable* (which could be pronounced *peak-able*).

Exceptions to this are the following words, which retain the -e, or may do so:

blameable	nameable	timeable
giveable	rateable	tuneable
hireable	saleable	unshakeable
likeable	sizeable	
liveable	tameable	

See also **spelling reform in Australia.**

Aboriginal/Aborigine. The recommended use is *Aboriginal* for one such person, *Aboriginals* or *Aborigines* for more than one.

The word, like the word *Negro* or the word *Black*, always takes a capital letter. John Lloyd, at the time editor of the London *New Statesman*, said that "it's both daft and patronising to think you're doing people a favor by giving them a capital letter," and there's a point to his remark, but if an Australian or German, Arab or Jew can have a capital letter, then so can an Aboriginal or a Negro.

Many are puzzled as to why *Aborigine* is not favored for the singular, and it seems worth explaining this. There is certainly a Latin phrase *ab origine* which means *from the beginning*, but it is not *ab origine* from which the word *Aboriginal* directly comes.

Our word *Aboriginal* comes from the Latin plural noun *Aborigines*, a word which meant the people who were in Italy before the Romans. This Latin word does not have a singular form, and to impose one on it is equivalent to saying *a scissor*. In other words, there is no such thing. If a singular is required, it is considered best by many that we avoid doing violence to the Latin derivation of this word, and use the adjectival *Aboriginal* as a singular instead.

So, if you want to be strictly correct, the simplest thing is to avoid the word *Aborigine* altogether and always use *Aboriginal,* both in the singular and plural.

The word *Black* or *Blacks* is also used in Australia to denote Aboriginals. This is not because the word was common in the nineteenth century and therefore has some historical justification, but because American Negroes in recent years have preferred the word *Black* to the word *Negro*, and some Aboriginals see virtue in the strength of the *Black/White* juxtaposition. *Black* is not, however, accepted by all Aboriginals.

The word *aborigines*, used in a generic sense to mean the original inhabitants of any country, should be spelt with a small *a*.

See also **gin; half-caste; Koori; lubra; Murri; Nunga.**

Aboriginal names. The following is the recommended pronunciation of the names of some Aboriginal language groups:

Pitjantjatjara	*pi-jen-je-JAH-er* (the shortened pronunciation *pi-jen-JAH-er* is also permissible)
Pintupi	*PIN-too-bee*
Yankuntjatjara	*YAHN-koon-che-jah-er*
Luritji	*LOO-re-jee*
Arrernte (Aranda, Arunta)	*AH-ren-de*
Anmatyira	*ahn-MAH-je-er*
Katitye	*KY-di-je*
Walpiri	*WAHL-be-ree*
Waramungu (Warramunga)	*WO-re-moong-oo*
Ngatjatjara	*NAH-je-jah-er*

abridge/bridge. A gap cannot be *abridged.* The verb *to abridge* has only one meaning, *to shorten, condense, curtail: The manuscript was most skilfully abridged before publication in the 'condensed book' series.*

abstruse/obtuse. Something that is *abstruse* is *hard to understand.* The word comes from Latin words meaning *thrust away, out of reach. Obtuse* has several meanings, the main one being *mentally slow, stupid, slow to feel or comprehend.* An *obtuse pain* is, in medical circles, one that is *indistinct, hard to locate,* and the word comes from the Latin word for *dulled.*

absurd. This word is sometimes pronounced *absurd* and sometimes *abzurd.* Both pronunciations are found in British English, American English and Australian English. *Absurd* is more common and has the more general approval. To this writer, at least, *abzurd* sounds affected.

abyss. An *abyss* is *a deep gorge.* It is pronounced *a-BISS,* though a frequent Australian mispronunciation is *ABB-iss.*

academic/academe. An *academic* in Australia used to mean a member of the teaching staff of a university. The word has now also been adopted by the teaching staffs of colleges of advanced education to describe themselves. There is undoubtedly an element of status-seeking in this, but the matter will not arouse opposition from those who believe that the distinctions imposed between sectors of higher education in Australia are illegitimate.

Academe (pronounced to rhyme with *sack a team*) as a synonym for *the ambience of existence in a university setting* is strictly speaking incorrect, as *Academe* is in fact a shortened form of the name of the Greek hero *Academus*. Plato and his successors taught in a grove of olive trees near Athens sacred to Academus. Milton wrote in *Paradise Regained* of "the olive grove of Academe," and the phrase *groves of Academe* (with a capital A) is correct.

academic/academician. An *academic* (see above) is not an *academician*. An *academician* is *a member of an academy*, defined as *an institution or society concerned with the advancement of literature, art, science etc.* Perhaps the most famous academy is the French Academy of forty of the most distinguished figures in French cultural life, founded in 1635 but by no means the earliest of the great academies. Australian academies are the Australian Academy of Science, the Australian Academy of the Humanities and the Australian Academy of Technological Sciences. The word *academies* is also, somewhat confusingly, used to refer to universities and colleges of advanced education in Australia.

academic English is a horrible corrupt dialect of the English language, used by teachers in tertiary institutions in order to sound cleverer than they really are and thus to win promotion, power and money.

The following are examples taken from just *one* recent academic article written in Australia. The preferred wording is in brackets.

characterised from a number of positions [seen]
provide ways of understanding [understand]
the extent of the hegemony [the dominance]
To look back from a developmental point of view [to look back]
reveals the degree to which the incidence of oppositional stances [reveals that opposition]
the struggles documented in the past [the struggles of the past]
Such social conditions as we now enjoy [Present social conditions]
It is a familiar thematic [It is a familiar theme]
The extent of the callousness [The callousness]
the political construction of its subjects' lives [the politics of its characters' lives]
which questions the natural views of reality [which questions reality]
This is happening, apparently currently [This is happening]

it deals with particular, often marginalised, sections of that context [it deals with its margins]

They may collectively indicate a renovation of the cinematic representation of life in Australia [They suggest a new way of looking at Australia in film]

Consensual views of Australian life do not interest them [They are not looking for consensus]

It proposes a more radical reading position of questioning [It suggests questioning]

given the established convention of realism's signification of historical truth [given the established realist conventions]

Formally, it is a benchmark of the value of departing from the established norms and practices [Its originality is a milestone]

foregrounding its function [emphasising its function]

operated as a provocation for the production [led to production]

appropriation of generic conventions from overseas to make entertaining spectacles [to make entertaining spectacles on overseas models]

accent. Many words in English are spelt the same but are pronounced differently, according to meaning and function.

Accent or *stress*, the force with which a part of a word is pronounced, is of considerable importance in English, although not, for instance, in French. Try asking someone what an *up-hols-TERer* is.

The noun *increase*, for example, has the accent or emphasis on *in-*, the first syllable. The verb, however, has the emphasis on *-crease.*

Many speakers in Australia today seem to be unaware of such distinctions.

The following are both nouns and verbs, distinguished in pronunciation by the noun's having the stress on the first syllable, the verb on the last syllable:

abstract	convert
accent	convict
collect	convoy
combat	defect
comment	descant
compound	desert
compress	detail
concert	dictate
conduct	digest
conflict	discharge
consort	discount
content	entrance
contest	escort
contract	essay
contrast	exploit

7

export	pervert
extract	present
ferment	progress
import	project
impress	rebel
imprint	refuse
incense	second
increase	suspect
insult	survey
interdict	transport
object	transfer

The following also differ:

ADJECTIVE	VERB
AB-sent	ab-SENT
alt-ERN-ate	alt-er-NATE
con-SUMM-ate	CON-summ-ate
CON-verse	con-VERSE
FRE-quent	fre-QUENT
IN-tim-ate	int-im-ATE
PER-fect	per-FECT
PRES-ent	pre-SENT
NOUN	ADJECTIVE
AUG-ust	aug-UST
COM-pact	com-PACT
CON-tent	con-TENT
IN-stinct	in-STINCT
IN-valid	in-VAL-id
NOUN	VERB
AT-tribute	at-TRIB-ute

accent, Australian. *See* **pronunciation in Australia.**

accentuate. "The late arrival of trains was accentuated by signalling problems." This common use of the word *accentuate,* to mean *aggravate* or *made more acute,* is undesirable.

  Accentuate means *to throw something into prominence* or *to make it stand out more,* as in *The painter accentuated the figures in his drawing by deepening the shadows.*

accepter/acceptor. An *accepter* is simply someone who accepts something.

  Acceptor has two meanings, both specialised: (a) in finance, *the person or organisation who accepts responsibility for a draft or bill of exchange;* (b) in physics, *an atom or molecule able to receive an extra electron.* There are also other scientific uses.

accidie/alienation/anomie. These three words have overlapping meanings, at least as they are used in contemporary discourse about the relationship of the individual to society. It would be hard to avoid coming into touch with at least one of them in the average day's stroll through the groves of pop sociology and psychology.

Accidie is a word with origins in medieval religion and comes from a Greek word meaning *couldn't care less.* From its original meaning of *spiritual sloth,* a very damning vice indeed in medieval times, it has been revived recently to mean *a feeling of 'what's the use?'* Pronounce *aks-sidi* or (if you want to use the Latin pronunciation) *ak-kid-ee-ay.*

Alienation is a formidable word; indeed Raymond Williams, in *Keywords,* has called it "one of the most difficult words in the language." Simply defined, it means *estrangement, the feeling of being an outsider.* In psychiatry it means *the feeling that both yourself and the outside world are unreal* (the feeling or belief that only you exist, and that the outside world is unreal, is called in philosophy *solipsism*). *Alienation* is also seen as a consequence of the artificiality of civilisation, cutting us off from our original human nature. (In this sense, of course, it relates to the influential teachings of Rousseau.) In Marxist terminology the word means that, while man creates himself by creating his own environment, in class society he is alienated from his essential nature by the inhumanity of the capitalist production process, which changes him from one who uses to one who is used, from one who owns to one who is owned, and from one who belongs to one who has no place consonant with the dignity of his own nature.

Anomie (or *anomy*) literally means *without laws.* It is used where the individual or society loses touch with normal social or moral standards. It is characteristic of a society where large numbers of breaches of the law occur, and are reported, but where nothing is done about them: "the true meaning of the erosion of law and order," says Ralf Dahrendorf. *Anomie* means much the same as *psychopathic* but is not used in the same way. *Psychopathic* is a medical judgement relating to anti-social or criminal behavior, while *anomie* rather refers to a generalised state of having no particular norms to relate to, and hence drifting through life.

accommodation. Frequently misspelt *accomodation.*

accord. "Comedians don't get the accord they deserve," says an actor.

The actor means *acclaim* or *recognition,* not *accord. Accord* means *agreement, consent, harmony,* as in *We reached accord on the new proposals.*

acid test. "This is the big acid test," said Tom Hafey, coach of the Sydney Swans football team, prior to its big match against Carlton in May 1986.

Gold, it is said, cannot be dissolved by any acid except *aqua regia* or 'royal water', a mixture of nitric and hydrochloric acids. Therefore it was by applying an 'acid test' that it was possible to distinguish gold from inferior metals.

The phrase has had a long history. In 1920 H. W. Fowler called it a "popularized technicality" and a vogue phrase brought into prominence by President Wilson during the first world war. George Orwell called it a "lump of verbal refuse" fit only for the dustbin. These judgements seem harsh. *Acid test* is a vivid and economic phrase with an interesting history. It deserves to survive.

acquaint. *Acquaint* has two meanings.

It can mean *to be familiar or conversant with,* as in *She was acquainted with Dame Joan Sutherland.*

It can also mean *to tell* or *inform: I acquainted him with the bad news.* In this sense prefer the simpler words.

acronym. An *acronym* is a word formed from the initial letters of other words or phrases, as for instance *UNESCO,* which stands for *United Nations Educational, Scientific, and Cultural Organisation,* or *NATO,* the *North Atlantic Treaty Organisation.*

Australian examples are *ANZAAS* (Australian and New Zealand Association for the Advancement of Science), *ANZAC* (for which there is a separate entry) and *QANTAS* (Queensland and Northern Territory Aerial Services).

Many familiar acronyms gradually become ordinary words. It is therefore more common to see Unesco, Nato, Anzac and Qantas than to see them written throughout in capital letters.

See also **laser; radar.**

acrostic. An acrostic is a word or phrase formed by certain letters hidden within another piece of writing. An acrostic is commonly formed by the initial letters of each line of a piece of poetry.

Australia's most famous acrostic was devised by the poet Gwen Harwood, writing under the name of Walter Lehmann, and published in the *Bulletin* of 5 August 1961. The magazine was unaware of the message spelt out by the first letters of each line:

> ABELARD TO ELOISA
> Far above memory's landscape let the fears
> unlatched from thundering valleys of your mind
> carry their lightning. Stare the sun up. Find
> kinetic heat to scotch your mist of tears.

All that your vision limned by night appears
loose in dismembering air: think yourself blind.
Louder than death in headlines the unkind
elements hawk my passion: stop your ears.

Deny me now. Be Doubting Thomas. Thrust
into my side the finger of your grief.
Tell me I am an apparition frayed
out of the tattered winding-sheet of lust.
Recall no ghost of love. Let no belief
summon me, fleshed and bleeding, from the shade.

activate/activation are words best left to the realm of science, where they belong.

actor/actress. There is a general movement towards abandoning the female form of words (see **(the) female critique**). This is because in many cases, such as **poet/poetess**, **Negro/Negress**, it is felt that the female form of the word is slighting or diminishing.

This tendency is welcome, though opposed by those who hold that there is nothing *intrinsically* wrong with the female form of words, that we use many all the time without any concern *(sister)*, and that, in enabling us to make useful distinctions, they add strength to the language.

Taste, sensitivity and common sense will guide each of us in the decisions we take on individual cases. *Authoress* and *poetess*, for instance, have been used as sneer words for a long time and are best discarded. *Actress*, however, has no sneer connotations. It is hard to imagine a woman objecting to being called "a great actress." It seems sensible to leave this word alone, unless and until it takes on pejorative tones.

For all that, some actresses in Australia now prefer to be called *actors*.

adage. Pronounce this word *AD-ij,* not *a-DAHZH.*

adaptation/adaption. In the introduction to this book we wrote about the dependence of Australians on guides to the English language "which do not approach that language through two hundred years of cultural adaption."

Later we changed *adaption* to *adaptation*. Why?

Both *adaptation* and *adaption* have long histories in English. *Adaption* was used by Swift. Both mean *the process of adjustment to different conditions.*

Adaption, however, has dropped out of modern use except in one specialised connection, where sociologists talk of the slow modification of the cultural characteristics of a community.

Adaptation, therefore, is the more appropriate word for general use.

adapter/adaptor. An *adapter* is a person who adapts something. An *adaptor* is an electrical device.

address. A simple little word, yet there's much to be said about it.

First, let us take the noun *address*. This has two main meanings: (1) the *address* that you put on a letter, and (2) the *address* that you make to the Amalgamated Society of Pudding Thieves, or whatever other body is to suffer.

Note that an *address*, in the second meaning, is a weightier word than *talk* or *speech*. *Addresses* are given on formal occasions. If a university gives you an honorary degree, you may be asked to make, in response, an 'occasional address'. To use the word where a simple talk or speech is involved is to be guilty of a pretentious inflation of language, an inflation beloved of the municipal mind.

The verb *to address*, apart from *addressing* an envelope, means *to direct a protest or petition to a person or organisation, to apply oneself to a task, to speak or write to an occasion, to apply one's attention to*. This is all fairly straightforward, but such phrases as *We will now address the question of...* have become unpleasant pieces of political and bureaucratic jargon. Let us try *not* to *address* questions but to *consider, approach* or *deal with* them.

In English and Australian usage both the verb and the noun are pronounced the same way: *add-DRESS*. In American English the noun is pronounced, when it means the address on an envelope, as *ADD-ress*.

address of Earth. For the correct address for the Earth, see **earth.**

ad hoc. *Ad hoc* is a Latin phrase meaning *for this particular purpose and no other*.

Let us set up an *ad hoc* committee to examine this particular issue.

It was an *ad hoc* decision (meaning a decision of a special nature taken outside normal channels or precedents).

The slang phrase *adhockery* is used to satirise the process of trying to meet problems by stop-gap methods, instead of sitting down to think seriously about the principles involved in order to establish some general rules.

adjacent/adjoining/contiguous. Things are *adjacent* when they are close to other things: my neighbor's house is *adjacent* to mine. This means that it is close to mine but not actually touching it, or joined to it.

If things are *adjoining*, however, they are actually attached. If Room A *adjoins* Room B it shares a common wall or walls.

Contiguous means the same as *adjoining*, though it tends to be used for large things: *the boundary of his station is contiguous to mine; Papua New Guinea is contiguous to West Irian. Contiguous to* is preferred to *contiguous with*.

adjectives. An *adjective* is one of eight **parts of speech** in traditional grammar.

Adjectives describe, or give information about, nouns and words that stand in for nouns. Adjectives in the following sentences are in italics:

> He was the *last* runner in the *first* marathon of the season.
> *Lucky* you, to have won the *biggest* lottery this month.
> *This* river is the *longest* in the *fifth* continent.

Adjectives are described in different ways. These include:

PREDICATIVE ADJECTIVES. Adjectives which do not come before the noun, but which follow the verb, as in *The wind is* furious *tonight.*

ATTRIBUTIVE ADJECTIVES. Adjectives which stand with the noun, as *the* red *door.*

(Note that, while most adjectives can be used in either an attributive or a predicative way, some can only be used in one way or the other. We can talk about *a leading question* but can not say *the question is leading;* we can mention *two men abreast,* but not *two abreast men.*)

POSSESSIVE ADJECTIVES, such as *my, our.* (See also **determiners.**)

DEMONSTRATIVE ADJECTIVES, of which there are four: *this, that, these, those.* (See also **determiners.**)

COMPOUND ADJECTIVES, such as *quick-fingered, swift-footed, time-expired.*

ADJECTIVAL CLAUSES. These are clauses, usually introduced by a relative pronoun, which qualify a noun or pronoun in another clause and hence perform the function of an adjective. Examples are:

> This is the road *down which we first explored.*
> The bank manager *whom he visited* was exceptionally pleasant.
> What was the name of the town [*which*] *we visited last year?*
> Do you remember the time [*when*] *we first saw Vesuvius?*

admission/admittance. These words have various meanings. Here we are concerned with the meanings related to *going in* to a place. Both words mean the same thing when the meaning is *the permission or right to enter.* In other words, you may say *by reason of her position in the organisation she had admission* (or *admittance*) *to the stadium.* But when the meaning is *a charge for entry* you may only use the word *admission: admission cost a dollar,* not *admittance cost a dollar.* Similarly, an *admission charge,* not an *admittance charge.* Finally, and just to make things harder, for *the act of allowing to enter* use only the word *admittance: admittance was through the green gate.* In summary:

> *Admission:* permission to enter, or a charge for entering.
> *Admittance:* permission to enter, or the act of giving entrance.

admit. Prefer *She admitted the offence* to *She admitted to the offence.*

Advance Australia Fair. The Melbourne wit John Bangsund has argued that it is desirable for national anthems to be silly "in words, music and divisive function." He regards the Australian National Anthem as perfect. In July 1987 the anthem was printed in the program for the nurses' graduation ceremony at the Central Gippsland Hospital in Traralgon, Victoria. The fourth line was given as "Our home is dirt and sea." In order to assist patriotic Australians we print here the first verse of our National Anthem, pointing out as we do so that the first line has now been changed, in the interests of 'inclusive' language, from the original *Australia's sons, let us rejoice:*

> Australians all, let us rejoice,
>> For we are young and free,
> We've golden soil and wealth for toil,
>> Our home is girt by sea;
> Our land abounds in nature's gifts
>> Of beauty rich and rare;
> In history's page, let every stage
>> Advance Australia fair,
> In joyful strains then let us sing
>> Advance Australia fair.

adventitious/adventurous. *Adventitious* is a word used to describe something that happens *accidentally* or *unexpectedly:* "Just as they were about to be overwhelmed, reinforcements arrived adventitiously." Or, in answer to the question "Did you arrange for things to turn out that way?", the answer "No, it was adventitious." The word has the same meaning as *fortuitous.*

Adventurous means *possessed of a daring spirit.*

adverbs.
"If you get the verbs right you don't need adverbs at all. I think adverbs are absolutely bloody." — Graham Greene.

A fine sentiment, even if Graham Greene does need three adverbs to make it.

The *adverb* is one of eight **parts of speech** in traditional grammar. Most adverbs end in *-ly,* but many do not. And some adjectives, such as *early,* end in *-ly* also. Examples of adverbs are *slowly, fast, perhaps, seldom, finally, gradually, incessantly, today, reasonably.*

The adverb limits the scope of verbs, adjectives and other adverbs. It says how far they can go. Here are some examples:

> He advised him to work *carefully* at the job. (Here the scope of the *verb* is limited.)
> You are *most* kind. (Here the scope of the adjective *kind* is defined.)
> She behaved *extremely* kindly towards me. (Here one adverb, *extremely,* is modifying another adverb, *kindly.*)

The adverb can perform so many grammatical functions that cynics have suggested that it is the word used by grammarians for what is left over after other parts of speech have been defined.

Adverbs are sometimes placed in categories for the purpose of convenience. Categories used include:

ADVERBS OF MANNER: *They yielded* gracefully.
ADVERBS OF TIME: *Do it* immediately.
ADVERBS OF PLACE: *Take it* away.
ADVERBS OF DEGREE: *It is* quite *obvious that she went* too *far.*
ADVERBS OF REASON: *It is* therefore *possible.*

On adverbs, note:
1. In general, adverbs should be placed before verbs, and not between the verb and the object. *We then finally abandoned the position* is preferred to *We then abandoned finally the position* or *We then abandoned the position finally.* However the general rule in all such matters, 'put it where it sounds best to you as long as the sense is not affected', holds good here as elsewhere.
2. Where both an adjective and an adverb end in *-ly*, the adverbial use looks and sounds awkward, as in *He treated her beastly.* There is no alternative in such a case but to change the sentence around: *He treated her in a beastly fashion.*
3. *Adverbial clauses and phrases* are groups of words which function as adverbs. Examples are:

> They walked *along the road in full view* of the observers.
> *When thieves fall out,* honest men rejoice.
> Is she wise *as she is fair?*

4. The tendency to 'kill' the adverb by dropping the *-ly* with which most adverbs end is to be opposed. *Not* "He is batting very slow this morning" *but* "He is batting very slowly this morning."

adversary. Pronounce *AD-versary*, not *ad-VERS-ary*.

adverse/averse/aversion. These words are easily confused.
Adverse means *contrary* or *hostile*, and it is not used of people. One speaks or writes of *adverse weather, adverse opinions.*
Averse means *disinclined: He was averse to finishing the climb*, or *She was averse to the idea of returning home.* It is often used in the form of *not averse to. She was not averse to oysters* would usually mean that she was happy enough to eat them, without being passionately addicted to them, though Australians sometimes use the phrase to understate a strong addiction to something.
Write *adverse to, averse to.*
Adverse may be stressed on either the first or second syllable. *Averse* is stressed on the second.
The noun *aversion* may be followed by *from, to* or *for.*

advertisement tends to have both an 'educated' and an 'uneducated' pronunciation in Australia.

15

The approved pronunciation is *ad-VERT-is-ment*. The uneducated variant is *ad-ver-TISE-ment*, no doubt a back-formation from the verb *advertise*.

advice/advise. To *advise* someone is to give *advice*, and therefore the word should not be used as a synonym for *inform*. *He was advised that the flight was cancelled* is incorrect; he was *informed*.

Note that *advice* is the noun: *He gave me some excellent advice. Advise* is the verb: *I was advised to come in out of the sun.*

adviser/advisor. The word is *adviser*, but a very common error is to make it *advisor*, presumably by back-formation from *advisory*. *Advisor* is in fact an American spelling, but there is no particular reason that we should adopt it, and nor do many Americans.

advocate. The verb *advocate*, meaning to *recommend* or *urge*, should not be followed by the word *that*.

She advocated that seat-belts should be compulsory in all vehicles is incorrect. It should rather read *She advocated compulsory seat-belts for all vehicles.*

-æ-. The traditional spelling of words such as *mediæval*, *encyclopædia* and *primæval* has been with the *ae* (*oe* in some words) fused into what printers call a *ligature* (two letters joined together) and linguistic scholars call a *digraph*, thus: *mediæval*. This is a signal to the reader that mediaeval is not pronounced *media-eval*, that the two vowels represent a single sound, usually the sound *ee*.

The *æ* digraph has given way to a simple *ae*, partly because it is easier to write and to set in type, and partly because there is little need in practice to signal to people how to pronounce such words.

The spelling of these words is now taking another step towards simplification: *medieval, encyclopedia, primeval, pederast, pedagogue*. This is now standard American usage, and is creeping into Australian usage (though the older form still holds out in words such as *paediatrician*).

Sensible in some ways, the development is open to the objection that the sound *ee* is not necessarily preserved when we abandon the digraph, that a word that should be pronounced *peederast* comes to be pronounced with the *ped-* rhyming with *head* rather than *heed*.

Words in which the *ae* at present shows no signs of disappearing include *archaeology* and *aesthetics*.

See also -œ-.

aegis. "There is of course an essential incongruity in the wild plaintive instrument of the rugged ragged clans of highland Scotland providing the aegis for a showpiece of Victorian propriety and formality" (*Age*, 18 June 1985).

Aegis means *a protection, a shield.* In ancient Greece it was a goat skin worn over the shoulder, or like a shield over the left arm. What the author of the above means, in his convoluted way, is that the bagpipes were providing a *background* or *accompaniment* to the ball in question, not that they were *protecting* it.

The word *aegis* is usually found in the phrase *under the aegis of,* where it means *under the protection or auspices of.*

aeon/eon. An *aeon* or *eon* is *an immeasurably long period of time.* The American spelling is *eon,* the British generally *aeon.*

Since (a) there is a general tendency for words spelt with the digraph (two vowels representing one sound) *ae* to move towards the simpler spelling with *e,* and (b) since the move in this case does not affect the pronunciation of the word, the spelling *eon* is recommended for standard Australian use.

See **-ae-.**

aerodrome/aeroplane. *Aerodrome,* standard in Australia until the second world war, has now yielded to the American *airport. Aeroplane* has proved sturdier, and is still the standard Australian term, though probably *airplane* and *aircraft* (now both singular and plural) will make headway.

aesthetic/ascetic. *Aesthetic* means *relating primarily to pure concepts of beauty,* as in *It was aesthetic rather than material considerations which determined her choice of the house.* Pronounce *ees-thetic* or *a-sthetic.*

Ascetic means *self-denying, abstemious, uninterested in material comfort.* You can be *an ascetic* or you can be *ascetic.*

affect/effect. *Affect,* as a verb, means *to influence, to have consequences,* as in these examples:

The decision affected workers in all industries.

I was very much affected by the glorious singing of "O Sole Mio."

Affected, as an adjective, means *artificially showing-off, putting on an act:*

He spoke with an extraordinarily affected English accent, as though he had been born in Hampstead rather than Wollongong.

Affect, affected and *affective* also have psychological meanings, which need not concern us here but which may be consulted in dictionaries.

Effect, as a verb, means *to cause something to happen, to bring it about:*

He was well out of the crease, but effected a brilliant recovery to avoid being stumped.

After much litigation, a settlement of the dispute was effected.

Effect, as a noun, means a *result* or *consequence,* as in:

The effect of this decision was lamentable.

17

afflict/inflict. If you are *afflicted* by something it is *causing you distress*. People are *afflicted* by disease. If something is *inflicted* on you, however, it is *imposed* on you: punishment, unpopular visitors, extra duties and the like.

afforestation. See **reafforestation/reforestation**.

Afrikaans, Afrikaners. See **boar/Boer/boor/bore**.

again/against. The preferred pronunciation of these words is *agen* and *agenst*.

aged. When speaking of an *aged woman* we pronounce the word with two syllables: *age-ed*. But when simply saying that *The child is aged six* the word is pronounced as one syllable.

ageing/aging. Both these forms of the word are correct, but most important Australian newspapers prefer *ageing*, which is recommended.

ageism/ageist. These ugly words are not yet in the dictionaries, but are in common use, at least in Australia. They form a trilogy with *racism/racist* and *sexism/sexist* as exemplary sins of our day.

Or at least they should. *Ageism* is *discrimination against the aged for no other reason than that the aged are aged*. An *ageist* is *one who takes this position or performs such discrimination*. Although it is as sinister and unwelcome as sexism and racism, a campaign against *ageism* has none of the popular appeal of campaigns against racial or sexual discrimination. And it is accepted unthinkingly by many who would be horrified at being accused of being racist or sexist.

Universities, for instance, though supposedly dedicated to the indivisibility of scholarship, happily discriminate against retired members of staff who wish to continue thinking — for instance, making it hard for them to borrow books. Section 74 (2), sub-section (a), of the New South Wales Anti-Discrimination Act of 1977 states that persons are not eligible to be members of the Anti-Discrimination Board if they are of, or above, the age of 65. Presumably such persons are regarded as no longer mentally competent. Other boards have similar rules. Cults of innovation and experimentation in the arts are frequently manipulated to discourage participation by the older and to reinforce a 'hegemony' of the young. Divorce, marriage and sex are looked upon by many in society as inappropriate for the elderly. Even association between elderly men and women is frowned upon in some institutions for the aged.

So, ugly or not, the words are needed.

agenda. Pedants who argue that *agenda* is a plural noun and should therefore not be applied to a single list of items show a poor understanding of Latin.

Agenda means *things to be done*, which is certainly a plural concept. But a list of business to be transacted at a meeting is a statement of things to be done, and therefore rightly called *an agenda*.

aggravate. The original, and many would hold the proper, meaning of *aggravate* is *to make worse*, as in *His illness was aggravated by exposure.*

The word, however, is now widely used to mean *irritate*, or *annoy: His manner aggravated me to the extent of making me hit him.*

There is a derivative from this usage, the noun *aggro*, meaning *deliberate incitement.*

Aggravate in its original meaning is a useful word, and there are plenty of other words to convey the meaning of *irritate* or *exasperate*. It is far too late to stop *aggravate* being used in the second sense, but the survival of the original sense of this word should be fought for.

ago.

> The mightiest moments pass uncalendared, and over a year ago, towards the end of 1924, Hugh had experienced . . . the greatest single stroke of good fortune of his whole life.

The *and*, in the above sentence from Rupert Hart-Davis's biography of Hugh Walpole (1952), should have come before the comma and not after it, but that is another matter. Here the argument is about the word *ago.*

The dictionary definition of *ago* is *in the past*. To that extent Hart-Davis's use of *ago* seems correct. We believe, however, that Hart-Davis should have written *over a year before*, not *over a year ago*. The point is that *ago refers to a point of time in the past but reckons back from the present*. If, as Hart-Davis is here, you are reckoning back from the *past*, not from the present, *before* should be used.

Never use the words *ago since*, as in *It is fifteen years ago since they were married*. Prefer *It was fifteen years ago that they married*, or *They were married fifteen years ago*. Nor should you write *They were there since four years ago*. Say, rather, *They have been there for four years.*

The use of *back* in the sense of *ago* (*a few days back*) is slangy, and undesirable in serious writing.

agreeance/agreement. *Agreeance* will be found as Australian office jargon for *agreement: I'm in agreeance with that*. Whatever the Town Clerk may think, there is no such word as *agreeance.*

AIDS. Prefer *Acquired Immuno-deficiency Syndrome* to the more common, but less scientifically accurate, *Acquired Immune Deficiency Syndrome*. The *deficiency* is not immune; there is a deficiency in the *immunity.*

air force. For air force ranks, see **ranks in the armed forces.**

aitch/haitch. Australian speech is more democratic than English speech, in the sense that there are fewer words, and fewer pronunciations of words, which readily identify the 'class origin' (for want of a better phrase) of the speaker.

We also care less about the matter when such a word does come along. Fritz Spiegl, in the BBC's *Listener* (23 May 1985) wrote of his delight at hearing a distinguished Australian gynaecologist in England talk about the "Haitch Factor" in his research. In Britain, Spiegl said, "if he put his haitches in the wrong place, he'd hardly have passed his exams, let alone got a consultancy."

Fine. But probably the most common Australian class 'identifier' is the pronunciation of the letter *h*. The received pronunciation is *aitch*, and the middle classes almost always adhere to this pronunciation. Many, however, of working-class and lower middle-class origin pronounce the letter as *haitch*. It has been suggested that this pronunciation is Irish in origin and has been spread in Australia through the influence of Catholic schools.

Use which pronunciation you wish, but remember that (as Fritz Spiegl has reminded us) it *is* an 'identifier'.

See **indicator words.**

Alas, poor Yorick. The quotation is often given as "Alas, poor Yorick, I knew him well." The actual words of Shakespeare are "Alas, poor Yorick. I knew him, Horatio; a fellow of infinite jest, of most excellent fancy . . ." (*Hamlet*, act v, scene i).

albeit. This is a word to be avoided. The writer Barbara Jefferis has, properly, called it a "terrible, tedious, trendy archaism."

ale. Originally beer was flavored with hops, and ale was not. Today the distinction is that *ale* is brewed with top-fermentation yeasts and *beer* with bottom-fermentation yeasts. For the first century of European settlement in Australia all beer was in fact ale. From about 1890 the Continental type of bottom-brewed lager beer started replacing ale in Australia.

Virtually all Australian beer is now lager beer, not ale. The exceptions are the famous Cooper's Ale of South Australia, Carlton Old, sold as a draught ale in New South Wales, and Toohey's Hunter Old Ale.

Apart from these correct usages of the word *ale* in Australia, it is normally heard only as a fancy-genteel name for *beer*. In this sense it is a **poseur word** and should be avoided.

alfresco. "We looked into the next room and saw that an alfresco press conference was under way" (press report). Whatever they saw was not an *alfresco* press conference. *Alfresco* comes from the Italian *al fresco* and means *in the open air*. Picnics are *alfresco* but press conferences are normally not. The writer perhaps meant that they observed an **impromptu** press conference.

In English *alfresco* is written as one word, not two.

alibi. "We had a sensational drop to $37,000 (takings) last week which is sinister but, all alibis apart, everything in New York has dropped."

An *alibi* should mean one thing only, and that is *a plea that one could not have done something because of being elsewhere*. Although it is sometimes used, as Noel Coward does here, as a synonym for *excuse*, this should be avoided.

alienation. See **accidie.**

a little knowledge is a dangerous thing. Properly:

> A little learning is a dang'rous thing;
> Drink deep, or taste not the Pierian spring . . .

From Alexander Pope's "Essay on Criticism." Pieria, home of the Muses, is on the slopes of Mount Olympus.

all. "All libraries, research institutions, universities, colleges, high schools, and government departments cannot afford to be without the *Australian National Bibliography 1901-1950.*" Unfortunately it is the National Library of Australia itself that writes this. The statement is an inclusive statement in itself and does not need the *all*, an attempt perhaps to give added pungency to the message, but which in fact detracts from it. The writer should have either omitted the *all* or written *No library, research institution, etc.* A minor blemish is the unnecessary comma after *schools*.

All of the people, all of the excuses were idiotic. The use of the word *of* in such settings is superfluous: use *all the people, all the excuses*.

allergic. The use of *allergic* to mean *not liking* (*He's allergic to work*) is undesirable though widespread. Properly, *allergic* means *relating to an allergy*, an allergy being *a hypersensitive bodily reaction to some foreign substance*.

alligator. There are no alligators in Australia, except in zoos, though one of the two Australian species of crocodile, the saltwater or estuarine crocodile (*Crocodilus porosus*), is popularly referred to as an alligator.

all right/alright.
1. In such a sentence as *Are they all right?* when we are asking (for instance) if each of the cartons delivered is in good order, *all right* as two words has to be used.

2. When *all right* is being used as a unified term meaning *unharmed, satisfactory* (*Is she all right?*), the alternative spelling *alright* is common. *Alright* has a long lineage, firm backing and can not be called incorrect. It may well eventually become the standard form. In the meantime, however, *all right* is to be preferred, if only for the reason that to use *alright* leaves the literacy of the writer open to question in the minds of many.

all that glistens is not gold. The exact quotation is from Thomas Gray's "On the Death of a Favourite Cat, Drowned in a Tub of Gold Fishes," written in 1748:

> Not all that tempts your wand'ring eyes,
> And heedless hearts, is lawful prize,
> Nor all that glisters, gold.

all together/altogether. *All together* means a lot of people or things in proximity to each other, as in *The penguins were all together and not spread out over the beach.* In other words *all together* is an adjective, that is a word added to a noun (*penguins*) to describe an attribute of that noun. Just as in *The sky is red* the word *red* is an adjective.

Altogether is an adverb, and means *on the whole, totally. It was altogether an awful shambles.*

allude. To *allude* to something means *to refer indirectly to something already known: The politician appeared to be alluding to the scandal of last May.*

Allude does not mean *to mention directly. He alluded to the handsome donation by Mrs Cunningham* is wrong if the speaker referred to it specifically.

almost never. Prefer *hardly ever* or *very seldom.*

a lot. There is a word *allot*, and those who don't know its meaning may look it up in a dictionary.

There is, however, despite a growing impression to the contrary, no such word as *alot*, meaning *a lot*, as in *a lot of people.*

already. "Already two years ago the Prime Minister had made such an undertaking." This construction sits uneasily inside the English language, though no-one could say that it was actually wrong. Like the use of the word *hopefully* in the sense of "If all goes well", it has a German flavor. The German word *schon* can be and is used in the way *already* is used above.

It would sound and read better if the example above opened *As early as two years ago,* or *As long as two years ago* rather than the way it does open. Alternatively, the sentence would sound better if it were phrased *Two years ago the Prime Minister had already made such an undertaking. Already* should be avoided as the opening word of a sentence.

However, this does not solve the problem. It occurs again in such a phrase as *Three months ago already he was married;* as before, it is not so much the word as the placement of the word that grates: *He was already married three months ago* sounds inoffensive enough. The trick would seem to be to have the word *already* as close to the verb as practicable and not wandering around the sentence.

Note that *all ready* and *already* have different meanings, as in:

The troops were *all ready* for embarkation.

The troops had *already* embarked.

alright. See **all right/alright.**

alternate/alternative.

1. It is sometimes argued that there can only be *one* alternative in any given situation, because the Latin word *alter* means *one out of two.* This argument may be disregarded. You may have as many alternatives as you wish.

2. *To alternate* is a verb meaning *to do things by turns,* as in *The government in Israel has decided to alternate the prime-ministership.* (In other words, the prime-ministership will be shared, so many months for one and so many months for the other, between two people.)

Alternate is also an adjective (*the alternate prime minister*) and, as *alternately,* an adverb, as in *We alternately swam, and rested on the bank, the whole morning.*

3. The word *alternative,* noun and adjective, implies *the offering of a choice,* as in *The alternative to lighting the fire to get warm was to take a hot bath.* The word should not be used when no choice is offered. *Alternative accommodation will be offered at the Sydney Hilton* is wrong (use *substitute* or *other*), unless what is meant is that there are choices as to which room one may stay in. Similarly, *An alternative date has been set* is wrong, unless what is meant is that persons may choose between dates. Say rather that *Another date has been set.*

4. The phrase *no other alternative* should be avoided. Since *alternative* already means *other,* it is an unnecessary doubling-up. *No alternative* is the correct form.

5. Finally, and to summarise, note that there is an important difference between *an alternate prime minister* and *an alternative prime minister. An alternate prime minister* is a person who shares the position of prime minister with someone else, on a 'now it's my turn' basis. An *alternative prime minister* is someone standing by waiting for the chance to displace the present prime minister: in other words, and in the Australian system, normally the Leader of the Opposition.

23

although/though. These words are interchangeable, except that (1) *though* has to be used at the end of a sentence (*It wasn't a good day, though*) and (2) also should be used in such idioms as *even though, as though*.

aluminium is properly pronounced *alyoominium*, at least by the English. The Americans, who do not like the *yoo* sound in their words, spell the word *aluminum* and pronounce it *a-loo-min-um*.

Australians seem to have gone for a compromise, retaining the English spelling but pronouncing the first *u* as *oo*, or even as *i*, rather than *yoo*, thus: *aloominium, aliminium*.

See also **oo or yoo?**

amateur. This word may be pronounced *amater, amatsher* or as the French would, if you can get round to that. It is also frequently pronounced, even on the Australian Broadcasting Corporation's stations, as *amatchoor*, which should be avoided.

amaze. "Sutherland proceeds to amaze with details of the technology" (*Age*, 1 June 1985). *Amaze* is a *transitive* verb, which means that it has to take an object. The sentence should run, for instance, *proceeds to amaze listeners with details of the technology*.

ambiguity/ambiguous. See **ambivalent/ambivalence**.

ambivalent/ambivalence. These words do *not* mean *ambiguous/ambiguity*. To be *ambivalent* is to hold *two conflicting views or emotions at the same time*. These views may be far from *ambiguous*, which means *vague, obscure, capable of different interpretations*.

amenable. Pronounce *a-MEEN-abl*, not *a-MEN-abl*.

Americanisms. See **offensive intruders**.

America's cup. This is the "*America's* Cup," not the "Americas' Cup" or "American Cup." A yacht named *America* was the first boat to win this famous race, and the cup is called after it.

America/United States. For every time the *United States of America* is called that, or even called the *United States*, it must be called *America* a hundred times.

It is not only easier, shorter and more euphonious to say *America*, but the usage is reinforced by the fact that we never refer to anyone as *a citizen of the*

United States (except in officialese), but as *an American*.

It's all unfair, of course. An Argentinian is an American just as much as someone from the United States is. All we can do is to reflect on the situation, be conscious of its implications, and consider that life wasn't meant to be fair.

Latin America comprises all those countries in North and South America in which Spanish and Portuguese are spoken. There are a number of Latin American countries which are not in South America, but in what is sometimes called *Central America*. *Latin America* does *not* mean *South America*.

Since the correct name for Brazil is the *United States of Brazil*, Latin Americans refer to the United States of America as the *United States of North America*.

among/amongst. Both of these words mean the same thing, and they have equal status, although *among* is more common. *Amongst* seems easier to say before vowels: *amongst others* comes off the tongue more easily than *among others*. This may be the reason that these two words, unusually, co-exist peacefully.

amoral/immoral. If you are *amoral* you have *no moral code of behavior whatsoever*. But if you are *immoral* you act against a moral code in some particular way.

anagram. An anagram is a word or phrase the letters of which can be rearranged to make another meaning.

A most interesting anagram is the following:

```
R O T A S
O P E R A
T E N E T
A R E P O
S A T O R
```

This Latin inscription has been found on tiles and walls at Manchester and Cirencester in England, near Budapest, at Pompeii, in Saxony, on the Euphrates and in Alexandria. It dates from the first and second centuries A.D.

First of all, this is a complex **palindrome**. It can be read from top to bottom, from left to right and (with letters reversed) from bottom to top. But there is far more to it than that.

On the face of it, the message is clear, and reads *Arepo, the sower, guides the wheels with care*. No thought-police could object to that. But hidden within the anagram are two secret Christian messages, dating from the time Christianity was proscribed in the Roman empire.

The first Christian reference is the word *tenet, guides*, which forms a cross within the anagram: in other words, *the cross guides*. The second reference is

that the letters in the anagram can be re-arranged to make the word *paternoster*
(Our Father) twice. A cross may thus be formed with the letters *A* and *O* (Alpha
and Omega, the Beginning and the End) at each tip:

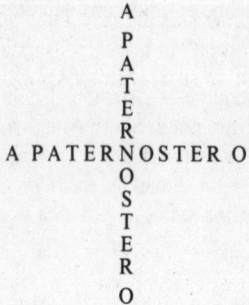

```
              A
              P
              A
              T
              E
              R
A PATERNOSTER O
              O
              S
              T
              E
              R
              O
```

Rather more secular anagrams are *The nudist colony* (no untidy clothes),
Desperation (a rope ends it) and *The lost paradise* (Earth's ideal spot).

analogy/analogous. An *analogy* is *a suggested partial similarity between two
different things,* as in such sentences as:

> There is an analogy between the bone structures of apes and of humans.

> An analogy has been suggested between the economic collapse of Argentina and
> the present economic trend in Australia.

Note that an analogy is a *comparison* only. It does not suggest that one of the
phenomena described necessarily follows from the other.

Analogous is the adjective from *analogy*, as in the question *Is the economic
history of Argentina analogous to that of Australia?*

Analogy is pronounced with a soft *g*, in other words like the *g* in *gee-up*. The
catch is that *analogous* is pronounced with a hard *g*, as in *get*.

androgynous/epicene/hermaphrodite. These are all words which describe the
co-existence within one organism of male and female sexual characteristics.

Androgynous is primarily a scientific, especially a botanical, word. It is an
adjective which conveys the same meaning as the noun *hermaphrodite*. Both
words may be applied to human beings, but normally only in a strictly
physiological sense.

Androgynous should not be confused with *androgenous*, which means *bearing male offspring only.*

Epicene is primarily a grammatical term describing nouns *which have the
same form to denote either gender.* By extension it is also used to mean *having
mixed male and female sexual characteristics.* Thus, when applied to people, it
can mean *sexless, effete* or (of a man) *effeminate.* Although it is in itself a useful
word it is also, like most words dealing with unorthodox sexuality in our

prejudiced society, usually a sneer word.

See also **effete; homosexual.**

angle. "We have a new angle on the problem." *Angle* used in this sense of *viewpoint, approach to* or *aspect to* is racy, idiomatic and descriptive. It is still regarded, however, if not as slang then as slangy, and should be used with caution in writing.

Anglo-Celtic. See **Celt, Celtic.**

Anglo-Indian. Originally (and still sometimes) the word *Anglo-Indian* meant *a person from Britain who was domiciled in India.* In 1900, however, the word was officially adopted to distinguish persons of so-called 'mixed' descent, with both British and Indian forebears, formerly called *Eurasians.*

an historian/an hotel? There are a few words, notably *historian* and *hotel,* which you sometimes see written or hear spoken as *an historian, an hotel,* and sometimes as *a historian, a hotel.*

The confusion stems from the fact that the letter *h* in these words was at one time unaspirated — that is, it was not sounded.

Some people still do not sound the *h* in these words. In that case the word will be preceded, of course, with *an.* Most of us, however, do now aspirate these words. In such cases *a* must be used.

What *is* wrong is to say *a historian, a hotel,* and at the same time to drop the *h* in your pronunciation. Or to say *an historian, an hotel,* sounding the initial *h.* In other words:

an 'istorian	a *h*istorian
an 'otel	a *h*otel

There is, as Mr Arthur Phillips in his inconvenient way has pointed out, just one catch. That is that most of us *think* we sound the *h* in such words, but in fact don't.

In writing, of course, one has the choice of *a* or *an* with such words, depending on the way one hears them in the mind. However, to write *an historian, an hotel* does give a somewhat mannered impression.

animal. In the Australian idiom an *animal* is a pretty nasty piece of work, someone so anti-social that their behavior is animal-like. Many would consider this a slur on animals.

But what about, say, a *political animal?* During 1987 Mr Wilson Tuckey, a member of the House of Representatives, was suspended by the Speaker, Mrs Joan Childs, for referring to her as "just a political animal." The seven-day suspension was a heavy one for what was an innocuous phrase.

Animal is often used merely facetiously, as in the term *no such animal*: "Where will I find an honest person?" "There's no such animal." In the same way it is used as a synonym for *specimen* in such phrases as *She's just a political animal*, meaning someone whose drive is essentially politically based. Surely this is to be expected in a Speaker of the House of Representatives? It would have been a different matter had Mrs Childs been referred to as a *partisan* political animal.

Perhaps Mrs Childs got her animals mixed up, and as a consequence Mr Tuckey got a holiday.

announcement to. The ABC's news on 3 October 1987 referred to the political crisis in Fiji, and to "Colonel Rabuka's announcement to abolish the Constitution."

The only way the word *to* can follow the word *announcement* is with the phrase *She made an announcement to this effect*. The ABC should have reported "Colonel Rabuka's announcement that he intended to abolish the Constitution."

anoint is one of the trickiest of words to spell. It means, of course, *to smear with an oily substance*, and is often used in a religious context. For some reason, possibly because of the existence of verbs such as *anneal, announce, annex* and *annotate,* many find it hard to avoid giving *anoint* a double *n*.

anomaly/anomalous are so spelt. *Anomoly* and *anomolous* are wrong.

anomie. See **accidie.**

Antarctic/Antarctica/Antarctic Circle. *Antarctic* is perhaps an uninspired place name, meaning simply *opposite the Arctic*. The word does, however, have the distinction of having been invented by Aristotle in the fourth century B.C., when in his *De Mundo* he refers to "the Antarctic Pole." The word *Arctic* comes from the Greek word for *bear*, thus the constellation of the Great Bear, hence the north.
NOTE
1. The tricky spelling.
2. That, being proper names, *Antarctic* and *Antarctica* both take a capital letter.
3. That one must say *the Antarctic* but must never say *the Antarctica.* Either "I should like to visit Antarctica" *or* "I should like to visit the Antarctic."
4. That the letter *c* in the middle of *Antarctic* and *Antarctica* is supposed to be pronounced. The *ct* sound is, however, an awkward one to get the tongue around, especially in rapid speech, and it is likely that the *c* sound, though remaining in the printed word, will eventually be dropped in pronunciation, as the *i* in *parliament* has been dropped. Indeed this is already happening, and is

not to be deplored. The *c* is not present in the Italian (*Antartico*) or Spanish (*Antartida*) forms of the word.

The *Antarctic Circle*, at 66 degrees 33.5 minutes South Latitude, is the point at which the sun may be seen not to set in the summer and not to rise in the winter. Considerable portions of the Antarctic continent are in fact north of the Antarctic Circle.

Antarctica is sometimes referred to as *the sixth continent*.

ante-/anti-. *Ante-* as part of a word means *before*. If my birthday *antedates* your birthday, I am older than you. An *antedated* cheque is a cheque bearing a date earlier than that on which it was actually written. In other words, *ante-* means the same as *pre-*, in such a word as *precooked*.

Anti- means *against*. There is no difference in sound between *antewar* (*antewar*) and *antiwar* (*anti-war*). If there is any possibility of confusion in speech, use *pre-* instead of *ante-*. The opposite of *anti-* is *pro-*.

A common *ante-* phrase is *ante bellum*, meaning *before the war*. The opposite of *ante-* is *post-*, *after*, as in *the post-invasion fighting*.

antennae/antennas. Use *antennae* for the feelers of insects, *antennas* for radio installations.

anticipate.
THE HARD LINE
Anticipate does *not* mean *expect*. *Anticipate* is often used as though it meant *expect*, for instance in such a sentence as: "They anticipated no trouble, but trouble they got," but this is wrong.

Anticipate means *to do something which affects a future occurrence*. Thus:

> They anticipated the trouble by going elsewhere.
> He anticipated his inheritance by getting heavily into debt.
> The police anticipated his flight from the country by closing every airport.

It is true that the meanings can be close, but there is a difference, a difference that adds flexibility to the language, and it is a difference that should be fought for, even if the battle may be a losing one.
THE SOFT LINE
Only pedants will now argue that *anticipate* may not be used to mean *expect*. The dictionaries allow *expect* as *one* meaning of *anticipate*. This is not a sudden, unexpected blow at the language. The broadening of the meaning of the word *anticipate*, perhaps even the eventual replacement of the original meaning of that word, has been going on for a long time. This is what happens in languages and what is supposed to happen in languages.
SUMMING UP
It is pointless to fight the use of *anticipate* to mean *expect*, but at least we can be aware of the history of the word, and at least we can endeavor to keep the

original meaning of the word still in use. And perhaps remember that there is a difference between *expecting* a marriage and *anticipating* it.

antipodes comes from the Greek and can be rendered *opposite one's feet*. It is used by Europeans to refer to the places you would come out at if you dug a tunnel through the centre of the earth. There are even some Antipodes Islands near New Zealand.

When used by the people of Europe to refer to countries such as New Zealand and Australia the word *antipodes* often has the suggestion of a faint sneer about it.

There is, however, no reason whatsoever why we should not refer to Europe or parts thereof as the *antipodes* if we wish to, just as there is no reason except convention that the southern hemisphere is placed at the bottom of maps rather than the top.

Why let them get away with it?

antisemitic. *Antisemitic* actions are *actions displaying prejudice towards Jews.* An *antisemite* is *one who has such beliefs or makes such actions.*

There is a slight illogicality in usage here, for a *Semite* or *semite* is a member of that group of caucasoid peoples who speak a Semitic (or semitic) language. This group includes both Jews and Arabs.

Prefer the form *antisemitic/antisemitism* to *anti-Semitic/anti-Semitism.*

antivenene/antivenom. The World Health Organisation agreed in 1979 to call the serum preparation injected into human veins or muscles as an antidote for snake-bite and other animal poisons *antivenom.* This word has been accepted by the medical and scientific professions in Australia and elsewhere, and *antivenene* is a word no longer used.

antivenom. See **antivenene/antivenom**.

anyone/anybody. *Anyone* and *anybody*, being short for *any one person*, should be followed by a singular verb: *Anyone* is *entitled to play the game*, not *Anyone* are *entitled to play the game.*

There is, however, an idiomatic construction in which *anyone*, *anybody* is followed by a plural, in this case a plural pronoun. An example is: *If anybody calls, tell them I'm designing St Paul's.*

This useful idiom avoids the *he/she* problem and is to be encouraged. See **(the) female critique**.

Anzac is an **acronym**: a word formed from the initial letters of other words. It came into use in January 1915 as a code name for the Australian and New

Zealand Army corps, then preparing in Egypt for the landing at Gallipoli which took place on 25 April 1915.

The members of the Anzac corps were only a part of the force that landed at Gallipoli, but the name quickly became famous. Edgar Wallace, the thriller writer, was moved to comment:

I'd count it the greatest reward
That ever a man could attain;
I'd rather be "Anzac" than "lord",
I'd rather be "Anzac" than "thane",

which was a rather labored rhyme. Members of the corps were allowed to wear a small brass 'A' on their color patches. The word has been protected from exploitation by law, in both Australia and New Zealand.

The word in popular usage primarily has meant *a person who served with the Anzac corps on Gallipoli.* Even at the time, however, those who served with the corps but did not reach Gallipoli considered themselves entitled to the word. After the first world war the word *Anzac* tended to be used generically to describe Australian and New Zealand troops who served overseas in that war. Since then it has been developed further through journalism, often to describe joint Australian and New Zealand defence activities.

Aotearoa. This name for New Zealand is sometimes used by New Zealanders when in a poetic mood, and when they wish to forget that the first Australian name for their country was the Pig Islands. *Aotearoa* is a Maori name. *Aotea* means *dawn* or *cloud, roa* means *long,* hence *The Land of the Long White Cloud.*

apartments/condominiums/flats and the terminology of the Australian real-estate industry.

With no guarantee that these following terms are used by all Australian real-estate agents in the same way, the following are the definitions we have been able to extract:

APARTMENT: a fancy name for a flat, an adopted American usage. Used for a better-than-average flat.

COMPANY-SHARE FLAT: those occupying a block of flats do not buy the flats but buy shares in the company owning the block of flats. This entitles them to occupy a flat. The original form of flat-ownership, with the disadvantage that, since money cannot be borrowed against shares, the rights to a flat must be bought with cash.

CONDOMINIUM: not widely used in Australia, but creeping in from the USA. A condominium (or "condo") is a block of strata-title flats which share recreational and other facilities, such as a spa, swimming pool, a tennis court and even (in the USA) a shop or shops.

DUPLEX PAIR: a building comprising one flat on the ground floor with one flat above. In Western Australia, often a pair of single houses with a common wall.

FLAT: a residence, usually on one floor, within the same building as other such residences.

MAISONETTE: a flat of two storeys joined to another similar.

STRATA-TITLE FLAT: a flat to which the owner has a firm title, facilities shared with other flats in the same block being jointly managed through a 'body corporate'.

STRATUM-TITLE FLAT: a block of flats owned by a service company, differing from a company-share flat in that there may be individual titles to units.

TOWN HOUSE: flats, usually of two storeys, built in association with similar units, often with small individual gardens or plots of land.

UNIT: as with *apartment*, used as a name for a better-quality flat.

HOME UNIT: These are usually bigger than flats, with at least two bedrooms. They have strata titles and are designed for permanent living, but by a couple rather than a family.

VILLA UNIT: a row or terrace of single-storey, normally two-bedroom flats, detached or semi-detached, sometimes separated from each other by garages; the units often occupying both sides of a central driveway.

apocalypse. An *apocalypse*, or *an apocalyptic event*, does not mean *a great culminating disaster*, or need not mean this. An *apocalypse* is a great, revealing event. It can be a violent one, and this is the meaning that has become popular because of the film "Apocalypse Now," but it could be a revelation about the Second Coming of Christ, or the event itself. The original words from which we have our word *apocalypse* suggest *a message that is both hidden and disclosed.*

apologia. If you or I make an *apologia*, we do not make an *apology*. An *apologia* is *an explanation of one's beliefs and actions*, an argument in defence of one's point of view. It can be argued that many autobiographies are *apologias*. They may contain apologies for mistaken ideas or bad behavior, but they are in no sense themselves apologies. Perhaps the most famous apologia in the English language is Cardinal Newman's book *Apologia pro Vita Sua,* which may be translated from the Latin as *An Accounting for his Life.*

A poor thing, but mine own. Actually "A poor virgin, sir, an ill-favored thing, sir, but mine own . . ." (Touchstone, in *As You Like It*, act v, scene iv.)

apostrophes. An *apostrophe*, or raised comma, is found in words such as *don't*.
1. In such cases it represents a letter left out of the word for purposes of shortening it:

don't (do not)	I'd (I would)
he's (he is)	fo'c'sle (forecastle)

2. It is also used to indicate a *possessive:*

    John's car   My brother's wife

3. The possessive of words ending in an *s* or *z* sound can either have the normal *'s* ending or simply take an apostrophe without the *s:*

    St James' name-day   conscience' sake

    St James's Palace   conscience's sake

Except when it sounds awkward or ugly the full *'s* ending is preferred. See **(the) possessive and the 's' sound.**

4. Note that plural nouns ending in *s* or *es* take the apostrophe *after* the word:

    the boys' playtime   the fishes' scales

    my brothers' wives   the ladies' hats

5. In such phrases as *Melbourne Teachers College* or the *Butchers Union* the apostrophe may be dropped because it is inconvenient (and because teachers, as well as butchers, may be unsure how to use it). There is a grammatical rationalisation for this: that the words *Teachers* and *Butchers* are being used, not as nouns (which would require an apostrophe) but as adjectives (or adjectival nouns, properly speaking), much as one would say *a brick college.* It is a shaky argument.

    Note that when we write *the Menzies government, the Whitlam government,* we are using *Menzies* and *Whitlam* as adjectives and they therefore take no apostrophe, but that an apostrophe is necessary when we write *Menzies' government, Whitlam's government.*

6. It is sometimes necessary to use an apostrophe simply to avoid puzzlement: *Mind your p's and q's.* Otherwise omit them in such cases and write *M.P.s* (or *MPs*), *1940s.*

7. *Brian and Mary's party* or *Brian's and Mary's party*? In a case where Brian and Mary are separate and distinguishable people, the latter is formally correct: it is short for *Brian's party and Mary's party.* However, most of us would use *Brian and Mary's party,* and while this may be idiomatic it is not incorrect.

    With two names which are linked in a recognised phrase, however, the correct usage is:

    Bryant and May's match factory   Lea and Perrin's sauce

    Angus and Robertson's bookshop

8. Many Scottish names used to be spelt *M'Arthur* rather than *McArthur,* *McArthur* or *Macarthur.* The mark in the first example is not an apostrophe but a *turned comma,* as with the first of the two double **quotation marks** (see **quote/unquote**). Typesetters seldom take the trouble to distinguish the turned comma from the apostrophe in setting these Scottish names. *Mc* and *M^c* are, in fact, lazy modern attempts to reproduce the turned comma without going to too much trouble. The correct style will, however, invariably be found in old books and newspapers.

9. Note *hers, yours, theirs, ours* and *its* (except where *it* means *it is,* where the contraction is *it's*); but *one's, someone's, everybody's, nobody's.*

10. The use of the apostrophe in such sentences as "Pie's and Pastie's sold here" is a sordid illiteracy, known as the *galloping apostrophe* or *signwriters' stutter*. It is there because the writer does not know anything about the apostrophe and puts one in just to be safe.

THE APOSTROPHE HAS NOTHING TO DO WITH THE FORMATION OF THE PLURAL.

See also **(the) geographical possessive**.

apotheosis/epitome. Tricky words, especially *apotheosis*. They are sometimes used as though both meant the same thing. But they don't.

Apotheosis literally means *deification*, the *making of a god*. Figuratively it is used to express the concept of the *highest ideal*, as, for instance

> To many, Captain Oates, who sacrificed himself for his comrades in Antarctica, was the apotheosis of nobility.

Epitome often means a summary, or a condensed account of something, but here we are concerned with its other meaning, the *representation of something in miniature*, the *embodiment of a certain quality in a person*. To say that

> In his time, Lord Kitchener was looked upon by many as the epitome of the soldier,

means no more than that Kitchener represented the *essence* of the soldier. If you think poorly of soldiers the remark is not flattering, and could be a long way from meaning that Kitchener represented the highest ideal of the soldier.

In other words, *epitome* has the sense of the *condensed average* of something, while *apotheosis* has the sense of *abstract virtue of the highest order*.

apparatus may be pronounced *apparaytus* or *apparartus*. The former is more common in Australia, though not in Britain.

appendices/appendixes. Use *appendices* or *appendixes* for attachments to books and documents, *appendixes* for the anatomical use of the word.

appraise/apprise. President Reagan, we were told in the press, was kept "appraised" of the Libyan situation in March 1986.

To appraise something is *to assess its worth*. We *appraise* the potential of a horse, the value of a house or the quality of a short story. To *apprise* or *apprize* (prefer the former) is *to inform*. President Reagan was *apprised* of the Libyan situation by people who had *appraised* the nature of the relationship between the United States and Libya.

appreciate. Take these two sentences:

> Those who have attempted to spend some weeks in utter isolation with a selected group of friends will appreciate that small does not necessarily mean beautiful.
> It is on Martin Martin's book of 1698 that much of our appreciation of the history of the island of St Kilda depends.

Now consider the dictionary definitions of the word *appreciate* (*appreciation*):

    (a) *To increase in value: The dollar appreciated against the yen.*

    (b) *To feel grateful for: I appreciated your letter.*

    (c) *To take full account of,* not commonly found as a verb but familiar as a noun: *A close appreciation of the German positions was made before the beach landings.*

(d)   *To value highly: They appreciated Beethoven's late quartets more than his symphonies.*

Now, which of those meanings applies to the use of the words *appreciate* and *appreciation* in the examples above?

The only near meaning, of the four given, is (c), but even this meaning is not an easy fit with the sense of the quotations.

In the first quotation *understand* or *recognise* or *admit* would have been preferable to *appreciate*. In the second quotation *understanding* or *knowledge* would have been more precise and less inflated.

In other words, the loose use of the words *appreciate/appreciation* to mean *understand/understanding* is to be opposed.

a priori/prima facie. These are two well-used Latin phrases with similar but not precisely corresponding meanings.

A priori in the strict sense means *reasoning deductively, from causes to effects.* A European arriving in Australia might say: "All trees lose their leaves in the winter. This eucalyptus is a tree. Therefore it will lose its leaves next winter." This example of *a priori* reasoning happens to arrive at a false conclusion, but *a priori* reasoning sometimes does. More loosely, the phrase means that something is *known to be true*, that *it does not need validation:* "We can agree on *a priori* grounds that water is wet."

Prima facie is a simpler term. It means *at first sight, without further examination.* "*Prima facie*, there would seem to be grounds for sending such a person to gaol." The inference is that there may also be reasons, as yet unexamined, why this should not be done.

The difference is that *a priori* is more of a precise, philosophical term than *prima facie*, and is a definition of a way of arguing a case: that there are enough facts to start with and no more are needed. *Prima facie*, on the other hand, while it agrees with *a priori* in saying that 'things look this way,' also has within it a built-in doubt or qualifier 'on further investigation they may not be this way at all.'

There is no point in trying to pronounce these terms as the Romans would have, one reason being that we do not know how the Romans would have pronounced them. We need not and should not even try to pronounce them as classical scholars would today. In English *a priori* is pronounced *ar-pry-or-eye* and *prima facie pry-ma fay-shee* or *pryma fay-see*.

apropos. A handy term, from the French *à propos de*, meaning *in respect of*, as in: "The English used to say, apropos international trade, that ..."

As used in English the word is spelt *apropos* and may be pronounced with the *s* on the end of the word.

apt/likely. *This is apt to happen. This is likely to happen.* The distinction is that *apt* implies that *it often does happen*, while *likely* simply suggests that *the chances are in this case that it will happen.*

archive/archives/archivist. *Archives* are *places where collections of public or corporate records are stored.* They are also *those records themselves.* Most dictionaries consider *archives* to be a plural noun and do not admit that it is possible to have *an archive.* Among these is the *Macquarie Dictionary*; it is surprising that that dictionary did not recognise that *archive* as a singular noun is a common Australian usage: *Her literary papers constitute a fine archive.* Pronounce *archive* as *ARK-ive* but pronounce *archivist* (somone in charge of archives) as *ARK-ivist.*

Argentina/The Argentine. The correct name of this country is *Argentina*, though it is sometimes called *The Argentine.* A national of Argentina is an *Argentine*, the adjective *Argentine*, not *Argentinian.* Pronounce *Argentine* to rhyme either with *seen* or *syne.*

arguable. "It is arguable that increasingly in Australia differences between lifestyles in different cities and the various States are becoming marked and permanent."

The writer of this presumably means by *it is arguable* that *there is a case for saying.* However he could just as easily be stating that *there is a case for not saying.* In other words, the phrase *it is arguable* is an ambiguous phrase, the sense of which, with luck, will emerge from the context in which it is used.

This is fudging, though; and the phrase *it is arguable* is best avoided. It should be replaced with a more precise phrase, such as the one suggested above.

aristocrat. In American English *a-RIST-o-crat*, in Australian English *AR-ist-o-crat*.
Armadale/Armidale. *Armadale* is the spelling for the Melbourne suburb of that name and for the outer suburb of Perth. The New South Wales country town, and capital of the New England district, is spelt *Armidale.*

army. For army ranks, see **ranks in the armed forces.**

aroma. This word comes from the Greek for *spice*, and should preferably be used for *pleasant* smells. To say "This is a foul aroma" is to disturb the aroma of this pleasant word.

artefact/artifact. An *artefact* or *artifact* is *something made by art*, in other words anything constructed by a human being. The word is, however, usually confined to the specialised meaning of *a stone tool or implement created by Stone Age humanity.*
The preferred spelling is *artefact.*

articulate/inarticulate. If you are *articulate* you express yourself fluently and clearly in words, either spoken or written. *Inarticulate* means that *you have difficulty in so expressing yourself,* or that *you speak unintelligibly,* or that *something cannot be expressed at all (inarticulate distress)*. The noun is not, as many Australians believe, *articulacy/inarticulacy,* but *articulateness/ inarticulateness.*

artist. Never *artiste.*

arts, the. See **culture.**

artspeak. From an essay in a catalog for the exhibition "The Forbidden Object" at the Roslyn Oxley Gallery, Sydney, on the occasion of the sixth Sydney Biennale, 1986:

> The order of nature itself is instated through a perverse historicity, installing an anterior condition to the colonising order of culture . . . Prescription and interdiction establish a culture of liminal positions and regulating dimensions. The articulated order of culture forbids the pluri-dimensional universe of nature . . . The discourse of culture is a discourse of rupture. It is also a highly derivative discourse: appropriating, ingratiating, making over, stitching together, quoting and referring . . .

-ary, -arily. Attempts to give words ending in these syllables an American inflection, by pronouncing them *airy, airily,* should be opposed in Australia.

ascetic. See **aesthetic/ascetic.**

ascribe/subscribe. "Modernism in architecture had reached such a point that it had forced every principle it ascribed to."
Not so. For *ascribed* read *subscribed.*
To *ascribe* something is *to attribute it to a source or cause,* as in *They ascribed the poor harvest to the unexpected hot winds.*

37

Translated literally from the Latin, *to subscribe* is *to write beneath.* You may thus *subscribe* your name to a letter, or to a *subscription list.* From here *subscribe* moves on to adopt the meaning, not of signing your name, but of the act of *ordering a magazine, making a donation,* or *lending your support.*

as far as. "As far as this technology, we have had no major problems." This from the Australian Broadcasting Corporation's "New Technology" program.

The speaker clearly means *As far as this technology is concerned, we have had no major problems.* The use of *as far as* without a verbal structure to complete the phrase is incorrect, inelegant and illogical.

Asian/Asiatic. *Asiatic,* especially when applied to people, is now a word under a cloud. It is supposed to have a derogatory sound, and should be avoided. The logic is not clear, and there is a perfectly respectable organisation in the United States called the Asiatic Society, but words do fall in and out of favor. Probably the association of *Asiatic* with such phrases as *the Asiatic menace* is the reason for the discarding of this word.

asphalt. Although no doubt the pronunciation *ass-falt* is more strictly correct, the common, indeed almost invariable Australian pronunciation is *ash-felt,* which should be regarded as acceptable.

assassinate. Do not use this word lightly. Do not, for instance, say *Captain Cook was assassinated by the inhabitants of the Sandwich Islands.* The word should be restricted to the murders of heads of state, monarchs and the like. It is not normally used for the kind of death that Captain Cook died, in a fracas on a beach. It conveys the sense of a planned, deliberate, political action.

assuage. To *assuage* is *to relieve pain, thirst and so on.* It is pronounced *a-SWAYJ,* not *a-SWAHZH.*

as such does not mean *so,* or *thus. As such* means *in the capacity specified,* as in:
> Policemen, as such, do not have any law-making capacity.

This is saying that policemen, as policemen, have no say in the making of laws. On the other hand they may have a voice through their trade union or when in an advisory capacity to ministers, etc.

But take this sentence from a student essay:
> John Adams said that the end of government is "the Happiness of the People", and as such by existing, government is very beneficial.

The student clearly believes that *as such* means *thus,* or *so.* Her sentence would work if this were so. But it is not so, and the sentence therefore makes nonsense.

assume/presume. Broadly speaking these two verbs have the same meaning: *to take for granted,* or *to suppose.* There is, however, a shade of difference. One *presumes* that the world is round, in the sense that one believes it, on the basis of informed opinion, until it is proved otherwise. One *assumes,* however, that the plumber will finish the job on time; there is an element here of a personal proposition, a proposition which may or may not be disproved.

as to. *I wondered as to the whereabouts of his car.* In such cases use *about* rather than *as to.* Say or write *The question whether the ship would sail remained undecided* rather than *The question as to whether the ship would sail remained undecided.*

as well as. This simple-looking phrase conceals a sting. Take this sentence:
The pilot, as well as all but one of his passengers, have survived the accident.
This is incorrect, for the phrase *as well as all but one of his passengers* is not considered part of the subject, *pilot,* but simply an additional piece of information, as though it were in brackets. It is outside the main sentence, and therefore the subject, *pilot,* remains singular:
The pilot, as well as all but one of his passengers, *has* survived the accident.
If, however, the sentence had had *and* instead of *as well as,* then that *and* would have created a plural subject, *The pilot and all but one of his passengers,* and this would have had to be followed by *have.*
As well should be avoided when used, generally at the beginning of a sentence, to mean *also, in addition.* The ear is expecting an *as* to follow, and meaning can become confused.

as what. "... as good as what I'd seen in the Netherlands" (Donald Horne, ABC television, 21 March 1985). Mr Horne should have said "as good as I'd seen in the Netherlands." See **indicator words; (the) wandering what.**

ate. *The cat* ate *the rat.* Well-bred English people pronounce this *et.* Australians pronounce it *ate.*

at large. (1) This is a perfectly appropriate term when it means *unconfined,* as in *There are three prisoners at large.* (2) It is, however, a most undesirable term when it is used in a meaningless way simply to mean *in general,* as with *the public at large.*

at the best of times. "It's a lively and tuneful work at the best of times," the ABC told us on 27 March 1988, "but taken as Sir Georg Solti conducts it, it becomes a showpiece."
For *at the best of times* read *at any time.*

attribute/character/property/quality/trait. These words all relate to the *nature* of a person or thing. But note the distinctions.

An *attribute* of someone or something is an aspect of personality, behavior or nature which is *attributed* or *ascribed* to them. It is a less prescriptive word than *property*, vaguer and less precise, with a hint of maybe-so, maybe-not-so about it. *Bad temper is said to be one of his attributes.* Many believe that an *attribute* must be a *good* quality, but this is not necessarily so.

The *character* of someone or something covers distinctive features seen as a whole: *His character, sunny, straightforward and honest, was an appealing one; The general character of the climate is forbidding.*

Properties, in this sense, belong to things and not to people. A *property* of a substance is a basic characteristic, often one which makes it behave in a certain way: *a property of iron is its tendency to oxidise.*

Quality has several meanings. When we talk of the *quality* of an article, or of someone's intellect, we mean its superiority measured against other examples. The word can also mean *personal traits: She was a mixture of good and bad qualities.* It is unusual to hear someone described as *a man or woman of quality*, though once this would have meant a person of high social standing. *Quality* can also be used as a synonym for *property.*

Trait (which is pronounced in Australia either *tray* or *trayt*) refers to some particular feature of a person, some *aspect* of their character or behavior: *His redeeming trait was his generosity. Trait* originates in a word meaning *a stroke of the pencil*, as in a sketch. See also **trait**.

aural/oral/visual. *Aural* communication is by *hearing*, from the Latin word *auris, an ear.*

Oral communication is by *speaking*, from the Latin *os, a face.*

Visual communication is by *seeing*, from the Latin *visus, sight.*

In speech, *aural* and *oral* are easily confused.

See also **verbal communication**.

Australasia. The word *Australasia* was coined in 1756 by the French savant Charles de Brosses, to encompass the lands known or believed to exist below the continent of Asia.

This was the first meaning. Later the word came to mean *Australia and the islands of the south-west Pacific, including New Zealand.*

Today the term, when used, generally means *Australia and New Zealand.*

The New Zealanders, however, object strongly to the term, which they think diminishes their national independence, and *Australasia* is falling into disuse. The Australasian Association for the Advancement of Science, for instance, changed its name many years ago to the Australian and New Zealand Association for the Advancement of Science (ANZAAS).

The word *Australasia* should therefore be avoided.

The islands and seas of the south-west Pacific are now referred to collectively as *Oceania*. (Note that J. A. Froude's well-known book on what used to be known as the Australasian region is called *Oceana*, not *Oceania*.) The word is imprecise, but does not normally include Australia and New Zealand.

Oceania may be pronounced *oseania* or *osheania*.

Australia. The word *Australia* or *Austrialia* as applied to a large, hypothetical land-mass in the southern hemisphere crept into use from about 1600 onwards. It originates, of course, from the Latin word for *south*, or *the south*. In the eighteenth century, however, the continent of Australia, as it became increasingly known to Europeans, was commonly referred to as New Holland or *Terra Australis*, the 'Southern Land'.

The first reference to *Australia*, meaning the continent of Australia, in a printed book appeared in Sir George Shaw's *Zoology of New Holland* in 1794. By 1814 Matthew Flinders was writing that in his opinion the word *Australia* was "more agreeable to the ear" than the term *Terra Australis*, though the word was not yet in use, and the word appeared on his charts.

The first official use of the word *Australia* appears to have been in the journal of Governor Lachlan Macquarie for 30 September 1816. From this time *Australia* rapidly replaced *New Holland* as the accepted name, though until Federation in 1901 it was often held that the word did not include Tasmania.

Australia Felix means "Fortunate Australia" or, perhaps better, "Favored Australia" — even, if you like, "The Lucky Country". Major Thomas Mitchell applied the term to the country he traversed in 1836 in central Victoria and the western district of Victoria, from the Murray River to Portland:

> We traversed it in two directions with heavy carts, meeting no other obstruction than the softness of the rich soil; and, in returning, over flowery plains and green hills, fanned by the breezes of early spring, I named this region Australia Felix, the better to distinguish it from the parched deserts of the interior country, where we had wandered so unprofitably, and so long. (*Three Expeditions* . . . London 1839, vol. 2, p. 333.)

Australia Felix was (and is) used either to describe the Port Phillip District of New South Wales before Separation in 1851, or to describe the fertile areas of what is now western Victoria.

Australiana. "Royal Park with its Australiana character" (Channel 9 News, Melbourne, 17 July 1984).

The traditional use of the *-ana* ending was for the description of a collection of anecdotes and other biographical items relating to an established figure: *Baconiana, Johnsoniana*. More recently the *-ana* ending has become appropriated to meaning *a collection of books devoted to the same topic*. Thus, *Australiana* for a collection of Australian books, *Antarcticana* for a collection of books on the Antarctic, *Furphiana* for a collection of books on, or by, Joseph Furphy. The suffix normally implies some degree of scarcity or desirability.

This is a useful term with a specialised meaning which, like other specialised meanings, should be adhered to in the interests of a vigorous, accurate language. Such terms, however, are always in danger of being taken over by the semi-literate simply because they sound specialised, arcane, up-market.

With the rising interest in recent decades in Australian traditional artefacts and the like, *Australiana* has extended its meaning from "a collection of books" to "a collection of objects of virtu, furniture, folk-art and the like, created in Australia and illustrative of the Australian experience." Such an extension may be regrettable but, all things considered, may be condoned.

What is *not* excusable is to use the word *Australiana* as a synonym for "naturally Australian," "home-grown" or "indigenous". There are many words and phrases which can economically express these meanings. To use *Australiana* in the sense in which it was used by the broadcaster above is mindless, pretentious, and destructive of language.

"Australiana books" is of course an offensive tautology, and "Australiana paintings" is a puffed-up way of describing *Australian* paintings.

An *Australianum* is an unusual, but sometimes used word for a single item of *Australiana*: *Governor Phillip's* Voyage to Botany Bay *is a desirable Australianum*.

Australian accent. See pronunciation in Australia.

Australian Broadcasting Commission/Australian Broadcasting Corporation. The Australian Broadcasting Commission started broadcasting in 1932. It was replaced by the Australian Broadcasting *Corporation* in 1983.

Australianist. It is odd indeed that the word *Australianist* as a noun does not appear in any of the four dictionaries of Australian English. The word does appear in the *Macquarie Dictionary*, but only as an adjective meaning *consciously Australian.*

An *Australianist* is (1) *an academic working in a specifically Australian field*: *Her teaching and research is in British history, but he is an Australianist*; (2) *one who advocates policies in a specific Australian national interest*: Lieutenant-General Legge:

> was a victim of a conflict within the pre-war army between the imperialists, who sought to lock the army into a grand scheme of imperial defence in which the forces of the dominions would constitute a kind of imperial reserve, and the Australianists, who wished to shape a national force for the defence of Australia.
>
> *Canberra Times*, 7 May 1988

autarchy/autarky. *Autarchy* means *the government of a country through the absolute authority of a single person or group.* On the other hand *autarky* is *an economic system whereby a country is completely self-sufficient and there is no need for imports. Autarky,* except sometimes in wartime, is an impracticable doctrine in a world where individual economies are increasingly interdependent. *Autarky* is sometimes spelt *autarchy,* but this should be avoided, to obviate confusion with the other word.

author/authoress. The word *authoress* should no longer be used. See **(the) female critique.**

availability. Do not use *availability* to mean *lack,* as in *The availability of resources to complete the project was serious.*

average/mean. To reckon the *average* of anything you add all the numbers or quantities and then divide by the number of members. The *average* of 3, 4 and 8 is 5. The *average* temperature in Brisbane in January is obtained by adding the 31 maximums and then dividing them by 31.

The word *mean* can be used different ways. One dictionary definition is *the mid-point between the two extremes,* which is not necessarily the same as the *average.* By this definition the *mean* of 3, 4 and 8 is 5½. There are also *weighted means* and *geometric means,* matters of concern to mathematicians.

The important point, however, is that in general use, including scientific work and weather reporting, the word *mean* means the same as the word *average.*

aversion. "My aversion to life in the tropics proved unendurable," said Madame Melba as she appeared in the 1988 television series. Furthermore, she said it at the very opening of the second episode. If Madame Melba meant what she said, she found life in the tropics agreeable. Otherwise it was not her *aversion* she found unendurable, but *life in the tropics.*

a voice in the wilderness. Strictly, a voice *crying* in the wilderness. The quotation is from Matthew, chapter iii, verse 3: "For this is he that was spoken of by the prophet Esaias, saying, The voice of one crying in the wilderness. Prepare ye the way of the Lord."

await/wait. "Mr Lange is awaiting on a statement from the French government" (ABC news).

The sentence should read either *Mr Lange was awaiting a statement from the French government* or *Mr Lange was waiting on a statement.*

If you are *waiting on* someone you are serving them a bowl of soup.

See also **waiter/waiting/waitress.**

awful Australianisms. The following are claimed to be specific Australian contributions to the debasement of the English language:

> *Wage fixation* as a pompous way of saying *wage fixing.*
> *Industrial disputation* instead of *industrial dispute.*
> The use of *enormity* to mean *difficulty* or *bulk.*
> *Finalise,* meaning *to bring to a conclusion.*

awhile/a while. *Awhile* is an adverb meaning *for a short time. A while* is a noun meaning *a period of time* (which may be short or long). Note:

> They then rested awhile (correct)
> They then rested for awhile (wrong)
> Let us pause for awhile (wrong)
> Let us pause awhile (right)
> Let us pause for a while (right)

In other words, do not use *for* with *awhile.*

axis. The plural of *axis* is *axes.*

Ayers Rock. *Ayers Rock* is so spelt. It was named after Sir Henry Ayers, premier of South Australia. Do not spell *Ayer's Rock* or *Eyre's Rock.* The Aboriginal name of *Uluru* is rapidly gaining acceptance as the name for Ayers Rock.

B

bach. Pronounced *batsh*, to rhyme with *catch*. A visitor to Australia, C. E. Jacomb, who published his book "*God's Own Country*" in 1914, pointed out that Australians had coined a new word, *baching*, which "expresses vividly, if crudely, the ugly life it gives a name to." Actually the use of the word in Australia dates back to the 1880s or earlier.

Australians then have the verb *to bach*, meaning *to live on one's own, often in makeshift quarters*. The New Zealanders go one better and have a noun. Where Australians refer to *a weekender*, for a second or holiday house, New Zealanders refer to *a weekend bach*.

back. For use as *ago*, see **ago**.

background. "We'd better background all this," said the film reviewer John Hinde on the ABC, 17 March 1986. *Background* is a noun. Its use as a verb (as John Hinde was using it) has only a slender dictionary backing. It should be regarded as informal. *We'd better put all this into perspective* would be a more acceptable way of saying the same thing.

backward/backwards. Either word is correct, though *backward* is now more common.

bacteria/bacterium. One such organism is a *bacterium*, a number are *bacteria*. See **lost singular**.

bail/bale. Here we have a pretty kettle of fish. Let's try to get it sorted out.

Bail in the legal world is *a deposit paid as security against the non-appearance of an accused person in court*. It stems from the Old French word *baillier, to hand over*.

Therefore, if we are getting someone out of a mess, we talk metaphorically about *bailing them out*. Some dictionaries say that you can spell this *baling out*, but since the derivation seems clearly from the legal word *bail*, we cannot agree.

Next, we come to the *bailing* or *baling* out of a boat. The word is from the Old French *baille* (bucket), and may be spelt either way. Since it seems at least as likely as not that the action of jumping out of an aeroplane is an imaginative extension of the action of baling out a boat, then that too can be spelt either way.

Bail, in the sense of *a device to restrain cows during milking*, is said to be a specifically Australian usage. From it we get *to bail up*, meaning (a) *to put a cow into a bail* (b) the bushranging use of *to accost or threaten for the purpose of robbery* (c) *to accost a person and impede their escape for the purpose of talking to them*. The word comes from Old French again, in this case *baile* (stake).

Then we have the word *bale*, as in *wool bale*, meaning *a large package*. This word comes from the same root as *ball*, the Old Norse word *böllr*. Hence *I've got to bale up this load of books, He was baling up the hay*.

We should also note the word *baleful*, meaning *harmful* or *menacing*. This comes from an Old Norse word meaning *evil*.

banal. Something that is *banal* is *so commonplace that it is not worth repeating*. The word may be pronounced *ban-NAL*, *BAN-nal* or in the French mode, *ban-AHL*. The word came into the language from Norman French, and occurred in the term *bannal mill*, the mill belonging to the lord of the manor which the common people were obliged to use. The *ban-AHL* pronounciation is a latter-day affection which should be avoided, as should *BAY-nal*. Prefer the pronunciation *ban-NAL*, to rhyme with *canal*, which is consistent with the pronunciation of *banality*.

bandicoot looks like an Aboriginal word and is often taken to be one. The word has certainly been around in Australia a long time: the phrase *poor as a bandicoot* was familiar in the early 1840s. The word comes however from India, the Telegu *pandi-kokku*, which means *pig-rat*. As *bandicoot* it is recorded in Anglo-Indian English from 1789.

The bandicoot has had, as they say, a bad press. Not only can you be as poor as a bandicoot, but as miserable or as bald as one. Sir Henry Parkes once said of an opponent that he was "as miserable as an orphan bandicoot on a burnt ridge."

In fact one is not *as bald as a bandicoot* but *as bald as a coot*. The *bald coot* is a vernacular name for the purple gallinule, *Porphyrio porphyrio*, found in many parts of Australia.

barracouta. This well-known Australian fish is now frequently referred to and marketed under the South African name *snoek*, in an attempt to mask its rather low reputation in the kitchen (too many bones; often wormy). This kind of manipulation of the language in the interests of commerce should be opposed.

barbecue. For a nation which has elevated the barbaric cult of the backyard barbecue to an art form we have considerable difficulty in spelling the word correctly.

It very often appears as *barbeque*, presumably a back-formation from the jocose Bar-B-Q.

Barbecue is from a Haitian word meaning *a wooden framework mounted on posts*.

basic. The more educated pronunciation of this word is *BASE-ik*. However the American pronunciation *BASS-ik* is also common in Australia. Prefer *BASE-ik*, as many Americans do.

basically. Basically, *basically* is a useful word.
  However, this from a story by Shirley Hazzard:

> Mr Bekkus frequently misused the word "hopefully." He also made a point of saying locate instead of find, utilise instead of use, and never lost an opportunity to indicate or communicate; and would slip in a "basically" when he felt unsure of his ground.

basis. The plural of *basis* is *bases*.

bas-relief. A *bas-relief* is *a sculpture in which figures project slightly from a background.* It may be pronounced with the *bas* as *bar* or to rhyme with *has*. The former is preferred.

bastardry. When Eric Lambert's famous novel about the second world war, *The Twenty Thousand Thieves*, was published in London in the early 1950s, his publishers assumed that his chapter heading "Short Pause for Bastardry" was a mistake, and to Lambert's fury printed it as "Short Pause for Bastardy".
  Bastardy is, of course, a standard English word meaning *the condition of being illegitimate by birth.* It has no close relationship to the Australian word *bastardry*, which means *deliberate provocative, irritating and malicious behavior, especially on the part of authority.*
  Lambert saw himself as the victim of some British bastardry.

B.C./A.D. The *Christian era,* as it is sometimes called, dates from the birth of Christ supposedly in the year A.D. 1. In fact it is now believed that Jesus Christ was born in 12 B.C. There was no year 0, and the year 1 B.C. was followed immediately by the year A.D. 1.
  B.C. stands for *Before Christ* and A.D. for *Anno Domini*, which is Latin for *in the Year of the Lord.*
  Jews do not of course accept the divinity of Christ, and have their own system of chronology, dating from the supposed foundation of the world in 3760 B.C. Muslims date their era from 622 A.D. In practice non-Christian societies often have to use the Christian reckoning for convenience, in such cases frequently adding to the Christian date the letters B.C.E. (Before the Common [or Christian] Era or C.E. (Common [or Christian] Era).
  A new chronological measurement increasingly in use by archaeologists, historians and scientists is B.P. (Before the Present). It is important to note that B.P. is *not* a calendar date. If archaeologists and others wish to refer to a *specific*

date in the past they will use B.C. and A.D. like the rest of us, for instance in such a statement as "We shall now discuss what might have been happening in Egypt in the year 4500 B.C."

B.P. is a *carbon-age* date, based on the technique of radio-carbon dating. Since solar radiation has not been constant over the millennia, and since there is still much dispute about variations and inaccuracies in such dating, radio-carbon dates are given as (say) 18000 B.P., plus or minus 800 years. This means that the date has two out of three chances of being right within 800 years.

Since *Before the Present* is an unsatisfactory way of measuring accurately, for of course it changes all the time, it has been agreed that B.P. will mean *before 1950*. The year 1950 was chosen because the radio-carbon content of the atmosphere was then approximately what it had been before the Industrial Revolution. At that date some two hundred years of pollution by the burning of fossil fuels had been neutralised by the effect of the atom tests held since 1945.

The abbreviations *k.yr.* (thousand years) and *m.yr* (million years) are also in use by archaeologists and others, as in such a sentence as "Bass Strait was created by rising waters some 12 k. yr. ago." Again, it is important to note that these measurements relate, not to calendar computations, but to radioactive dating techniques with standard errors necessarily applied.

beat up. We are used to the phrase, firstly as an adjective to describe *something showing the signs of wear*, and secondly as a verb, meaning *to assault viciously*.

The word has however another, colloquial meaning or meanings, at least in Australia. It can mean *to put together a tendentious, manufactured case* against someone or something. In a closely related sense it can also mean *to systematically organise supporters*.

"It was a great political beat-up," said Michelle Grattan on ABC television in October 1985, meaning that it was a cobbled-together, would-be sensational story. This usage was current at least as early as the early 1970s, when the magazine *Nation Review* inaugurated an Eggbeater Award for the worst *beat-up* of the week. In the second sense of *drumming-up support* we have found it used in a Victorian parliamentary enquiry as far back as 1911: "Were your friends beaten up to pay their half-crown subscriptions?"

beer glasses. One of the few areas in which Australians obstinately adhere to regional variations in nomenclature is that of beer glasses and beer measures. A *pot* in Western Australia is, for instance, twice the capacity of one in Victoria, Tasmania and Queensland. Conservatism among drinkers is so strong that in New South Wales, Tasmania and the Northern Territory beer measures are still in fluid ounces rather than millilitres.

Glass Size	115 ml 4 oz	140 ml 5 oz	170 ml 6 oz	200 ml 7 oz	225 ml 8 oz	285 ml 10 oz	425 ml 15 oz	575 ml 20 oz
N.S.W	–	pony	–	seven	–	middy	schooner	pint
VIC	–	pony	small	glass	–	pot	schooner	–
QLD	–	small beer	–	–	glass	pot	–	–
S.A	–	pony	–	butcher	–	schooner	pint	–
W.A	Shetland pony	pony	–	glass	–	middy	schooner	pot
TAS	small beer	–	a beer six	–	eight	ten, or pot	–	–
N.T.	–	–	–	seven	–	handle	schooner	–

before the present (B.P.). See **B.C./A.D.**

begging the question. "I'd like to beg that question," said a professor on ABC radio on 15 August 1985.

From the context of the discussion the professor appeared to mean that he wished to *postpone consideration of the matter*. The dictionaries say that this is wrong. If the professor wished to use the phrase in a colloquial sense, that sense would be that he wished to *evade* the question.

Begging the question doesn't mean this. Its primary meaning is that the person concerned *unwarrantably assumes that the matter under discussion is already proved*. To put this another way, *it is trying to prove an argument by using an argument that is itself open to argument*. Examples are arguing that *Australia needs an aircraft carrier because Indonesia is planning to invade us*, or arguing that *there is nothing cruel in catching fish because they feel no pain*.

behind the eight ball. To be *behind the eight ball* means *to be in a disadvantageous position, not an advantageous one*. The player of snooker whose ball is behind the eight (black) ball is not allowed to hit it when making a shot.

benthic/demersal/pelagic. The development of marine science in Australia in recent years is bringing some scientific terms into greater prominence. These three adjectives are now frequently seen, and not only in the scientific literature. They are worth noting.

Benthic means *living in or on the bottom of the sea*; the flounder is a benthic fish.

Demersal means living *above the bottom of the sea but not on it*, as with the whiting.

Pelagic means the rest — the fish that swim merrily *in the middle and upper reaches of the ocean*.

bereaved/bereft. Both are correct. In general, *bereft* is used in normal discourse (*Imaginatively, he was quite bereft*) and *bereaved* when the reference is to death: *a bereaved son.*

berm. New Zealand English for *a nature strip.*

berserk. "When the Queen dropped her handbag we went berserk to see what was inside it," said a journalist.

Berserk does not just mean *frenetic activity*, as the journalist appears to believe. It means *violent, uncontrolled and destructive activity*. The word is Icelandic; it means *wearing a bear's coat.*

bête noire. In French a *bête noire* (plural *bêtes noires*) is, literally, *a black beast*. We use the term in English to identify something we particularly dislike, particularly a person: *He's my* bête noire. Note (1) that the term is not yet sufficiently anglicised for italics not to be used; (2) that one frequently sees it incorrectly *spelt* as *bête noir*, especially in newspapers.

between. It is still held by some that *between* (which is related to the word *twain*) should only be used when talking of *two* things, and that *among* should be used for more than two.

This argument holds that one should say, for instance, *She slipped a number of leaflets* among *the pages of the book,* not *between the pages.*

This argument no longer holds validity, if it ever did. *Between* expresses a relationship to surrounding things which have a specific identity, *among* expresses a more collective and general relationship. So:

> Treaties were then drawn up between the six nations.
> It was difficult to distinguish between the three leaders in the race.
> They had to select between four applications.
> The children danced among the flowers in the field.

Note that, if *between* is associated with a following conjunction, then that conjunction must be *and*. Do *not* write *Australian voters have to make the choice between Mr Hawke or Mr Howard*; write *Australian voters have to make the choice between Mr Hawke and Mr Howard.*

See also the two entries following.

between each, between every. "There was an interval of half a mile between each car." This sounds all right at first hearing but, looked at more closely, we see that you cannot have a gap *between a car* unless you cut it in half.

Say rather "There was an interval of half a mile between all cars in the procession", or "between one car and the next."

Note that such a sentence as *She was between 25–30 years old* is incorrect. The hyphen between *25* and *30* means *to*, and the sentence should read: *She was 25–30 years old*, or *She was between 25 and 30 years old*.

between you and I is *wrong*. A preposition, *betweeen* in this case, must be followed by the objective case. *I* is subjective. The objective of *I* is *me*, and the phrase (and others like it) must read:

    between you and me

    between him and her (not between he and she)

    between them and us (not between they and we)

Nevertheless Shakespeare uses "between you and I" in *The Merchant of Venice*.

beyond the pale. "It's not beyond the pale that this could be the real thing," said a member of the panel of the ABC's antiques program, "For Love or Money."

Clearly the speaker meant that it was not beyond the bounds of possibility. She was quite wrong.

Originally the phrase *beyond the pale* meant *beyond the limits of administrative settlement*. The word *pale* comes from Latin and French words meaning *a fence post*. (Compare our word *paling*.) The other side of the fence was where the Wild Ones were.

The meaning has now shifted to mean *over the odds, beyond the limits of decent behavior*.

biannual/biennial. *Biannual* means *happening twice a year*, *biennial* means *happening every two years*. To avoid confusion *twice-yearly* and *two-yearly* may be used.

bicentenary/bicentennial. Note the variation in spelling.

bid. The noun *bid* has as its first meaning *a price offered for something in a contest for purchase*.

A secondary use is as a synonym for *attempt* or *endeavor*. "New Zealanders make bid for *America's* Cup."

This use of the word *bid* has been popularised by the need for journalists to find short words for headlines. It should be avoided.

billion. Those who went to Australian schools were always taught that *billion*, following English and German usage, meant *a million million*.

This is no longer so. Both in Australia and in Britain the American and French definition of *billion*, i.e. *a thousand million*, is now virtually standard. It was adopted generally by the press in the 1970s.

This is a sensible development, and one foreshadowed by Sir Ernest Gowers, in his edition of Fowler's *Modern English Usage*, where he wrote that the word *billion* in the traditional English sense was "useless except to astronomers" and should be dropped.

When confusion between the two meanings of *billion* is possible, it is necessary to make the meaning clear. It is now common, particularly in the Australian press, to avoid the word *billion* altogether, to prevent confusion, and to print *2,300,000,000* or *2,300 million* rather than *2.3 billion.*

Mathematicians, scientists and engineers have their own way of avoiding confusion. Their way of writing a million is 10^6, which is easily remembered if we reflect that a million contains six noughts. (What it actually means, of course, is that if we multiply 10 by 10 we get 100, and if we multiply 100 by 10 we get 1000, and if we do this six times we get a million.)

	British	American	Mathematical
million	million	million	10^6
thousand million	milliard	billion	10^9
million million	billion	trillion	10^{12}
thousand million million	–	quadrillion	10^{15}
million million million	trillion	quintillion	10^{18}

The American usage as given above was adopted internationally in 1948 and reaffirmed in 1982. It is officially recognised in Australia under what is known as "Australian Standard 1000".

Although the British definitions as given above are still upheld in the *Oxford English Dictionary* they should now be regarded as obsolete and only of historical interest.

It is wise to avoid the use of the words *billion* and *trillion* altogether, and to use *a thousand million* (billion) or *a million million* (trillion), or the numerical equivalents, instead.

Note the use of the terms *kilo-*, *mega-* and *giga-* in an increasing number of scientific and other contexts. We are familiar with *kilo-*, meaning a thousand, as in *kilogram*, a thousand grams. *Mega-*, from the Greek *megas* (great) means a million, as in *megawatt*, a million watts. *Giga-*, from the Greek *gigas* (giant), means a thousand million, as in *gigahertz*, a unit of frequency.

bi-weekly/bi-monthly. *Bi-weekly* means either *every two weeks* or *twice a week*. Similarly with *bi-monthly.* The words should be avoided, and *twice-weekly*, *fortnightly*, *two-monthly* used instead.

bizarre. *Bizarre* behavior is behavior that is *unusually unusual*, behavior that is *out of character* or *totally unexpected in the circumstances*. It is somewhat bizarre that the word appears to be one of the few in the English language that come from that most unusual language, Basque, where it means *a beard*. The days, however, when beards meant Bohemia seem to have passed. Often pronounced *biz-AIR*, the correct pronunciation is *biz-ARE*.

Black. For the word *Black* to denote an Aboriginal, see **Aboriginal/Aborigine.**

blame. You can blame a person or a thing *for* something, but you cannot blame a thing *on* a person:

> He blamed the faulty steering for the accident. (correct)
> She blamed her husband for the failure of the marriage. (correct)
> They blamed the delay on the contractors. (wrong)

You cannot *blame* a *delay,* though you can *blame* the *contractors.*

bloc/block. The word *bloc* is used to denote a combination of people, parties, organisations or nations which have joined together with some common interest in mind. One might write of *the Third World bloc at the United Nations* if these countries adopted a united stand on an issue.

The word is closely related to *block.* Both come from the French, *bloc* being a more recent import than *block.* It is, however, naturalised, and does not need italics.

blond/blonde. The usual practice is to use *blonde* to describe a fair-complexioned woman, but otherwise to use *blond,* as in *the blond-haired Swedes.* It would be sensible to use *blond* in all cases, and this is now starting to happen in the Australian press.

blood, sweat and tears. Winston Churchill's famous wartime challenge to the British was, in fact, "blood, toil, tears and sweat," the phrase thus ending on a positive note.

bludger. This admirable Australian word for *an idler, someone not pulling their weight,* originally meant *a man living off the earnings of a prostitute.*

The original sense has not completely disappeared, and some people are sensitive to it. Caution is suggested in the use of the word, whether jocular or not.

blueprint. In origin, of course, *a technical drawing.* From this, by extension, *a master-plan.* Eric Partridge warns: "subtly dangerous [for] its implication that mankind can be satisfactorily arranged for, therefore put out of mind, by devising for it some plan that sounds well and is insanely impractical ..."

boar/Boer/boor/bore A *boar* is a male pig.

A *Boer* is the old — and now considered derogatory — name for the original

boat or ship?

European settlers of South Africa, predominantly of Dutch descent. They are now called *Afrikaners* and their language is *Afrikaans*. The word *Boer* is related to the German word *Bauer*, meaning a farmer or peasant.

A *boor* is *an unmannerly person, a pain in the arse.* The origin of the word is the same as that of *Boer.* Many words of abuse relate back to the image of the land-worker: *peasant* itself, *villain* (= villein), are examples. *Boor* is pronounced to rhyme with *do-er.*

A *bore*, as well as meaning *a hole drilled in the ground*, is also a word for *an earbasher*, someone who pins you down and talks to you until your head spins. It could be related to the old East Anglian word *bor*, meaning a neighbor or gossip.

boat or ship? Technically a *ship* in nautical parlance is a sailing vessel with square-rig sails on three or more masts.

This is worth knowing but is not the main problem, which is when to call a vessel, in ordinary speech, a *boat*, and when to call it a *ship.*

To the seaman a *boat* is *a small open craft* propelled by oars, or a motor, or a small mast and sail. It may be said that, to a seaman, a *boat* is something that can be lifted aboard and carried on a *ship.*

To call a seaman's *ship* a *boat* is a nautical solecism of the first water. A *ship* is *an ocean-going vessel*, which answers for most purposes, except that it's stretching things a bit to refer — say — to someone's blue-water yacht as a *ship.*

The Navy is particularly sensitive to its *ships* being called *boats*, except that we also have to remember that in the Navy submarines and patrol vessels are called *boats.*

Nor does the Navy like its vessels being called — say — *THE Melbourne*, or *THE HMAS Melbourne.* The definite article is not used. "Are you going aboard *Melbourne*?" is the form.

Still, worse things happen at sea.

boffin.

> The ABC's new literary series, "The Book Program", like its new arts series, "State of the Arts", will probably polarise the viewing population. Both share the same problem. If they are too lightweight, the boffins will jump out of their ivory towers in boredom. If they are too esoteric, everyone will turn off.
>
> *Age,* 6 May 1986.

The word *boffin* entered the language just before the second world war, becoming familiar towards the end of that war. Originally Royal Air Force slang, it is said to have been used by fliers to describe their scientific colleagues working on the development of radar. From this the word came into general use to mean *a scientist, particularly one working on abstruse, defence-linked matters.* (And there was another meaning also, lesser known: *boffin* as a naval term to describe an older officer.)

The origin of the word is not clear. Eric Partridge has suggested it may be related to "the bafflers", or to the name of a series of children's books, but there is no agreement.

The use of the word, as in the example above, to mean *intellectuals* is not justified, although it is heard from time to time. It is likely that younger people hear the word as the slang of an older generation and misinterpret its meaning.

The Melbourne film-maker David Parker, in an interview in the *Age* (10 May 1986), talks of a character in his film who is "a 30-year-old boffin who works for the Melbourne tramways":

> He's simple in the sense that his mother did a really good job on him, in an adverse way. He is highly intelligent, very good with his hands, but totally inept socially. To the outside world, he would seem retarded.

Questioned on this, Mr Parker stated that he was using the word *boffin* to mean someone obsessed with a particular activity to the exclusion of normal social behavior. Mr Parker's boffin is not a scientist but a man who builds his own tram. In this case the meaning is still fairly close to the original.

In the *Sydney Morning Herald* of 4 April 1987 Phillip Knightley reviews Richard Hall's book on Peter Wright and the *Spycatcher* trial, *A Spy's Revenge*. Here David Parker's sense of an *outsider* (and not necessarily a scientist) is developed. "A true boffin has to be a bit of a rebel," writes Hall. "His bright ideas are often not given the recognition they deserve. Although perhaps they won't admit it, they can be pretty savage fighters." Knightley adds:

> They are touchy, proud, resentful of colleagues with flash university degrees, prepared to be as savage about the Establishment as any left-winger, and bitter about the influence of the old school tie, because they know it has been used to put down their kind of people.

bogey/bogie/bogy. *Bogey* means (a) one stroke over the standard good score for a hole in golf (par), (b) an evil spirit, as in *bogey man*, (c) to swim, in some Australian colloquial speech, (d) in *bogey-hole*, a swimming-hole.

Bogie means the sets of small wheels seen on railway locomotives and coaches. Items (c) and (d) above may also be spelt *bogie*.

Bogy is an alternative spelling for *bogey* or *bogie*.

bona fide/bona fides. *Bona fide* means *in good faith*, and is an adjective. *Bona fides* means *good faith*, and is a noun. *It was a bona fide agreement; her bona fides was never in doubt.* However *bona fide* used as a noun was common in Australia, and perhaps still is, when applied to a traveller who had to vouch that he or she had covered a certain distance before asking for alcohol at a pub outside normal hours: *Only bona fides served on Sundays.* Here the word was short for *bona fide travellers* and was pronounced *bon-a fides*, the *fides* rhyming with *sides*. Otherwise pronounce *bone-a fidy* (rhymes with *tidy*) and *bone-a-fidies* (rhymes with *tidies*).

bonus A *bonus* is *something extra, paid or given, over what is expected or required.* It is not, however, or should not be, a word meaning *something nice that happens,* as in such a phrase as *It was a bonus that she came early.*

The point of such an objection is not to force people to use words in ways the dictionaries approve, but to try to preserve useful word meanings before they are swallowed up by adaptations. If the original sense of *bonus* is lost, then it will be necessary to find another word to do that job.

The living language is stronger than lexicographers, but part of the job of lexicographers should be to try to preserve aspects of language which they feel are important.

book. There are many definitions of a book, from the dictionary's "portable written or printed work" onwards. The National Library of Australia holds, for purposes of its definitions, that a book should be more than four pages long. The body that administers 'public lending right' in Australia defines a book for its purposes as being more than forty-eight pages. What all definitions of a book would seem to have in common is that a book is an object entire in itself, not forming part of an indefinitely continuing series.

For objects which may sometimes look like books but which in fact are continuing series we have other words, notably *magazine* and *journal.*

It is common in Australia to hear a magazine referred to as a "book," so much so that this usage may be regarded as part of the Australian language. To many people, in other words, the *Australian Women's Weekly* is a "book."

This cannot be called incorrect, if it is part of the living language, as it is. Two points about the usage may, however, be made. The first is that it obscures a useful distinction and thereby may give rise to confusion. The second is that it is an **indicator word** — that is, a word which identifies the speaker as less literate and less educated than others.

The words *book* and *magazine* should be kept separate.

book titles.
1. The title of a book is always *the title that appears on the title page*, not the title that appears on the spine or the dust-jacket. They frequently differ.
2. Titles are often printed either in capital letters or in a mixture of capital letters and small (lower-case) letters:

　　　A Dictionary of MODERN ENGLISH USAGE

This presents problems when it is desired to quote such titles in the text of another work, or in a bibliography. The problem is that we may not be sure what capitalisation would have been used if the title had appeared in upper- and lower-case (capital and small) letters.

To overcome this it is now common, especially in library practice, for all titles to be quoted in lower-case, except of course for proper names:

　　　A dictionary of modern English usage

3. In writing titles for books, short stories etc., follow these rules where both capitals and small letters are being used.

Capitalise the first and last word, and all other words *except*

(a) *the, an, a, and, or, nor*

(b) prepositions (*by, for, to,* etc.)

as shown in the following examples.

The Man Who Loved Children	*What Are We Waiting For?*
My Friends and Other Animals	*Not by Bread Alone*

4. Capitalise each segment of a hyphenated word:

A Damned Close-Run Thing.

boor/bore. See **boar/Boer/boor/bore.**

Botany Bay. When Governor Arthur Phillip sailed for New Holland with the First Fleet in 1787, he expected to establish the convict settlement at Botany Bay, south of Sydney. Captain James Cook had found Botany Bay in 1770 and surveyed it, and it was recommended for settlement by Joseph Banks, who had been with Cook.

At the time of the arrival of the First Fleet in Botany Bay in 1788 the existence of Port Jackson was not known to the Europeans, but Phillip soon located it and, as every schoolchild knows, landed his expedition at Sydney Cove. Port Jackson was a harbor greatly superior to Botany Bay.

Botany Bay, however, remained the general term in use by outsiders for the settlement for many years, even being extended generally to cover all subsequent European settlements in Australia. It was still being used as a misnomer fifty years and more after 1788, and gave rise to many expressions such as *Botany Bay swell* and (of the emancipist Samuel Terry) *Botany Bay Rothschild.* In England it even acquired metaphorical meaning, remote fields on English farms being named "Botany Bay".

Mr Ian Mair has recited for us an old Australian limerick thought daring in its day because of its references to aperients:

There was an old woman of Botany
Who took physic whenever she'd got any,
  With calomel pills,
  And syrup of squills,
And jalop, to break the monotony.

Botany Bay is still sometimes used lightly or jocularly to refer to the European settlement of Australia in the early days, and there is no objection to this.

both/each. Be careful. Take the following sentences:

The annual literary prizes offered by the Premiers of New South Wales and Victoria are both worth about $50,000.

The annual literary prizes offered by the Premiers of New South Wales and
Victoria are each worth about $50,000.

On the face of it to many these sentences mean the same. In fact they are very
different.

The first sentence is saying that the two prizes, taken together, are worth
$50,000 (say $25,000 each). The second sentence says that *each* prize is worth
$50,000, in other words $100,000 in all.

A lot of money to drop on the way to the bank!

bouquet. A *bowkay* of flowers or a *bookay* of flowers — both pronunciations are
correct.

bourgeois literally means a rate-payer, a full citizen of a borough. It is related to
the word *burgess*, which also means this. The word is seldom used in this sense,
however. More commonly it is used as a term of contempt and so used, as
George Orwell pointed out, exclusively by the bourgeoisie itself. It is an
adjective as well as a noun.

The word is used now (a) to denounce those who adhere to materialistic and
conventional middle-class values (b) by Left intellectuals as a synonym for
middle-class.

This raises the vexed question of what, in our society, the middle class is. Is it,
for instance, the class to which people think they belong? Or is it the class that
exploits the working class by standing in a certain economic or ideological
relationship to it? This debate has kept many Australian academics in gainful
employment for years past.

And, of course, by being used instead of the simpler term *middle-class*, and
because it has to many a certain unfamiliar and even mystic air about it, it is also
a **bully word.** It is meant to sound scientific, but in fact it is evaluative and used
as a weapon.

So too is its offshoot *petit-bourgeois*, another way of saying *lower middle-
class*. This is even more of a sneer word, and there is probably even less
agreement about its definition than there is about *bourgeois*. To be *petit-
bourgeois*, a term often applied to self-employed shopkeepers and the like, in
some political, social and academic vocabularies is to be rootless, lost between
the values of the proletariat and the values of the exploiters. A *petit-bourgeois
radical* is a dreadful thing for one member of the Left to say of another. It means
that the object of this scorn is politically untutored, an enthusiast without the
steadying influence of either working-class experience or of theoretical understanding, and altogether a pretty nasty piece of work.

Unfortunately social debate can hardly go on without convenient, even if
misleading, terms for such categories as people find it useful to construct. We
will continue to talk, each of us with our own view of what the terms mean, of

middle-class, *lower middle-class* and *working-class* this-and-thats. *Bourgeois*, however, is a word best avoided if possible.

It is, however, true that for precise use in various Marxist, historical and political contexts the words *bourgeois* and *bourgeoisie* probably remain indispensable. The problem is that *middle-class* in a strict sense most conveniently relates to an earlier historical period when there was a ruling *upper* class as well as a middle class. To convey the sense of a ruling *middle* class the term *bourgeois* has its justification.

The history of this interesting word is covered in some detail in Raymond Williams' admirable *Keywords*.

See also **working class.**

brace in the sense of *a brace of quail*, does not mean *several*, but *two*, or *a pair of*.

bracket. The use of this inoffensive word to mean *group*, as in the sentence *The inhabitants of Double Bay may be assumed to be in the upper income brackets*, is a pretentious example of what has been called *economese*.

brackets. There are three kinds of brackets: the *round bracket* ( ), called *parenthesis* (plural, *parentheses*) in American English and by typesetters and printers; the *square bracket* [ ], sometimes called simply a *bracket*, and the *angle bracket* <>. The printing devices {} are not brackets but *braces*.

ROUND BRACKETS

The chief use of the ordinary round bracket is to remove from a sentence material which is relevant (otherwise it would not be there) but which does not form part of the main thrust of the argument or narrative.

The comment in the paragraph above is an example. The words *otherwise it would not be there* are not really necessary to the sentence, which flows perfectly well without them. However, those words do make a reinforcing argument.

Another example, from Alan Moorehead:

> It is from Howitt's excellent transcription and from Wills' field-books (which were recovered from his grave a day or two later) that we can now piece together the story of how the explorers lived out their last weeks on the Cooper.

The material here enclosed between the brackets is a *parenthesis*, something 'put in beside' the main body of the sentence. Note that a parenthesis does not have to be between round brackets. Parentheses may also occur between commas, or dashes. Although either commas or dashes would serve instead of round brackets in the quotation from Moorehead, in many cases this is not so, and the bracket distances its contents from the rest of the sentence more than do the commas or even the dashes. For this reason material in brackets may more easily be omitted from sentences than parentheses within commas.

However the round brackets can be used for a deliberate literary effect, adding apparently extraneous material which in fact is central to the story:

> Ney provided a pleasing example of soldierly honour — after solemnly pledging his word to Louis XVIII that he would be faithful unto death and capture Napoleon (with the entirely unnecessary addition that the Corsican should be brought captive to Paris in an iron cage) Marshal Ney, Prince de Moskowa, went over to his old commander the moment he saw him, and the two gentlemen roared with laughter over the jest at dinner.
>
> Richard Aldington

Round brackets are also used for straightforward explanatory purposes: *I shall see you next Friday (June 3rd)*; *He then said that it was he (Richard) who was coming.*

SQUARE BRACKETS

Square brackets signify that what is being interpolated is an author's comment or addition to what appears, usually a quotation.

Here are examples:

> "The moon is now [read *not*] made of green cheese," said the astronaut.

Since the author's comment on this statement is made inside the actual quotation marks, square brackets are necessary to show that what is within them is not the astronaut's statement.

Again, you might see in a bibliography an entry such as the following:

> [Thomas Wells?]: *Michael Howe, the last and worst of The Bush Rangers of Van Diemen's Land* (Hobart Town, [1818]).

In this example, the author's name is in square brackets because it does not in fact appear on the book, which is only thought to be by Thomas Wells. The date appears in square brackets because, while we in fact know it was published in 1818, it does not say so on the book. In other words, we do not have a direct authority for saying so.

Note that brackets, round or square, stay *within* the full stop at the end of the sentence if what is in brackets is only part of the sentence, but *outside* the full stop if the whole sentence is in brackets:

> "This is not so," he said (but he was lying).
>
> (He said it was not so, but he was lying.)

ANGLE BRACKETS

Angle brackets are rarely used, and may be disregarded. In the editing of texts they are used to indicate words which are absent but which the editor feels should be present: *Now is the time for <all> good men to come to the aid of the party.*

See also **sic**.

bridal/bridle.

> The parachute is constructed with a stainless-steel bridal cord.

Bridal means *relating to a bride.* Joseph Furphy said of Australia: "Our virgin continent! how long has she tarried her bridal day!"

Bridle, as in a horse's bridle, is *a device for restraining something.* The example above should have been:

> The parachute is constructed with a *bridle* cord.

A *bridle path* is a path so constructed that horses may be ridden along it.

Britain. *Britain* as a word has no official recognition. Indeed the English historian A. J. P. Taylor is scathing about it. The "Scotch," as he calls them — he says this is the English word for the people who live in Scotland, whatever they care to call themselves — "seek to impose 'Britain' — the name of a Roman province which perished in the fifth century and which included none of Scotland nor, indeed, all of England."

The country we often call *Britain* is either *Great Britain* (England, Wales and Scotland) or the *United Kingdom* (England, Wales, Scotland and Northern Ireland). The *British Isles* is a geographical, not a political, term. It refers to a group of islands off the north-west of continental Europe, including Great Britain, Ireland, the Isle of Man, the Shetlands and Orkneys and the Channel Islands.

The official title of the country is *the United Kingdom.*

The use of the words *England* and *English* to denote Great Britain or its inhabitants frequently causes resentment among the Welsh and the Scots.

Scotland used to be known as *North Britain.*

Northern Ireland is sometimes called *Ulster*, though this is a dubious usage, since part of the historical Ulster is in fact a province of the Republic of Ireland.

See also **England/English; Scotch/Scots/Scottish.**

brutalise. The primary meaning of the verb *to brutalise* is *to make someone brutal*, or *to become brutal:*

> In the course of his military training he was brutalised, his moral judgement undermined.

Note that this does *not* mean that he was knocked about.

The sense of this word which means *to treat brutally, especially in a physical sense* is still not accepted by many.

Either an *-ise* or an *-ize* ending is allowable.

Buckley's chance. This Australian expression means *no chance at all.* Many are puzzled because they believe the idiom must refer to William Buckley, the "wild white man," who escaped from the abortive settlement at Port Phillip Heads in 1803 and lived for thirty-two years with the Aboriginals. Buckley, they reason, surely beat the odds and established that an escaped convict had some kind of chance. In fact the phrase comes from the Melbourne store of Buckley & Nunn, established in the 1850s and, until recently absorbed by David Jones, a leading establishment of its kind. There is no documentary evidence for this — or any other — derivation, but the author bases his remarks on the evidence of his family, one of whom worked in Buckley & Nunn's in the 1890s. So — Buckley's chance means *none*, the once-familiar usage being "You've got two chances — Buckley's and none."

bullet/cartridge. See **gun/rifle.**

bully words. Language, like the police force, is a means of social control. Those who have a command of words and can write the right kind of letters have a big advantage in getting their own way, especially with their own kind. The so-called 'unlettered' usually get on well enough simply by not playing the game of words, but even they in the long run come up against the power of language. The medical practitioner who writes a fluent letter to the shire council on his surgery letterhead has more chance of being taken notice of than the man or woman who uneasily tries to make a case across the counter.

Those who do play the game of words strive for advantages against each other. One way is to terrorise, or bully, or to seek to impress with words that sound 'superior'. The use of Latin tags for this purpose, or long unfamiliar words, is passing out of fashion, mainly because hardly anyone now is familiar with either, even to use them against someone else.

The big stick in the game is now words imported from scientific and semi-scientific disciplines, the military, etc. These include:

Interface (from cybernetics and computers), meaning *connect.*

Viable (from biology), meaning *able to stay alive.*

Liaison, liaise (from the military), meaning to *consult,* or *exchange information.*

Ethnic (from anthropology), meaning *pertaining to a linguistic or cultural group.*

Bourgeois (from Marxist political debate), meaning *middle-class.*

Trauma (from medicine), which does *not* mean *a personal crisis.*

Parameter (from mathematics), meaning *limitation.*

Echelon (from military use), meaning *level,* as in *The upper echelons of the business community.*

Context (from language studies), meaning *setting.*

Problematic (from philosophy), meaning *difficult,* or *a question.*

It is well to be on watch for such words, and to realise that they are being used for a special effect, in other words as *bully words.*

Officialdom is fond of bully words, the use of which is intended to *make* people act in certain ways. For instance,

proceed *instead of go*	communication *instead of* letter
report to *instead of* visit	optimum *instead of* best

bureauspeak. The following note describing the "general framework" of the Australian Bicentennial Authority was distributed to branch offices of that body in 1985:

> The authority is an organisation created for a specific purpose and as an organisation has a relatively short and identifiable life span. However, some of the projects and processes established during this short life are intended to continue well beyond 1988. Notwithstanding its unusual features, the authority may be viewed as a socio-technical system operating dynamically in the cultural, social, economic, technological, political and religious environment of Australia. Its operation is essentially one of input, conversion process, and output with these elements linked in a cyclic fashion by a feedback mechanism.

burned/burnt. Prefer *burnt*, except when striving for some special effect, when *burned* may be more suitable.

bus/bused/busing. According to the rules for doubling the final letters of words when they become parts of verbs, *bus* should theoretically become *bussing*, *bussed*, and this spelling is almost standard in the United States.

In British and Australian English, however, the words are an exception to the rule, and the verb forms are *buses/busing/bused*.

bushwhacker. This word, which signifies in Australia *a character from outback, usually one lacking urban skills and graces*, is of quite recent origin in this country. It does not appear in Edward Morris's diligent dictionary, *Austral English*, in 1898, but it is used in a Henry Lawson story published in 1900. Thereafter it moves into common usage, and P. R. Stephensen called his collection of outback sketches (1929) *The Bushwhackers*.

The word probably comes from the United States where, from the middle of the nineteenth century, *to bushwhack* was *to assault from ambush*. Sidney J. Baker, in his *The Australian Language*, says the term *bushwhacker* was used originally in the American Civil War to describe deserters who raided towns and homes for supplies and valuables, and sometimes to mean *guerrillas*. The *guerrilla* meaning continues to survive in the United States, where a *bushwhacker* is also someone *who cuts his or her way through the woods* or *travels or lives in the woods*. In New Zealand the word is used of *someone who clears the bush, especially an axeman*.

The word is spelt either *bushwhacker* or *bushwacker*. Prefer the former, which is closer to the idea of *clearing one's way* and is also far more common.

business/busyness. A *business* is a form of organised activity, especially in trade and commerce. *Busyness* is the state of *being busy*.

by the skin of my teeth. The exact quotation is "I am escaped with the skin of my teeth," from Job, chapter xix, verse 20.

C

cache/cachet. Russell Barton, in a despatch from Canberra in the Melbourne *Age* of 18 July 1987, referred to the approval of Prime Minister Hawke's governmental reorganisation by Mr David Block, a financial strategist from the private sector, as "a cache worth having".

A *cache*, pronounced *cash*, is *a hidden store* — of food, weapons, stolen goods and the like. It is also a verb meaning *to place in such a store: We cached the remainder of the food for our return journey*. It comes from a French word meaning *to hide*.

Russell Barton meant that David Block's approval was a *cachet* worth having. (Perhaps this is what he wrote, and it was the typesetter's fault.) *Cachet* may mean a *seal* or *postmark*, in both French and English, but in both languages it is more commonly used in a figurative sense, to mean that something has *character, style, a seal of approval: That dress has a certain cachet*. It is pronounced *CASH-ay.*

caddie/caddy. A *caddie* carries golf-clubs. A *caddy* contains tea.

cadre. A *cadre* is *a trained, professional nucleus of personnel capable of creating an effective, expanded organisation.* The word is used especially in the armed forces and in industry. It should be pronounced to rhyme with *harder*, not with *staider*, and certainly not as *card-ray.*

calendar. See **perpetual calendar**.

calibre. The *calibre* of a piece of artillery or a firearm is *the measurement across the bore.* Therefore one can have *large calibre* guns or *small calibre* bullets but not *heavy calibre* or *light calibre.*

camp. For the use of this word in its homosexual sense, see **gay.**

can/could. *Can* expresses the *ability* to do something, whereas *may* (or *might*) expresses *possibility.*

Thus the answer to the question "Can we go when we finish our work?" may well be "You *can* go, but you *may* not."

In other words, if a request is being made for a permission which may be refused, the correct version of the above question is "*May* we go when we finish our work?"

cannabis

Similarly, "Could you join this committee?" invites the answer "I *could* but I *will* not." The question should be "*Will* you join this committee?"

cannabis. See **marijuana**.

can not/cannot. Contrary to a widespread belief, there is a difference between *can not* and *cannot*, and both are proper forms. Many believe that *can not* must always be spelt *cannot*.

Can not is used where it is desired to place a special emphasis on the *not*.

It would, for instance, be normal to have *I'm sorry, but she's away interstate, and cannot come tonight.* On the other hand *can not* is needed, rather than *cannot*, in such a sentence as *You can not go round the streets hitting people on the head with a stick.*

cantaloupe. A *cantaloupe, cantaloup* or *cantalupe* is a kind of melon. It is *not* spelled *cantelope* and it is *not* pronounced to rhyme with *antelope*, but with *loop*. The word comes from Cantaluppi ("wolves' song"), once the site of a papal village near Rome, where it was first cultivated.

canvas/canvass. *Canvas* is *a heavy cloth used for sails, tarpaulins and the like.*

To canvass is a verb. It means *to seek out voters and solicit votes*, or *to investigate something thoroughly, especially by discussion.*

capital/capitol. The word *capitol* is used only to refer to (a) a certain temple in ancient Rome, (b) the United States Congress building in Washington D.C., (c) the seat of an United States State legislature. In this last case it is spelt with a small *c*.

Capital Hill in Canberra, the site of the new Parliament House, is so spelt, although *Capitol* is sometimes erroneously seen.

capital letters. In old printing shops, where type was hand-set, each compositor had two boxes of type. The upper box contained capital letters and the lower box the others. Thus capital letters are often called *upper-case letters,* the rest *lower-case letters.*

1. Capital letters are of course used at the beginning of sentences and for proper names such as *George, Samantha, Melbourne, Ansett Airlines, the Germans, the Windsor Hotel, Auntie Mabel, General Brown.*

2. Traditionally we allow capital letters to the *Prime Minister* and the *Premier,* the *Governor-General* and the *Governor,* and the *Church* when we are referring to a specific religious organisation, such as the *Catholic Church.* In politics we also allow capitals to portfolios, for instance the *Minister for Social Security.*

3. Capitals will be used to start a sentence that is quoted within another sentence:

> She turned to him and said: "Drop dead."

4. Capitals *may* be used for an independent question within a question:

> The issue now is, Will we return?

5. Capitals *may* be used for Yes and No within a sentence when used in such a way as to stress their importance:

> Although many voted Yes, many more favored No.

6. Beyond this, the tendency is to use capitals very sparingly. Note these examples:

> The *University of Melbourne,* but *He went to the university.*
> The *Minister for Social Security,* but *The minister said . . .*
> The *Archbishop of Sydney,* but *The archbishop said . . .*
> The *Ford Motor Company,* but *the company's headquarters are at Broadmeadows.*
> *The board of directors of ICI, and its chairman.*
> *A professor of engineering at the University of Adelaide.*
> *The Victorian parliament meets at Parliament House.*
> *The wind came from the south-west.*

7. Some special cases:

(a) Use a capital letter for the word *State* where it refers to an Australian State or a State of the United States of America. This is to avoid confusion with the more general meaning of the word *state.*

(b) A capital letter is normally used for the name of a university course: *She studied Education at the University of Queensland.*

(c) A capital letter is used to distinguish a special geographical region, institution, or historical period: *the Far East,* *the Age of Reason,* the Perth *Bar.*

(d) *The Bible,* but *a biblical reference.*

(e) Capitals are usual for deities: *God the Father and His Son Jesus,* *the Almighty,* *Allah.*

(f) An *Act* of parliament, and a *Bill* before parliament.

8. Do *not* use capitals for the points of the compass, *unless* they are part of a proper name: *South Carolina,* but *southern California.*

9. For the capitalisation of book titles, see **book titles**.

cappuccino. The Italian work *cappuccio* means a hood, or cowl. Thus we get Capuchin monks, who wear a hood; capuchin monkeys, with hair on their heads like a hood; Flinders Island in Bass Strait, called by early explorers the Grand Capuchin, presumably because of a hood of cloud; and a coffee termed a *cappuccino,* because it is topped with hot milk.

The Italian plural of *cappuccino* is *cappuccini,* but Australian custom favors *cappuccinos.*

carburetter/carburettor. Prefer the spelling *carburettor*.

carcase/carcass. This word means *the dead body of an animal* or is used (contemptuously) of a human being who, for instance, *thinks only of his own carcass.*

Either spelling is correct. *Carcass* is preferred, as being closer to the original Italian *carcassa,* but *carcase* is probably more common in Australian usage.

careen/career. *To careen* is a nautical term meaning *to lay a ship over,* especially *to put a ship ashore deliberately so that she may be exposed by the tides for cleaning purposes:* hence *Careening Cove* in Sydney Harbor.

It is however not uncommon today to read of a car *careening* down a street. This is because of a confusion with the word *careering,* meaning *to move rapidly and out of effective control.*

Caribbean. The Caribbean Sea is bounded by the West Indies, Central America and the north coast of South America. Pronounce *karrib-EE-an,* not *karr-IBB-ian.*

caricature. A *caricature* is a portrait of someone which purposely distorts some feature of that person for comic effect. It may be drawn, written or acted.

The word is pronounced with the stress on the first syllable: *CAR-ic-ature.* The pronunciation *car-IC-ature* is incorrect. As is the spelling *characterture.*

carillon. A *carillon* is a set of bells hung in a tower. There is a carillon at Lake Burley Griffin in Canberra. The word is, curiously, pronounced not as spelt, but as *carillion,* with the stress on the second syllable.

carousal/carousel. A *carousal* is *a merry drinking party.* Pronounce *ka-RAUZ-al.*

A *carousel* is (a) an alternative name for a *merry-go-round,* widely used in Europe and also in the United States; (b) in olden times, *a form of tournament;* (c) *a circular magazine for the projection of slides;* (d) *a luggage sorter used in airports.* Pronounce *ka-roo-SEL.*

Cartesian. See **Descartes.**

cartridge. See **bullet/cartridge.**

case. In many foreign languages the form of a noun, adjective or pronoun changes according to its relation to other words in the sentence.

English is very largely an uninflected language and examples of case changes in words are few. However, when we argue whether we should say *It is I* or *It is me* we are arguing about the case that the personal pronoun *I* should be in, nominative or accusative (or, as it is more trendy to say these days, subjective or objective).

Examples of words that change their form according to case are:
ACCUSATIVE OR OBJECTIVE (sometimes called the *direct object*)
Pronouns show the accusative case: *me, him, her, us, them, whom.*
GENITIVE OR POSSESSIVE (*of* whom or *of* what?)
1. Nouns in English change when entering the genitive case by adding *'s* or *s'*: *of the book* becomes the *book's*, and *of the books* becomes the *books'*, thus:

> This is the cover of the book
> This is the book's cover.

In a case such as this *the book's* has the function of an adjective.
2. Pronouns show the genitive case: *mine, yours, his, hers, ours, theirs, whose.*
DATIVE (*to* whom or *to* what, sometimes called the *indirect object*)

In a sentence such as *He sent me away* the word *me* is in the objective (accusative) because it is the object of the verb. But in *He sent me a handkerchief* the word *me* is dative because it answers the question *to whom?* It is the word *handkerchief* that is the accusative of the sentence. *Me* is said to be the *indirect object*, which is always in the dative case.

Datives include the words listed under *accusative* above. They have the same form.

On the genitive, see also **double possessives**.

caster/castor. A *caster* is a person who casts something, or a machine which casts metal. It is also the name of *a dispenser which sprinkles (casts) sugar*, the sugar therefore being *caster sugar*. *Castor* has several meanings, the most familiar being *a form of wheel attached to furniture*, and in the phrase *castor oil*.

casuarina. This name for the (predominantly) Australian species of tree comes from the Malay word for a cassowary, *kasuari*. The connection is the fine, drooping leaves of the tree, supposedly like the feathers of the cassowary.

The tree is often called *she-oak* (from the resemblance of the wood to oak) or *beef-wood* (from the red color of the wood).

Bernard O'Dowd told the author of this book that it was the sound of wind in the she-oaks that inspired the words in his famous sonnet "Australia": "or trail uncanny harp-strings from your trees."

catalog/catalogue. Our word *catalog/catalogue* comes via Old French from the Latin *catalogus* and the Greek *katalogos*, which words mean *a list* or literally, *to collect completely*.

The *-us* and *-os* endings in such cases are normally dropped when the word is adopted into English. The *-ue* ending on *catalogue* is, in English, merely a flourish taken over from the French. It serves no purpose in English and the American spelling *catalog* is preferred and recommended.

Catch-22 does not just mean an unexpected difficulty. It means a *no-win situation,* but it also means more than this. It means that *the very fact that you meet a pre-requisite is a sufficient reason in itself for your not being able to achieve the goal for which you met the pre-requisite.* There is an element of the crazy logic of *Catch-22* in Groucho Marx's famous statement that he would not want to be a member of any club which would admit him as a member.

Catch-22 is very seldom used in its proper and pure sense. We tend to use *Catch-22* to describe a situation where initiative and reaction simply cancel each other out: *You can't have a swim until you've signed this form and you can't sign this form until you've had a swim.* It is true that common both to this use of the phrase and the 'pure' use of the phrase is that a situation is created from which the victim can not escape, but the cruel irony of the original meaning, that the victim has by doing the right thing achieved his own downfall, is missing.

There is no doubt that *Catch-22* will be used almost exclusively in the debased sense, and nothing much can be done about that.

It is worth turning to the source, Joseph Heller's great anti-war novel, *Catch-22*:

> Orr was crazy and could be grounded. All he had to do was ask; and as soon as he did, he would no longer be crazy and would have to fly more missions . . . If he flew them he was crazy and didn't have to; but if he didn't want to he was sane and had to . . . "That's some catch, that Catch-22," [Yossarian] observed. "It's the best there is," Doc Daneeka agreed.

categorical. This word, when found in such a phrase as *The firm issued a categorical denial,* does not mean *emphatic,* but means *unconditional, unqualified.*

Heard on the radio: "He quite uncategorically said . . ." The speaker meant that *he said without any qualifications.* But he messed it up.

A *category* is *a division in a system of classification.* Items associated with the steering assembly in a car constitute a *category* within the total parts necessary to construct a car. If something is placed in a category it is clearly stated that it *belongs to the system,* that there is no argument or doubt about it. Thus to state something *categorically* is *to state it quite certainly and positively.* On the other hand to speak *uncategorically* is *to introduce the element of doubt and uncertainty.*

categorise/categorisation. To categorise something is to *place it in a category,* to *classify* it: *We no longer believe in categorising people on the basis of the shapes of their heads.*

The words *classify* and *classification* are much to be preferred: they are simpler, and have less air of pretentiousness about them.

category. A *category* is *a grouping of things or people.* It is a word imported into general English from philosophy, and conveys the sense of *a grouping more restricted than a class.* The use of the word simply to mean *a class* has been criticised.

Catholic/Roman Catholic. Catholic means *universal, all-embracing.* It comes from the Greek word *holos,* meaning *whole.* When applied to a woman or man it can mean broad-minded, of wide sympathies or interests.

In religion the Catholic Church was originally the whole body of Christians. When that Church split between the Latin or Western branches and the Greek or Eastern branches, *Catholic* applied to that section of the Church, the Latin section, which was based on Rome.

After the Reformation sections of the Catholic Church which became independent maintained that it was they who remained in essential continuity with the earlier Catholic Church, and that the Catholics centred on Rome were not true Catholics but were Roman Catholics.

However self-serving and even silly this now appears to us, sects and splitters almost always have to maintain that it is *they* who represent the pure doctrinal line of this-or-that.

So, to call Catholics *Roman Catholics* was, and remains, a shot in a religious war. It is true that the Catechism of the Church of England says "I believe in the Holy Catholic Church" (some Anglicans keep their mouths shut at this point) but, whatever this may mean, it does not mean that Anglicans adhere to the Church of Rome.

Good manners and the increasing respect that Churches are showing each other both dictate that those who claim to belong to the Church of Rome should be called what they want to be called, which is *Catholics.*

If *Roman Catholics* is to be used at all, it should be used only where there is a real need to distinguish them from others who may also call themselves Catholics.

caviar/caviare. Should you move in the appropriate circles, the spelling *caviar* is to be preferred.

The phrase *caviar to the general* needs to be seen in context. Hamlet, in act II, scene ii, is speaking to the players, and telling them that one of their performances did not please the multitude, but won approval from the discriminating:

for the play, I remember, pleased not the million; 'twas caviar to the general: but it was . . . an excellent play . . .

Caviar, then, is assumed to be an acquired taste, not something everyone would like, and the phrase in fact means *caviar to the general* [*multitude*].

cello. The word *cello* (pronounced *chello*) is used for one of the larger members of the violin family of string instruments. Like the word *piano* it is a fully anglicised word. A recent development among musicians and the writers of concert programs is to use *celli* for the plural, but this is both affected and incorrect. In Italian *cello* is an adjective meaning *little,* and the plural is *celli*. In English *cello* is a noun and the plural is *cellos*.

The full name of the cello is *violoncello,* meaning *little big violin.* The explanation of this oddity is that the *big cello* is what we call the *bass* or *double bass.* Cello should not be written *'cello.*

Celt, Celtic. The Celts were the early inhabitants of Great Britain and Ireland. Many Celts were dispossessed by the Anglo-Saxons and driven west and north, to survive in the mountain fastnesses of Wales and the Scottish Highlands, in remote Cornwall, in Brittany and, of course, in Ireland. Except in Cornwall, their languages have survived too.

Australian society has often been called *Anglo-Celtic,* meaning that the origins of most of its settlers — apart from the Aboriginals — have been in England, Scotland, Wales and Ireland. It is mainly because of the number of Irish migrants to Australia since 1788 that this is a more appropriate term than *Anglo-Saxon.*

Celt and *Celtic* may be pronounced either *kelt, keltic* or *selt, seltic.* The *selt* pronunciation is uncommon in Australia, and even sometimes ridiculed, but it is acceptable and, incidentally, *seltic* is the correct pronunciation of the leading Scottish soccer team, Celtic.

censer/censor. A *censer* is a container for incense used in religious ceremonial. A *censor* is one who seeks to influence or suppress the opinions, writings etc. of others.

centenary. Pronounce *sen-TEEN-ary.*

Central Australia. Officially there is no such place as Central Australia, which is included in the Northern Territory. It did, however, exist as a separately administered territory between 1926 and 1931, the centre being Alice Springs. *The Centre,* however, is a common way of describing the interior regions of Australia around Alice Springs.

centre round. *The interests of sports-loving Australians centre round the coming* America's *Cup races off Fremantle.* Matters cannot be *centred round* something, but they can be *centred on* or *centred in* it.

centrifugal/centripetal. A *centrifugal* force is *a force moving away from a centre.* In other words, when things rotate there is a tendency for them to throw things outwards, as with a garden spray. The opposite is *centripetal* (not *centripedal*), *a force acting inwards towards a centre.*

centuries.

> So, toward undreamt-of-destinies
> He slouches down the centuries

said one of our poets of the Australian.

This being so, we may as well get the centuries correct.

The 20th century began on 1 January 1901, which as it happened was the day of the inception of the federated Australian nation. This century will end at midnight on 31 December 2000.

In other words, the year 2000 belongs to the 20th century, not to the 21st. The third millenium of our era will *not* commence until the dawning of the year 2001.

And the same applies to all other centuries.

The reason for this quickly becomes apparent if you count the years in a century, starting with the first year in that century.

Similarly the *third decade* (let us say) in the 20th century did not run from 1920 until 1929, but from 1921 to 1930.

NOTE: a newspaper informs us of alluvial mining in Victoria *in the 18th century.* The writer clearly believes that because ninety-nine of the hundred years in the last century started with the figures *18*, it must be the *eighteenth* century. This is not so. It was the *nineteenth* century.

See also **(the) turn of the century**.

cerebral. *Cerebral* is an adjective meaning *relating to the brain.* Australians pronounce it *SER-e-bral*, Americans *ser-EEB-ral.*

ceremonial/ceremonious. A *ceremonial* occasion is one that involves the use of *ceremony.* A *ceremonious* occasion is one that is *excessively polite and formal,* one in which the organisers *pile on the agony.*

chairman/chairperson. *Chairman* is the traditional word for a person presiding over a board or meeting of some kind. The trouble is that the syllable *-man* suggests that the word favors the male as against the female. Or so we have come to see since, during the last generation or so, this and many similar matters have been pointed out to us by a large number of angry women.

There are women prepared to continue to accept *chairman* as a satisfactory description of the post and the person occupying it, even for women, but the need to find an alternative is widely recognised.

The possibilities include:

1. abolish the word *chairman* and substitute *chairperson;*
2. keep *chairman* for a male holder of such an office, *chairwoman* for the female;
3. refer to the office as *the Chair,* the office-holder as *Mr Chair* or *Madame Chair.*

The word *chairperson* is an ugly and self-conscious neologism, an insensitive language atrocity. One of the other solutions is recommended.

See **(the) female critique.**

chameleon. This animal's name is pronounced with a hard *ch* and the stress on the second syllable, thus: *ka-MEEL-eon.* The first syllable is not pronounced *sham.*

chamois/shammy. *Chamois* should be pronounced in the French way (approximately *sham-wah*) when referring to the animal, but *shammy* when referring to the leather used for cleaning cars. In Australia the leather is made from sheepskin.

Shammy is acceptable in Australia as the spelling of the cleaning leather.

The plural of *chamois* is written the same: *chamois.*

chaperon. A *chaperon* is *a female escort, especially for a young girl on a social occasion.* Spell this way, not as *chaperone,* but pronounce to rhyme with *bone.*

character. See **attribute/character/property/quality/trait.**

charismatic. It is not good enough to mean, when you talk of someone as *charismatic,* that that person appeals strongly to you.

Charismatic means *having a special personal quality which makes a person capable of influencing and inspiring large numbers of people.*

charted/chartered. A trap for the unwary, as witness the following, from an article on the musical "Cats" in the *Sydney Morning Herald* (13 July 1985): "The idea of intrigue and innovation took us into previously uncharted areas . . ." Or Maximilian Walsh on the Tokyo economic summit: "We are moving into unchartered territory" *(Age,* 5 May 1986).

The writers of course meant *uncharted,* in other words *unmapped.* To be *unchartered* means to lack a *charter,* which is a document conveying rights and privileges, or a legal agreement covering the conditions of hire of some form of transport: *The ship had recently been unchartered, and a new agreement was under discussion.*

chasm. A *chasm* is *a deep cleft in the ground.* Some who appear on television believe that it is pronounced with the *ch* as in *cheese.* The word is, however, pronounced *kasm.*

chauvinist/chauvinism. These useful words are in danger of being filched by those who use them in a feminist context: "He is a male chauvinist." In fact the word comes from Nicholas Chauvin, a vociferous patriot of Napoleonic times, the kind of person Rudyard Kipling referred to as a "jelly-bellied flag-flapper." Since there are still plenty of these around, we need to hold on to the word in its primary sense. When used to apply to the sexes, the word is best qualified: a *male chauvinist,* a *female chauvinist.*

chemist/pharmacist. The word *chemist* in Australia, like the word *engineer,* is not protected by legislation. Anyone may tell the world that they're a chemist. In practice two sets of people are called *chemists*: a certain kind of scientist, and *pharmacists.* There is some confusion and unhappiness about this.

A professional *chemist* in Australia has completed a science course, majoring in chemistry, at a tertiary institution. Chemists work in an area concerned with the composition, properties and reactions of substances. There is a professional body, the Royal Australian Chemical Institute, to which they may belong. If they do so, they are entitled to call themselves *chartered chemists.*

A pharmacist has completed a course at tertiary level in the properties of pharmaceutical substances, in other words drugs, as they relate to the treatment or prevention of human disease. He or she is registered with a State pharmacy board, and may belong to the Pharmaceutical Society. *Pharmacist* is a legally protected word.

Both in Australia and in Britain science chemists are cross because most of us call pharmacists *chemists* and their shops *chemist shops,* rather than *pharmacies.*

The complaint is of long standing. The great German chemist Justus Liebig wrote in 1838 that "England is not the land of science: their chemists are quite amateurish and ashamed to call themselves chemists because the pharmacists — whom they despise — have appropriated the name."

Pharmacists these days say that they *want* to be called *pharmacists,* in order to be recognised as health specialists and not just as purveyors of hot-water bottles.

It may be logical, and even sensible, to call our local 'chemist' a *pharmacist* and his shop a *pharmacy.* We could even adopt the American *drugstore* and *druggist.* But it is very hard to persuade people to change the way they use words by high-minded appeals to do so.

chic means *stylish, elegant, fashionable.* This word is preferably pronounced *sheek*, though *shick* is allowed.

childish/childlike. If we say that someone's behavior is *childish* we disapprove of it. But if we say that it is *childlike* we shall probably be approving: *Her artistic vision was movingly childlike.*

Chinaman/Chinese. *Chinaman* is 'old Australian' for a *Chinese.* It is not now, nor has it been for many decades, an acceptable term.

The word *Chinaman* remains in use in cricket, where it refers to *a ball from a left-handed bowler to a right-handed batsman that spins from off to leg.*

chivalric. A *chivalric* action is an action which is in conformity with the manners of a medieval knight: courage, honor, helping the weak, being courteous to women (and, one would hope, to anyone else as well).

Chivalric has been heard pronounced on ABC television as *chiv-AL-ric.* This is wrong, and the stress is on the first syllable: *CHIV-al-ric,* as it is with *CHIV-al-rous.*

choice. "Fellow citizens, you have the choice today of voting for the Australian Labor Party!"

In fact the unfortunate citizens were offered no choice, though they did have an *opportunity* of voting for the Labor Party.

Choice implies *choosing between two or more offerings.* The sentence would have been correct if it had been phrased *you have the choice of voting for the Australian Labor Party rather than any other.*

choler/collar. *Choler* means *anger* or *ill humor: The rude reply intensified his choler.* Because *to be hot under the collar* is an idiom which means *to be angry or ill humored,* it is sometimes — and incorrectly — written as *hot under the choler.*

chook is the admirable Australian word for a *domestic fowl.* Although essentially a vernacular, that is an informal, or slang, word, it is steadily moving into the position of being an accepted, proper usage, though it is not quite there yet.

Christian name/first name/given name. Until quite recently in Australia it was generally assumed that everyone's 'baptismal' name, their name or names other than their family name or surname, was a *Christian name.*

We now realise that not everyone is a Christian, and the usage has been dropped. We now ask people *What are your first (or fore) names* or *What are your given names?* Take your pick. We rather prefer *first names,* on the ground that we are all 'given' surnames as well as first names.

chronic. *Chronic*, as in the phrase *she had a chronic dose of the flu*, or *it's been a chronic winter*, is an illiteracy.

In those phrases *chronic* is being used as though it meant no more than *severe*. But *chronic* has a precise meaning and no other. It comes from the Greek word for *time* (hence *chronometer*) and means *something that lingers on*, is *constantly present or recurring*. To say that people have *chronic malaria* does not mean that they have acute or severe malaria but, to the contrary, that they have recurring bouts of the illness.

circa is a Latin word meaning *about*, in the sense of *about ten years ago*. It is frequently used with dates, for instance accompanying photographs in books or notices about historical sites, such as this:

This building was erected *circa* 1825.

More frequently it is abbreviated, so that the above notice would read:

This building was erected *c.* 1825.

(The abbreviation for *circa* is sometimes *c.*, as above, and sometimes *ca*.)

Strictly speaking, since it is a foreign word simply on loan to us, it should appear (as it does here) in italics.

claim. To *claim* that your car does two hundred kilometres an hour, that the police investigation was unfair, or that you are the fastest gun in the West, is regarded by many as an unfortunate misuse of the word. You may *claim* a goldmine, a share of the moon or the rights that properly belong to you. In other words, you may assert, by using the word *claim*, that you are entitled to something. Because of this 'strongness' about the word it has come to be used as a stand-in for more appropriate words: properly, you *assert* that your car does two hundred kilometres an hour, you *allege* or *maintain* that the police investigation was unfair, you *declare* that you are the fastest gun in the West.

Clark/Clarke. Marcus *Clarke*, the author of *His Natural Life*, but Manning *Clark*, the historian. Professor Manning Clark's surname is *Clark*; the name is not hyphenated, and Manning is a first name.

classical/romantic. *Classical* has two meanings. The first relates to ancient times, and broadly means the literature and other arts of the ancient Greeks and Romans.

Classical virtues in the arts, as exemplified by the ancients, came to be identified as balance and restraint; they were intellectual rather than emotional, concerned with form, precise, harmonious. In European culture the eighteenth century is often identified as the period in which the classical ideal was sought after. So *classical* is also used for the period in modern times which preceded the *romantic*.

Romanticism is less easily defined. Firstly, it was opposed to many of the classical precepts, which were seen as artificial, limiting, placing emphasis on collective taste rather than individual expression. Reason — a classical ideal — is not all; the emotions also need to be brought into play. Man is naturally good, and the forms of civilised behavior, so important to the classical vision, may inhibit the search for freedom, truth and beauty. Spontaneity rather than restraint is important.

There is a vast literature on romanticism, the dominant intellectual mode of the nineteenth century and of our own. In English literature Pope is seen as the archetypal writer of the classical period, Wordsworth as the first major writer of the romantic.

Used narrowly, *the Romantics* is used to denote the English painters and writers of the first half of the nineteenth century.

clause. A clause is a group of words containing a subject and other words, including a verb, that tell us something about the subject. *The man was dead* is a clause. If it has a full stop after it it is also a sentence. If, however, the sentence is

The man was dead, and we called the police,

here *The man was dead* is a *main clause* of that sentence, but *we called the police* is another, because it too can stand alone. Sometimes these are called *co-ordinate clauses,* because each is of the same rank. Co-ordinate clauses are usually joined by the conjunctions *and, but, or, nor.*

However, with a sentence such as

This is the man who ran in the race,

only *This is the man* is the *main* clause. The *subordinate* clause is *who ran in the race, subordinate* because it cannot stand by itself. (Some authorities prefer the *main clause* to be called the *main sentence,* and wish the word *clause* to be used only for *subordinate* clauses.)

The important thing about subordinate clauses is that, however many words they may have in them, they always operate as in effect a single word influencing a word or words in the main clause. In the sentence

They dawdled as they trudged to school,

as they trudged to school is an adverbial clause which influences the verb *dawdled.* It tells us that they didn't necessarily dawdle all the time, but they did dawdle as they went to school. It really is five words giving us one piece of information. We can imagine it, as also other subordinate clauses, in a box, a box we can often move around the sentence:

They dawdled | as they trudged to school |.

Subordinate clauses are classified into three kinds — not to make life harder, but because to do so helps us to understand the jobs they are doing. This helps us to understand the ideas behind the words we are reading. Unfortunately there is always a gap between the ideas we want to express and the words we want to express them in.

1. The *relative*, or *adjectival*, clause. This kind of subordinate clause does the work of an adjective. In other words, it gives information about the *noun* or *pronoun* to which it relates. Examples are italicised in the following:

>Melbourne is the city *where I was born.*
>
>The girl *who had just arrived* was Italian.
>
>What color dress was that woman *[whom] we met yesterday* wearing?
>
>This is the gate *that always sticks.*
>
>This is not as good a car *as I thought it was.*

Relative clauses are introduced by relative pronouns, such as *where, who, whose, which, that, what, as,* sometimes in association with a preposition (*in whom, up which*). *When, why,* and *where* may also introduce relative clauses, and are sometimes called *relative adverbs,* though there is a good case for simply considering them relative pronouns when used in this way. *Do you remember the day when we went to the beach?* contains the relative clause *when we went to the beach* which governs, or restricts, the noun *day.* The important thing to remember is that if a group of words in a sentence qualifies the *noun* (or *pronoun*) in that sentence, it is a relative clause. If it does not, it is some other kind of clause.

2. The *adverbial* clause does the work of an adverb. That is, it qualifies some verb, adjective or adverb by stating time, place, manner etc. Note that some adverbial clauses may start with words such as *that* or *as,* just as relative clauses do. The essential point is not the word that introduces the clause, but the *function* performed by that clause.

>The uproar ceased *when the police arrived.*
>
>The party-goers went home *as they were told to do.*
>
>*Because my clothes were missing,* I went home in a towel.
>
>I walked so slowly *that the sun was up before I got home.*
>
>*Though I am very fond of parties,* I shall think carefully before I go to another.
>
>*Let them say what they like,* I have learned a lesson.
>
>I shall go again, *but only with much forethought.*

3. The *noun* clause does the work of a noun in a sentence. It may be the subject of the verb or the object of the verb, or may perform other functions in the sentence, but it is *a group of words which performs the function of a noun.* In the sentence *That she will dance is certain, That she will dance* is a noun clause that is the subject of the verb. In *It is certain that she will dance, that she will dance* is a noun clause that is the object of the verb. Note that the clause must contain a subject and a verb. Examples:

>*Whatever we do* is going to be unpleasant. (*Whatever we do* is the subject of the verb *is.*)
>
>I had forgotten *that she was coming.* (Here the noun clause is the object of *had forgotten.*)
>
>I asked them *when they would be leaving the town.* (The noun clause is the object of *asked.*)

> *What is good* and *what is bad* must remain the highest questions. (The italicised
> words are standing in place of the nouns *good* and *bad*.)

See also **that/which/who/whom.**

clematis. This plant, sometimes called *traveller's joy*, is generally pronounced
clem-ATE-is in Australia. This pronounciation seems peculiar to Australia. The
English and Americans call it *CLEM-atis.*

clichés. A *cliché* (pronounced *klee-shay*) is a word or phrase which has become
so tired that it is no longer capable of performing its job properly. Originally,
perhaps, an amusing and lively turn of language, a fresh and distinctive way of
saying something, the cliché has become boring, because you can hear it coming.
The origin of the word is significant: it comes from the French printers' term for
a stereotype, something cast from a mould.

In Australian English some examples of the cliché are:

in this day and age
in my humble opinion
in due course
that's for sure
at this moment in time
not to worry
for starters (meaning *for a start*)
ongoing (meaning *continuing*)
interface (meaning *connect*)
in-depth (as in *an in-depth talk,* meaning *searching*)
have a nice day!
getting past first base (from American baseball)
across the board (meaning *the conclusion, or the final cost*)
part and parcel
the name of the game
into (as *he's into cricket*)
highlighted (meaning *emphasised*)
bench-mark (as *this bench-mark decision,* meaning *precedent*)
coming on stream (meaning *starting production*)
in my book
by the same token
I'll wear that (meaning *I accept that*)
I'll take that on board (meaning *I'll give that some thought* or *I'll accept that*)
it would have to be (*What do you like best in men? It would have to be a love of
music*)
doing your own thing
to militate against

render inoperative
life-style
in this time-slot (meaning *at this time*)
the bottom line (meaning *the final cost*)
each and every
make contact with (meaning *meet*)
on the back burner (meaning *in abeyance*)
answer to a maiden's prayer
sticking out like a sore thumb
a meaningful relationship
to take a dim view of
pay it up front
at the end of the day (meaning *in the final assessment*)
in any shape or form
that's further down the track (meaning *that's to come*)
at the present juncture
a total experience
grind to a standstill

There are, of course, hundreds more. Many, perhaps most, of the above are American in origin. This does not, however, affect their status as Australian clichés.

The cliché, however, has its defenders. "Often," Arthur Phillips has written, "it is sheer affectation to avoid the established verbal stereotype. The basically important things to avoid are not clichés, but dead metaphors." "Let not your son be afraid of the hackneyed phrase," Somerset Maugham told the mother of an aspiring writer. "It may very well be the most suitable." Nicholas Bagnall has published a whole book called *A Defence of Clichés* (London, 1985), pointing out among other matters that many old and favored phrases in our language and literature *are* old and favored because it's hard to say them better, and that it's better to hang on to the best of what we've got than to pursue originality for its own sake. David J. Enright has written (*Times Literary Supplement*, 28 June 1985) that "We need repetition, which signifies what we have in common, as well as novelty, which indicates what makes us different and separate." He adds:

> The girl who tells her boyfriend, as the train draws out of the station, that he should take care, not do anything rash and so forth, really means that she loves him and will miss him. And he does not say: "Ah, she has used a ridiculously trite remark, therefore she does not love me." He says: "Ah, she loves me after all."

For all that, there are clichés *and* clichés. Phrases such as *a deafening silence, conspicuous by her absence, a tower of strength* and *one fell swoop* are likely to stay in the spoken language, at least, indefinitely. Others, such as those in the list above, are 'worn-out trendy' in any terms. In the written language, particularly, we should always ask ourselves if the familiar phrase we want to use is so familiar that it has lost its punch and its point.

Much of our common store of literary and historical allusion is being lost as a result of the democratisation of education and the drive for 'relevance'. The study of English language and literature in the schools is under constant pressure from the 'levellers', who appear to be unaware that facility in the use of their own language is the most effective of all supports to those who are struggling to establish themselves in the world. The American writer Saul Bellow has said that "Words are a poor boy's arsenal." We may regret the inability of young people today to recognise a biblical or other allusion which was part of the stock of common discourse only a generation or so ago, and this undoubtedly weakens the language. There would be some compensation if the vernacular language were flourishing. The main objection to the mindless cliché is that it has the opposite effect, that it is reductive and limiting, and that by impoverishing the words we use it impoverishes originality and impoverishes thought.

clique. A *clique* is *a small and exclusive group of friends or associates*. It is pronounced to rhyme with *bleak*. To pronounce this word as *click*, the only pronunciation given in the *Macquarie Dictionary*, will be viewed by many as inelegant and even incorrect. The *click* pronunciation, though widespread in Australia, is an **indicator word.**

Strangely enough, though, the word probably came from the Old French *cliquer, to click*, the sound of the latch as it shut out unwanted persons.

The adjective is *cliquey*.

clothes. For pronunciation, see **fortune**.

cloud no bigger than a man's hand. In I Kings, xviii. 44 the actual phrase is "There ariseth a little cloud out of the sea, like a man's hand."

coconut. *Coconut* is the word, not *cocoanut*. The coconut has nothing to do with the cocoa plant.

cohabit/cohabitate. Kerry Stokes, television takeover entrepreneur, when interviewed about his latest acquisitions in August 1987 said that there were two policies which "can not cohabitate."

Firstly, there is no such verb as *to cohabitate*. The word is *cohabit*. You may also have *cohabiter, cohabitant* and *cohabitation*.

Secondly, the dictionaries seem to agree that *cohabit* means *living together in a sexual relationship, married or otherwise*. There is no support for Kerry Stokes's meaning, which is roughly *work together, get on with each other, support each other*. But Mr Stokes's use here of the word *cohabit* as applied to policies (and by extension to ideas) is not only a perfectly sound extension of the more narrow meaning, but a common one. It is strange that it is not reflected in the reference books.

cohort. Originally a *cohort* was one of ten units in a Roman legion, and numbered from 300 to 600 men. From this it came to be used for any band of warriors or people with a common cause, as in *the cohorts of Satan*. But whether the word should be used simply to describe *any* gathering is disputable. One distinguished Australian novelist uses *cohort* to describe customers in a post office. The word fails in its purpose here, for an essential part of it is the sense of *a defined common goal* and, while the people in the post office may have a common goal in their desperate efforts to gain the attention of the clerks so that they may buy a stamp, this is an individual goal rather than one to which all have pledged. The use of the word *cohort* to mean nothing more than *companions* or *a group of people* is particularly common in the United States, where it is criticised as journalese. It can also be because many people imagine the word means *colleagues*, as when the politician Steele Hall was attacked on the topic of his *cohorts in the National Party* (*Age*, 19 February 1987), or when Charles Sriber in the *Australian* (14 November 1987) writes of having "a chat with Laurie or his cohorts."

In biology the word is used to describe certain subdivisions of species, while it is also common in sociological writing, where a *cohort* refers to *a group within a group*: *Of those surveyed, the cohort born in 1968 was of special interest.*

collective nouns. *The cast is at the moment involved in another play*, or *The cast are presently involved in another play*? There are a number of kinds of collective noun, but the kind we are concerned with here has been called a *noun of multitude*, a *group noun* or an *abstract singular*, standing in for a *concrete plural*. (In this case the concrete plural would be *actors*.)

There are many such collective nouns and we use them all the time: *crew*, *committee*, *group*, *team* and so on. The point is, however, that they may be followed by either a singular *or* a plural verb. In other words, both the examples given above are correct.

The British tend to use plurals in such cases: *the government have decided*. The Americans tend to use the singular: *the administration has committed itself*. Australians may decide for themselves, and will do so on the basis of what sounds better in each case.

Where, for instance, the speaker or writer has in mind a *collection of individuals*, rather than a single entity, the collective noun will be followed by a plural: *the audience was enthusiastic*, but *the audience were predominantly older people*.

Avoid, if possible, sententious collective nouns where they are not necessary: for instance, *the readership* where *the readers* would do as well, *the leadership* instead of *the leaders, the management* for *the managers.*

Note, incidentally, that you cannot have *these kind of people. Kind* is a singular noun, and therefore the phrase must be *this kind* or *these kinds.* See **kind.**

colleges of advanced education. See **post-secondary education.**

collision/collusion. A *collision* occurs when two or more objects hit each other. A *collusion* occurs when two or more people conspire with each other to deceive or defraud.

Colombia/Columbia. Colombia is the country in South America. British Columbia, Columbia University (New York) and the District of Columbia in the United States are thus spelt.

colonial/colonialist. A *colonial* is a person who lives in a colony. Until 1901 all Australians lived in colonies and were *colonials.*

Colonial, when applied in an Australian context to — say — *colonial architecture, colonial literature,* refers to the period between 1788 and 1901. (Some would argue, however, that while that may be formally correct Australian life started moving out of a phase of colonial dependency in the 1880s or earlier.)

Colonialist means *a person who believes in the colonial system.* A person, perhaps, who believes that the British should still be ruling India, or the Australians Papua New Guinea. It is a political and ideological term, whereas *colonial* is simply a description.

The two words are sometimes confused.

colons. The colon, printed thus : , is a very useful punctuation mark, but it is frequently avoided because people are not sure of just what its function is. The colon has a role to play which no other punctuation mark can. That role is to prepare the reader for what is to come, to indicate that what follows the colon buttresses what has gone before. Some examples:

> The good ship had withstood many vicissitudes in its time: storms and tempest, wind and ice, the impact of great seas and the occasional grounding.
>
> And most marvellous of all: the astonishing silhouettes of animals from the ends of the earth, falcons from the Nile, greyhounds, green parrots, magnificent horses, camels from the far south.
>
> On numerous occasions Mr Cupitt repeats the same basic idea: "there is no longer any privileged point from which the earth can be seen objectively and as it really is."

In such cases many writers will use the dash, printed —, as a replacement for the colon. The dash, however, has other functions in punctuation and does not carry the essential power of the colon, which may be summed up as a momentary pause for assessment.

The colon will also be used by writers seeking for a pause more telling than a semi-colon, but less final than a full stop:

> And so I betake myself to that course, which is almost as much as to see myself go into my grave: for which, and all the discomforts that will accompany my being blind, the good God prepare me!
>
> Samuel Pepys

The colon should only be used where there is already an obvious pause in the run of a sentence. It should not come between a verb and its object. For instance, this is wrong:

> The best-known cities in India are: Calcutta, Delhi and Bombay.

No colon is required here at all.

The colon will usually be found after *said*, in such a phrase as *Tonight the President then said: "It is time to face the facts. We have been living in a fool's paradise."* It will also often be found after *for instance*, as in *There were a great many animals on the Ark, for instance: pigs, monkeys, guinea-fowl, bandicoots and aardvarks.*

The colon is not followed by a capital letter, except of course in the case of a proper noun.

combat/combatant/combative. The nouns *combat* and *combatant* ("The combatants met in combat") are pronounced with the stress on the first syllable, thus: *COM-bat, COM-bat-ant.* So is the adjective *combative.*

The verb *to combat* ("We shall combat this decision") may take the emphasis on the second syllable (*com-BAT*), but does not have to.

In all these words the *com-* part may be pronounced either *com* or *cum.*

commando. The plural is *commandos.*

commas. The *comma* is the most frequently used mark of punctuation. It has a number of uses. They include:

SETTING OFF INTRODUCTORY WORDS

> Good heavens, it's happened again; Rebecca, come here this instant!

SETTING OFF INTRODUCTORY PHRASES

> Courageous though it seemed, it was an action deplored by all.

SEPARATING MAIN CLAUSES

This is especially useful when the clauses are somewhat elaborate:

> The book has been out of print for many years, but it has remained of very considerable interest to the profession.

BEFORE SHORT EXPRESSIONS INDICATING REINFORCEMENT
>That's the right way, isn't it?
>
>It's not at all wise, you know.

WHERE A SYMMETRICAL CONTRAST IS BEING MADE BETWEEN IDEAS
>The higher, the fewer!
>
>The more she protested, the less we believed her.

TO SEPARATE ITEMS IN A LIST
>Tom, Dick, George and Harry were all pains in the neck.

Note that these days it is considered desirable not to have a comma before *and* or *or*, unless there seems to be a good reason for having one.

TO MAKE THE SENSE CLEAR

Note these misuses of the comma:

>Soldiers, who run away, are not welcome in any army. (The comma here after *soldiers* makes the sentence mean that all soldiers at all times run away.)
>
>I was not angry with him, because I detested him. (The comma here means that, because the speaker detested the man, he was not angry with him. This sounds silly. What the speaker should have said was *I was not angry with him because I detested him* [but for some other reason].)
>
>This thesis was the first historical work on Monaro which I read, to my very great profit. (Note how completely the sense is altered by placing the comma after *Monaro* instead of after *read*.)
>
>The French, having set off a nuclear explosion in the Pacific, Pacific nations protested. (As it stands this sentence leaves the words *The French* up in the air, with nothing following them, then says that Pacific nations set off a nuclear explosion and protested about something. To make it clear that it was the French who set off the nuclear explosion, the comma after *The French* has to be removed.)
>
>And inky clouds like funeral shrouds sail over the midnight skies. (From the Gilbert and Sullivan light opera "Ruddigore". Note the ludicrous effect of two commas: *And inky clouds, like funeral shrouds, sail over the midnight skies.)*

TO DO THE SAME WORK AS A PAIR OF BRACKETS
>They were accustomed, or had been in earlier days, to walk to the township each morning.

The most useful rule to remember here is that *a comma brackets off subordinate material* (as in the example just above) *and that two commas will be needed unless the subordinate clause is ended by a full stop.*

The following example, is therefore, *wrong*:

>He wanted to make clear that he would be coming later, and that whatever the others might have thought he was not going to resign.

This is the *correct* punctuation:

>He wanted to make clear that he would be coming later and that, whatever the others might have thought, he was not going to resign.

This list of functions does not exhaust the work of the comma, but is sufficient to demonstrate what a variety of important jobs it performs.

Note the following examples of misplaced commas from recent Australian writing:

> Straight from there to Fern Tree on the slopes of Mount Wellington, where, newly married, we rented a holiday shack.

> He uses his quotation, not to illuminate an assertion, but, rather, to pacify misgivings.

The commas after the words *Wellington* and *assertion* are not required. They spoil the flow of the sentences. They are put in by the writers because they would be needed, or at least allowable, did the phrases *newly married* and *rather* not appear. But once you have those qualifications to the second part of these sentences, you must return the *where* and the *but* to the first part of the sentences.

For the use of commas in numbers, see **numbers**, and for their use in relative clauses, see **that/which/who/whose.**

commence. The word *commence*, which means the same as *begin* or *start,* has its place, as do all words in the language. It is an appropriate word to use instead of *begin* or *start* in somewhat dignified contexts: *the commencement of hostilities*, for instance, or perhaps even *the play will commence at 8 p.m.*

Generally, though, the simple, more direct words *begin* and *start* are to be preferred.

commensurate/consummate. Commenting on the Budget of 1987 the managing director of the National Mutual Royal Bank, Mr Bill Gurry, said that the Treasurer, Paul Keating, was "a commensurate politician" (*Sydney Morning Herald*, 17 September 1987).

Commensurate means *having the same or a proportionate extent or duration or size as does something else.* One may say, for instance, that *the number of teachers in New South Wales is commensurate with the number in Queensland*, which simply means that the categories concerned — in this case the number of teachers — have enough in common to be able to be usefully compared or contrasted.

The number of teachers in New South Wales is not, however, *commensurate* with the length of time it takes to fly across the Tasman Sea. These are different categories and cannot be compared.

The word Mr Gurry was seeking for was *consummate*, which means (in this case, and used as an adjective) *highly accomplished.*

The adjective, as here, is pronounced *KON-sem-it*, though *kon-SUM-it* is also allowed.

See also **consummate.**

commentate. So-and-so was *commentating* at the cricket, the ABC news told us. There is certainly a noun, *commentator*, which is an accepted word. But there is dispute about whether someone who makes a commentary on an event is *commentating*. Many prefer *commenting on* or *providing a commentary for*. The verb is well established in sports reporting, however, and although it may sound inelegant there *is* a difference between Alan McGilvray's *commenting* on the cricket and his *commentating* on it.

common sense/commonsense. Use *common sense* for the noun (*She had a lot of common sense*) and *commonsense* for the adjective (*It was a commonsense solution*).

Commonwealth. Australia not only has a euphonious and appropriate name for itself, but also has an unusual and effective 'describer' in the name *Commonwealth*. We may not *be* a commonwealth in all respects, but the word implies a sharing and a mutuality which few would reject, at least as a goal.

We could have had much worse. The Dominion of Australia, the Federated States of Australia and the Federal Dominion of Australasia were amongst alternatives suggested.

The word was adopted at the 1891 Federal Convention in Sydney, but only by one vote in the relevant committee. It was in fact adopted because of the support of New Zealand delegates who had no serious interest in any proposed federation. Alfred Deakin wrote that the word was received "with scanty favour by the Committee because of the flavour of Republicanism and the suggestion of Separation that it was considered to convey."

This was because the republican government of Oliver Cromwell in England, 1649-1660, was called a Commonwealth. In fact the word has a much more ancient lineage, and a much less pointed meaning, than Cromwell's usage indicates. The word, as Sir Keith Hancock has pointed out, "is associated pre-eminently with the nation-building work of the Tudor monarchy." Like the word *republican* itself at this time, it was perfectly compatible with monarchical government. The original emphasis of *commonwealth* leant heavily towards the concepts of national unity, office and duty, against the belief that any man or rank — as Hancock has put it — "possessed a natural right to power and wealth."

By derivation from *common weal* the word *commonwealth* came to signify the common good, the body politic, the people at large, a society in which the general welfare is regarded as more important than the interests of a single class.

J. A. La Nauze has written at length on the Australian origins of the word. In particular he has drawn attention to the many texts which, in the second half of the nineteenth century, may directly or indirectly have influenced the reception of the word, including its use by J. A. Froude in his *Oceana* and the very title of

Bryce's famous *The American Commonwealth*. He believes that it was these assonances, rather than any direct emotional sympathy for the English revolutionists, that led Henry Parkes to the increasing acceptance of the term and its espousal, deftly supported by Alfred Deakin, at the 1891 Convention, causing Edmund Barton, later the first prime minister of the Commonwealth of Australia, to say at the Convention that "Commonwealth is the grandest and most stately name by which a great association of self-governing people can be characterised."

Despite this, the word Commonwealth was sharply criticised in several of the colonial parliaments subsequent to the 1891 Convention. Victoria rejected the name in favor of *Dominion*. The word was, however, now in the documents, over the succeeding years it became more familiar and became increasingly accepted, and under the Commonwealth of Australia Constitution Act, chapter 12, clause 3, the colonies became "a Federal Commonwealth under the name of the Commonwealth of Australia."

The word has been well received by subsequent commentators. Quick and Garran, in their work on the Australian Constitution, wrote that "this grand old word, rich in meaning and tradition, and intimately associated with the literature and history of the English people, did more to arrest the public attention and kindle the public imagination than any other word in the English language could have done." Keith Hancock wrote in 1932 that:

> It is indeed truly extraordinary that, notwithstanding the enormous differences of "tyme and place", the ideas of Tudor England should have found, three centuries later, a new home in a land which to the sixteenth century was but a speculative *terra australis incognita*. Those same aspirations which in the first decade of the twentieth century made "the settled policy of the Commonwealth" — an exclusive nationalism, protection, distributive justice, a high standard of living, care for the "under-dog" — were the very breath of Tudor idealism.

John La Nauze, more waspishly, has written that *Commonwealth* is "a noble word which will survive in Australia when its misapplication to the ghost of the deceased British Empire sitting crowned upon the grave thereof has long since been abandoned."

Many Australians will share La Nauze's irritation that 'our' word has been appropriated for the British Commonwealth of Nations, but his view that it will be Australia's national use of the word that will survive, rather than the other, is now open to doubt. As early as 1965 Prime Minister Menzies told the House of Representatives that "I myself have been in the habit of referring to the 'Australian Government' wherever I go. This is something I commend to all honourable members" (*Parliamentary Debates*, p. 1976). E. G. Whitlam, then deputy leader of the Australian Labor Party, argued to the House on 20 October 1966 that the proper use of *Commonwealth* was to describe the British Commonwealth, not the Australian one, and that the term *Commonwealth of*

Australia conveyed to other nations, particularly in the Pacific, the sense that Australia enjoyed self-government rather than independence and was still tied to Britain. He added that confusion could be caused by such titles as "Commonwealth [of Nations] Games," that the Australian States did not call themselves, for instance, *the State of New South Wales* but simply *New South Wales*, and that in any case the usage was inconsistent, some federal bodies calling themselves "Australian" (such as the Australian Universities Commission) and some "Commonwealth" (the Commonwealth Scientific and Industrial Research Organisation).

On taking office in 1972 Whitlam discouraged the use of the word *Commonwealth*, for instance changing the title of the Governor-General to *Governor-General of Australia*. The Reserve Bank of Australia was persuaded to adopt the simple *Australia* on our banknotes, where it still remains. Senator James McClelland discussed the matter, in reply to questions, in the Senate on 13 May 1975. He repeated Whitlam's arguments of 1966, stating:

> My proposition is that we should use none of the words "Australian", "Commonwealth", "Federal", or "National" unless they serve to identify or distinguish and that we should prefer the geographic term to the others, particularly to the word "Commonwealth".

The general policy of the Australian government, McClelland said, was "that the word 'Commonwealth' should be avoided as far as possible in referring to Australian bodies." Canada and New Zealand had dropped the word *Dominion*.

In his book *The Whitlam Government* (1985) E. G. Whitlam returns to the issue, mentioning the preference of R. G. Menzies, and Menzies' description of himself as prime minister *of Australia*. In a private letter (1985) he has said that "I do not overlook the virtues of the word 'Commonwealth', since it is the English translation of 'Republic'. It also is appropriate in a constitutional sense in distinguishing 'the Commonwealth of Australia' and 'the State of New South Wales', etc." Apart from such cases, Mr Whitlam said, he felt its use should be limited.

The Fraser government which replaced the Whitlam government in 1975 reinstated the use of the word *Commonwealth* in the Governor-General's title, and enacted legislation referring to the Queen as the Queen of the *Commonwealth of Australia*. The subsequent Labor government of R. J. L. Hawke has remained quiescent on the issue, though in 1984 the title of the Commonwealth Crown Solicitor, a post once held by E. G. Whitlam's father, was changed to Australian Government Solicitor.

The use of the word *Commonwealth* to describe the central government of Australia as distinct from the State governments has been frowned on and termed "secondary" and "inartistic". Since the Commonwealth of Australia incorporates the whole of Australia, including the State governments, it may be argued that it is a solecism to say, for instance, "This legal case relates to a clash between Commonwealth and State powers", and that in such a case the word *federal* should be used instead of *Commonwealth*.

Further material on the origins, and adoption by Australia, of the word *Commonwealth* will be found in J. Quick and R. R. Garran, *The Annotated Constitution of the Australian Commonwealth* (Sydney and Melbourne, 1901), pp. 131, 136, 311-314 and 368; W. K. Hancock, *Politics in Pitcairn . . .* (London, 1947), chapter entitled "A Veray and True Comyn Wele;" and J. A. La Nauze, "The Name of the Commonwealth of Australia," *Historical Studies*, vol. 15, no. 57, October 1971.

communist/communism. See **political terminology in Australia.**

commuter is an American word, originally meaning *someone who lives in the suburbs and travels to work using a season ticket.* (The American for a season-ticket is a commutation ticket.)

The use of the word has now widened to mean *someone who lives in the suburbs but travels by any means to his or her work in the city.*

And, of course, there is also a verb: *They commute three times a week.*

Only twenty years ago it could be said that this word "has not been heard much in Australia". It is now an accepted part of our language and, since it meets a need, a desirable one.

Attempts to apply the word in such ways as *a small train commutes frequently between Flinders Street and St Kilda* should be opposed. This is changing the meaning of the word. The appropriate verb here would be *shuttles.*

A sentence such as *She commutes to work* is saying the same thing twice, and thus is a **pleonasm.**

comparable. Pronounce *COMP-re-ble*, not *com-PAIR-able.*

comparatively/relatively. *Comparatively* and *relatively* are often used to mean *fairly*, or *rather*, as in *She was a comparatively good runner*, or *It was a relatively unpleasant experience.*

The objection to this is that we don't know what the happening is being *compared* or *related* to. If we read *It was a relatively poor village even by Bangladesh standards*, or *This is comparatively poor by your usual performance* we at least know what is being compared or related to, even if we may argue that the words *comparatively* and *relatively* are not needed in those sentences at all.

The objection to the loose use of these words applies also to *comparative* and *relative.*

compare/contrast. Generally speaking objects rather like each other are *compared*, objects unlike each other *contrasted.* One will therefore *compare* the texture of two cakes, but *contrast* night to day.

Compare may be followed by either *to* or *with*. Some authorities recommend *to* when the intention is to emphasise similarity, *with* when there is no close affinity. Thus:

> In praising Billy Graham, the speaker compared him *to* Jesus Christ.
>
> In comparing the French plane *with* the American, the panel felt that the former was far superior.

In other words, use *compared with* if an argument is involved, *compared to* if no argument is intended.

The noun *contrast* is usually followed by *between*:

> Many visitors make a strong contrast *between* Sydney and Melbourne.

In such a sentence as "In contrast *to* other leaders of his time, Roosevelt was never posturing or vainglorious," Americans will prefer *to*, but British usage prefers *with*.

The verb *to contrast* should normally be followed by *with*, as in "She contrasted the absence of amenities *with* those in the neighboring suburb." The use of the verb *contrast* on its own, without a *with*, is frowned upon, as in such a sentence as "The colorful clothes contrasted the dull day," and should be avoided.

Contrast as a noun is pronounced *CON-trast*, as a verb *con-TRAST*.

Do not say or write *as compared with* or *as compared to*, in such a sentence as: *As compared with Italy, the Soviet Union is a vast country*. The *as* is unnecessary.

compass points.
1. The actual points of the compass, referred to as such, should be written or printed thus: *south-east, north-west-by-north*.
2. When used, however, as adjectives, or as nouns with a meaning beyond that of a compass-point, print thus: a *northwesterly* [wind], a *sou'wester* [hat], *Northwest Territories, Southwest Island, Southeast Asia*.

compeer/compere. A *compeer* is *a person of equal rank or status*, or *a companion or comrade*. It is sometimes used of things, as in:

> Most of these expressions are, or soon will be, in Collins, Longman and Chambers [dictionaries], together with their American compeers.

Compere is a British, not American, word. It comes from the French *compère*, meaning *godfather*, and it refers to the master (or mistress) of ceremonies at some form of presentation in the entertainment industry, often a television show. The word is widely used in Australia, though not widely welcomed, perhaps because it is thought to be American. It fills a need: it is hard to think of another suitable word, unless it be *presenter*.

Compere is pronounced with the stress on the first syllable: *KOM-pair*. It makes *compered, compering*.

compelling/compulsive. *Compelling* means *to arouse strong feelings of interest or admiration: it was a compelling plot, his arguments were compelling.*

Compulsive goes further than this. It implies *that a person is driven to accept something or do something without being in control of the matter: She is a compulsive liar,* or *The book is compulsive reading.*

compensatory. Most people, in Australia at any rate, want to say *com-pens-AT-ory,* because it seems easier to pronounce the word this way. Dictionaries, however, will allow us *COM-pens-at-ory* or *com-PENS-at-ory* but will not allow us to say *com-pens-AT-ory.*

The dictionaries will have to change.

complacent/complaisant. These words are pronounced similarly, but have quite different meanings.

Complacent means, of course, *unmoved, self-satisfied, happy with things as they are.*

Complaisant means that a person is agreeable to a proposition, acquiescent. *When asked if she would accept a new position, her attitude was complaisant.* As can be seen from this example, while the distinction is clear enough in print, it can be ambiguous in speech, and if the less common word of the two, *complaisant,* is used in a context where it may be misunderstood, it would be wise to find another way of saying the same thing.

complementary/complimentary. Something that is *complementary* is something that *completes or balances something else to make a whole.* Ham is complementary to eggs as a breakfast dish; one shoe is complementary to the other in the same pair; violins, viola and cello are complementary parts of a string quartet.

The word *complimentary* means (a) expressing a compliment (*She made some complimentary remarks*), (b) something given away free (*They received complimentary tickets for the gig*).

complex. A *complex* is *an assemblage of related parts,* as in *the complex of buildings within the University of Sydney,* or *This is a complex matter.*

It does *not* mean *a fear or phobia about something or someone: She's got a complex about entering trams* is incorrect. This debased use of the word stems, of course, from the psychological use of the word (in its correct sense) to denote *a system of feelings towards a certain matter.*

complex/complicated. There is a shade of difference between the meaning of these two adjectives. Something that is *complex* is *made up of a number of interconnecting parts,* is *intricate* or *involved. Complex* though the article or matter may be, there is no necessary suggestion that it is *hard to work out, difficult to comprehend. Complicated* has the same sense of being *intricate*, but carries also with it a sense of *difficulty in understanding.*

compose/comprise. *To compose* has of course several meanings, but the one we are concerned with here is *to be the component elements of.* Thus *a brigade is normally composed of three battalions, a string quartet is composed of four players.*

To comprise means *to consist of,* as in *a full cricket team comprises eleven players.* It is not to be confused with *compose,* and it is incorrect to say *a full cricket team is comprised of eleven players. Comprise* is never followed by *of,* while *compose* usually appears in the form *composed of.*

composite. This word is both an adjective (*this is a composite substance*) and a noun (*this is a composite*). The word means *made up of distinct parts, a compound.* In Australia it is pronounced *COMP-osit,* in the United States *com-POS-it.*

compound nouns. See **trades unions or trade unions?**

computer. The name for the calculating machine is *computer,* not *computor.* A person who adds figures is also a *computer.*

computerbabble. See **technobabble.**

conditioned. In its primary, psychological sense, *I have been conditioned to like porridge* does *not* mean *I have become accustomed to porridge and now I like it,* but properly means *I have been subjected to a process of rewards and punishments which has resulted in my coming to like porridge* (or *give up smoking,* or whatever).

The use of the word *conditioned* to mean no more than *accustomed* is now built well in to the language and will remain. We should not, however, lose sight of the original meaning.

conduit may be pronounced to rhyme with *bond it,* or *fund it,* or as *con-dew-it.* The most 'approved' English pronunciation is the *fund it* one, but this is rarely heard in Australia.

conference. "The teachers will conference" is a gruesome imposition of a verb function on an inoffensive noun. Its use in this sense is no tribute to those teachers who conference. "The teachers will meet" is preferable, even if this does not sound so important. Or, indeed, "The teachers will confer."

But what of the word *conferencing* in such an example as *The conferencing process is a useful way of teaching writing by mutual discussion*? Here the noun is being made to play a verb/adjective function. It is argued that, in this sense, the word fills a need. Certainly it sounds better than "The teachers will conference," and certainly what we say here will not stop its being used, and certainly we have to accept that in a living language words should and will expand their functions. Perhaps we should just lie back and think of Fowler.

Or should we again say that *the conferring process* is the obvious, unpretentious answer?

See **noun to verb: is change decay?**

congruent. "I don't think this particular action is congruent with what the Minister said about the matter in his paper."

Is it not, indeed. How shocking.

Used in this way the adjective *congruent* is an import from geometry. There it means *having identical shapes.* But the secondary use of *agreeing, corresponding,* is well established, and although the word may sometimes sound pretentious it has not degenerated to the point of being a **bully word.**

conjunctions. The *conjunction* is one of eight **parts of speech** in traditional grammar. As the name suggests, it is a *joining word.* Conjunctions such as *and, but, because, when, if, however, therefore* join together words, phrases and clauses to supplement and expand meanings.

For convenience, three divisions of conjunctions are often recognised. These are:

CO-ORDINATING CONJUNCTIONS

These are *and, but* and *or,* and they join words and groups of words which are equal in status, such as *ham* and *eggs, Richard* and *Barbara, she was poor* but *she was honest.*

SUBORDINATING CONJUNCTIONS

These force a part of a sentence into an inferior position to another part of that sentence. Thus, while *He mounted and he rode* shows *he mounted* and *he rode* as equal partners in that sentence, connected with the co-ordinating conjunction *and,* if we write instead *When he mounted, he rode* the *when* subordinates *he mounted* to *he rode.* In other words, *he rode* is still a sensible statement on its own, but *when he mounted* now depends on *he rode* to make sense of itself.

CORRELATIVE CONJUNCTIONS

These are pairs of words which, together, act as single conjunctions. They include *either ... or, not only ... but also, neither ... nor.*

He *not only* rode to hounds, *but also* kept a pack of the beasts.

Some modern grammarians hold that words such as *however* and *therefore* are not true conjunctions, which may only appear as the first word in a clause, and are better termed *sentence connectors.*

connection/connexion. If we spelt words according to how they have evolved in the language, we would spell *connection* as *connexion* in deference to its root word, *nexus*. Many, especially sticklers for 'correctness', do. In Australia (and the United States) the word is, may be, and should be spelt *connection*.

connoisseur. A *connoisseur* is a person who has a special knowledge of some field, especially in the arts. The word tends to be applied rather to a collector or one who is knowledgeable than to a critic. It comes to us from the Latin and French words meaning *to know*. The pronunciation gives public figures in Australia a lot of trouble. It is *kon-is-ER*, not *conno-syooer*.

conservative. See **political terminology in Australia.**

consonant. See **vowel.**

consortium. The English and Australian pronunciation of this word is *con-sort-ium*, plural *con-sort-ia*. The American pronunciation is often *con-sor-shum*, plural *con-sor-sha*. The latter pronunciation is making some inroads in Australia.

constable. The first syllable in *constable* rhymes with *bun* rather than with *bon*. This is the case with several older words in the language, such as *son*, *done*, *money*. But, since no other word starting with *con*, and with the stress on the first syllable as with *constable*, has the *cun* pronunciation, the tendency is for many to pronounce it *con*, as with *constant* and *continent*. This pronunciation is not fully accepted, and the *Macquarie Dictionary*, for instance, does not even record it.

consummate. *To consummate* something is *to bring it to completion or perfection*. It is frequently used of a marriage, where the word does *not* mean *to celebrate a marriage*, but *to complete it legally by sexual intercourse*.

The *Barrier Daily Truth* at Broken Hill is famous in journalistic history for printing the statement in 1947 that the wedding of the then Princess Elizabeth and Prince Philip was *consummated* in Westminster Abbey.

A *consummate* artist or a *consummate* fool is one who brings the attributes of such persons to the highest level. Pronounce the verb *KONS-sim-ate*, with a secondary stress on the final syllable.

See also **commensurate/consummate.**

contagious/infectious. A *contagious* disease is one that is transmitted by contact between persons. An *infectious* disease is transmitted by any means, including *contagion*.

contemplative. There is often argument about whether this is pronounced *CON-tem-play-tiv* or *con-TEM-play-tiv*. Either is acceptable, and both pronunciations are in general use.

contemporary. "The contemporary photographs are by Josiah Shutter." What does *contemporary* mean in this context? The trouble is that it can have two meanings, opposite to each other, and dependent on context.

Contemporary can mean that the photographs were taken *at the time of the other events described.* On the other hand it can mean *now, today, of the present time.* Usually the sense is clear from the context, but not always, and in general the word is best avoided if there is any likelihood of ambiguity. Words or phrases such as *at the time* or *present-day* may be used instead.

contemptible/contemptuous. Something that is *contemptible deserves contempt: His actions in this matter were contemptible.* However to be *contemptuous* of something is *to view it with disdain and contempt: I was contemptuous of his actions in this matter.*

context. In the Australian Opera's program for "Boris Godunov" (1986) we read ". . . we see the Tsar in the context of his family."

The meaning is clear enough. The phrase means that we see the Tsar *in his family setting,* and some such wording as this should have been used. For *context* is a word stolen from a specialist area, language studies, and used here because it sounds impressive.

It is true that *context* is now used more widely than its original specialist meaning, especially in such phrases as *Let's look at these issues in context.* In such a sentence it may pass without comment, even though there are alternatives: *Let's look at this matter in perspective,* for instance, though it could be argued that that has a slightly different meaning. But the word should always be used with caution, and not used for effect.

See **bully words.**

continual/continuous. Both words can, and often do, mean the same thing: *happening all the time, without remission, unceasing.*

However *continual,* for those who care about the finer points, also has another meaning: *recurring frequently,* as in:

> He had continual bouts of malaria.

This does not mean that he had them all the time, without intermission, but that he had them frequently.

It seems worthwhile to attempt to distinguish between these words. It adds a little word-power to the language.

contrast. See **compare/contrast**.

contribute. She *con-TRIB-uted* to the magazine, not She *contrib-UT-ed* to the magazine: a common Australian mispronunciation.

controversy. There is a tendency in English for the stress to move forward in words towards the first syllable. For instance, in adopting into English such French words as *plateau* and *charlatan*, where in the French there is equal emphasis on all syllables, we tend to place it on the *first*.

Against this, however, is the difficulty of actually *saying* some words which theoretically should be stressed on the first syllable. Words such as *corollary*, *laboratory* and *disciplinary* tend to be pronounced *co-ROLL-ary*, *la-BOR-a-tory* and *dis-cip-LIN-ary*, however much the dictionaries frown on this.

Thus the 'correct' pronunciation of *controversy* is *CON-tro-versy*, and this is the one the textbooks prefer. But *con-TROV-ersy* is winning, simply because it is easier to say. Both are acceptable.

What is *not* acceptable is the pronunciation sometimes heard from Australian Broadcasting Corporation announcers, *con-tro-VER-sy*.

convener/convenor. Either.

conveyer/conveyor. A *conveyer* is a person who conveys something from one place to another. A *conveyor* is a machine for moving articles.

convince/persuade. The two words mean much the same thing: *to prevail on someone to accept a point of view*. There is however a big catch. You *convince* someone *of* something, but you *persuade* someone *to do* or *to believe* something. We may *convince* a sucker *that* the brick is made of gold; we may *convince* him *of* the validity of this belief. We cannot, at least in standard English, *convince* him *to believe* our assertions. But we can *persuade* him *to believe* them.

In other words, *convince* may not be followed by *to*, even at some remove. *The Prime Minister had been persuaded by his advisers to attend the rally* is preferable to *The Prime Minister had been convinced by his advisers to attend the rally*.

Note that *a persuasive argument* is not the same thing as *a convincing argument*. You may well regard the con-man's argument that the gold brick is real to be *persuasive*, and at the same time not *believe* it. But if you regard the argument as *convincing*, then you do believe it.

If the gold-brick buyer shows signs of being *convinced*, is he then *persuasible* or *persuadable*? The answer is either, with *persuasible* now more widely used.

coolie. An epigram by Bartlett Adamson:

> So long as one last coolie lies,
> And in an Asian gutter dies,
> There cannot be, beneath the sun,
> Security for anyone.

The word *coolie*, meaning *an unskilled worker in Asian countries*, will properly be avoided by Australians, as suggesting an affront to human dignity. It may, however, be worth noting that the word as it is used in, for instance, Hong Kong, carries no derogatory overtones or suggestions of savage exploitation. Its resonance is neutral, and it simply means an unskilled worker.

copy/duplicate/facsimile/replica. The essential meaning behind all of these words is the same, that something is being copied exactly. There are, however, shades of difference.

A *copy* of something need not be an exact reproduction of it: you may *copy* a letter in different handwriting, but it is still a copy. Painters often *copy* the works of great artists, and there is no suggestion that the copy must be indistinguishable from the original, though clearly the closer to the original it is the better copy it will be.

A *duplicate* (the word originally meant *to fold in half*) is not necessarily an exact copy of an object, but may be *another precisely similar example of an object*. When locks are provided with *duplicate keys* it does not necessarily mean that one has been copied from the other, but that both were manufactured in the same way in the same machine. When we say that *This shoe is a duplicate of that shoe* we mean it has been *made in precisely the same way*.

A *replica*, however, *is* an *exact* copy. One might, for instance, give a swordsmith a beautiful sword, and ask him (or her) to make a *replica* of it. It may not have the same worth as the original (though a *duplicate* normally would). Note however that a replica, for instance of a famous statue, may vary in one respect: frequently there is an alteration in size, though not in other details.

A *facsimile* is *a copy that is exact in every respect*. (The Latin means *made the same*.) There should be no way of telling the difference, which is why facsimiles which are identical with originals often have a mark of some kind on them to show that they *are* copies. Rare books are reproduced *in facsimile*, which means they are copied by photographic means and printed as far as possible with the same paper and binding as the originals.

These words are not necessarily mutually exclusive. If, for instance, you copy a document in a copying machine, you will have a *copy*, a *duplicate*, a *replica* and (if it remains the same size) a *facsimile*.

copy/issue. "I found the four latest issues of the Sydney *Bulletin* especially interesting."

Correct. The latest *issue* of a periodical is the latest example of that publication to appear. You should not say "in the last four *copies* of the Sydney *Bulletin*.

Each *issue* of a periodical contains as many *copies* as the printer put through his or her machines.

So, if you buy two *copies* of a magazine, you bought two identical specimens of the same *issue*.

A moment's thought about what the word *copy* actually means will make the point clear.

cordial. In Australia *cordial* means *a syrup to which water is added to make a soft drink*, or *the drink itself*. In American usage, however, cordial means *an alcoholic liqueur*. Teetotal travellers should bear this in mind.

cortege. A *cortege* is *a solemn procession*, often *a funeral procession*. It is frequently pronounced *KORT-age*. The correct pronunciation is *KORT-ayz*, to rhyme with the words *sort-beige*.

council/counsel. *Council* means an *assembly* of some kind. There is no such verb as *council*. Nobody can be *councilled*.

Counsel means *advice* or *consultation. I went to see my doctor and got good counsel from him.* It is also a verb: *The police counselled him to stay clear of that particular hotel.*

councillor/counsellor. A *councillor* sits on a council. A *counsellor* is someone who gives advice.

cousins. Your aunts' and uncles' children are your *first cousins, full cousins* or *cousins german*. Their children are *second cousins* to your children, but *first cousins once removed* to you. Similarly, the next generation are *third cousins* to your grandchildren, but *first cousins twice removed* to you. Draw a family tree to make this clearer.

The *german* in *cousins german* is the same word as *germane* in a phrase such as *a germane consideration*, meaning *relevant* or *related*. The word comes from the Latin for *a sprout*, from which we also get *germ* and *germinate* and *the Germans*. The Germans were, to the Gauls and Romans, a number of tribes *related* to each other.

covert, as in *covert operations*, has the first syllable as in *cover*. It does not rhyme with *overt*.

crafts. See **culture**.

crayfish/lobster. In recent years attempts have been made to compel Australians, and particularly Victorians, to use the word *lobster* instead of their traditional and home-grown *cray*, or *crayfish*. (*Lobster* is the more common word in Sydney.) The Atlantic lobster is clawed, whereas the Australian crayfish is not. When the South Africans started marketing their crayfish to the Americans as "rock lobster", someone decided the Australians should do so also. This may suit the marketing managers, to whom the word *lobster* is best left. Attempts to change the way we use words by bureaucratic edict must be opposed.

The *-fish* in *crayfish* is in the word in error. Our *crayfish* comes from the Old French *crevice*, and the ending of that word has been confused in English with the word *fish*.

credible/creditable. "The exhibition was very credible," we read. The writer meant that the exhibition was very *creditable*: that it brought *credit* on its organisers. *Credible* means *believeable*.

crescendo, pronounced *cre-SHEND-o*, does *not* mean the *climax of something*, as in *the roars of the crowd rose to a crescendo*.

A *crescendo* is *the process of rising*, not the end result. It means *a gradual increase in loudness*. It would be correct to say *The crescendo of the crowd's cries resulted in a final mighty roar*.

crippling. This word is pronounced as two syllables, and not as three. Radio and television announcers do not agree. Strikes are always *cripp-el-ing*.

crisis. The plural of *crisis* is *crises*.

criterion/criteria. The former is the singular. See **lost singulars**.

critic/critical/criticism. A *critic* is a judge of the work of others, especially of literary and artistic work. He or she is *not* necessarily a fault-finder. A critic may indulge in passionate praise of something criticised. The phrase *She criticised my work* does *not* mean that she disapproved of it. It means that she took the trouble to look at it carefully and tell me what she thought of it, which was perhaps nothing but good.

I received a critical assessment of my essay does *not* necessarily mean that I received any barbs.

It is true that the words above can also be used in the sense of *fault-finding*, and indeed are very commonly used this way. But this should not blind us to the fact that they can be, and frequently are, value-free. *He was very critical of my riding* has only one meaning, of course: he found many faults. But *Here is a critical report on your proposal* may well mean no more than *I have read it carefully and made a few comments.*

Apart from the two, somewhat contradictory, meanings above, *critical* also has two other meanings. It can mean *relating to a crisis*, as in *Dunkirk was a critical event for Britain in the second world war*, or *The injured woman was in a critical condition.* And in science it can mean *a point at which a qualitative transition takes place*, as in *A nuclear chain reaction only takes place when a critical mass of material is present.*

cuisine is pronounced *kwis-een*, not *koos-ine*.

culinary. Pronounce the *cul* part of this word as *cull*, not as *cool*.

culture. *Culture* is a word with which the English language has never been very happy. Dictionaries distinguish a number of meanings for the word, which itself of course is a problem.

We mention here the two most common uses of the word. These are (a) *culture*, as in *Aboriginal culture*, meaning *the complete range of beliefs, activities and creations of a people*, and (b) *culture* meaning *paintings and books and the 'refinements' of a given society at a given time.*

The first, or 'anthropological' sense of the word *culture* is no problem. It is with the second sense that difficulties arise.

One of the problems, of course, is to define just what *culture* in the second sense comprises. We may accept Patrick White, Richard Meale or Fred Williams as part of Australian cultural life in the second sense, but will we accept Paul Hogan or Barry Humphries? Broadly speaking we may define *culture* in this sense as *productions of the creative intellect* (which would certainly bring in Humphries and Hogan), but what about inventors, teachers, farmers, cricketers, also applying a creative intellect to the solution of problems which have an aesthetic significance?

We tend to avoid such awkward matters by using the word *culture* in the second sense as little as possible, which is why in English-speaking countries there is no such person (so far as we are aware) as a *Minister for Culture*. We are also uneasy in English about the use of the word *culture* in other languages, with their ominous Ministries for Culture.

So we fall back on *the arts*, a term we find acceptable. It's unsatisfactory in that it tends to be applied rather narrowly, often reaching little further than painting, literature, theatre and music, and even then often being interpreted in a specialised and elitist sense. In industrial society the 'artist' has set himself or herself apart from the craftsman and craftswoman and from the designer, has claimed a special status as the repository of true creativity, and as a result is vulnerable to the charge of catering for the privileged.

We thus end up with the phrase *the arts and crafts*, a dubious distinction unknown to our forebears.

cupola. This word, meaning *a small dome*, is pronounced *KEW-po-la*.

curate's egg. Many Australians, when they see a headline such as "Summit lays a curate's egg on agriculture" (*Age*, 10 May 1986) must wonder what on earth a curate's egg is.

There are, or were, a host of 'in' jokes and side-references in the English language which help, or helped, to make it the rich and versatile instrument it is. All great languages, perhaps all languages, have these inbuilt cultural quirks. It makes them harder to learn, but very much more effective and interesting to speak.

A number of factors are tending to weaken the earlier cultural affinities of the language. The democratisation of education has weakened the old middle-class referents — the classical tags, for instance, which made much nineteenth-century writing almost the private language of a subculture. Again, it seems likely that 'educated' people are not as well-read as they once were, not as 'literary,' though they may be better informed in other ways.

To come to the point. *The curate's egg* is a phrase stemming from a famous joke in a November 1895 issue of London *Punch*. A terrified curate is breakfasting with his bishop. The bishop asks if the curate is satisfied with his boiled egg. The curate answers, to the effect that the egg is good, "in parts."

Thus the phrase *curate's egg* suggests that a proposal or solution or experience is only partially satisfactory; that, indeed, taken overall, and to adopt an Australian phrase, it may well be "on the nose".

curb/kerb. A *curb* or *kerb* is where one steps up from a street onto a footpath. The Australian use is *kerb*, the American *curb*.

The verb *to curb* means to restrain, as in *curbing your emotions* or *curbing a horse*.

currency. In the early years of the European settlement of Australia there were two forms of money in circulation: the coins and notes emanating from Britain, known as *sterling*, and coins and notes from other sources, adapted for use specifically in Australia, known as *currency*. The most famous items of currency were the holey dollar, a Spanish silver dollar overstruck, and the "dump" which was punched out of its centre.

The terms *sterling* and *currency* came to be widely applied to the European inhabitants of Australia. Those born and brought up in England and

Scotland — the great majority — were termed *sterling*, the locally born *currency*, hence the term *currency lads and lasses*. There was much curiosity as to how the locals, born into a convict colony, would turn out. (As it happened, they turned out well.)

The currency is a term still in occasional use to refer to the early generations of the Australian-born.

See also **pounds, shillings and pence.**

cyclic/cyclical. *Cyclic* or *cyclical* means *recurring in a regular pattern or sequence.* Halley's Comet is a *cyclical* phenomenon.

The *cyclic* may be pronounced either *saiklik* or *siklik*.

cyclone. A *cyclone* is a meteorological name for *a wind system rotating* (clockwise in the southern hemisphere, anti-clockwise in the northern) *around a centre of low barometric pressure.*

Cyclone is the usual name for this disturbance in Australian and Indian Ocean areas. In the West Indies and much of the Pacific the same phenomenon is called a *hurricane*, and in the China Seas a *typhoon*.

czar/tsar. Some authorities prefer the spelling *tsar*, on the ground that it is closer to the Russian original. This seems to us a pedantic argument, seeing that the word is more frequently spelt *czar*, and that this spelling has received much support from the extended use of the word in such phrases as *czar of industry*, *czar of crime*. Early in this century the famous G. D. Delprat, general manager of the Broken Hill Proprietary Company Ltd from 1898 to 1921, was known to his employees as "Czar" Delprat.

It would seem sensible to accept the spelling *czar* as the standard English form. In either case the word is pronounced *zar*.

Czechoslovakia. One word, not *Czecho-Slovakia*, a form which annoys Czechoslovaks considerably. Czechoslovakia consists of three parts: Bohemia, Moravia and Slovakia. Bohemia and Moravia are known as "the Czech lands."

The adjective is *Czechoslovak*, not *Czechoslovakian*.

D

dais, meaning a raised platform, is pronounced as two syllables, thus: *day-is*.

dance/darnce. How should Australians pronounce such words as *dance* and *castle*? With the long *a* (*darnce*) or with the short *a*, to rhyme with *pants*?

Other words of the same kind over which Australians differ include *chance, circumstance, lance, grasp* and *telegraph*.

The short answer to this question, of course, is 'any way you like'. The question, however, is of some interest.

A sentence such as *They climbed the path to the castle to take a bath* would be pronounced by an American with short *a's*, as in the words *pat* and *bat*. Most English people (except in the north of England) would pronounce the sentence *They climbed the parth to the carstle to take a barth*.

This latter pronunciation was unknown in Elizabethan times. Shakespeare would have pronounced the words as the Americans now do. Until some time early last century, indeed, any other way of pronouncing them was considered low-class and vulgar. The *parth/barth* pronunciation was, in fact, the pronunciation of the London streets.

The broad *a* displaced the clipped *a* in polite society in the mid-years of last century. Since Australian speech was in any case strongly influenced by the street pronunciation of London (as American speech replicates the twang of the Puritans from East Anglia who colonised the east coast), the broad *a* pronunciation was probably common in this country by that time. Subsequently it would have been reinforced by 'polite' usage.

So the pronunciation of *dance* to rhyme with *pants*, and similar pronunciations still heard here, are probably 'polite' relict pronunciations from the time of the First Fleet which have somehow survived.

It is commonly said that the *darnce* pronunciation is a characteristic of Adelaide speakers and of Melbourne public-school products. The *Macquarie Dictionary*, however, says that *cassle* for *castle* is "quite common" in Melbourne but rare in Sydney, where *carstle* "is almost universal."

This would, of course, support our suggestion that the *darnce* pronunciation was of convict origin.

See also **regionalism in Australian language**.

dangling phrases. See **hanging participles**.

dashes. It is a secret known to few authors of manuscripts that there is a distinction between a hyphen (-) and a dash (—).

See under **hyphen** for the use of that punctuation mark.

The dash has four functions in written English:

1. It may be used to indicate an involuntary break in a sentence, especially where a speaker is interrupted:

> "Of course, dear Florence wouldn't have —"
> "Don't spoil it . . ."

> Christina Stead

2. It may be used to indicate a pause in a flow of words:

> "Oh, no. Only by Mrs Aspinall—when she comes."

> Patrick White

3. It may be used, on occasion, in place of a colon:

> They were all there on deck—the sailors, the passengers, even the ship's cat.

4. It may be used, with another dash, instead of brackets:

> They were dressed in the height of larrikin fashion—tight-fitting suits of dark cloth, soft black felt hats, and soft white shirts with new black mufflers round their necks in place of collars—for the larrikin taste in dress runs to a surprising neatness.

> Louis Stone

NOTE

1. In typescript the dash is indicated by *two* hyphens, not one and not three.
2. Leaving the hyphen aside, some printers make a distinction between a short dash (the *en rule*), used in such contexts as *the Johnson–Burns fight of 1908*, *the 1939–1945 War*, and the longer dash (as in 1–4 above) known as the *em rule*. Current practice, except in fine printing, tends to equate the short rule and the hyphen, thus giving us that mysterious Australian politician, Bruce-Page.

data/datum. *Datum* means, in the Latin, *something given*. It is almost entirely used, however, in the plural, *data*, which means *pieces of information*.

It is important to remember, however, that *data is* plural. We must therefore say *these data*, not *this data*. We cannot talk about *a data*, though the statement *This is an interesting piece of data* is so ingrained that we simply have to accept it and treat it as an idiom. It is undesirable to say *the data is significant*: prefer *the data are significant*.

Datum survives in a few specialised usages, such as *datum point*, the point from which all subsequent measurements are to be made.

Data is *not* pronounced *datta*, or to rhyme with *sonata*, but with the first syllable sounding like the word *date*.

dates.

1. The form for the writing of dates which is generally accepted today is *13 June 1979*, not *13th June, 1979, June 13th, 1979* or *June 13, 1979*. It is clear and economical.
2. The general convention in editing and printing today is to use the form

1943–4 to express the meaning *1943–1944*. Since there is an exception to this (that 'teens' numbers are expressed *1917–18*), and since it is not as immediately clear as *1943–1944*, we prefer the latter. Financial years are normally referred to as *1971/2*.

3. Prefer *the 1960s* to *the 1960's*.

4. Dates are sometimes written like this: *12.1.1983*, or *12/1/1983*. It is important to note that in Britain and Australia this means 12 January 1983. In the United States of America, Canada and other countries whose daily language practice is influenced by the USA, this way of writing the date would mean 1 December 1983.

5. For establishing what days of the week specific dates have fallen on since 1800, or will fall on until 2000, see **perpetual calendar**.

dead reckoning does not mean 'dead-on' or 'spot-on' reckoning. If you are navigating by *dead reckoning* you are navigating by estimates of distance and course which have not been checked by sun or star sights. *Dead reckoning* may therefore be a dangerous and inaccurate way of reckoning your position.

debris. Meaning *broken bits and pieces*, may be pronounced either *DAY-bree* or *DEBB-ree*.

debut. This word may be pronounced *day-byu, debb-yu, day-boo* or *debb-oo*. *Day-boo* is closest to the original French pronunciation, while *debb-yu* is probably the most common Australian pronunciation. *Day-boo* is recommended.

decade, meaning *a period of ten years*, may be pronounced either as *decayed* or as *deckered*.

See also **centuries**.

decimate. "By 1933 the moth *Cactoblastis cactorum* had decimated the cactus hordes and cleared the land again for crops and pastures." Strictly speaking, to *decimate* is to select every tenth man in a group for execution, as a form of group punishment. By extension it may be used to mean the destruction of some part of a whole. It should not be used to suggest total destruction or extermination. The above usage is therefore wrong.

Nor should the word *decimate* be used as a synonym for "played havoc with", as in this statement made in the House of Representatives on 18 April 1985: "You decimated the steel industry." The same comment applies to the description of parts of northern Australia as "country which until recently was being decimated by wandering buffaloes" (ABC "Countrywide" program, 20 June 1986).

deductable/deductible. Prefer *deductible*.

de facto/de jure. These are commonly used Latin phrases with opposed meanings.

De facto (pronounce *dee facto* or *day facto*) means *in fact*. A *de facto* relationship is a relationship which does not have formal legal status but which nevertheless exists. A relationship which is in all respects a married relationship, except that the formalities of marriage have not been complied with, is called a *de facto* (or *common-law*) marriage.

A situation that complies with the formalities of the law is called a *de jure* (pronounced *dee jury* or *day jury*) relationship.

These days *de facto* marriages may be recognised by the law even though they do not formally comply with the requirements of the law.

defect. *Defect* as a noun—*There is a defect in this torch*—carries, in Britain, a preferred pronunciation which is the same as the verb (*to defect*): that pronunciation is *de-FECT*, with the emphasis on the second syllable.

In Australia and the United States, however, the pronunciation of the noun and the verb differ. The noun is normally pronounced *DE-fect* and the verb *de-FECT*.

defence/defensive. Note the difference in spelling of these two words. The American spelling of defence is *defense*, but not the Australian.

defer, following normal rules (see **doubling up**), makes *deferred, deferring*, but is anomalous in making *deferable*, though *deferrable* is also acceptable.

definite/definitive. *Definite* means *clear* or *precise*, as in *She made a definite offer to buy the house*.

Definitive means *having the character of finality*. A *definitive* offer is a *final* offer, one that marks the end of the road, so to speak. A *definitive* edition of the poems of 'Banjo' Paterson would be, or should be, an edition comprising all the poems which the author wished to be regarded as his work, in the form he wished them printed. A *definitive* edition of the letters of Mary Gilmore would include all surviving letters, not just a selection of them. A superb performance of *Hamlet*, or of a violin concerto, might be termed *definitive*, in this case meaning *setting a standard by which other performances will be measured*.

definitely. *Not definately*, one of the commonest spelling errors.

defuse/diffuse. To *defuse* a bomb is *to take the fuse out of it*. To *diffuse* something is *to spread it around*. The ABC news was in error when it told us in March 1987 that *anxiety on the matter was diffused*. At least, that was what it sounded like. Perhaps the speaker was just mispronouncing the word *defused*. Both words are stressed on the *fuse*, but *de* is clearly pronounced with *defuse*.

deign. "In 1836 he deigned to settle in Gippsland." The speaker meant that the pioneer in question *elected* to settle in Gippsland, or *decided* to settle there.

This is not what *deign* means. *Deign* means *to do something because one thinks it worthy of one's status or attitudes to do it, to condescend to do something.* "After some reflection, he deigned to dirty his hands by changing the tyre." The verb is almost always used in a sarcastic sense.

deity. Is *deity* pronounced *dee-ity* or *day-ity*? And what about other words ending in *-eity*, such as *homogeneity* and *spontaneity*?

The short answer to this question is that the 'approved' pronunciation of all these words is *ee-ity*, but that *ay-ity* has become so common in the last fifty years or so that it may now be more popular than *ee-ity*. There seems to be a shift in pronunciation here, apparent throughout the English-speaking world.

deli, short for *delicatessen*, is commonly used in all States except New South Wales, Victoria and Tasmania to describe a small shop selling bread, milk, confectionery and some groceries. In New South Wales, Victoria and Tasmania such shops are called *milk-bars* or *corner shops* (sometimes *mixed businesses*), the word *deli* is seldom heard, and the word *delicatessen* is used (as elsewhere) to mean a specialist shop selling cooked meats and the like.

delusion/illusion. There are subtle but important differences between a *delusion* and an *illusion*.

One is *deluded* by something that actually exists but which is *wrongly seen or interpreted*. You can, for instance, be *deluded* by a sense of optimism when there are no grounds for such a feeling, just as you can be *deluded* about the real speed of the car you collided with.

In the sense that optimism exists, or the speed of a car exists, an *illusion* does not exist at all. If you think you can see the Man in the Moon, you are suffering from an *illusion*, for he is not there. A conjurer, by *delusion*, creates an *illusion*.

demean. This confusing word has two meanings.
1. In the first sense the verb means simply *to behave*, thus:
>   She demeaned herself with credit.
>   He demeaned himself poorly.

The word of course is related to *demeanor*.
2. The verb is also used in the sense of *to debase*:
>   They would not demean themselves to apologise.

demi-monde. A distinguished Australian literary figure once got himself into legal trouble by referring to someone as a member of the *demi-monde*. The word is French and means "half-world" and our friend apparently believed that it meant being on the fringe of things, in this case of the arts.

Sadly for him, *demi-monde* means no such thing. It relates, primarily, to what used to be called women of doubtful reputation; secondarily, to any group behaving with doubtful legality or propriety.

Watch it!

demise. Apart from certain legal meanings as both verb and noun, *demise* is a noun meaning *death*, as in *The demise of the Prime Minister of Sri Lanka has been reported.*

Prefer *death* to *demise* in such cases, and in phrases such as *after the demise of.*

There is an increasing tendency in Australian political reporting to apply the word *demise* to the fall or replacement of a public figure: *the demise of Andrew Peacock; the demise of Sir Brian Murray.* It is true that the word can be used figuratively, as in *the demise of my hopes*, but there is little or no justification for its being made to mean *downfall*.

The word may certainly not be used as an adjective, as at a recent public function in Melbourne, where the chairman referred to *our last two demising secretaries*.

Pronounce *demise* to rhyme with *pies*, not with *mice*.

demur/demurring. *To demur* about something is *to raise objections*. It is pronounced *de-MERR*, to rhyme with *purr*. The word *demurring* follows, in being pronounced *de-MERR-ing*.

dependant/dependent. *Dependant* is a noun. It means *a person who depends on another. She was hard-working and had many dependants.*

Dependent is an adjective and means *depending on a person or thing*: *Her children were under-age and were totally dependent on her.*

dependent clauses. See **that/which/who/whom.**

deplete. "Rainwater household supplies in Girilambone have long been depleted."

The sense of this statement in its context in the *Australian* is that the house tanks have long been *exhausted*.

This is a proper use of the word *deplete*, which means in Latin *to deprive of that which fills.*

There is however another meaning, which is *to partially reduce* the stock of something. It is our view that, in general use, *to deplete* normally means *to partially reduce* rather than *to exhaust*.

deprecate/depreciate. These two verbs are sometimes regarded as meaning the same thing, *to disparage, to belittle, to express disapproval of.* In fact there is a distinction which should be preserved. *Deprecate* is a stronger word than *depreciate.* It originally meant to *pray against* someone. One may *deprecate* terrorism but *depreciate* someone's role as an architect. It is desirable to regard *deprecate* as meaning *disapproval,* and *depreciate* as meaning *of less value than usually regarded.* You can *depreciate* your achievements as a painter without *deprecating* them.

Depreciation as an intransitive verb (one which does not take an object) means *to lose value,* as most Australians know to their cost: *The Australian dollar has depreciated against many other currencies.*

Descartes. The adjective from the name of the French philosopher and mathematician René Descartes (1596-1650) is *Cartesian.* One would thus talk of *Cartesian principles.*

desiccate. To *desiccate* is to *dehydrate,* from the Latin word *siccus, dry,* which of course is also related to the French *sec. Siccus* is also related to other Indo-European words, such as the Czech *suchy, dry.*

It is said that the Czechs are called Czechs because they lived on the dry flats along the river Vltava or Elbe. In other words, *suchý* is said to have evolved into "Cechy," the Czech name for *Bohemia.*

Leaving the digression aside, *desiccate* is often misspelt *dessicate.* It can be helpful in spelling the word to remember the root, *siccus.*

despatch/dispatch. Either is correct, though *dispatch* is favored by most authorities.

deteriorate/deterioration. It is common, but incorrect, to drop the fourth syllable of *deteriorate* and pronounce it *deteriate.*

Similarly *deterioration* should not be pronounced *deteriation.*

determiners. Some modern grammarians describe words such as *that, this, my, his, these, those,* classified traditionally as *demonstrative pronouns, demonstrative adjectives* or *possessive adjectives,* as *determiners,* defined as *a word that determines the referent or referents of a noun phrase.*

The word *determiner* is also used to replace more traditional classifications for such words as *the, a, some, many* when used in such a sentence as *There's some men on the beach.*

See also **modifiers.**

deviate/divert. Attempts, we were told, were being made *to deviate public disapproval from the Australian Labor Party. To deviate* is *to turn aside.* A ship

111

can *deviate from a course* and a person can *deviate from her faith in religion*. The verb is usually intransitive and you cannot *deviate something*, though you can, as we have seen, *deviate from something*.

The word that should have been used in the above example, and which was being sought for, was *divert*, which also means *to turn aside* but which is transitive and can be used with an object such as *public disapproval*.

See also **divergence/diversion**.

device/devise. *Device* is the noun: *She had constructed an admirable device.* *Devise* is the verb: *She had devised an admirable construction.*

There is also a legal meaning of the verb *devise*, meaning *to assign, to give: I hereby devise my possessions to my daughter.*

devil quoting scripture. Actually "The devil can cite scripture for his purpose" (*Merchant of Venice*, act I, scene iii).

devil's advocate. In its classical sense a *devil's advocate* is an official of the Catholic Church appointed to collect evidence and argue *against* a proposed canonisation (declaring someone a saint).

A *devil's advocate* is *someone who presents, for the purposes of a specific argument, the case against someone or something.*

A *devil's advocate* is *not* someone who tries to make bad things sound good, but someone who presents the *worst case* against a proposal as a given responsibility, rather than out of conviction.

devotee. A *devotee* of something is *devoted* to it: *She was a devotee of fine wines.* The word is pronounced *devot-EE*, not *dev-OAT-ee*.

diaeresis. See **hyphens**.

dial. We are familiar with *dialling* a phone number. But what word do we use to describe the action of pushing buttons on more modern phones?

Dialling will no doubt remain in use, even for button-phones, but *keying* will probably in time become the standard word. It will, however, take longer for *key tone* to replace *dial tone*.

diametrically. Kenneth Hince (*Age*, 14 April 1986), in reviewing a performance of the opera "Boris Godunov," wrote that the producer "both offset and complemented Mussorgsky's tendency to be monumental by using his huge chorus in diametrically opposite ways."

We meet *diametrically* most often in the phrases *diametrically opposite* and *diametrically opposed*. These terms are, let's face it, clichés. (So is *let's face it.*)

A *diameter* is *a line that goes from one side of a circle to the other through the centre of the circle*. Something that is *diametrically opposed* is *exactly opposed*, as far away from the other side of the circle as it can get.

Whether any great strength is added to the simple word *opposed* by attaching *diametrically* to it is very much a matter of doubt. If something is opposed to something else we normally assume that it is directly opposed, rather than being opposed at an angle. If not, we say *somewhat opposed*.

Diametrically, except when a real geometrical point is being made, should be given a rest.

different from/different to. *Different from* is the form to be preferred, though many distinguished writers have used *different to*, and *different to* should be used when it feels natural to do so, as in a situation where *similar to* and *dissimilar to* are being used:

The horse she rode was similar to his, but different to the one she rode a week ago.

Different than is also found in the best authors, is common in American English, but nevertheless is frowned on in British and Australian usage.

digraphs. See -æ-, -œ-.

dilemma. A *dilemma* is *a choice between two equally unattractive arguments*, or more simply *a problem that appears difficult of solution*. Pronounce *dill-EMM-a* or *dye-LEMM-a*, but prefer the former.

dilettante. A *dilettante* is a person who flutters around, cooing interest and affection for a topic (usually in the arts) without in fact doing anything substantial about it.

The plural may be either *dilettanti* or *dilettantes*.

The catch is that this is not a French word, though it looks like one, but an Italian one. Therefore the final letter is sounded, thus: *dil-et-ARNT-e*.

diminish/minimise. The two words do not mean the same thing. To *diminish* is to *make less* or *become less*, while to *minimise* is to *reduce to the lowest degree*.

Thus to *diminish* your claim to a share of the cake does not mean that you have *minimised* it. *Diminishing* may simply be a stage in the *minimising*.

dim sim/yum cha. To Australians, and particularly to Melburnians, the *dim sim* at its best is one of the most delectable Chinese delicacies: cylindrical, the size and shape of a short thumb, spicy mince-meat lovingly folded into its integument of paste, and steamed in a basket.

Literally translated from the Cantonese, the word means *a slight touch on the heart*. How true and how fitting! But the Chinese use *dim sim* or *dim sum* (the

113

same thing) rather as a group name for a variety of small delicacies of many kinds served as a meal, typically as a Chinese breakfast.

Yum cha, literally *drink tea,* means the same as the Chinese definition of *dim sim.* In Australia it is used to describe a kind of Chinese smorgasbord.

dinghy/dingy. A *dinghy* (also spelt *dingy* or *dingey*) is *a small boat,* usually a rowing boat. Pronounce *DING-y.*

Dingy, an adjective which probably comes from the same root as *dung,* means *drab, dirty, discolored.* Pronounce *DINJ-y.*

dingo. The plural is *dingoes.*

dinner/lunch/supper/tea. These words for meals are, in Australia, reliable indicators of social class.

Australian educated speech normally refers to the midday meal as *lunch* (*luncheon* is regarded as affected in Australia, except in the term *luncheon party*), and to the evening meal as *dinner. Tea* will normally mean *afternoon tea,* and *supper* will normally mean a light meal late in the evening.

Others will speak of the midday meal as *dinner,* and the evening meal as *tea* (sometimes, *supper*).

It is probable that the 'received' usages are gaining ground.

Received usage accepts *dinner* (sometimes *Sunday dinner* or *Sunday lunch*) as an appropriate word for the midday meal on a Sunday, when that meal is regarded as the main meal of the day, and *tea* (once, *high tea*) or *supper* as terms for the evening meal on Sunday.

The pervasive working-class and rural use of *dinner* for the midday meal is in fact the traditional meaning, standard until last century, as in Alexander Pope's:

> The hungry judges soon the sentence sign,
> And wretches hang that jurymen may dine.

	'Received' usage	'Common' usage
morning	breakfast	breakfast
mid-morning	morning tea	no agreed usage; smoko, tea break, in working situations; also morning lunch; at school playlunch
midday	lunch	dinner
mid-afternoon	afternoon tea	no agreed usage
evening	dinner	tea (sometimes supper); dinner used when dining out or having guests
late evening	supper	no agreed usage; supper; sometimes late supper

dinosaurs. Let us remember, when we smile at the dinosaur as a failed evolutionary experiment, and use the word to describe a *non-survivor*, that dinosaurs ruled the Earth for 150 million years and were wiped out by a cataclysm, not because of their own stupidity. We have been around about two million years and may not be around much longer.

diphthongs. (1) The ligatured letters *æ* and *œ*, found in such words as *encyclopædia*, used to be called *diphthongs*, because that was the way they were pronounced in classical Latin. They are not pronounced that way in English words, however, and the term now used for them is *digraph*. See -æ- and -œ-. (2) For the use of the word in phonetics, see **vowels**.

directly. "I'm going home to England, directly," the early Melbourne identity Charles Ebden used to say. (His Aboriginal servant used to mimic this, to the great pleasure of Ebden's friends.)

Directly, according to all the dictionaries, means *immediately, straight away*. There is no doubt that in many cases that is just what it does mean: *I rang her up directly I received the letter*. However there are other usages, such as that of Ebden above, where *directly* means, rather than *straight away*, *very soon*, *before long*. The word *directly* in answer to such a question as "When *are* you coming?" suggests at least a momentary delay.

Directly can also mean, of course, *in a direct line: I then strode directly to the town hall*.

See also **presently**.

dirigible/dirigisme/dirigiste. These words all come from the French verb *diriger, to direct*, and they all contain the meaning of *control, direction*. Indeed in German the conductor of an orchestra is the *Dirigent*. In English a *dirigible* is *an airship which can be steered*.

Dirigisme and *dirigiste* are French words slowly making their way into English, where they will eventually become naturalised as *dirigism* and *dirigist*. When we speak of *dirigisme* or *dirigiste* policies we mean *policies laid down and controlled by a central state apparatus*. Thus the economies of the communist countries are sometimes referred to as *dirigiste* economies, in theory fully planned and controlled from the centre. We have seen a government White Paper referred to as *dirigistic*, that is, *strongly prescriptive* or, to use an Australian expression, *standover*.

disabuse. To *abuse* someone is *to berate them, to direct words of condemnation against them*.

Disabuse, however, does not mean *to withdraw such words*. It means *to be successful in changing someone's mind*, as in *I disabused him of the idea that the world was flat*.

disappoint. All too often, says the wine-writer Mark Shield in the *Age* (13 May 1986), one hears of a great Australian *pinot noir*, "but, when they materialise, they invariably disappoint."

In the dictionaries *disappoint* is a *transitive* verb, which means it needs an object. Mark Shield should have written *they invariably disappoint me*, or *they invariably disappoint one.*

The tendency for transitive verbs to become intransitive (not requiring an object) is part of the living reality of the English language, in the same way as nouns are turned into verbs. *Disappoint* is, at least in Australian usage, well on the way to becoming an intransitive verb, and Mark Shield has helped it along the way. He has been criticised for doing so. At the point where none notice the way he has used *disappoint*, or consider it worth commenting upon if they do, then *disappoint* will have successfully gone through its metamorphosis into a slightly different kind of word.

disassemble/dissemble. On the analogy of *associate* making *dissociate*, and similar formations, it might be expected that the opposite of *assemble* would be *dissemble.*

This cannot be, for there is another word *dissemble*, with another meaning. *Dissemble* means *to conceal one's real motives by pretence*, or simply *to pretend*: *When asked to explain his motives he dissembled, and told a series of lies.*

The opposite of *assemble* therefore has to be *disassemble.*

disassociate/dissociate. *Disassociate* is a common, but illiterate, form of the correct word, *dissociate.*

It is worth saying why this is so. In *associate*, the *sociate* part of the word has the sense of *coming together*, and this is reinforced by the *as* which commences the word. It may be said that *associate* in terms of its origins means something like *together-join*. To write *disassociate*, however, introduces the *dis-* and creates a hybrid word meaning something like *un-together-join*. This is illogical and rather silly. What we want to say is *un-join*, and this is just what we do say when we write *dissociate.*

disastrous is so spelt. *Disasterous* is wrong.

disc/disk.
1. For a *gramophone record*, prefer *disc* to *disk*, which is the American spelling. Perhaps rather strangely, the word *disc* for a gramophone record has not made the inroads in Australia that—given the strong American influences in popular music—it might have been expected to. The use of the new term *compact disc*, for a special kind of gramophone record, may assist the retention of the word *record* for *long-playing records.*

2. The American spelling *disk* is now common in Australian computer technology. Although in the first edition of this book the spelling *disc* was preferred, this seems a lost cause, and we may draw what comfort we can from the fact that, if we spell the computer *disk* that way, it at least distinguishes it from the gramophone record *disc*. An additional argument is that the associated word *diskette* is an IBM proprietary name and presumably therefore has to be spelt that way.

discomfit/discomfort. *Discomfit* means *to make someone uneasy*, or *embarrassed*, or *to frustrate their intentions*, as in *They were discomfited by the court's ruling*.

Discomfort, of course, means (as a verb) *to make someone or something uncomfortable*.

discovery and exploration. Who 'discovered' Australia, or the islands in the Pacific for that matter? Since humanity did not evolve in Australia, Australia was 'discovered' by the first immigrants, presumably the ancestors of the present-day Aboriginals, perhaps a hundred thousand years or more ago.

So Captain Cook did not discover Australia, and nor did the Dutch, who reported the existence of the continent a hundred and fifty years before Cook. To suggest that Europeans 'discovered' Australia is, in a roundabout way, to suggest that the Aboriginals were and are not really people.

What we *can* say is that the Dutch brought Australia into the thought-world of Europe, in the same way that Cook (and others) did for the Pacific islands and the east coast of Australia. But that is all we can say.

We should also remind ourselves frequently that the great European explorers of Australia, both by sea and land, were 'first' only in a limited sense, and were in fact following in the tracks of countless generations of earlier explorers, equally human even if from a different culture.

discreet/discrete. *Discreet* means *prudent, circumspect, careful what you say*. *Discrete* means *distinct, separate, discontinuous: Although they appeared identical, the phenomena were discrete*. For words so far apart in meaning, the number of times they can be confused in speech is surprising, and *discrete* is best confined to writing or print.

discriminate/discrimination. As a verb *to discriminate* usually means *to single out a group or quality for special favor or disfavor:*

> In selecting the team they discriminated against Eddie Gilbert, who was an Aboriginal.
> In selecting the bouquet I discriminated in favor of the violets, which I especially admire.

117

It is time for us to discriminate between right and wrong.

The verb can also mean *to be discerning in matters of taste: In selecting the portraits she discriminated intelligently.*

Because of the popularity of 'anti-discrimination' legislation (see **ageism/ageist**) *to discriminate* and *discrimination* are being used to suggest that the activities they convey are always undesirable and unpleasant activities. This is not so, as we see above, and as is conveyed by that other modern term, *positive discrimination*, which means *favoring people or groups because they have not had justice in the past.* The very fact that we have had to attach the word *positive* to the word *discrimination* is an indication of the general misuse of the word to mean *negative discrimination.*

disfranchise/disenfranchise. The word is *disfranchise. Disenfranchise* should be avoided.

The reason is that *dis-* and *en-* when put together are contradictory. *En-* means, in effect, *to let in*, and *dis-* means in effect *to shut out*, of the position of being able to vote. Thus *disenfranchise* would mean *to shut out to let in to being able to vote*, when all we want to say is *to shut out of being able to vote.* The word that says this is *disfranchise.*

disinformation/misinformation. *Misinformation* is *information that is misleading, but not intentionally so. Disinformation* is *information that is deliberately, intentionally misleading.*

When the Swedish Prime Minister Olaf Palme was assassinated in 1986, the investigating authorities in Stockholm blamed Kurdish malcontents. In the *New York Times* magazine of 1 March 1987 they were accused of "police disinformation," of attempting to divert attention from other possibilities, including Palme's private life and the secret sale of Swedish arms to Iran.

The prefix *mis-* conveys the sense of *wrongly*, the prefix *dis-* the sense of *the opposite of.* Thus *misplace*, to put in the wrong place, and *displace*, to substitute.

In the second world war all participants engaged in disinformation, though it appears the British were most successful. *Disinformation* was then known as *black propaganda.* The word *disinformation* was apparently adopted by American intelligence agencies in the 1950s from the Russian *dezinformatsiya*, said to be the name of a division of the KGB. Dirty tricks are always what the *other* fellow is up to.

The noun has now become a verb, *to disinform.* Oddly, *disinformation* appears neither in the supplement to the *Oxford English Dictionary* nor in the *Macquarie Dictionary*, though it has now been in common use for twenty years.

disinterested means *free of bias.* It does *not* mean *lacking in interest.*

See **uninterested/disinterested.**

disparate. *Disparate* means *utterly different: These are disparate issues.* Pronounce *DIS-prit, DIS-pirit.*

dispute/disputation. A *dispute* is *an argument.* A *disputation* may also be an argument, and Australians love to use it instead of *dispute* because it sounds more impressive, but in almost all cases prefer *dispute. Disputation* may be reserved for *a formal argument on a thesis.*

dissect rhymes with *his sect,* not with *bisect.*

distasteful. A sea creature, we were told on an ABC wildlife program, "resembles a distasteful flatworm" in order that other creatures do not eat it.

The author would have been better to write *an unpalatable flatworm* or *an unsavory flatworm. Distasteful* is not the opposite of *tasteful,* but means *repugnant* or *disgusting* or *immoral.* It is used in a moral rather than a physical sense.

distract/detract. *To distract* is *to cause someone's attention to be diverted: It is important not to distract the driver's attention by talking to her.*

To detract is *to take away from, to diminish: His behavior detracted from his earlier reputation for responsibility.*

dived/dove. Australians and the British say *She dived off the end of the pier.* Americans may say this, but they are just as likely to say *She dove off the end of the pier.* The *Macquarie Dictionary* says that this is an American colloquialism, but *dove* now appears in standard American writing. It is not acceptable in Australian English.

See also **plead/pleaded/pled.**

divergence/diversion. Although the meanings of these two words overlap, use *diversion* for *a traffic detour, divergence* for *the act of diverting* (*They then made a divergence*) or *the degree by which something diverges* (*The divergence between the two series of readings was extreme*).

See also **deviate/divert.**

doctor. The title of *doctor,* abbreviated to *Dr,* used to be almost solely confined to *medical practitioners who were not surgeons.* In academic fact most medical practitioners hold bachelors' degrees from a university and very few have a *doctorate* in medicine. For all that, the title of *Dr* has been traditionally accorded to doctors and legally protected as such. It was then, and is, in most cases a courtesy title. It is sometimes jokingly said that medical practitioners are not 'real' doctors. (Note that surgeons traditionally call themselves *Mr,* not *Dr.*)

'Real' doctors are those who hold a doctoral degree from a university. There is, however, a catch here. There are two kinds of doctoral degrees. The 'junior' doctorate is called a Doctorate of Philosophy (Ph.D.), is earned after post-graduate research which extends for a number of years, and applies to all academic fields. Thus the puzzle, for the uninitiated, of coming up against a doctor of philosophy who has never heard of Plato.

The senior academic doctorates either are earned by submitting a corpus of learned publications or are awarded as distinctions of honor. In the latter case they are termed *honorary doctorates*. These 'senior' doctorates are identified by field: Doctor of Engineering, Doctor of Music, Doctor of Science, Doctor of Dentistry, Doctor of Letters and so on.

The courtesy title of *Dr* accorded to medical practitioners has in recent years been extended to dentists and veterinarians.

The likelihood that other occupational groups will also demand the title of *Dr* is demonstrated by the recent actions of the Californian legislature, which is largely composed of lawyers and has decreed that all law graduates in that State will be know as doctors of law. This also applies retrospectively. In Australian terms such professionals hold only a bachelor's degree (or, as the Americans would say, a *baccalaureate*). Traditionally all American medical practitioners hold the degree of Doctor of Medicine (*M.D.*), gained at an educational level which, in Australia and Britain, would qualify only for a bachelor's degree. It should be noted, however, that Americans in the professions normally complete a first degree in the liberal arts before entering their professional studies.

The most apposite comment on all this is from W. S. Gilbert: "When everybody's somebody then no-one's anybody."

See also **honorifics**.

dollar. See **pounds, shillings and pence.**

dolphin/porpoise. No *porpoises*, members of the family *Phocoenidae*, are to be found in Australian waters. The animals which we sometimes call *porpoises* are all *dolphins*, members of the family *Delphinidae*. Four species are commonly found around the coastline of Australia.

donate. *Donate* is, as A. P. Herbert once pointed out, something of a snob-word. Lady Muck *donates* a cup for the mile race at her son's public school, while Bert Brown *gives* ten dollars to help his football club along.

Don Quixote. The *Quixote* in this word is pronounced *kwiksot* or *kwiksit*. Attempts to approximate to a Spanish pronunciation of this word are affectations designed to disguise lack of familiarity. They have as little—and as much—justification in English as the pronunciation of Cervantes as

Thervantes, with the Castilian lisp. In other words, they are showing off. We do not pronounce **quixotic** as *keyotic*.

dots. Three dots, thus ..., have two useful purposes in the written language. They are sometimes called *an ellipsis* (plural, *ellipses*) or *leaders*.
1. The dots may express an unfinished thought, an invitation to the reader to fill in what the author has left unsaid, or a broken ending, as when a character is saying something but is interrupted by another:

> If he dared to touch her I could shoot him and be justified ...

George Turner

2. Dots may also express, in a quotation, something that has been left out:

> There comes a tide in the affairs of men
> Which ... leads on to fortune.

3. Note that dots have a clear space after the word that precedes them and before the word that follows them.
4. Never use more than three dots.
5. Where dots indicating an excision follow on from a complete sentence, the order is (a) last word of sentence, (b) full stop, (c) space, (d) three dots, as with:

> And so it happened. ... We agreed it was wrong.

6. What if, in quoting something, you wish to make it quite clear that the dots do indeed represent something left out, and are not in the original? Here it is wise to place *your* dots within square brackets, thus: [...].

double negative. The double negative is a grammatically correct aspect of certain languages—Czech is one, Modern Greek another—but is often thought to appear in English only in vernacular speech: "I didn't have no ticket," meaning logically that *I had a ticket* but accepted to mean *I had no ticket.*

In fact we use the double negative in English all the time, without recognising it. When someone says "That won't appeal to the taxpayers, I don't believe", we know that the speaker *believes* it won't appeal to the taxpayers, not that he does *not* believe this.

Similarly, when we say "She didn't come, I don't think", we mean that we *do think* she didn't come.

The double negative has to be accepted as part of correct, if idiomatic, English.

double possessives. We may talk of *the child of my sister*. Here *of my sister* is a possessive phrase. It says that the child belongs to my sister. Why then have another acceptable phrase, *the child of my sister's*, which says the same thing all over again but says it twice?

First, let us make the point clear: *both forms are correct*.

It is something of an oddity in the language. One historical argument is that some way had to be found to avoid having to say *this my plate* and *that your horse;* that *this plate of mine* and *that horse of yours* were found very convenient; and that eventually they came to be used much more broadly: *the child of my sister's.*

NOTE

1. The double possessive is not used of inanimate objects. One should not say *the regenerative effect of the rain's,* but *the regenerative effect of the rain.*
2. Do not use the double possessive if *that* is in front of the *of:*

    a fountain very similar to that of the bishop, *not*
    a fountain very similar to that of the bishop's.

doubling up. A problem we all run into in spelling is when, in adding suffixes to words, we double the final letter. Is it *occured* or *occurred, regrettable* or *regretable, benefitted* or *benefited.*

The three answers to this problem normally adopted are (a) to guess, (b) to learn the ones that trouble us most by heart, or (c) to look up the dictionary.

There are, however, rules. We set them out here in three forms, an Instant Guide, a Quick Guide and an Expanded Guide.

INSTANT GUIDE

If the last syllable before the consonant is stressed (and this includes, of course, all words of one syllable), and if it contains only one vowel, then *double.*

QUICK GUIDE

1. Is the word one syllable? (Yes)
Does it have only one vowel before the final consonant? (Yes)
    Then double that consonant.
2. Is the word one syllable? (Yes)
Does it have more than one vowel before the final consonant? (Yes)
    Do not double the consonant.
3. Is the word more than one syllable? (Yes)
Is the last syllable accented? (Yes)
Does that syllable have only one vowel? (Yes)
    Then double the consonant.
4. Is the word more than one syllable? (Yes)
Is the last syllable accented? (Yes)
Does that syllable have more than one vowel? (Yes)
    Do not double the consonant.
5. Is the word more than one syllable? (Yes)
Does the accent fall on a syllable other than the last? (Yes)
    Do not double the consonant.

EXPANDED GUIDE

1. The problem only arises when there is a vowel immediately before the final consonant. Thus words like *start, evict* and *effect,* which do not have a vowel

before the final consonant, stay as they are when a suffix is added.

2. Where the vowel immediately before the final consonant is a single letter (or a single letter preceded by *qu*, as in *quiz*), in all single-syllable words double the consonant: *rot* becomes *rotten*, *bed* makes *bedded*, *trek* makes *trekking*, *club* makes *clubbable*, *quiz* makes *quizzed*. (Exception: *bus* makes *bused*.)

3. If in single-syllable words there are two immediately preceding vowels, do not double. Thus *soot* becomes *sooty*, *flair* becomes *flaired*, *head* makes *heading*. (Exception: *wool* makes *woolly*, *woollen*.)

4. With words of more than one syllable decide where they are accented. If the last syllable is accented, then follow the sames rules as above. Thus *repeat* (two vowels) becomes *repeated*, equip (a *qui* word) becomes *equipped*, *regret* (only one vowel) becomes *regretted*. (Note however that, while *prefer, transfer, confer, defer, infer* and *refer* follow the rule in becoming *preferred, preferring etc.*, they do not follow the rule with the *-able* ending, becoming *preferable*, etc.)

5. Words of more than one syllable, *not* stressed on the last syllable, do *not* double. Thus *biased, womanish, lettered*.

Exceptions: (a) *Worship* becomes *worshipped*. (b) In words ending in the letter *l*, the letter is doubled *wherever* the stress falls in the word (e.g. *devil, devilled, channel, channelled*) except where the *l* is preceded by two vowels or a long vowel sound such as *ur, ow* (*curl* becomes *curled, appeal* becomes *appealed, fail* becomes *failed*). There is a body of opinion which holds that we should, in the interest of consistency with the treatment of other final consonants, drop the rule which says that the *l* must be doubled on an unstressed syllable, and adopt the American system which gives us *traveled, signaled*. This would be desirable.

6. Some words, often compound words where the last syllable has the full vowel sound of a single-syllable word, are also exceptions: *handicapped, hobnobbed, kidnapped, horsewhipping, zigzagging, humbugged, leapfrogged, nonplussed* are examples.

7. Where a final consonant is silent, it is not doubled. Thus *précis* becomes *précised*.

See also **spelling reform in Australia**.

dove. For *dove* in the sense of *dived*, see **dived/dove**.

doyen/doyenne. "You have to admit that the leadership of the waterside workers has, over the years, provided the doyens of intellectual thought in the trade union movement."

Thus Mr Stewart West, a Minister in the Hawke government, and himself a former waterside worker (*Age*, 5 April 1986).

It is not clear what Mr West means by *doyens*, but it seems likely that he means something like *the most outstanding examples*.

If so, he was wrong. *Doyen* means *the most senior member of a group*. The *doyen* of the diplomatic corps in Canberra is the ambassador who has been longest in his or her Canberra post. The *doyen* of recognised Australian poets was Robert D. FitzGerald of Sydney, until his death in 1987.

The female form, *doyenne*, may be disregarded, because there is now a general tendency to get rid of specifically female forms (see **(the) female critique**) and because the word is now effectively anglicised in any case. Pronounce *doyen* as a normal English word, not a French one.

draft/draught. These are in origin the same word, related to the verb *to draw*, and are pronounced the same way. While in the United States the spelling *draft* has become dominant, in British and Australian usage a distinction is made.

One *drafts* a Bill for a parliament, a detachment of soldiers or a financial document in a bank.

In architecture and building, however, a *draughtsman draughts* a plan. Beer is kept *on draught*, a current of air is a *draught*, *draught-horses* pull drays, we refer to a ship's *draught*, and we play the game of *draughts*.

Note, however, that many Australian newspapers prefer a *draftsman* or *draftswoman*.

dramatic. "There will be a dramatic reduction in train services tomorrow ... new regulations will dramatically streamline shunting operations."

Thus a television news-reader on the ABC (15 December 1985).

If *dramatic* means anything it must surely mean that an event is *startling, heightened in impact, a bit larger than life*, in other words, as we would expect to see in at least some dramas. A reduction in trains running of one in every four is no *dramatic* news, at least to the Victorian public at the time of the news bulletin. Nor is the general public going to find anything at all to do with railway shunting operations of *dramatic* interest.

This unfortunate word is being used here, as so often, in a lazy way. Some tired journalist is trying to force this news to be interesting by using a 'dramatic' word, in this case the word *dramatic*. The practice is, of course, self-defeating. People stopped listening to the boy who cried "Wolf!" and if words like *dramatic* are over-used they will lose the meaning they are intended to convey.

draw. One of the meanings of the word *draw* is *to move towards or away by pulling*.

Curtains are *drawn*, which may mean that they are either *opened* or *closed*. We normally assume that the word means *to close*, and it may be wise to make the alternative meaning clear by writing *to draw open*.

dreamed/dreamt. Prefer *dreamt*, except in poetry and 'heightened' usages.

drove. I *drive* a car, I am *driving* a car, I have *driven* a car, I *drove* the car. But I *drove* the sheep, I am *droving* the sheep, I have *droved* the sheep, I *droved* the sheep.

While the noun *drove*, meaning *a herd or flock being driven together in some direction*, is familiar enough in Britain and the United States, the verb *to drove* is not. Nor is the noun *drove* when it means *the act of droving: it was a long drove we made that year*.

dry. Note *drier, driest, drily, dryish, dryness, drying*. For the political use of this word, see **wet/dry**.

due is a word peculiarly vulnerable to mispronunciation, and to do so is often taken as an indicator of sloppy speech. It is *not* pronounced as one would pronounce the word *Jew*, but as *dyoo*. In other words, sound the *d*.

duel. The Australian Broadcasting Corporation talks of a *duel* between *three* golfers. Although the word is, surprisingly, not related to the Latin *duo* (two) but rather to *bellum* (war), a duel may only be between *two* people or parties.

due to/owing to. Traditionalists often argue that, while it is correct to write *The cancellation of the football match was due to a downpour*, it is incorrect to write *Due to a downpour, the football match was cancelled*.

This is because the football match was *not* due to the downpour. It was *the cancellation* that was due to the downpour, and the *due to* must therefore relate grammatically to *the cancellation*.

The grammatical arguments are complex, and the purists claim that *due to* is an adjective which means *caused by* and that it must have a noun to agree with; and that to use it as a synonym for *because of* is to change it into a compound preposition.

The arguments may be passed over, but what can not be passed over is that the issue is a live one and still inspires heated debate.

The simplest way out of the problem is to avoid the use of *due to* altogether (except in such a context as *She had $240 back-pay due to her*) and use *because of*. Another is to remember that unless *due to* is used in the sense that means *caused by*, it is under suspicion. A third help is to remember that *due to* can very rarely be used, in the purist sense, to start a sentence.

The objections to the misuse of *due to* will no doubt in time pass away, as the same objections to the use of *owing to* have almost disappeared.

dunny. See **(the) smallest room**.

duplicate. See **copy/duplicate/facsimile/replica**.

dwarf. The plural is either *dwarves* or *dwarfs*.

dye. Note *She is now dyeing the cloth red.*

dyke is a vernacular word for *a female homosexual*, a *lesbian*. Though not Australian in origin it is well established in use in Australia. A *bull-dyke* is the dominant partner in a lesbian relationship.

dynasty. A *dynasty* is *a sequence of rulers from the same family or background*. On Australian television this word is frequently mispronounced so that the first syllable rhymes with *pine*. It does not. It rhymes with *pin*.

E

each/either. Can we say "The car has bumper-bars at either end"? The short answer to this is Yes, but it has to be regarded as an idiomatic construction. Many would hold that *either* means *one or the other*, not *both*, and that the proper wording here is *The car has bumper-bars at each end.*

each/every. *Each* and *every* (and also *anyone, anybody, everybody, nobody, somebody*) are singular. It is useful to remind ourselves that *each* stands for *each one*, *every* for *every one*.

Thus a sentence such as *Each student has to bring their own writing implements* is, in theory, wrong, and should read *Each student has to bring his or her own writing implements.*

This, of course, is clumsy. If you have to keep on doing it in the one piece of writing it becomes unworkable. So what is the solution?

The first solution is to put the whole sentence into the plural if possible: *All students must bring their own writing implements.*

The second solution is to accept the fact that such a sentence as *Each student must bring their own writing implements* is commonly used, perfectly understandable and helps to overcome the *he/she* problem, in other words the absence of the badly needed unisex third-person singular pronoun, as does the word *they* used in the same way.

In other words, to say *Each student must bring their own writing implements* should now be regarded as less than idiomatic and perfectly acceptable. There will be rearguard actions fought over this but the angels are on the side of the innovation. To refer to a point made in the Introduction to this book, this is a desirable mutation rather than an excrescence.

earth. *Earth* should be spelt with a capital *E* when referring to the planet *Earth*.

The address of the Earth, according to Dr Robin Hirst of the Melbourne Planetarium, is:

    The Earth,
    The Solar System,
    Orion Spiral Arm,
    Milky Way Galaxy,
    Local Cluster,
    Local Super-cluster,
    The Universe.

This, at any rate, is the way things stand (or float?) about 18,000,000,000 years after the Big Bang.

ebullient means *full of enthusiasm*: it comes from a word meaning *to boil*. The *bull* part of the word may rhyme with *pull* or with *cull*.

eccentric. The pronunciation of this word as *escentric*, heard on the Australian Broadcasting Corporation's transmissions, is incorrect. Pronounce *eksentric*.

eclectic. To have an *eclectic* approach to, say, the collecting of paintings is *to ignore theories and doctrines* and to operate on the basis of a more relaxed attitude — to collect what you like, or what comes your way, for instance. You can have an eclectic philosophy, or eclectic architecture: a philosophy or architecture which draws from a number of styles, as do many modern buildings, including the Melbourne Shrine of Remembrance.

Whether it is desirable to announce, however — as New Zealand's famous Huka Lodge does — that its wine list "is truly eclectic" is another matter. Dedicated drinkers prefer their wine suppliers to be discriminating rather than eclectic. Here *eclectic* is being taken over, as so many words are, as a word to impress. Not only are the proprietors not sure what the word means — they are pretty confident that the client will not know either. Obviously the hope is that *eclectic* means something like *wide-ranging*. Well, it does. But it also carries a sense of generous picking rather than careful choosing. A little learning *is* a dangerous thing.

ecology/environment. These two words do not mean the same thing. It is wrong to say *Woodchipping is affecting the ecology in Tasmania*. Woodchipping may be affecting the *environment* in Tasmania, but *ecology* is, properly, *the study of the relationships between living organisms and their environment*. It is not those relationships themselves.

edition/impression. A book is first written and then it is published. The entire number of copies thus produced is an *edition*; if it is the first time it has been published, then it is a *first edition*.

If demand for this book is greater than expected, there will be a call for a further printing. So long as the text of the book remains essentially unaltered, this second printing of the book is *not* a second edition but a *second impression* (that is, a reprint) of the first edition. And so on.

If, however, after some time a number of errors have come to light, or new information has materialised, the author or publisher may wish for a substantially amended version of the book to appear. This will then be known as the second *edition*.

It will thus be seen that to talk of the *first edition* of a book as an invariable rarity is misleading. Some first editions (including subsequent *impressions*) may run into hundreds of thousands of copies. In such cases it will be the *first edition, first impression* that may be sought after.

editor/editress. The word *editress* should no longer be used. See **(the) female critique**.

editorial. In standard English *editorial* has only two meanings: (a) an adjective relating to the function of an editor, as in *the editorial office;* (b) a noun describing an unsigned statement of opinion prominently printed in a newspaper or magazine to indicate the views of the publication itself: *The editorial in the* Age *supported the re-election of the Labor government.*

Other uses of *editorial* now seem to be creeping in. "You sent editorial to every newspaper in Australia," complained one person being interviewed on the ABC (28 August 1985) to another. In this sense *editorial* is being used as a synonym for *press statements*, or as a shortened form of *editorial matter*.

In the *Australian Book Review* of November 1985 publishers Hilary McPhee and Diana Gribble say "We do books Penguin wouldn't do in a fit because our editorial is different." Here the word *editorial* appears to be shorthand for *editorial approach.*

These new uses of *editorial* conflict with (b) above, may cause confusion, and should be discouraged.

educational nomenclature. Australians are used to referring to steps in the educational system as *primary, secondary* and *tertiary.*

Primary education is carried out in *primary schools* which educate children from the age of about six until the age of about twelve, and usually consist of about six *grades* or *years.* In referring to education at this level before the advent of secondary education, the schools should be called *elementary schools.*

Secondary education, if government-run, is usually carried out in *high schools, technical schools* or (sometimes) *secondary colleges.* Private secondary schools are usually called *colleges* or *grammar schools.* Secondary education is usually regarded as running through six *forms* or *years,* following on from primary education. If *years,* they run on from primary education, so that formal education runs from *year one* to *year twelve.*

The term *tertiary education* is, apparently, restricted to Australia and New Zealand. It is a somewhat ambiguous term, and is best reserved for education within a *college of advanced education* or a *university.* For other forms of education after the completion of formal schooling, such as education within the *technical and further education* segment, the term *post-secondary education* is now preferred, though *post-secondary education* also clearly will include *tertiary education* when used in a more general sense.

See also **post-secondary education; schools**

educationist/educationalist. Prefer *educationist* of these two, but prefer *educator* to either.

Edwardian means *relating to the period of the reign of King Edward VII, 1901-1910.* In Australia it is applied to a period of architecture (often now called **Federation**), and is used in such phrases as *Edwardian society, the Edwardian era.* The usage transfers somewhat oddly from Britain to Australia, but there were then much closer affinities to the British Crown than now exist. It is also more succinct than having to say, for instance, *before the first world war.*

-ee endings. See **interviewee.**

effectuate. The use of pretentious words is a sign of insecurity. When Western Australians wanted to secede from the Commonwealth of Australia they asked the British parliament *to effectuate the restoration of Western Australia to its former status.* They were, of course, trying to show the Mother Country that they knew long words too.

They would have done better to ask Britain *to restore* Western Australia to its former status.

effete. Originally *effete* did not mean what it commonly means today, which is *effeminate,* but meant rather *drained of vitality, ineffectual, decadent,* and it is still frequently found in this sense. The word is related to the word *foetus,* and once meant *worn out by childbearing.*

e.g. The abbreviation *e.g.* stands for *exempli gratia,* meaning *for the sake of example.* It should not be confused with *i.e.,* which stands for *id est,* and means *that is.*

The terms are used correctly in this sentence:
> There are many species of macropods (*i.e.* kangaroos and wallabies) in Australia, *e.g.* the Grey Forester.

The abbreviations may or may not be in italics, but in any case need a comma before them.

Note that *e.g.* may not be followed by *etc.,* as in *there are many species of macropods,* e.g. *The Grey Forester* etc.

egregious. Long words are *not* necessarily bad words. They may express a meaning, or a shade of meaning, which no other word can do. They are there, in short, because the language needs them. Long words, like all other words, can of course be misused. They can be used to create a smokescreen, to intimidate, to confuse and control other people. If they do this, they are being used badly. But short words can be used in this way too.

Nor need long words be "words I don't understand." If you don't understand normal, useful English words simply because they are long and sometimes a bit unusual, that's your fault and not the word's fault.

Egregious is not a particularly well-known word but it is a very useful one (pronounce it *e-gree-jus*). You will always remember its meaning if you remember that it's a Latin word that means *separate from the flock*, and think of a flock of geese with one member of that flock some distance from it and likely to be grabbed by a fox.

It means, then, *outstanding*, but with perhaps a special sense of *outstanding within a group of people or things*. An *egregious* error is an error that is quite obvious. Some other examples:

> Among architects Robin Boyd was egregious, in that he could write well.

> Among the *prima donnas* of her day was the egregious Madam Melba.

These days *egregious* is usually used in a negative sense, such as *an egregious liar*, but there is no reason why it should not be used in a positive sense as well.

ei and ie. One of the simplest and most useful rules in English spelling is "*i* before *e* except after *c*".

Following this rule, *siege* (for instance) is spelt with an *ie*, but *receive* is spelt with an *ei* because it comes after a *c*.

NOTE
1. This only applies to words where the *ie* or *ei* sound is pronounced as *ee*. The rule therefore does not apply to words such as *neighbor, freight, neither, heir, leisure* or *inveigle*.
2. Exceptions to the "*i* before *e* except after *c*" rule include *weird, deity, seize, counterfeit, weir* and *plebeian*.

See also **spelling reform in Australia.**

eidetic. *Richard Roe has an eidetic memory*. This does not mean, as it is often taken to mean, that Richard Roe has a *photographic* memory, that everything he sees or reads imprints itself on his memory.

Eidetic means that *the images imagined to be seen are actually unreal, but so vivid that they are taken as real.*

either.
1. The word may be pronounced *ee-ther* or *eye-ther*. *Ee-ther* is the more common American pronunciation, *eye-ther* the British. The four dictionaries which have paid attention to Australian usage give precedence to *eye-ther* in Australian pronunciation.
2. To write *neither one or the other* is incorrect. *Either* must always be followed by *or* and *neither* by *nor*.
3. *Either* is singular, because it stands for *either* [*one*]. Thus *either of them is suitable,* not *either of them are suitable.* Similarly with *either . . . or: either Jack or Jill is going to come,* not *either Jack or Jill are going to come.* But, when the alternatives are both plural, then the verb is plural: *either the soldiers or the sailors are going to form the guard.*
4. What about the situation where you have a mixture of singular and plural?

An example is: *either the two women or Rebecca are coming to help*. Again we use the plural *are* because it sounds better, though the conflict should be avoided, by rewording, if possible.

5. Strictly speaking, *either* can refer to only two choices. It is considered undesirable to write *This painting appears to depict either oranges or tangerines or mandarins*. Such an idiomatic use of *either* is, however, common even in practised writing.

6. *Either* is frequently used to mean *both*, as in *the guests sat on either side of the table*. Many consider this inelegant and prefer *both sides* or *each side* in such a case.

7. In old-fashioned English *or . . . or* is sometimes found instead of *either . . . or*. Shakespeare writes of "When yellow leaves, or none, or few, do hang / Upon those boughs . . ."

-eity. For the pronunciation of words ending in *-eity*, such as spontaneity, see **deity.**

eke out. To *eke out* is *to supplement*, not *to prolong* or *extend*. You can eke out your income by taking on extra work (the sense is usually that it won't amount to much if you do), but you can not *eke out an existence*.

elder/eldest and older/oldest.
1. *Elder* and *eldest* are now used only for family relationships, as in *She is my elder sister*.
2. Note that a sentence such as *She is my elder daughter* must imply that the speaker has only two daughters. If the speaker has more than two, and he or she was speaking of the first-born of those three, the sentence would be *She is the eldest of my daughters*, or *She is my eldest daughter*. (Similarly with *younger* and *youngest*.)
3. In other words, note that, when there are only two items in a category, only the *comparative* ending (*-er*) can be used:
   Of two children, one is the *elder*.
   Of two buildings, one is the *older*.
   Of two apples, one is the *redder*.
4. Outside family relationships, and with the occasional exception such as *elder statesman*, use *older* and *oldest*:
   Sylvia was the *older* of the two girls.
   The *oldest* city in Australia is Sydney.

the electronic media. A pretentious and inflated way of saying *radio and television*. It would be handy if we had a short word which encompassed both, but as yet we do not. Prefer *radio and television*. See **media.**

elegant. Normally *elegant* means *graceful in style or design or behavior: It was a most elegant room, It was an elegant gesture.* But it is also used by scientists and others to describe *an ingenious and simple solution,* substituting for an old solution a new solution that is less involved and more effective.

eleventh commandment. In general cynical conversational use the *eleventh commandment* is *Thou shalt not be found out.*

In religious circles, however, the eleventh commandment was stated by Jesus at the Last Supper (John xiii. 34): "A new commandment I give unto you, That ye love one another; as I have loved you, that ye also love one another."

elicit/illicit. *Elicit* means *to draw something out: He elicited the truth by cross-examining the offender; She elicited the right answer by a close study of the text.*
Illicit means *unlawful: Sly-grog trading is an illicit activity.*

elite. Henry Lawson sighed for the day when "the rich an' educated shall be educated down," though admittedly he also asked for "higher education for the toilin' starvin' clown." It is often argued that Australians resent outstanding achievement in areas other than sport. Certainly *elitist* is often found in this country as a term of abuse, invariably used as such by those who themselves have had special benefits in educational or social background.

An *elite* is *a special group distinguished by intelligence, wealth, power, skills* etc. The word comes from an Old French word meaning *chosen,* and further back from the Latin for *to elect.*

In his professional life the author of this book has observed with interest highly qualified colleagues in the educational world attempting to prevent programs being instituted for specially gifted children who sometimes languish for the lack of extra stimulation in the schools. Successive Australian governments have been as reluctant to finance the development of high levels of academic attainment as they have been eager to subsidise generously the Australian Institute of Sport.

While it is true that an aware democracy must beware of military and political elites, and must firmly associate *achievement* with the *opportunity to achieve,* the use of the words *elite* and *elitist* as terms of abuse is childish and tells us more about the user of the words than the supposed objects of scorn.

Elite may be either singular (*the elite is*) or plural (*the elite are*), depending on context. An acute accent (*élite*) on the word is optional.

See also **tall poppies.**

ellipsis. The plural of *ellipsis* is *ellipses.* For the printer's mark, see **dots.**

embarrass/harass. Just say to yourself a hundred times "One *r* in *harass,* two in *embarrass*" or "the longer word has two" and, with luck, you won't forget it.

embargo. There are two main uses of this word in the English-speaking world, including Australia. And, for some reason, one of these uses is not given in any English dictionary we have seen, and of Australian dictionaries only in the *Australian Pocket Oxford.*

In the first instance is *a ban on something: an arms embargo, the forbidding of ships from a certain country to enter one's ports,* and so on. This meaning is covered in the dictionaries.

The other meaning, which is not referred to, is *an injunction stating that a certain piece of information may not be published or acted upon until a certain date or time.* This use of *embargo* is a commonplace in journalism in particular. The Prime Minister may be planning to fly to Japan on an urgent diplomatic issue next Friday. It is desirable to let the press know in advance, for a number of reasons, but the Japanese would be offended if the news were announced before Wednesday. The press release is, therefore, issued as early as possible, but *embargoed* until Wednesday.

The plural is *embargoes.*

emigrant/immigrant. An *emigrant* is someone who leaves a country, an *immigrant* is someone who comes into a country.

Thus it is necessary to be both at the same time! When Sir Charles Court, former Premier of Western Australia, arrived in Australia at the age of one in 1912, he was, for instance, both an *emigrant* from Britain and an *immigrant* to Australia.

And similarly, of course, with *emigration* and *immigration.*

Migrant, as a word to describe an *immigrant,* is an Australian innovation.

empathy/sympathy. Both *empathy* and *sympathy* involve association with the feelings of others. Sympathy, however, may mean that, while one does not necessarily *share* the feelings of another, one does feel compassion and concern at the state of mind or the problems of another. Empathy goes further. If you have *empathy* or *empathetic feelings* towards another person, you are actually able to enter into their feelings and share them.

empirical/imperial. University students have recently been referring to *the empirical policy of the Venetian state* and to *Britain's empirical policy in the nineteenth century.*

It is, perhaps, just possible that they *really* meant *empirical,* a useful and common word that means *being guided by experience rather than by theory.* But it is far more likely that they meant *imperial.*

Imperial, from the word *empire,* means *relating to an empire.* In countries, such as Japan, which have a monarch actually designated an *emperor,* everything related to that monarch is by definition *imperial:* the *imperial palace,* the *imperial wish,* the *imperial egg-cup.* (In the case of Japan, though it would no doubt be theoretically correct to refer also to the *imperial navy* and the *imperial government*, such usages have been tactfully avoided since the collapse of the Japanese empire in 1945.)

Presumably the fact that the adjective from *empire* confusingly starts with an *i* instead of an *e* leads many into the *empirical* mistake.

employe/employee. *Employe* used to be the normal English form of the word and is still used in certain newspapers. However it has long been supplanted in general usage by the spelling *employee*, which is recommended.

The justification for *employé* is that it is the French for *an employed male*, while *employée* is the French for *an employed female*. Since neither meets the unisex requirements urged on us today, we may as well stick with *employee*.

enclave. An *enclave* is *a territory which is completely surrounded by another territory.* The Australian Capital Territory is an *enclave* within the territory of New South Wales. Pronounce as spelt and not as *onclave*.

encumbrance/incumbent. An *encumbrance* (sometimes *incumbrance*) is *something that is found burdensome*, as in *He was no help but a confounded encumbrance*. The word also has a legal meaning, of *a charge upon property; This house is freehold, but there is a mortgage encumbrance.*

The word *incumbent*, when it is used as an adjective, means *something that is morally binding: It is incumbent upon you to do what you can for your illegitimate child.* When used as a noun, *incumbent* means *the holder of an office*. It is used especially of clergymen: *The present incumbent at St Prude's is the Rev. Mr Uptight.*

Although the splendid word *encumbrant* is sometimes heard, and although it should exist, in fact it does not.

endeavor. In the magazine *Books & Bookmen* of October 1985 Mr Brian Masters quotes the following lines from James Lee-Milne's *Midway on the Waves*:

> [Another personality is] like some big, floppy sunflower with a radiant face which one watches slowly unfold when recognition of what one is endeavouring to impart slowly dawns upon him.

Masters comments: "to use the word 'endeavouring' (normally to be avoided) perfectly depicts the struggle of getting anything at all through to this character. It is a word of toil, which 'trying' is not."

engineer. Whereas words like *doctor* and *architect* and *solicitor* have a legal definition and protection in Australia (that is, laws lay down who may call themselves such), the word *engineer* has no such protection.

Anyone may set up a backyard workshop and call themselves an *engineer*.

Some tradesmen and many technicians called themselves *engineers*. So do fully-qualified, professional engineers.

In certain contexts, then, the word may have to be used with caution.

See **technologist/technician/tradesman**.

England/English. The word *England* is by custom used as an adjective in one context only, that of cricket, where the correct name for the English test team is *the England team* or *the England XI*. This is no doubt at least in part due to the fact that there may be Scots, Welsh and others playing in the team, and that therefore it may not be strictly *English* at all.

The use of the word *English* when in fact the Welsh and Scots as well as the English are meant is resented by many, though admittedly it is reinforced by such terms as *the English language, the Queen of England*. *British* is the appropriate adjective, though there is no simple and satisfactory way of describing a *British person*. The word *Briton* is not used in this sense.

England is prounounced *INGland*, not *ENGland*.

See **Britain**.

enormacy/enormity. A writer in the Melbourne *Age* of 5 November 1985 writes of "the enormacy" of a problem. An ABC television commentator covering the opening of the new parliament building in Canberra talks of the "sense of enormity" provided by the view from parliament to Mount Ainslie.

Firstly, there is no such word as *enormacy*. Secondly, *enormity* does not mean *grand, sweeping, spacious*.

Enormity means *the character of being outrageous or wicked* or *an act of great wickedness:*

> The enormity of Hitler's racial policies defies rational analysis.
>
> The assassination of President Kennedy was an enormity even by American standards.

Further, *enormity* should not be used to mean *bulkiness* or *difficulty*. The word is often misused in this way:

> The enormity of the problems facing the company chairman led to his resignation.

While it is true that words change meaning and acquire new meanings as well as the old, and it is also true that it is stuffy to oppose this in many cases, nevertheless when a new usage tends to diminish or drive out of the language an old and important usage it must be opposed.

Oppose, then, the enormity of using *enormity* to mean *enormous*. Use *extent, size, weight, difficulty, bulkiness, immensity* or whatever word fits what you have to say.

enquiry/inquiry. Either is correct, but the tendency is to reserve *enquiry* for the meaning of *question*, and *inquiry* for the meaning of *an investigation*.

In Australia, governments hold *inquiries*, not *enquiries*.

The American pronunciation tends towards *inkry,* and the British are following suit. The *Times Literary Supplement* informs us, however, that Australians still pronounce each syllable.

enrol/enroll. The English and Australian usage is *enrol, enrols, enrolled, enrolment.* The American forms are *enroll, enrolls, enrolled, enrollment.*

ensue. *Ensue* and *ensued* are pronounced *in-SYU, in-SYUED*, not *in-SOO, in-SOOED*, unless you are American.

See **oo or yoo?**

enthuse. "Yes, I had a look at his pictures, but I didn't enthuse about them." So remarked our publisher to us over a pleasant lunch.

Being nice to publishers is the beginning of wisdom so we did not comment on the phrase at the time. But courage!

The verb *to enthuse* is a back-formation from the noun *enthusiasm* and has already entered some dictionaries. Indeed it first turned up in the United States in 1827. It's a part of the language and unlikely to be eradicated. If people want to use it that makes it – so many would hold – a legitimate usage.

But it's certainly still part of sub-literate English and unlikely to be found in writing that attempts to be serious or standard writing. It is heard mainly in conversation. It grates on many. And the fact that it still grates on many is a good reason for avoiding it.

entitled. To be entitled to something is *to have the right to it*. People in employment are *entitled* to holidays, for instance.

There is a developing tendency in Australia to use the word *entitled* as though it meant *obliged*. "I'm not entitled to work seven days a week," we heard a lighthouse keeper say recently. He meant, of course, that he was not *obliged* to work seven days a week.

That this misuse of the word is not restricted to lighthouse keepers emerges from the remarks of the Perth lawyer Ronald Cannon, who represented Brian Chambers, hanged in Malaysia in July 1986. Mr Cannon said:

> When a client tells a criminal lawyer that he is guilty then the criminal lawyer is
> not entitled to defend him on the basis of being not guilty. He is entitled to stand
> back and let the Crown prove their case and that is about all he is entitled to do.
> (*Australian*, 19 July 1986)

The first *entitled* in this quotation is used in its proper sense, the third perhaps so. But the central use of the word clearly means *obliged* rather than *entitled*.

See also **obligate/obligatory/oblige.**

envelop/envelope. *Envelop* is a verb meaning *to surround, to cover*. The stress is on the second syllable: *en-VEL-op*.

Envelope, with a final *e*, is a noun meaning *the covering around a letter*. The stress is on the first syllable, and the word is pronounced in Australia either *EN-vel-ope* or *ON-vel-ope*. The former is preferred.

eon. Prefer this spelling to *aeon*.
See **aeon/eon** and **-æ-**.

ephemera/ephemeral. The word *ephemera* means *something that is short-lived*. The original Greek means *lasting for one day only*. As we use it the word usually means *printed material such as handbills and catalogs* which, like the mayfly (of the genus *Ephemera*) vanish overnight. Libraries collect books as a matter of course, but often have difficulty in acquiring collections of *ephemera*. The word is plural, except when used of the insect, when *I caught three ephemaras* is correct.

The word is altogether more familiar in its adjectival form *ephemeral*. We may speak of *an ephemeral event*, one that disappears swiftly without consequences.

The word in either form may be pronounced with the *phem* rhyming with either *them* or *theme*, the former being preferred.

epicene. See **androgynous/epicene/hermaphrodite**.

epigram/epigraph/epitaph/epithet. An *epigram* is *a short, usually witty comment in the form of a poem or a phrase*. Sir Robert Helpmann's statement that "I think you can be contemporary without taking off your clothes" is an epigram. So too is Rudyard Kipling's notorious comment on Sydney:

> Greeting! My birth-stain have I turned to good;
>   Forcing strong wills perverse to steadfastness;
> The first flush of the tropics in my blood,
>   And at my feet Success!

An *epigraph* may be an inscription on an object such as a statue or a coin, but is more normally used to mean *the short quotation often to be found at the beginning of a book or at the head of chapters in a book*.

An *epitaph* is a message on a tombstone, or written to commemorate someone's death. Part of the epitaph on Governor Lachlan Macquarie's tomb on the island of Mull is "The Father of Australia."

Epitaphs and epigrams often go well together. A splendid example is to be found in St Anne's graveyard, Wardour Street, London:

> Near this place is interred
> Theodore King of Corsica
> who died in this parish Dec 11 1786

> immediately after leaving
> the King's Bench Prison
> by the benefit of the Act of Insolvency
> in consequence of which he registered
> his kingdom of Corsica for the use of
> his creditors.

> The grave, great teacher, to a level brings
> Heroes and beggars, galley-slaves and kings.
> But Theodore this moral learn'd ere dead:
> Fate poured its lessons on his living head,
> Bestow'd a kingdom, and denied him bread.

An *epithet* may be (a) a short description attached to or substituted for a person's name, as in *Spofforth the Demon Bowler*, or (b) a curse or phrase of abuse, as *You contemptible animal!* The primary or 'proper' meaning is the first, and there are many who object to the suggestion that *epithet* means *a term of abuse.*

epitome. See **apotheosis/epitome.**

eponymous is a word often heard, simple in meaning, but puzzling to many. It means *called after*, and is best understood from examples:

> We visited the grave of St Sebastian, and the eponymous cathedral. [That is, the cathedral was called St Sebastian's Cathedral.]
> We viewed a documentary film on Bass Strait and its eponymous discoverer. [That is, the film was also about George Bass himself.]
> The eponymous authors of *Grimms' Fairy Tales.* [That is, the brothers Grimm.]

Eponymous is, of course, the adjective. The noun is *eponym*.

equable/equitable. Something that is *equable* is *even-mannered. Equable weather* is *pleasant, unchanging weather.* An *equable personality* is one that is *easy to get on with.* The word is of course related to *equal.* And when a Central European says "That's *egal* to me," he or she means "That's all the same to me." *Equality* and *egalitarian* are part of the same family.

Equitable is rather different. It is more of a political word, a word that relates to *fairness in dealing: The contract between them was in fact equitable.* An arbitrator's *equitable* judgement is one that is *reasonable and fair to both sides.*

ra. An *era* is *a period of time*, usually a protracted and an important one. We talk of *the Christian era, the era of discovery in the Pacific, the post-Hiroshima era of atomic power.* It is pronounced *ear-a* not, as frequently heard, *error.*

-er/-est. See **elder/eldest and older/oldest.**

139

-er/-or. Are there any rules explaining why *adviser* is spelt with an *-er* ending and *abettor* with an *-or* ending?

The answer is, not really. There are explanations, such as that *-er* is the ending for words of English origin, but *-or* for words of Latin origin, but they do not help us much, and in any case there are many exceptions.

What we can say is that:

(a) it is easiest to treat the *-or* words as exceptions, for most new words of this kind being formed today (except in the law) take *-er*.

(b) words with *-ate* endings seem to be consistent in taking, and holding on to, the *-or* ending (*calculator*).

The following lists are not exhaustive. Words often misspelt are printed in italics.

-OR WORDS

abductor	creditor	juror
adaptor (thing)	demonstrator	monitor
agitator	*defector*	prosecutor
auditor	*distributor*	purveyor
calculator	*divisor*	sailor
censor	ejector	spectator
collector	governor	sponsor
contractor	illustrator	*supervisor*
conqueror	instructor	surveyor
corrector	inventor	tailor
counsellor	*investor*	*transistor*

-ER WORDS

adapter (person)	*dispenser*	preventer
adviser	*eraser*	*promoter*
computer	*idolater*	propeller
conjurer	protester	*protester*
corrupter	presenter	seller
decanter	presser	singer
deserter		

See also **adapter/adaptor; adviser/advisor; convener/convenor; spelling reform in Australia.**

err. The dictionaries recognise only one pronunciation of *err*, and that rhymes with *cur* or *purr*. *Erring* follows, in rhyming with *purring*.

It is certainly true that *err* is often pronounced *air*, perhaps by back-formation from *error;* so much so that dictionaries, which these days at least pretend to *listen* to what people say, might have been expected to recognise this. In this case few, if any, do.

eruption/irruption. An eruption is *something that breaks through*: a volcanic explosion, a boil, a tooth, anger. An *irruption* is *something that rushes in*: *a sudden entry*, sometimes *an explosion in population. He irrupted into the room in great excitement* — here his entry is an *irruption*.

eschew. Professor David Caro, Vice-Chancellor of the University of Melbourne, is quoted in the *Age* of 8 March 1986 as stating that his university is "a place where staff eschew scholarship."

We doubt that Professor Caro said this. *To eschew* is *to shun, to avoid, to steer clear of*. Some academics *do* eschew scholarship, even at the University of Melbourne, but we suspect that Professor Caro said that his academics *espouse* scholarship.

Eschew comes from an ancient German word meaning *to frighten away*. It is a rather highfalutin word, satirised in the T-shirt slogan "Eschew obfuscation."

esoteric/exotic. The root of *exotic* is *exo*, Greek for *outside*. Something that is *exotic* is, traditionally, *something that hails from afar, something unfamiliar, something foreign*. The use of this word in a loose sense, meaning little more than *unusual* (as in *He was smoking an exotic brand of cigarettes*) is to be watched.

By contrast the word *esoteric* comes from the Greek word meaning *inner*. Something that is *esoteric appeals only to the initiated*, is *private, obscure, abstruse*. (The opposite of *esoteric* is *exoteric*.)

The words balance each other. In essence they both refer to the unfamiliar, but one word defines the unfamiliar as something that is too far from our reach, the other as something that is too deeply buried within.

especial(ly)/special(ly). *Specially* is now well on the way to displacing *especially* for all purposes. It is worth noting, however, that strictly speaking *especial/especially* means *to an especial degree*, while *special/specially* means *for one purpose and no other*. Thus:

It is my especial [*not* special] pleasure.

She took especial [*not* special] care of my house.

You need a special [*not* an especial] ingredient for this dish.

There was a special [*not* an especial] clause in the agreement.

The welcome was especially [*not* specially] effusive.

She came specially [*not* especially] to see him.

espresso/expresso. It is *espresso* coffee, not *expresso*. *Espresso* is Italian for *express*, as in *express train*. There would be no objection to saying *express coffee*.

the Establishment. The phrase was invented by Henry Fairlie, who has defined it (*Guardian Weekly*, 3 February 1980) as "a number of men and women with

141

certain very strong assumptions of their own, and with the influence to make these assumptions prevail in society as a whole." *The Establishment* does not consist of people, such as politicians, who hold and exercise power; it consists of those who create the climate of opinion within which it is possible to exercise power. Neo-Marxists would call this **hegemony**.

Fairlie doubts whether the phrase can be easily transferred to countries other than England, though it has certainly been widely adopted.

The phrase was not originally intended to have a specifically political meaning, and has in fact been used by conservatives against their opponents. But, however used, it is desirable to remember that it refers rather to those who set the rules than to those who put the rules into action.

et al. See **referencing**.

etc. is short for *et cetera*, which literally means *and the rest*. The use of *etc.* in formal written work is to be discouraged. Such a sentence as:

> He grabbed his suitcases etc. and made a bound for the train

is not acceptable except in conversation. Either omit the *etc.* altogether or find a way round the difficulty, for instance:

> He grabbed his suitcases and other gear and made a bound for the train.

Note that *etc.*, being an abbreviation that does not end in the same letter as the full phrase which is abbreviated, takes a full stop after it wherever it appears. See **abbreviations**.

Do not pronounce *eksetera*.

ethnic. *Ethnic is both a noun (She is an ethnic)* and an adjective *(She is ethnic).* The use of the word as a noun is apparently uniquely Australian. *Ethnic* is the current OK word for a member of a distinguishable migrant community in Australia, replacing such discarded usages as "New Australians." In time *ethnic* will itself be found offensive and will be replaced; indeed the word is accruing pejorative overtones already, and is being replaced by **multicultural**. Ethnic is a useful enough reach-me-down word but will not stand up to much examination, though the word itself has been adopted, of course, because it has a (spurious) anthropological flavor about it.

Is an Englishman an ethnic? Is an Irishwoman? Is a Canadian? If we rule them out because they are English-speaking and therefore of the linguistic majority, what about a mixed-race Indian or Sri Lankan whose first language is English? And so on. In fact, of course, all Australians have a distinguishable cultural and linguistic background which they have imported with them. We are all ethnics.

With, however, the exception of the Aboriginals, who decline the label of an 'ethnic minority' and argue that they are the original Australians.

et seq. See **referencing**.

euphemisms. *Euphemism* comes from two Greek words meaning *speaking nicely*. Euphemisms are ways of saying unpleasant things in the hope that the sting will be taken out of them. *Senior citizens* is a euphemistic way of saying *old people*, and similarly a *ratcatcher* becomes a *pest control officer*, a poor person *underprivileged*, and *slums* become *sub-standard housing*.

We will never get rid of euphemisms in the language, for at least three reasons. The first is that they help us to evade issues, and that is something we all do. The second is that their use is often motivated by a desire to be kind to other people, and this can be a worthy impulse. The third is that scorn for euphemisms is very much a 'class' phenomenon. The well-placed and well-heeled may well take pride in calling a *lavatory* a *shithouse*, and may smile at those who lack the social confidence, or perhaps the arrogance, to do the same.

Passed away, for instance, as a euphemism for *died*, is in Australia and no doubt elsewhere very much a lower middle-class and working-class usage. No doubt a great many people feel that *died* is too abrupt and hard-hearted a word. Others, however, will feel that *passed away* is a pussyfooting phrase, a dishonest attempt to evade reality.

Common euphemisms may be noted and thought about:

> restroom, lavatory, toilet, water closet
> perspire *for* sweat
> inebriated *for* drunk
> apprehended *for* arrested
> to be sick *for* to vomit
> pass water *for* urinate
> garbage collector *for* dustman, garbo
> intelligence gathering *for* spying
> electronic surveillance *for* bugging
> take out *for* bomb
> underprivileged *for* poor
> turf accountant *for* bookmaker
> remains *for* body
> ale *for* beer
> integrated harvesting *for* woodchipping
> lounge *for* living-room
> expectorate *for* spit
> dental cream *for* toothpaste
> lingerie *for* underwear
> desire *for* want

There are thousands more.

In the *Sydney Morning Herald* of 14 December 1987 a reporter referred to

Allan Border as "the little left-handed euphemism for Australian cricket for the past three years." Presumably the writer meant that Border's name was a *synomym* for Australian cricket — that Border and Australian cricket were the same thing.

See also **jargon.**

European. All Australians whose ancestors were of the European, 'White' or Caucasian section of humanity are, in a sense, *Europeans* by contrast with Aboriginals and Asians, no matter how long they have been here.

We also use *European* in another way, to describe *a present-day inhabitant of (or something that belongs to) the sub-continent of Europe.*

eventuate/eventuality. *Eventuate* dates from 1789 and *eventuality* from 1828, but they say that there's no fool like an old fool and these heavy-handed public-service words should be ordered to stay within the borders of the Australian Capital Territory.

the eve of. *The eve of* New Year's Day is not the late afternoon of New Year's Day, it is the *day before.* Similarly with *Christmas Eve*, and so on.

everybody. *Everybody* (or *everyone*) *must follow his* (or *her*) *own conscience.* Or *Everybody must follow their own consciences*?

Everybody and *everyone* are, strictly speaking, singulars, as we can see if we expand them to *every single body, every one person.*

So, *Everybody must follow his* (or *her*) *own conscience* is, in theory at any rate, correct.

This ruling, however, creates problems, not least that difficult business about *his or her.* Colloquially, and increasingly in serious writing, the tendency is towards *Everybody must follow their own consciences.*

If you don't want to be ungrammatical, change the wording: *All must follow their own consciences.*

See also **each/every.**

everyday/every day. *Every day* should not be written as one word except when used as an adjective in such a phrase as *It was an everyday occurrence.* Do not write *Smiles are free – use one everyday*, but *Smiles are free – use one every day.*

evoke/invoke. To *evoke* something is *to call it up*, as in these examples:

   The scenery *evoked* in him a memory of the Nullarbor Desert.

   The crisis *evoked* desperate energies on the part of the crew.

Usually, with *evoke*, outside agencies act on the person or persons concerned.

Invoke is usually something the person takes an active part in doing. It means *to call on something or someone for a response.* "Send her down, Hughie!" is an old Australian way of *invoking* rain. People may *invoke* the aid of God to get them out of a crisis. You may appeal to, or *invoke*, a witness, to help you win an argument.

The two words can at times converge to something like the same meaning.

The seance attempted to evoke *a response from the departed* suggests that they hoped the departed would respond, no more. But to say *The seance attempted to* invoke *a response from the departed* suggests that they actively sent out messages appealing for a response.

ex-. For the pronunciation of *ex-* at the start of a word, see the entry under **x.**

exceeding(ly)/excessive(ly). *Exceeding* and *exceedingly* mean *very much*, as in *He was exceedingly polite.*

Excessive and *excessively* mean *too much*, as in *He was excessively polite, to the point where I doubted his sincerity.*

except I/except me. The word *except*, when used as a preposition meaning *but*, takes the accusative, or objective, case. *No-one was there except me* (or *him* or *her* or *us* or *them*) is correct. *No-one was there except I* (*he, she, we, they*) is wrong.

exception that proves the rule. This expression, along with *There's an exception to every rule* and the like, is used only by people who do not know what it means. *Prove* has several meanings, among them *test* or *try*. The exception *tests* the rule — just as eating tests the pudding and galley proofs test the typesetting.

exclamation marks. Exclamation marks are rather graphically called "startlers" in some Australian newspaper proofreading rooms. The word defines their function well. They have two main purposes:
1. As a conclusion to an exclamation where special scorn or disgust is evinced, or an order being given, as in:

> You little bastard!
> How I suffer!
> May it rain cats and dogs!
> You wouldn't read about it in a book!
> God save the Queen!
> Keep quiet!
> What a way to run a railroad!

2. To show that the words being used by you are being used in a special way, a way which would be clear if you were saying them instead of writing them:

> My dear, the people, *and* the noise!

145

He never said a truer word!

And you thought it didn't matter!

Exclamation marks, however, should *not* be used indiscriminately to bolster simple statements and requests. These are *wrong*:

I had a perfectly lovely holiday!

There she was, waiting at the church!

I told him that the wrong horse won the Derby!

Please fetch me the knife!

The over-use of exclamation marks is a sure sign of writers who are not sure of themselves, and double and triple exclamation marks are never to be used.

exercise/exorcise. The New South Wales government advises car buyers to demand details of a car's history from sellers: "Otherwise, a finance company could exorcise its rights."

To exorcise (or *exorcize*) is *to expel evil spirits from a person or place by religious rites.* Perhaps there is a case for enlisting the aid of the Archbishop of Sydney in expelling evil spirits from used-car salesmen, but in the case quoted above the word *exorcise* is being confused with the word *exercise* which means, in this case, *put into action.*

exotic. See **esoteric/exotic.**

explicit/implicit. *Explicit* originally meant *unfolded.* If you make an *explicit* statement you *clearly divulge what you have to say.*

Implicit, however, originally meant *enfolded, hidden away.* An *implicit* attitude is *one which is not openly stated,* but which may be inferred from the general bearing, manner or circumstances of the person concerned.

When *implicit* is used in such a phrase as *implicit obedience* it means *complete* or *absolute,* in other words an acceptance so deep-rooted that it doesn't have to be stated.

expresso. See **espresso/expresso.**

extempore/impromptu. Both these are Latin, *extempore* meaning *on the spur of the moment* and *impromptu* meaning *in readiness.* In English usage they both mean the same thing: *to do something, such as to make a speech, without rehearsal or forewarning.* A distinction is sometimes made between *extempore* (not prepared) and *impromptu* (no previous notice).

extenuate does not mean to *excuse,* and you cannot *extenuate* a person. *He found cause to extenuate George* is wrong: the word means *to water down, to find reasons for modifying a judgement,* and therefore you can only extenuate

George's *behavior*, or find *extenuating circumstances* for his behavior.
  Extenuable, not *extenuatable*.

-ey/-y. There are a number of words ending in an unsounded letter *-e* which present some problem when being turned into adjectives by the addition of *-y* or *-ey:* for instance, *spike* (becomes *spiky*), *wave* (becomes *wavy*), *blue* (becomes *bluey*).

The rules are really very simple. All words which end in an unsounded *-e* drop that *-e* and add *-y.*

The exceptions are minor ones:

(a) When a noun ends in *-y*, add *-ey: clay* becomes *clayey.*
(b) When a noun ends in *-ue*, add *-y: glue* becomes *gluey.*
(c) *Hole* becomes *holey*, to avoid confusion with the word *holy.*

F

facile is one of many words which can be used either in an ordinary, 'unloaded' sense or as a term of criticism.

Facile comes from the Latin word meaning *easy* and in the first sense means that *someone is doing a job with easy, polished skill*, in a word, with facility: *It was a delight to watch the facile hands of the engraver at work.*

In the critical sense, however, the word means *superficial, showy, without depth: It was a facile solution to a difficult problem.*

It is pronounced with the second syllable rhyming with the word *aisle*.

facsimile. See **copy/duplicate/facsimile/replica.**

factitious/fictitious. Both those words have in common that they mean, in part, *removed from reality.* In use, however, they differ quite widely.

Factitious means *that something, supposed to be genuine, has been artificially contrived.* When John Colmer reviewed *The Autobiography of Kylie Tennant* (*Australian*, 12 April 1986), he wrote that her attempt to bring together the story of her lost grandson with

> her father's belief that he was a missing heir, that he was related to Lord Glenconner, the English Tennant family and Margot Asquith seems factitious.

By this Colmer — correctly — meant that Kylie Tennant was trying too hard to create something that did not, in the reader's eyes, carry conviction.

Fictitious applies to *an account that is completely made up, that is not true: The supposed alibi was fictitious from beginning to end.*

See also **fictional/fictitious.**

faculty. This word has, in the university context, quite different meanings in the United States and in Australia. In the United States *faculty* means the *teaching staff* of a university or department. In Australia it means the *governing body* of a university department or group of departments. This governing body will include teaching staff but will also include representatives of 'outside' interests.

fair. In such phrases as *play fair, fight fair, run fair*, the word *fair* is actually an adverb in its own right. *Fairly* is unnecessary and should be avoided.

fantastic is a very useful words which has been subjected to degradation.

Fantastic can properly mean *weird, strange in appearance or occurrence, unreal, something imagined.* (Indeed *fantastic* originally meant *something imagined.*)

Its use to mean *excellent, splendid* and so on is unnecessary and weakens a good word.

Far East. In 1939 R. G. Menzies, then Prime Minister, said "What Great Britain calls the Far East is to us the near north." It was a useful observation but, as events turned out, a bit late. In recent years the phrase *the Near North* has gained currency in Australia as referring to Southeast Asia, the Indian sub-continent, China and Japan. It is much to be encouraged.

One of the reasons the new coinage was slow to catch on was the outbreak of the second world war, the progress of which was reported to Australia in Eurocentric terms. Our troops fought in the *Middle East* (which was actually our *Far West*), and the *Far East* became a familiar war-time phrase.

It was all a bit of a mess because in fact the campaigns in north Africa were fought in what used to be called the *Near East*, which included the Balkans and the eastern Mediterranean. The original *Middle East* ran from what is now Iraq through India to Burma. However, in present-day British usage *Near East* and *Middle East* mean the same thing.

There is no objection to our continued use in Australia of the terms *Middle East* and *Far East* in the accepted British and European sense. The world is full of anomalies, thank God, everyone knows what the words mean, and only the sanctimonious will pretend to be shocked.

Although we are a European country, albeit in a somewhat bizarre geographical setting, we do have a small Asian and non-European component in our population. The use of the term *Near North* may be regarded as a courtesy to them, but more importantly as a reminder to ourselves of our own priorities. While *Near North* need not displace other terms, it should certainly be a common part of the Australian vocabulary.

far from the madding crowd. This famous phrase from Thomas Gray's "Elegy Written in a Country Churchyard" does *not* mean *Far from the maddening crowd* but *Far from the crowd which is acting madly*.

farewell. P. J. Kavanagh comments on this verb in the London *Spectator* (28 May 1988): "In antipodean newspapers I also noticed a new verb, 'to farewell': 'Last night the Magpies farewelled their long-time coach, Bruce Poniatowski.' I don't know whether I mind this verb, or care, but in my experience it is new and worth a mention."

farther/further. Both forms of the word are in common use in Australia, but it seems likely that *farther*, which perhaps sounds too stilted to many, will eventually fade away. Some argue for using *farther* when a distance is involved — *You must go three miles farther* — and *further* when the meaning is *additional, more advanced* — *There is a further consideration.* This is, however, too prescriptive, and in effect the words are interchangeable. For the verb, prefer *to further* to *to farther.*

fathom. The *fathom* is one of those sturdy weeds in the garden of the metrication bureaucrats which refuses to wither when instructed to.

Six feet long, the length of the stretch of a person's arms when counting the length of a rope, the word remains in common use among seafarers of all kinds. This is in part because, like many of the former imperial measures, and unlike many of the new metric measures, it grew out of, and was related to, human scales and needs, and not to **scientism.**

The word, pleasantly enough, is related to the Old Norse word for an embrace.

The Australian author Randolph Bedford once wrote a famous story entitled "Forty Fathoms by Quetta Rock." At some point in our well-planned future, readers may need to look this up under "Seventy-three point one five metres by Quetta Rock." This is not as facetious a remark as it may seem. An Australian government statistician once informed his readers that land in colonial days was sold for $4.97 a hectare, neglecting to add that this represented £1 an acre.

Fathom, of course, is also a verb, meaning not only *to measure depth* but also, by metaphorical extension, *to establish a meaning* or *to penetrate a mystery.*

See also **metrication.**

faze/phase. The Melbourne *Herald* informs us that a certain football team will not be *phased* by the new tactics employed by a rival team.

The verb *to phase* has the meanings of *to introduce in stages* and *to cause to function with*: *The new regulations were phased in over two years*; *The gears were carefully phased with other moving parts.*

The verb *to faze* is American in origin and means *to disconcert, to confuse.* The football team was, in the newspaper's view, not going to be *fazed.*

feasible does not mean *possible* or *probable*, but *able to be done.* In most cased *feasible* will also mean *possible*, for instance in such a sentence as *It is feasible* (possible) *to climb stairs to the top of that tower.*

On the other hand *feasible* cannot be used instead of *possible* in the sense *It is possible there may be an earthquake shortly.* Nor should *feasible* be used, as it often is, in such a phrase as *This is the most feasible explanation of the phenomenon*, when what is meant is *This is the most probable explanation . . .*

feature has become an overworked word, largely because of the influence of film: *featuring Marilyn Monroe.*

In this sense it has gone out of fashion and *starring* is now the word most often seen. However the word, as a noun, has passed into journalistic use. An *article* in a newspaper or book is dignified by the name of *a feature*, whether or not it really *is* a *feature* (in the sense of *something that stands out*) or a quite run-of-the-mill contribution. There is now a tendency to switch from *feature* in this sense to the simpler words *story* or *article*.

Feature has also been popular (and much mocked) in Australia when used in such phrases as *a feature window*, *a feature wall*: that is, as something more ostentatious than its surroundings.

The word is clearly a useful and versatile one which fills needs not easily met otherwise. It carries, however, an aura of pretentiousness, and should be used gingerly.

federation. The Australian colonies federated into the Commonwealth of Australia on 1 January 1901.

The word *federation* to describe this event is sometimes spelt *Federation*, with a capital *F*, but unless there is a special reason to do so the word should be written or printed with a small *f*.

Federation is used in Australian architectural and real-estate circles to mean the style in which buildings were often constructed around the period of the federation of the colonies. It replaces such terms as *late-Victorian* or *Edwardian*, which have a British rather than an Australian ring. *Federation* is more common in Sydney than in Melbourne, where *Edwardian* is still in use.

the female critique. A major aspect of the reappraisal of the place of women in society over the past twenty or thirty years has been the attention paid to language.

The argument is far more sophisticated than disputes about such matters as the word *chairman*. It looks to the way in which language both reflects the real structure of the world and at the same time has an important part in ordering and organising that world.

The feminist argument is that men have in large measure controlled the use of language, especially in formal settings, and that this has led to the domination of the language by male images and constructs, which diminish the role and participation of women in life as well as in language, and contribute to inexact expression and confused thinking. "Our disciplines," writes that admirable woman Katharine Whitehorn, "simply don't recognise the extent to which male assumptions — about what's normal, what's objective, even what *is* female — are built in; their practitioners think of them as totally neutral, simply because these have been the only ones around."

As long ago as 1949 Simone de Beauvoir wrote, in *The Second Sex*, that "man represents both the positive and the neutral, as in indicated by the common use of *man* to designate human beings in general; whereas women represent only the negative, defined by limited criteria, without reciprocity."

One obvious example of discrimination against women in language is the availability of the word *Mr* for *all* men, but the sorting out of women into married and unmarried classes by the use of *Mrs* and *Miss*. *Miss* not only implies unmarried status, but also immaturity. (See **(the) Mr/Mrs/Ms problem**.)

Another area of objection is the use of female forms of nouns where these have come, by use, to suggest inferiority or, at the best, a category for women which is not only sex-based but does not, unlike the male form, suggest an affinity to the whole world of achievement. The word *poetess* (which is now, and very properly, an outlawed word) suggests an amateurish, perhaps faintly comic figure. *Manageress* and many other words hold similar objections.

Books of ideological force and philosophical profundity have been written on these issues. We have no intention of summarising them here. There is no reason why we should accept the full range of feminist arguments about the alterations of the English language. That fine critic Dorothy Green, for instance, has written that "The zealots in favour of 'non sexist' English may find that in the end they have neutered women or made them anonymous, written them out of the language ..." Yet the feminists have made a great many users of the language more careful about the way they use words and about the implications of those words, and this has been a very considerable service. Their preference for the term 'inclusive' language rather than 'non-sexist' language makes a useful point.

1. Female forms of nouns should be avoided where they are likely to cause misunderstanding or give offence, and where there is an appropriate alternative form. Thus, use:

> artist, *not* artiste
> author, *not* authoress
> comedian, *not* comedienne
> editor, *not* editress
> executor, *not* executrix
> Jew, *not* Jewess
> manager, *not* manageress
> Negro, *not* Negress
> proprietor, *not* proprietress
> sculptor, *not* sculptress
> testator, *not* testatrix
> typist, *not* typiste
> usher, *not* usherette

and so on.

2. In cases where the male form may not be appropiate for the female, seek for an alternative word or form of the word: *bartender* for *barmaid*, *sailor* or *mariner* for *a female seaman*, *laundryworker* for *laundress*. The search for these

alternatives may become, however, an obsession of diminishing worth.

Insofar as there are male/female words which do *not* appear to carry a prejudice against the female form, we may as well go on using them, for they do perform a descriptive function which is always useful. In other words, providing there is no overriding objection, it can be helpful to know whether a man or women is under discussion.

Whether such words as *actress, waitress, stewardess, mayoress, heroine, policewoman, headmistress* and *conductress* are words 'loaded' against women is a matter that, in the final upshot, women will have to decide for themselves. The tendency will be for them to disappear. However the call for 'inclusiveness' can go only so far, as consideration of *queen, sister, aunt, wife* and many other exclusively female words which will stay in the language makes clear.

3. Sensitivity should be displayed towards the use of words which contain the word *man* and may be used in such a way as to convey the impression, at least subconsciously, that it is only the *male sex* that is involved.

Thus it is desirable to refer to an office's being *staffed*, rather than *manned*; to *a chairwoman* or to *the chair*, when a female is involved (*the chair*, of course, can apply to both male and female); to a *supervisor* rather than a *foreman*.

On the other hand, attempts to make English speakers abandon such a word as *manhole*, or to substitute *people-eating sharks* for *maneating sharks*, are likely to result in a derision which damages what is otherwise a worthy cause.

4. The use of words such as *he* and *his* in contexts where it is clear that women as well as men are involved is deeply offensive. The issue does not arise in the plural, for *they* and *their* are 'sexless'. Since it is unlikely a 'sexless' singular word will evolve, although *s/he* has been suggested, we have to (a) make sure that *he and she*, or *she and he*, are used in such contexts, or (b) try to turn the sentence round so that *they* or *their* can be used.

In general speech this problem has been partly solved already, in such a sentence as *If anyone turns up, tell them we'll be back tomorrow*. This is of course grammatically incorrect, because *anyone* should take a singular pronoun (*he* or *she*) rather than the plural *them*, but the use is idiomatically acceptable and should be encouraged and generally adopted. It is, after all, no more than what happened to the word *you* (see **thee/thine/thou**).

5. Care should be taken with words which imply criticisms of women's rather than both sexes' behavior. Obvious examples are *to bitch, to nag, henpecked, old maid, he's a bit of an old woman, slut*.

It is only fair at this point to summarise some of the more intelligent objections to drastic language revision in a feminist direction. These include:

> The debate is not about genuine misunderstandings so much as attempts to engineer a change in consciousness.
>
> Prescriptive attempts to force changes in language are rarely successful.
>
> The push to alter the way we use language comes largely from small groups of middle-class women.

Such aims are more divisive than forms they seek to replace.

Much of the proposed new usage offends against the principle of economy in language.

To follow reforms through to logical conclusions leads us to such perversities as "Man and woman the lifeboats."

Language is an aesthetic medium as much as an instrumental one. The right to say, in chosen contexts, *all men* rather than *all people* is more important than some imposed political or social concept of equity in language.

See also **chairman/chairperson**; **gender/sex**; **girls**; **mankind**; **spokesperson**; **the Mr/Mrs/Ms problem**; **tomboy**.

female/feminine. *Female* denotes the *sex* (or, as some would have it these days, the **gender**) of a woman.

Feminine, however, denotes *womanly qualities*.

You should therefore speak or write of a *female officer* (but only if it were necessary to establish that the person you were talking of was not a *male officer*) or a *female group*, or *female clothing*, but would talk of *feminine insights*, *feminine pursuits*, *feminine interests*.

A *female* room would be a room set aside for women. A *feminine* room would be a room which gave the impression of womanly concerns, whatever they may be.

It should be stressed, however, that the word *feminine* should be used with great caution. Any hint of patronage, or of attempting to establish innate distinctions between men and women, will be stongly resented by many, and not only by women.

feminism. See **(the) female critique**.

fetid/foetid. The adjective means *having a smell of decay*. It may be spelt either way, and in each case pronounced either *FET-id* or *FEE-tid*.

fewer/less. The Liberal Party slogan in the 1985 Victorian State elections was "More jobs – less taxes."

This would have been better put as "More jobs – fewer taxes," or "More jobs – less tax."

The basic rule is that *fewer* always means *a smaller number of*, while *less* means *a smaller quantity of*.

Another way of putting it is that, while there are exceptions, *fewer* should be used with plurals, and *less* with singulars. (The main exception is that *less* will be used with measurements: *less than ten kilograms*. The grammarians' argument here is that *less than ten kilograms* stands for *less than a weight of ten kilograms*, and hence is a singular.)

In publishing women get less perks than men says the Society of Editors

Newsletter (which should know better) for April 1985. *Less perks* should read *fewer perks*.

fictional/fictitious. *Fictional* means *relating to fiction*. *Fictitious*, however, means *not genuine, untrue*.
See also **factitious/fictitious**.

fifth continent. Although Australia is sometimes called the *sixth continent*, this is unusual and depends on accepting north and south America as two separate continents. The normal continent count is: Europe (strictly speaking not a continent but a sub-continent), Asia, Africa, the Americas and Australia. Antarctica is sometimes called the *sixth continent*.

figure is pronounced *figger*, but most authorities approve the long *u* sound in the word being sounded in derivatives such as *figurative*.

finalise or *finalize* means to put something in its final form. The word is said to be an Australian invention. Although it is accepted into the dictionaries it is an ugly word, which grates on many ears. Prefer *complete, finish* or *settle*.

finance. This word may be pronounced *fin-ance* or *fie-nance*. If used as a noun (*Do you have enough finance?*) it should be accented on the first syllable. If used as a verb (*She financed the enterprise*) it should be accented on the second syllable.
The *fin-* pronunciation is preferred in Britain and America, the *fie-* pronunciation in Australia. We prefer *fin-* to *fie-*.

finite verbs. See **verbs**.

first world war. Normally prefer *First World War* or *first world war* to *World War I* or *the Great War*.
But see also **Great War**.

fish. Many common names for Australian fish are wildly at variance with the same names which appear in dictionaries of British English. (The same applies also to other fauna: the English magpie, for instance, is quite different to the Australian magpie.)
The Australian *bass, catfish, cod, garfish, mackerel, mullet, perch, sole, tailor,* and *whiting* are not even of the same genus as the fish described in the *Shorter Oxford Dictionary. Sprat* and *anchovy* are different species. *Whitebait, tuna* and *salmon* refer to different fish. And there is further confusion between the common names for fish in different Australian States.

The Australian Fisheries Service has (1988) attempted to bring some order into the variant names of Australian fish. Here are some of their "recommended marketing names" with, in the second column, some of the variant names used in Australia:

Anchovy	whitebait
Australian herring	tommy ruff, roughies
Australian salmon	bay trout, salmon trout, kahawai
Barracouta	couta, snoek
Barracuda	giant sea pike
Blue eye	deep sea trevalla, sea trevally
Boarfish	duckfish, long nose
Australian bonito	horse mackerel
Black bream	golden bream, southern bream, silver bream
Butterfish	old maid, john dory
Southern calamari	squid
Rock cod	reef cod, gropei
Southern rock cod	beardy
West Australian dhufish	jewfish
John dory	kuparu
Elephant fish	elephant shark, ghost shark
Gemfish	hake, kingfish
Blue grenadier	whiptail, blue hake
Yellowtail kingfish	yellowtail
Luderick	blackfish, niggers
Jack mackerel	horse mackerel
Morwong	rubberlip, terakihi, perch, sea bream, jackass
Mullet	sand mullet, yellow-eye mullet, flat-tail mullet
Red mullet	goatfish
Mulloway	kingfish, jewfish
Orange roughy	sea perch
Golden perch	Murray perch, yellowbelly
Redfin	English perch
Redfish	nannygai, red snapper
Ribbonfish	frostfish
Northern scallop	scallop
Southern scallop	scallop, Tasmanian scallop
Blue whaler shark	blue shark
Bronze whaler	cocktail whaler, copper shark
Gummy shark	sweet william
School shark	snapper shark
Snapper (schnapper)	red bream, squire, cockney
Sweetlip	brown kelp, spangled emperor, brown emperor

Tailor	skipjack, bluefish
Silver trevally	trevally, silver bream, skippy
Trumpeter	bastard trumpeter, Tassie trumpeter
Striped trumpeter	Tasmanian trumpeter, common trumpeter
Blue warehou	Tasmanian trevally, snotty trevally, snotgall, sea bream
Grass whiting	stranger, rock whiting, blue rock whiting
King George whiting	South Australian whiting, spotted whiting
Sand whiting	silver whiting
School whiting	silver whiting, trawl whiting

fissiparous is a word, originating in the study of biology, which means *reproducing by splitting, or fission.*

It is often used in such contexts as *The Australian Left has a characteristic fissiparous tendency.*

A more accurate, word, however, is *fissile*, which means *having a tendency to split*. In the example above it is this that is meant, rather than that the Left has a tendency to reproduce itself by splitting. After all, in the case of a political split the party breaking away is doing so in order *not* to reproduce the existing system.

FitzGerald. The names of both the distinguished China scholar C. P. FitzGerald and of the equally distinguished poet R. D. FitzGerald take a capital *G*.

flaccid. *Flaccid* means *soft, limp, flabby*. Australians often pronounce the word *flaksid*. The correct and only pronunciation is *flassid*.

flammable/inflammable. It is an oddity of the language that these two words mean the same thing. Logically, it would seem that *inflammable* should mean *not flammable, not likely to catch on fire*. But, of course, it means the opposite.

The reason is that, while the prefix *in-* usually means *not* (as in *insincere*), it can also mean *into, towards, tending to*, as in *infiltrate, inflame*. (In this meaning the prefix was originally spelt *en-*.)

Because of the danger of *inflammable* being taken to mean *not flammable*, especially by those unaccustomed to the language, *flammable* is replacing *inflammable* on warning labels and the like. *Non-flammable* and *flammability* follow. *Inflammable* will remain in figurative contexts: *People with red hair do not necessarily have inflammable temperaments.*

flaunt/flout. To *flaunt* something is to display it in a conspicuous, showing-off kind of way:

The demonstrators flaunted their slogans in the faces of the police.

To *flout* is to make it clear that you don't give a damn about something:

The demonstrators flouted the police instructions to disperse.

So *flaunt* has the meaning of to exhibit proudly or conspicuously, *flout* has the meaning of disobey. For words far apart in meaning, they are surprisingly often confused, perhaps – as Sir Ernest Gowers has suggested – because flaunters and flouters are often the same people.

flautist/flutist. In Australia a person who plays a flute is a *flautist*, to rhyme with *flortist*. In the United States this person is a *flutist*.

flotsam, **jetsam and ligan**. *Flotsam* is floating cargo, stores or equipment, freed from a wreck or cast overboard to lighten a ship. *Jetsam* is sunken cargo which has been cast overboard to lighten a ship. *Ligan* is sunken cargo or gear which has been thrown overboard and buoyed. As with *flotsam* and *jetsam*, if claimed it is the property of the owners, otherwise of the Crown.

focus. The plural of *focus* may be either *foci* or *focuses*. If *foci* is used, it should be pronounced *fo-si* with the *i* as in *dive*.

The verb becomes *focused, focusing*.

Note that eyes can focus on something but that ears cannot. However, in more metaphorical usage, a phrase such as *attention was focused* is acceptable.

folklife is a nasty word imported into Australian from Americanese and now incorporated into an official "Committee of Inquiry into Folklife in Australia."

Folklore is an old-established English word. It means *the (originally unwritten and undescribed) songs, stories and customs of a people, patterns of thought and behavior handed down outside a formal framework from one generation to another.*

Folklife is a pretentious attempt to improve on an already existing and appropriate word.

following. The use of following to mean *after*, or *as a result of*, is widely regarded as undesirable. In other words, instead of writing *The bridge was built following extensive survey work*, write *The bridge was built after extensive survey work*.

footie or footy? In many Australian abbreviations and slang expressions, such as *aunty/auntie*, *bushy/bushie* (a bush dweller), the *-y* and the *-ie* endings seem to be used interchangeably over a long period of time, without one's tending to drive the other out.

Generally speaking, though, the *-ie* ending seems to be the preferred ending for the newly coined word or the word that is felt to be excessively slangy: *sickie*, *wharfie, softie, mozzie, quickie, Aussie*. Other words, becoming more assimilated to the general colloquial language, seem to change towards the more orthodox *-y* ending: *footy, aunty, hippy, cabby, telly, tranny*.

In some cases, such as *bushy/bushie*, there may be a tendency to preserve the *bushie* for the *bushman* meaning because there is already another meaning for *bushy*.

It's an open area of linguistic discussion, in which evolution is best left to take its course.

footnotes. See **referencing**.

forbear/forebear. *To forbear* is *to stop doing something or refrain from doing something.* It is of course a verb.

A *forebear* is *an ancestor, someone who has gone before.* It is a noun.

See **for-/fore-**.

forehead. The recommended pronunciation is *forrid*. The pronunciation *forehead* is often heard and is not incorrect, but the more 'educated' pronunciation is *forrid*. What has happened here, as with many words, is that the spread of popular education has led people to pronounce words as they are spelt, abandoning earlier and more idiosyncratic pronunciations. See **indicator words**.

foreign words and phrases. As the great Fowler – so great that he doesn't need initials – pointed out in his *Modern English Usage*, "The display of superior knowledge is as great a vulgarity as the display of superior wealth." The use of foreign words and phrases in English, and especially in Australian English, should be approached with caution. In Australia, fortunately, writers do not treat the common reader with the insolent superiority of the English who so often quote slabs of French (in particular) and other languages without providing a translation, thus establishing that they are interested in communicating only with that small section of the population able to make running translations of foreign languages. This is not so much a comment on bad manners as on the English class system.

Australian isolation and educational philistinism is such that no-one, either in talking or writing, can assume competence in a particular foreign language on the part of listeners or readers. This is why caution is necessary.

On the other hand there are many foreign phrases which are frequently used in educated speech and writing and which it is fair enough to assume people can learn the meanings of with little trouble. Obvious examples are *vice versa* and *et cetera*. It is true that they can be replaced with standard English phrases such as *the other way round* and *and so on*, but it would be a very boring language if we couldn't ring the changes a bit as the fancy takes us. Then there are other words and phrases which we use for which there is no effective, crisp English alternative: *bon mot, à la carte, ménage à trois.* Examples multiply as we move into more specialised literary or professional English: *ad hoc, fin de siècle, Weltschmertz, Schadenfreude.* It would be stupid to deny ourselves the richnesses or conveniences of languages other than our own.

George Orwell, in his essay "Politics and the English Language" published in *Horizon* in 1946, said that, apart from a few abbreviations such as *i.e.* and *e.g.*, "there is no real need for any of the hundreds of foreign phrases now current in English." In his famous essay on Newspeak, however, Orwell wrote that a "word which was difficult to utter, or was liable to be incorrectly heard, was held to be *ipso facto* a bad word ..."

Orwell may have been inconsistent, but he was a good enough writer to avoid using foreign phrases to impress, to bully or to confuse. Others, too, will be aware of their audience at all times, and will respect it.

forensic is an adjective meaning *relating to a court of law*. Speaking at the award to him of an honorary degree in December 1985, the Governor-General of Australia, Sir Ninian Stephen, spoke of *forensic craftsmanship*: "There is thus no higher praise of a judge than that he runs a good court ..."

Thus *forensic medicine* means *the application of medical skills to the purposes of the law*, as when pathologists report on the time of death. *Forensic skills* are abilities shown by advocates in court.

Forensic may not be used to describe anything of a technical nature done by police. Specifically, *forensic evidence* is *not* evidence of a scientific or medical nature presented in court. *All* evidence presented in a court is *forensic*.

forever/for ever. Traditionally *for ever* is regarded as *two* words, and must be two words in such uses as *Collingwood for ever!*; *for ever and ever, Amen*; *for ever and a day*; *she left the house for ever*.

When the phrase is used to mean *all the time*, however, there is now a tendency to write it as one word: *He was forever alluding to his grievances.*

If in doubt use two words.

foreword/preface/introduction. The *foreword* to a book or piece of writing consists of introductory remarks about the book and/or its author written by someone other than the author. It will normally remain unchanged in all editions, and precedes the contents page.

The *preface* to a book contains the author's personal remarks to the reader, and often includes the author's thanks to those who have assisted. It is usually changed from edition to edition, though previous prefaces may also be retained.

The *introduction* to a book consists of a statement about his or her intentions, viewpoint or subject matter by the author. It may be changed from edition to edition.

The normal order in which these are printed is *foreword, preface, introduction*.

for-/fore- *For-* is a prefix with the meaning of *against*, or *completely*. This meaning will be seen in:

forbear (to refrain from doing something)	forgive	forsake
	forgo (to give up, do without)	forswear
forbid		
forget	forlorn	

Fore-, however, has the general meaning of *before*, and this will be seen in:

forearm	forefront	forerunner
forboding	forego (to precede in time or place)	foreshadow
forebear (ancestor)		foreshorten
forecast	foreground	foresight
foreclose	forehand	forestall
foredoom	foreknowledge	foretaste
forefather	foreman	
forefinger	foretell	

for free. "I got it for free." This is an unashamed Americanism, quite a new arrival in the Australian language, and an unnecessary one. "I got it free" has been the standard Australian (and English) way of putting the matter. Presumably *for free* has derived by analogy from *for nothing*.

If only for the reason that *for free* reminds many who hear it of the inroads made into our language by a colonising force, it should be opposed. It will continue to be used, of course, like the word *gotten*, by those who are quite aware that it is an Americanism, and that to use it shows that one is in touch with the big exciting world over the other side of the Pacific. Ugh! See **offensive intruders.**

forlorn hope. This is a very interesting example of a phrase which has been mistranslated from another language without, however, doing the meaning of the phrase a great deal of violence.

Nineteenth-century military literature tells how fortresses were reduced, first by a breaching battery concentrating fire on a weak section of a fortress wall and then, when that collapsed, by sending in a storming party to clamber through the fallen wall and to engage the desperate defenders while the main body of the attackers followed, or assaulted the walls elsewhere. The storming party was known as the *forlorn hope*, from the Dutch *verloren hoop*, meaning *lost troop*. Eager young officers, anxious for death or glory, would volunteer to lead the forlorn hope.

In his remarkable memoirs of fighting in India, *The Path of Glory*, John Shipp writes: "The time for our next attack drew near, and as my wounds were now pretty nearly well, and I had failed in the first forlorn hope that I led, it seemed my duty to volunteer as leader of the second."

The mistranslation was obviously assisted by the nature of these exercises, forlorn hopes indeed.

formally/formerly. These two common words are almost identical in quick speech. This sometimes leads to their confusion in writing.

Formally means *in a formal manner,* as in *He then very formally bowed.*

Formerly means *once, in times past: She was formerly the world's leading* mezzo soprano.

former/latter. *Former* and *latter* are useful little words, but they can be tricky.
NOTE
1. Purists will hold that neither of these words should be used outside commercial or technical writing.
2. The words can only refer to *two similar items.* You *cannot* say, for instance, that

> Of the three daughters of the Haworth rectory, Charlotte, Emily and Anne Bronte,
> it was the former that wrote *Jane Eyre.*

You could, however say *it was the first of these that wrote* Jane Eyre.
3. The use of the words as adjectives presents no problems: *a latter-day genius, the latter part of the vessel, the former ambassador.*

See also **respective/respectively.**

formula. The plural of *formula* may be either *formulae* or *formulas.*

for real. ". . . before creating it for real" (ABC television, 18 August 1985).

For real is an ugly recent intruder into the Australian language. Presumably it is another import from American usage. The speaker above meant *before really creating it,* or *before actually creating it.* Better still, simply *before creating it.* See **offensive intruders.**

forte. A *forte* is a person's *strong point,* as in *Her forte was skilled metal work.* It may be pronounce either *fort* or *fortay.* It comes from the Latin word meaning *strong.*

fortuitous. See **adventitious.**

fortune. Pronounce as *forchin.* People who say *for-tyoon,* said the great H. W. Fowler, should be criticised for not accepting the "popular pronunciation of popular words." It may not be as easy to accept this agreeable generalisation in Australia as in England, but it does apply to *fortune, clothes* (pronounce to rhyme with *prose*) and *knowledge* (*NOLL-idje*), amongst others.

forward/forwards. Either is correct, though *forward* is now more common.

fracas. A *fracas* is a noisy brawl. It is *not* pronounced as spelt, but as *FRAK-ah.*

fraction. "He circled the course at a fraction of racing speed" (Clive James).

In fact we know what Clive James means – that the driver was circling the course at a speed much slower than racing speed. Strictly speaking, though, the word as used by Clive James is pretty meaningless. For all we can tell from the sentence, the driver could have been going at 99 per cent of racing speed. That is a fraction.

It would have been more precise to say *at a small fraction of racing speed*.

Frankenstein. The monster was not Frankenstein. Baron Frankenstein, in Mary Shelley's novel of 1818, was the man who *invented* the monster. The words *a Frankenstein* may therefore be applied only to *someone who invents and creates a monster*. The monster itself is *Frankenstein's monster*.

And let us put on record that the monster is at heart kindly, humble and socially responsible. He is also of course very strong and very clever. People fear and shun him because he *seems* monstrous. It is his desertion by Frankenstein that drives him to violence and destruction.

fraught is an adjective and is followed by *with*, as in such a sentence as *It was an enterprise fraught with danger. Fraught* means *filled*, or *charged*.

A sentence such as *She's fraught about the whole matter*, where *fraught* is being used to mean *filled with concern*, puts too heavy a load on the word. Although we expect *fraught* in this kind of use to mean *fraught with concern* or *fraught with fear*, it does not necessarily mean this. It could mean *fraught with the possibility of great happiness*.

Confusion presumably arises because of the similarity of the word *fraught* to the word *fright*.

fresh. The use of this word in the sense of *renewed* (*There has been a fresh outbreak of violence in South Africa*) is undesirable.

freshman is the American term for *a first-year student in a university or college*.

The word is understood in Australia but not used here. The word *fresher* is used in Australia, but mainly to describe a first-year student just entering on the year's work.

Nor does Australia have specific terms for students in other years of university and college work, except for such a usage as *She is a final-year student*.

Americans, however, have quite specific terms. There a second-year student is a *sophomore* (a joining of two Greek words meaning *wise* and *foolish*), a third-year student a *junior*, and a final-year student a *senior*.

fulfil. Normal English and Australian usage prefers *fulfil, fulfils, fulfilled, fulfilling, fulfilment*.

Rather surprisingly, considering the tendency in American English to dipose of unnecessary letters, the American forms are *fulfill, fulfills, fulfilled, fulfilling, fulfillment.*

full stop. Also called *a period, a stop, a full point* or *a point.*

The full stop may appear the simplest of the punctuation marks to use properly. After all, its function is crystal-clear: it ends a sentence. (So may **question marks** and **exclamation marks**.)

But the placement of a full stop may be critical. Knowing when to use one, and when to allow the sentence to run on further, is one of the marks of a precise and effective writer. (Most inexperienced writers do not use enough full stops.) The great Russian writer Isaac Babel once said that no iron can stab the heart more deeply than a full stop in exactly the right place.

The other common purpose of the full stop, apart from ending a sentence, is to indicate an abbreviation, as with *Rev.* for *the Reverend, etc.* for *et cetera* and *MS.* for *manuscript.*

Note however that the modern tendency is *not* to use a full stop when the abbreviation ends in the same letter of the alphabet as the full word. (The argument is that in such a case we have a *contraction* rather than an *abbreviation.*) Hence abbreviations such as *Mr, Mrs, Dr, st* (for *street*), *ave* (for *avenue*), *4th* need not take the full stop.

There is also an increasing tendency to omit the full stops between the letters of abbreviations of organisations: *RMIT* (Royal Melbourne Institute of Technology), *ACTU* (Australian Council of Trade Unions), *ICI* (Imperial Chemical Industries) and so on.

Nor is a full stop used with abbreviations regarded as symbols:

This was the S point of the island.
We travelled 345 km that day.
Over 40 m high.
A 10 ft rule.
Water is H_2O in chemical symbols.

See also **dots**.

fulminate. *To fulminate* is *to protest explosively and violently* against something. It comes from the Latin word meaning *a thunderbolt.* It may be pronounced with the *ful-* rhyming with *hull* or with *fool.*

fulsome. "Meals [are] reasonably cheap and fullsome" (*Age*, 3 May 1985). Bob Hawke has "a fulsome sort of personality" (Hazel Hawke on television, 6 July 1987). *Fulsome*, so spelt, does *not* mean *generous, outgoing* or *lavish.* It means *behavior which is cloying, unpleasantly servile, insincerely flattering,* as in *He made a fulsome speech of welcome.*

function. The use of the word *function* to mean a party, gathering, entertainment etc. -"We will be holding a function on the eighteenth of October"- is easily overdone and totters on the verge of the pretentious.

function/dysfunction. If something *functions* well it is working properly, or should be:

> The chief function of a hospital is to look after people who are ill.

If things are going wrong, however, we may speak of a *malfunction* or a *dysfunction*, the prefix *dys-* meaning *bad*, as in *dyspepsia*, bad digestion:

> The nuclear reactor was malfunctioning.

> The dysfunctions were such that the whole installation had to go.

Malfunction tends to be used of specific problems, *dysfunction* of more general ones relating to a whole installation or enterprise.

fungi. Pronounce *FUNG-eye* with the *g* hard (as in *get*) or soft (as the *j* in *jest*).

furore. *Furore* comes from the Latin for *to rave*, and its most common use is to describe *a widespread outburst of protest or resentment* at some action: *The government's announcement that it was closing the pubs caused a furore among drinkers.* Sometimes it means *an outburst of enthusiasm*: *The singer's performance of the aria caused a furore in the theatre.*

Pronounce *fyu-ROAR-ie*. The American spelling is often *furor*.

furphy. In August 1987 the Victorian Cabinet Minister Rob Jolly categorised Liberal Party claims that the sale of certain assets of the State Electricity Commission by the Labor government was illegal as a *furphy*.

Jolly did not mean by this that the Liberal Party's claim was *idle gossip, a rumor*, which is what a furphy is. He meant that it was *untrue*. His use of the word *furphy* was thus incorrect.

In 1873 John Furphy, brother to the author Joseph Furphy, established his iron-founding business in Shepparton, Victoria. The two-wheeled water-carts the firm made became familiar sights in the bush. By an engaging eccentricity they had cast into them, in Pitman's shorthand, the motto WATER IS THE GIFT OF GOD BUT BEER AND WHISKY CONCOCTIONS OF THE DEVIL COME AND HAVE A DRINK OF WATER, a slogan composed by John Furphy's son William.

After the outbreak of the Great War the water-carts became familiar objects in the big base camp of Broadmeadows, outside Melbourne, and subsequently on Gallipoli. From time immemorial the drawing of water has been a convenient opportunity for the exchange of information and speculation — *scuttlebutt* was a naval word for the lockable water cask on the deck of a ship — and from the meeting of mates around the water-tanks came the use of the word *furphy* to mean *a rumor*, and particularly *a rumor suspected to have little foundation in fact*. It was a coinage that caught on and has persisted.

further. See **farther/further**.

futuristic. *Futuristic* has only one meaning in English — or at least it did until the Melbourne football commentator Jack Dyer got to work on it. The dictionaries tell us that *futuristic* is an adjective we apply to *designs that are thought to be anticipating the future*: *It was a futuristic-looking car*. Jack Dyer praises *futuristic players* — ones who look like having a promising future in football.

G

gala/galah. A *gala* is *a festive occasion.* A *galah* is *an Australian parrot,* known for its cavortings when on the wing and for its habit of not deserting a companion in distress, and thus easily becoming another victim.

Because of these eccentricities the name of *galah* is also applied in Australian English to *a foolish person, someone who makes a bit of a fool of himself or herself.* Unjust to the galah, many would hold.

Gala may be pronounced *GAY-la* or *GAR-la,* with the accent on the first syllable. *Galah* is pronounced *ga-LAR,* with the accent on the second syllable.

galvanise. The word comes from Galvani, an Italian physiologist who died in 1798 and, by observing that muscles contracted when in contact with certain metals, laid an important basis for future electrical research.

In the industrial sense *to galvanise* is to cover iron or steel with a protective zinc coating. In the metaphorical sense *to galvanise* means *to stimulate into activity,* as Galvani stimulated his experimental muscles.

Mr Neil Brown, deputy leader of the Liberal Party, informed Australians in February 1987 that some incident, now forgotten, "had galvanised attention" on some issue. The form of words is, at the least, inelegant. Can one stimulate attention into activity? Abstract nouns such as *attention* should be handled gingerly, and here it would surely have been better to have used some such phrase as *galvanised the community into paying more attention to the issue.*

gambit. A *gambit* is *an opening move in a game of chess in which a piece, normally a pawn, is sacrificed to secure an advantageous position.*

From this the word is also used to mean *an initial manoeuvre or comment intended to secure an advantage in any situation.*

The word comes from the Italian for *a tripping up.*

Note (1) that a *gambit* is not simply any clever tactical move; it is one you start off with; (2) *opening gambit* is a **pleonasm**: all *gambits* are, by definition, *opening.*

Gandhi. The name of the Mahatma is frequently misspelt *Ghandi.*

gaol/jail. *Jail* is the American spelling. Prefer *gaol.*

garage. To rhyme with *barrage* or *marriage?* The two pronunciations coexist throughout the English-speaking world. The word is quite a recent one, and

garish

comes from the French *garer*, to dock a ship. Probably this is why the *barrage* pronunciation, the one closest to the French, is still the most common and the most 'approved' of the two ways of saying the word. The *marriage* pronunciation, which may be called the 'English' pronunciation, may gradually prevail, but is still under a cloud.

garish. *Garish* means *colorfully gaudy*, and comes from a word meaning *to stare*. Pronounce to rhyme with *bear-ish*, and not as *garrish*.

gay. It has often been said that homosexuals are not, on the whole, a very happy lot. For all that, the word *gay* (adjective and noun) to mean *homosexual* has been around for a longer time than most people realise. It was originally nineteenth-century thieves' cant for a prostitute. The sexual use of *gay* is well on the way to driving out of the language the use of the word to mean *merry*, or *happy*. "The Gay Gordons" can no longer be danced under that title, the Gay Nineties are suspect, and no doubt the old film "The Gay Divorcee" is being retitled for its umpteenth television repeat.

Gay or *a gay* is used for male homosexuals, not for female.

He (or *she*) *is camp* is also a way of referring to a homosexual, and can also be traced to the nineteenth century, where gentlemen in London's Hyde Park would slip into the army tents for amusement with the soldiery. They called it "going for a bit of a camp."

See also **dyke; homosexual; lesbian**.

gender. Gender is the *he, she, it* distinction in language. It is a commonplace of many, if not most, languages that the nouns in those languages are masculine, feminine or neuter. Fortunately English is almost free of such distinctions.

In German the word for *a young woman* is neuter, not feminine. Mark Twain said that "In German a young lady has no sex, while a turnip has." In French one refers to *Her Majesty the King* (because *majesté* is a feminine noun). Similar irrationalities (as they seem to us) are frequently found.

There is no gender in English nouns. There may be a word *actor*, and another word *actress*, but, although one of these words applies to a male, and the other to a female, the words themselves have no gender. You do not have to say, for instance, *a beautiful man* but *a beautifulle woman*, which is the kind of thing you have to do in other languages.

The only examples of true gender in English words are *he, she* and *it*, and the relative pronouns *who* (which applies to people) and *which* (which applies to neuter things).

For misuse of the word *gender*, see the following entry. For sexism in language, see **(the) female critique**.

gender/sex. "The Marginalization of Gender Disadvantage" is the title of a recent scholarly article arguing that the problems of girls in schools are not being taken seriously enough. In theory the word *gender* should have nothing to do with people. It is a grammatical term and its use should be restricted to grammatical contexts. Feminists, however, seem uneasy with the use of the proper word for the difference between male and female, which is the *sex* difference. It is the *sex* disadvantage, not the *gender* disadvantage, which the writers of the article are referring to. After all, the word *sexist* is commonly used, not *genderist*, and no-one imagines that a *sexist* is a *sex-maniac*.

It is, however, to be admitted that, though *sex* rather than *gender* should be used wherever possible, there are some situations where one must sympathise with the *gender*-users. Take this sentence:

> There are, in all modern societies, issues of regionalism and of ethnicity and, still, of gender which are discussable more usefully in cultural terms.

To use *sex* instead of *gender* in that sentence could be genuinely misleading. Maybe *male-female roles* would have been preferable to *gender* in that context, but it is a long way around the problem.

In the course of the preparation of this book Janet Mackenzie has suggested that the expansion of the word *sex* in the past fifty years to encompass the *sex act* ("We had sex last night") has made people nervous about the word, and has created the need for a word that means what *sex* used to mean. Since *gender* is available, and is only used in its grammatical sense without having many other meanings, it makes good sense to adopt it to mean *the difference between being male and being female*.

In any case it is increasingly being used that way, and it is most unlikely strictures will stop it. Insofar as it represents a concession to being mealy-mouthed, it is not to be welcomed; but against this is the fact that, as we have seen in the example above, it circumvents a confusion that has crept into the language.

What can be strongly opposed by men and women alike is the increasing use of such barbarisms as *gender-neutral language*. *Non-sexist language* is better than that. Perhaps best is the term *inclusive language*, to mean language which avoids offensive and unnecessary distinctions between women and men.

See **(the) female critique**.

genius. The plural of *genius*, when it means *a very brilliant person*, is *geniuses*.

When, however, we use the word to mean a *spirit*, as in *the genius of the Lamp*, the plural is *genii*, pronounced *jeen-ee-eye*.

genocide. To engage in *genocide* is to engage in *the deliberate extermination of a whole nationality or ethnic group*. It is a solemn word indeed, and should not be used lightly, or inaccurately. The Germans certainly practised genocide on the

Jews and Gipsies in the second world war. On the other hand, though they slaughtered hundreds of thousands of Poles, they did not attempt to wipe out the Poles as a whole group of people.

White Australian policy and practice towards Aboriginals after 1788 is sometimes called *genocide*. There were many settlers who advocated the extirpation of the Aboriginals, and there were countless appalling atrocities. Whole tribes disappeared, through disease, displacement, cultural attrition and deliberate killing. Yet official policy towards the Aboriginals was almost always well-intentioned; many efforts, misguided though they may have been, were made to 'protect' them; and settlers were occasionally hanged for atrocities. *Genocide* is a misleading and inaccurate word to apply to the Australian situation.

genre. Frequently heard in artistic circles, this word can acquire 'pseud' overtones. Pronounced (approximately) *ZHON-rer*, it usually means *a kind of painting or writing*, as in *The writing of lyrics was her main poetic genre*, or *His genre was watercolor painting*. When someone is called, however, a *genre* painter, it means that they specialise in painting domestic incidents or scenes from everyday life.

The use of *genre* in a context that is not artistic is inappropriate. To write *The audience last night was of a different genre to that of ten years ago* is asking the word *genre* to travel too far and work too hard.

gentleman. Pronounce as spelt, not as *gennelman*, frequently heard on radio.

genus. The plural of the word *genus*, used especially in biological taxonomy, is *genera*.

geographical names. The newspaper *Nation Review*, standard-bearer for radical chic, in its later demented days in the 1970s decided to refer to all names of foreign countries and cities by the native forms, so that bewildered readers found themselves reading about a country called *Shqiperia*, for instance. This turned out to be the Albanian name for Albania.

The English language contains a large number of recognised names for foreign places. *Italy* is the English name for the country the Italians call *Italia*, *Florence* the English name for the city the Italians call *Firenze*, and so on. *Peking* is the English word for the city the Chinese nowadays choose to call *Beijing*, and Canton the English name for the city the Chinese now call *Guangzhou*.

Unless we wish to impress our listeners or readers with our inside knowledge of the Middle Kingdom, there is no call on speakers of English to use other than the traditional English word in such cases as these. The Chinese have no intention of abandoning their traditional names for foreign parts.

We have been told that Prime Minister Whitlam, during his time in office in the early 1970s, received a request from the Chinese to adopt the new spellings and changed names they believed desirable, and that he insisted that Australia follow suit. It is not quite clear to us how Mr Whitlam could insist that non-governmental Australia should follow in this matter, but it is certainly true that in the wake of the uncritical Sinophilia that has affected Australia in recent years many Australian institutions have been anxious to do what the Chinese and Mr Whitlam wanted.

This same anxiety to be over-nice to our neighbors led many Australians, and many Australian institutions, to abandon the traditional English name for *Cambodia*, a name still used by most of the English-speaking world, and to adopt instead the name *Kampuchea*. There are no doubt other examples.

With the exceptions noted below, there are no better reasons for us to adopt the usages of other nations than there are for them to adopt ours. In 1945 Winston Churchill wrote a refreshing memorandum on this question, which reads in part: "If we do not make a stand we shall in a few weeks be asked to call Leghorn Livorno, and the BBC will be pronouncing Paris Paree. Foreign names were made for Englishmen, not Englishmen for foreign names. I date this minute from St George's Day."

It is no more, and no less, important for us to know that the Chinese call *Peking Beijing*, or refer to *Canton* as *Guangzhou*, than it is for us to know that the Greek name for *Greece* is *Hellas* or that the Russian name for *Moscow* is *Moskva*. Our atlases and guide books may include this information if they wish, and it would not go amiss. But that is as far as the matter need go.

There is, however, a grey area. In the case of countries formerly under colonial rule or influence, where a change of name is a political act underlining independence and enhancing self-respect, or where the former name (as with the *Dutch East Indies*) is clearly no longer applicable, there is every reason to accept a change of name. Few would object to *Rhodesia's* becoming *Zimbabwe* or *Salisbury's* becoming *Harare*, and to our use of those names. At other times traditional uses should not be lightly abandoned. It may be necessary and desirable to accept the change from *Batavia* to *Jakarta*, but there is no reason why we should change from *Mascassar* to *Makasar* or from *the Celebes* to *Sulawesi*.

Similarly there is no reason we should bow to the pressures being applied to change the name of the *Persian Gulf* in the interests of Middle Eastern politics. The *Persian Gulf* it has been in English for over four hundred years. Let others call it what they will.

It is common today, when using place names, to omit the apostrophe: *Milsons Point*. This seems sensible enough, if we remember the general rule that points of punctuation, grammar etc. are only worth retaining if they serve a useful purpose. Milsons Point no longer belongs to Milson, if it ever did, so there is no purpose in using the apostrophe to say that it does.

See also **(the) geographical possessive; place names.**

the geographical possessive. Bureaucratic busybodies in government offices are determined that the possessive will be dropped from place names in the interest of some kind of ideological tidiness. Thus they direct us to refer to, say, Benson's Valley as *Benson Valley*, to Cooper's Creek as *Cooper Creek*, and to Wilson's Promontory as *Wilson Promontory*. Whatever they put on maps, sensible people will write and use these names as they themselves wish; with, one hopes, a preference for the traditional forms, which there is no good reason for dropping.

Georgian. When used in Australia this usually applies to the buildings and architecture of the early colonial period (or to later copies). Authentic Georgian architecture in Australia is found almost exclusively in New South Wales and Tasmania.

The first four King Georges of Britain followed each other on the throne and reigned from 1714 to 1830. The Georgian period in Australia may be said to have lasted from 1788 until about 1850, overlapping stylistically with the **Victorian** period.

In Britain the word *Georgian* may also (but more rarely) apply to the reign of George V, 1910-1936, as in *the Georgian poets*, a school of poets at the time.

geriatric. In the mini-series "The Far Pavilions," seen on television, one officer in a British mess in India in the 1870s says to the other "He's a bit of a geriatric," or words to that effect.

Geriatric is, properly, an adjective, and means *relating to the health and welfare of old people*. *Geriatrics* is the branch of medical knowledge dealing with the problems of the aged, and a *geriatrician* is a medical practitioner specialising in that area.

Geriatric does not mean *old*, and it does not mean *an old person*. It is a piece of 1960s cant ("Never trust anyone over thirty") and is almost always used with a sneer. It was not used on the Northwest Frontier in 1878.

Organisations of the elderly in Australia are now protesting against the use of the word to refer to old people, not because of the argument about 'meaning' we advance above, but because it is so often used rather nastily.

See **ageism/ageist.**

germane. See **cousins.**

gerund. For notes on the gerund, see **to gerund or not to gerund.**

gesticulate/gesticulation. Pronounce with a soft *g*, sounding like *j*, not with a hard *g* as in *get*.

gibber. This Aboriginal word for *a stone*, commonly used in the interior of Australia, is pronounced with a hard *g*, as in *get*. The common English verb *to gibber*, however, has a soft *g* and is pronounced *jibber*. It means *to talk rapidly and unintelligibly*.

gibe/gybe/jibe. The verb *to gybe* is a yachting word meaning *the sudden shifting of the main-sail from one side of the vessel to the other*, an action which may be either deliberate or accidental, but which in both cases can lead to unwary yachtsmen getting bumped on the head by the boom. Gybe may also be spelt *jibe*. It is pronounced to rhyme with the *vib-* in *vibration*.

To *gibe* or *jibe* at someone is to *jeer* at them. It is similarly pronounced. *Gibe* is preferred, for there is another verb *to jibe* which means *to agree, to accord*: *Her proposals jibed well with mine.*

giga. See **billion**.

gigolo. A *gigolo* is *a man kept by a woman or paid to attend on women*. Pronounce *jigolo* or *zhigolo*, but not with a hard initial *g*.

gilding the lily. The actual quotation is *To gild refined gold, to paint the lily* (Shakespeare, *King John*, act III, scene ix).

gin. This word was used in the past for an Aboriginal woman. It is no longer acceptable.

girls. There is a strong feminist objection to the use of the word *girls* to mean *women*, as in *The girls are waiting to start work.*

The argument is that the word used in this way is demeaning, whether or not it is intended to be: that it is used to detract from the dignity and the equal status of women.

It can of course be argued that such phrases as *one of the boys, come and meet the boys, the old boys are sitting on the veranda* are also common in everyday usage, are used affectionately and have no other connotation than that.

However it is also true that one is more likely to hear such a sentence as *This is the men's lavatory, and this is the girls'* than *This is the boys' lavatory, and this is the women's.*

The case against the indiscriminate and patronising use of the words *girl* and *girls* is upheld.

See **(the) female critique**.

175

gladioli. The singular of *gladioli*, as Mr Barry Humphries would be happy to confirm, is *gladiolus*. So, one *gladiolus*, two *gladioli*.

goanna. The word goanna is a corruption of *iwana*, a word used by the Arawak Indians of the South American Guianas to describe a family of large lizards. The word, entering English through Spanish, became *iguana*, and was used for the first hundred years of white settlement in Australia to denote the Australian monitor lizards, a quite different group. The colloquial *goanna*, which gradually replaced *iguana*, therefore served a useful scientific purpose. The same process occurred with the American *opossum* and the Australian **possum**.

going to go. Many people feel uneasy about *going to go* in such a sentence as *He was going to go to the university, but he had this accident*. It certainly sounds a mite inelegant, and advice is sometimes given to prefer *going* to *going to go*. There is however a very considerable difference of meaning between *He was going to go to the university* and *He was going to the university*, and the construction is a correct and unavoidable one. Unless, of course, we take pains to substitute another verb for *to go*: *He was going to attend the university*, for instance.

Gondwanaland. This is the geologists' name for the supposed 'super-continent' existing during the Palaeozoic and Mesozoic eras in the southern hemisphere. Gondwanaland, it is argued, consisted of peninsular India, Australia, Antarctica, South America and most of Africa. The existence of Gondwanaland is supported by affinities in plant and animal life between now widely separated lands, and by the general acceptance in recent years of the Wegener theory of Continental Drift.

The Gondwana were an ancient tribe of South India. The name Gondwanaland was devised by the Indian Geological Survey during the nineteenth century.

good evening/good night. The standard usage is that *good evening* may be used either as an expression of greeting or an expression of farewell, but that *good night* is an expression only of farewell. For instance, to say *good evening* when you pick up the phone is welcoming; to say *good night* sounds as though you are saying "Good-bye; don't want to talk to you."

good night. See **good evening/good night**.

good/well. *Good* is an adjective meaning *having admirable qualities* and with many associated meanings: *a good engineer, a good winter, a good time*.

Well is an adverb meaning *in a satisfactory manner. She did it well*.

Being an adjective, *good* has a working relationship with *nouns*, as in the examples above.

Being an adverb, *well* has a working relationship with *verbs, adjectives and other adverbs*.

So: *she runs well* (not *good*); *he did it very badly* (not *bad*).

The two words do have one affinity. Just as you say *good, better, best*, so you say *well, better, best: She did it well, but he did it better.* So *better* and *best* act as *either* adjective or adverb.

There is one exception to the above. When Australians are asked "How are you?" they often answer "I'm *good.*" *Good* here is of course related to the verb *am*, and should be the adverb *well*: "I'm well." But the idiom is well established and is accepted.

good will. Prefer *women and men of good will* to *women and men of goodwill.*

got/gotten.
1. "In a few weeks I had gotten my passport," (Garrie Hutchinson in the Melbourne *Age*, 20 April 1985). In English English this use of *gotten* has been called "archaic and affected." In Australian English, however, it is certainly not archaic, being rather a novel use, and as for being affected, we must each judge for ourselves.

Gotten has been entering the Australian vocabulary, especially that of the less than middle-aged, and clearly from American English where, like so much else in the language, it is a relic of Shakespearian English. Some will see some irony in its use by Garrie Hutchinson, a conscientious objector to the Vietnam war. It has by no means taken over in Australia from *got* as the past participle of the verb *to get*.

Language changes all the time and there can be no objection on principle to this. American usages have as much right to enter the Australian language as any other, and it would be a sad day if the users of English ever became as touchy as the French about the mongrelisation of their language. Yet, for all that, *got* is shorter and causes no momentary surprise when it is used, as *gotten* still does. Perhaps *gotten* is an affectation, after all.

2. The use of the word *got* in such a phrase as *She has got the job* is often criticised. It would seem to have crept in because we *have* to use the word *got* when we shorten the phrase: *She's got the job.* Although certainly not wrong in *She has got the job*, it is perhaps undesirable, especially in written English.

gourmand/gourmet. Egon Ronay says in the London *Sunday Times* (30 March 1986) that:

> A gourmet is a connoisseur who exercises restraint and self-discipline, properties that, together with balance, are tenets of the Greek Epicurean philosophy. A

177

gourmand, on the other hand, is a hasty, impetuous eater, a glutton eager to stuff himself.

gradation/graduation. A *gradation* is *a series of stages in the progress of something.* A *graduation* (apart from its academic meaning) is *a series of marks on the side of a measuring vessel.*

graffiti. *Graffiti* – anonymous messages scrawled or painted on walls, in public lavatories, and the like – are, Ian Turner has written in his pioneering work *Australian Graffiti* (Melbourne, 1975), "one of the few remaining contributions to a living folklore."

Properly speaking, for Italians at any rate, *graffiti* is plural and the singular is *graffito: This is a nice graffito.* Many however will regard this as affected, and in Australia we have to accept *graffiti* as singular *and* plural.

grammar. See **parts of speech.**

grand. With names of relations do not use a hyphen *unless* there is a problem with the spelling or pronunciation. Hence:

grand-aunt	grand-dad
grand-uncle	grand-daughter

but:

grandchild	grandparent
grandfather	grandson
grandmother	

grandfather.

But in any event, Mr Holmes a Court would be grandfathered under the Broadcasting Act. He acquired his various licences when the test was *residency* in Australia (at the time he was both a resident and a citizen).

Age, 29 April 1986.

A *grandfather clause* was originally a clause in the constitutions of several of the southern States of the United States of America, added after the American Civil War, which stated that, although there would be literacy requirements for voting (designed to diminish the number of Negro voters), those who had ancestors voting before 1867 could continue to vote. This was a way of enfranchising illiterate whites.

Grandfather clauses are common in legislation, in Australia and elsewhere, relating to the establishment of qualifications for practice in a profession. Unqualified dentists, for instance, were allowed to become registered dentists if they had been practising before the registration Act.

The use of the word as a verb, as in the extract above, is new. What is being said in that extract is that, whatever the law today, at the time Mr Holmes a Court acquired his various media licences he was within the law and that, although the law has changed, he remains entitled to the licences he then acquired.

The word in this sense, either as noun or verb, does not appear in the *Macquarie Dictionary*.

gratis/gratuitous. *Gratis* was originally a Latin word meaning *by favors*. It is an adverb. If you are given a glass of port in a restaurant *gratis* you are given it *for nothing, as a favor*.

Gratuitous is an adjective. In one meaning it has the same sense as *gratis*: *Please accept these tickets. They are gratuitous*. The more common meaning, however, is *without reason*, especially in such phrases as *This was a gratuitous insult* or *A mere bystander, he received a gratuitous blow in the face*.

Great Britain. See Britain.

Great War. Conscientious copy-editors cross out the words *Great War* when they see them in manuscripts and insert *First World War*. Conscientious copy-editors sometimes get a little too big for their boots. *The Great War* was the name of the 1914-1918 conflict to all who took part in it, and for a generation afterwards. It remains a perfectly appropriate name for that conflict, and perhaps *the* appropriate name, when historians or others are writing about that *period*. Correlli Barnett, the distinguished British historian, has no problems with the term, nor do his publishers.

grievous. *Grievous* means *very severe or painful, causing grief* or *showing distress, serious*. As Mark Antony says in Shakespeare's *Julius Caesar*:

> The noble Brutus
> Hath told you Caesar was ambitious:
> If it were so, it was a grievous fault,
> And grievously hath Caesar answer'd it.

Grievous here means *serious*, *grievously* means *painfully*.

There is no such word as *grievious*, though it is sometimes heard, and we believe we even overheard Laurence Olivier using it.

grimace. A *grimace* is *a distorted facial expression*. *To grimace* is to make such an expression. Both noun and verb are pronounced *grim-ACE*.

grisly/grizzly. *Grisly* means *gruesome, causing horror*. "The battlefield was a grisly sight." The use of this word as a light-hearted slang word for *inconvenient* or *unpleasant* weakens the power of the word in the language.

Grizzly comes from quite another origin. It means *having grey or partly grey hair*, hence the *grizzly bear*.

Although no dictionary we have seen allows it, we believe there is another meaning of the word *grizzly*, with again a different origin. This is a word formed from the verb *to grizzle*, meaning *to fret, whine, grumble*. The dictionaries do not want us to talk of a *grizzly child* but of a *grizzling child*, but we believe the word *grizzly* is probably more frequently used in this context than is *grizzling*.

groin/groyne. The *groin* is part of the human body. A *groyne* is a breakwater.

grossly. The Opposition's views, said Treasurer Paul Keating in the election campaign of 1987, "grossly exaggerated" the real issues. Mr Keating said this not once but many times. The trouble is that Mr Keating believes *grossly* rhymes with *crossly*. It does not. It rhymes with *closely*.

guerilla/guerrilla. Either spelling is correct, the latter being the more traditional and the closer to the origin from the Spanish *guerra, war*. A *guerilla* or *guerrilla* is a member of an irregular armed force fighting regular units.

Guerrilla is the preferred British and American spelling and, although *guerilla* is common in Australia, it is not recommended.

gun/rifle. While people talk loosely and say "Guns should be banned," in fact they mean that *guns and rifles* should be banned.

A *gun*, properly *a shotgun*, fires *pellets* or *shot* and is used for the shooting of birds and small game. A *gun* has a smooth bore and, if of two barrels, often has one barrel which narrows slightly, or is *choked*. A *gun* has a short effective range of fifty to a hundred metres. It does not fire *bullets*. A gun is loaded with *cartridges*, or *shells*.

A *rifle* has a *rifled* barrel, which means that the inside of the barrel has helical grooves which grip the *bullet* the rifle fires, imparting a spin to it and ensuring greater accuracy. A rifle looks slimmer than a gun and normally has only one barrel. Rifles are used by armies and by shooters after large game. They may be accurate over long distances of a kilometre or more.

Note that, with rifles (and revolvers and pistols), the *bullet* is the *projectile* that leaves the barrel when the weapon is fired. You do not put *bullets* into a rifle or handgun, but *rounds*. The bullet is part of the round, the part that is propelled. The part that is then ejected by the weapon prior to the loading of another round is the *cartridge case*.

See also **pistol/revolver.**

gunwale. The *gunwale* of a boat or ship is *the top plank of its side* or, in the case of a metal or composition boat, *that part of the side of the boat you step over in* *climbing aboard.* It is pronounced, and sometimes spelt, *gunnel.* The word is frequently misspelt *gunwhale.*

gybe. See **gibe/gybe/jibe.**

gynaecology/obstetrics. Though often used as synonyms, these words mean different things. *Gynaecology* is the study of the specific medical problems of women, while *obstetrics* is concerned with pregnancy and childbirth. *Gynaecologist* and *obstetrician* follow. Pronounced *gynae* to rhyme with *shiny*, and put the stress on the *col. Gynecology* is the spelling in the United States.

gyrate/gyration. Pronounce with a soft *g*, as in *ginger.*

H

H. See **aitch/haitch**.

had have. Note the following inelegancies (the preferred form is in brackets):

> Do you think that if he hadn't have resigned ... (*hadn't resigned*).
>
> If Lendl had have missed the smash ... (*had missed*).
>
> If we had have won it (*had won it*).
>
> If he hadn't have done it (*hadn't done it*).

Technically, what is being done here is the doubling of a past perfect tense. It is a widespread habit in Australian English: the first three examples above are from Michael Schildberger, John Newcombe and John Bertram respectively.

halcyon. "Some people can look back to the halcyon days when petrol was a few cents a litre" (says an ABC announcer).

Halcyon comes from the ancient Greek word for a kingfisher, a bird fabled to build its nest on calm seas. *Halcyon days*, strictly speaking, are the fortnight of calm weather often associated with the winter solstice (the year's shortest day). More generally, *halcyon days* means a calm and pleasant period of existence. To associate them with nothing more than the low price of petrol is a rather mercenary interpretation of a colorful legend.

half.

1. *Half* may be singular or plural, depending on context:

> Half of the plank is rotten.
>
> Half of the travellers are absent.

The *of* in such examples may be omitted.

2. *Half an hour, half a dozen, half a kilo; but a half-hour, a half-dozen, a half-kilo, one-half.*

3. *The room was half full* but *a half-full room. We half expected this incident,* but *this half-expected incident.*

4. *Halfway, half past six, half holiday, half measure, half moon, half past, half pay,* but *half-day, half-hearted, half-brother, half-cock, half-baked, half-price, half-time, half-wit, half-yearly.* However in many such cases authorities disagree, so it is up to the writer to use a dictionary or to make up his or her own mind as to what form looks best.

5. Large numbers are often written as, say, 7½ million. Some authorities prefer

these numbers, when written, to appear as *seven millions and a half* rather than *seven and a half millions*.

6. To say or write *The interview lasted a half an hour*, and similar constructions, is regarded as a vulgarism. The *a* is not called for.

7. *Cut in half* or *cut in halves*? The latter is formally more correct, but *cut in half* has such idiomatic force that it has to be regarded as acceptable.

half-caste. There has always been a problem in finding an appropriate word to distinguish those Australians who are of part-Aboriginal and part-European descent.

There have been many offensive and racist terms in use in the past. The word *half-caste* was originally an attempt to escape from these terms, but has itself become an offensive word, and should at all times be avoided. In addition it is normally inaccurate; most part-Aboriginals have far less than 50 per cent of European or Aboriginal genes, if one may talk of genes in these terms.

The terms *mixed-blood* and *mixed-race*, though well-intentioned, are also to be avoided. Words like 'blood' and 'race' no longer have a place in discussions of ethnicity. Failing the evolution of a value-free word we shall have to continue to go the long way around the issue and use some such phrase as *persons of mixed descent*, though even this phrase is open to the objection that all human beings are members of the same species, and that therefore within that species descent can not be 'mixed'.

Probably the most acceptable usage today is *part-Aboriginal*, and this is recommended.

Many Australians of mixed descent now not only reject such a word as *half-castes* but also such coinages as *islanders* (for descendants of the hybrid community that developed in the Bass Strait islands), and prefer to call themselves *Aboriginals*, even if they are only to a minor extent in the Aboriginal line. It must also be added, however, that many of mixed descent prefer to consider themselves simply *Australians*, like the rest of us.

hallmark. In the first instance a *hallmark* is a stamp impressed on gold, silver and platinum objects designed to establish purity, date of manufacture, the name of the smith, and so on.

By extension *hallmark* has come to mean *a mark or sign of excellence or authenticity*.

Should, however, we be able to take the meaning further and say, for instance, "The Bicentennial is a hallmark in Australian history"?

The word is in fact being used in this way, almost as though it was a synonym for *milestone*. This usage is allowed by the dictionaries ("an outstanding or distinguishing feature") but it is at odds with the primary meanings of the word and, in our view, should be discouraged.

handful. A handful of what? *A handful of twenty-cent pieces* is fine. But *a handful of motor cars? A handful of horses? A handful of people?* Some hand!

hangar. The shed in which aircraft are kept is a *hangar*, not a *hanger*.

hanged/hung. The verb *to hang* may take as the past participle *hung* or *hanged*. The former, or 'strong' form has triumphed in every use of the word except that of execution, where we talk of a person's being *hanged*, not *hung*. This exception is probably due to the conservatism of the legal profession. This form of the word survives, of course, in the phrase *I'll be hanged if I will*.

hanging participles. The *hanging participle* or *dangling phrase* is best illustrated by example:
> Striding over the mountains, there came a clap of thunder.
> A brilliant journalist, his articles aroused wide praise.
> Like most mules, I found this one hard to get on with.

The first example suggests that the clap of thunder was striding over the mountains. The second suggests that somehow or other the articles were "a brilliant journalist." The third suggests that there is a mule speaking or writing.
  Correctly re-phrased, these sentences should read:
> As I was striding over the mountains, there came a clap of thunder.
> He was a brilliant journalist, and his articles aroused wide praise.
> I found this mule, like most of the breed, hard to get on with.

There are some idiomatic constructions which use dangling phrases but which are not considered ungrammatical:
> To be honest, she's quite useless.
> Speaking of holidays, we should be able to get away next month.

The *hanging participle* is a favorite target of those on the *qui vive* for misuses of English, but before shouting too much such persons may consider:
> 'Tis given out that, sleeping in mine orchard,
> A serpent stung me.
>
> Shakespeare
>
> Uncommonly conscious for a seaman, and endued with a deep natural reverence, the wild watery loneliness of his life did therefore strongly incline him to superstition.
>
> Melville: *Moby-Dick*
>
> Far from the madding crowd's ignoble strife,
> Their sober wishes never learn'd to stray.
>
> Thomas Gray.

Hansard. *Hansard* is an informal term used for the printed records of parliamentary debates. As a word it has no official standing in Australia, the proceedings of parliaments usually being called simply *Parliamentary Debates*. The original Hansard (and his descendants) compiled verbatim reports of the British Parliament until 1889.

Informal it may be, but it is more common to hear a politician say "Look it up in Hansard" than "Look it up in the *Parliamentary Debates*." The word is an acceptable synonym for records of parliamentary debates in Australia but, since it is not the official title of a publication, should not appear in italics.

happy Easter. Christmas is a festival of rejoicing and it is appropriate to wish others a *merry Christmas*.

Easter is a religious festival commemorating the death of Christ, and His rising again from the dead. Amongst believers the latter is of course a cause for rejoicing, but Easter seen as a whole is not, and is not intended to be, a 'happy' occasion.

The common wish, *Happy Easter*, is therefore religious nonsense and in bad taste.

hara-kiri. The Japanese form of suicide. This term is often misspelt and therefore mispronounced.

harass/harassment. For spelling, the old mnemonic is useful: *One 'r' in harass, two in embarrass.*

The preferred pronunciation of these words is with the accent on the first syllable, so that *harass* is pronounced like the proper name *Harris*.

An alternative pronunciation, probably now more common in Australia, is with the stress on the *second* syllable: *har-ASS, har-ASS-ment.*

hardly than/hardly when. It is wrong to say, for instance, *Hardly had we sat down to dinner than the telephone rang.*

Hardly has to be followed by *when: Hardly had we sat down to dinner when the telephone rang.*

The error probably stems from *no sooner than*, in which case the *than* is correct.

hard row. See **hoeing**.

hashish. See **marijuana**.

have a nice day. The reply to this of H. L. Mencken, the American critic of language, was: "I'll thank you to mind your own business; I'll have whatever sort of day I choose."

See **nice**.

Hawkespeak. Hawkespeak is a variety of the English language, perhaps not invented by Mr R. J. L. Hawke, but certainly popularised by him during his period of office as Prime Minister of Australia.

The main feature of Hawkespeak is its ability to say very little in the maximum number of words.

The following example was quoted in the *National Times* of 22 November 1985:

> And that tends to mean at times if you want to put it, there is no point in running away from it, it tends to mean at times that there's that there's a lack of specificity, or if you want to put it another way, there's a range of options which are put which are there to accommodate that indisputable fact about the social democratic parties such as ours.

See also **in respect of; upcoming**.

haywire. If things are haywire, they're *all over the place, in a mess*. The word is probably originally American, and the imagery that of a coil of wire accidentally released from its restraints and twisting itself into unmanageable confusion.

head up. *She was chosen to head up the new committee.* Why not *to head the new committee*, or *to be head of the new committee*? See **offensive intruders**.

heaps of is/heaps of are. See **half**.

heartache/heartburn. Jan Murray, wife of John Brown, a Minister in the second Hawke government, told a delighted public, on a television program in April 1987, that on her husband's appointment she and he had sexual intercourse on her husband's Ministerial desk.

Some time later (*Age*, 18 July 1987) Mr Brown remarked that his wife's statement "caused a lot of heartburn."

Heartburn is *a burning sensation beneath the breastbone caused by the regurgitation of the contents of the stomach.* Mr Brown and other politicians use the word *heartburn* when they are reaching for — or should be using — the word *heartache*, which means *a feeling of anguish.* Those who felt *heartache* because of Mr and Mrs Brown's pleasure felt it, we hope, not because of the innocent act itself, but because it was carried out on a public-service desk without Cabinet authorisation.

Hebrew. See **Jew/Jewess**.

hegemony means *the superiority of one state or power within a grouping of such states: Hegemony in the Nato alliance clearly rests with the United States of America.*

187

It may also mean *the ascendancy that one social class holds over others*. This is a recent application of the word, stemming from neo-Marxist texts and criticism. It is a legitimate extension, except that it has become a lazy piece of jargon in this sense, and of course Greek to the common man and woman who are being 'hegemonised'. One form of *hegemony* is to control people by using words they don't understand.

Any word which has become as tiresome as *hegemony* has in certain areas of political discourse should be given a rest.

The word can be pronounced in four different ways: *he-GEM-ony* (hard *g*), *he-JEM-ony*, *HEJ-emony*, HEG-emony (hard *g*). To the ancient Greeks a *hegemon* was a leader, and they pronounced the word with a hard *g*. If the second-last syllable of an English word is unstressed, then the stress tends to go on the antepenultimate, or third-last, syllable. It could thus be argued that the pronunciation *he-GEM-ony*, with the hard *g*, should be favored.

Normally common use would eventually sort this matter out. Since *hegemony* is, however, never going to be a word in common use, those who use it will continue to choose for themselves.

he/him, she/her. Heard on the ABC on 17 March 1986: "He murdered she and her daughter."

Why is this wrong?

Put simply, *He* in the above sentence is the *subject*, the person who *does*.

The person who is *done to* is the *object* of such a sentence. The objective form of *she* is *her* (and of *he* is *him*).

These sentences are correct:

> He murdered her and her daughter.
> She murdered him and his daughter.

Note the difference in meaning between:

> He likes icecream better than her.
> He likes icecream better than she [does].

height. Pronounce to rhyme with *bite*. Do not attempt to pronounce this word with a *th* at the end, a *th* which is not there anyway.

heinous means *atrocious, appalling*, especially in the form of *a heinous crime*. The word is pronounced *hayness*.

hence/hither. *Hence* and *hither* are old-fashioned words, especially in their once-common use of *from here* (hence) and *to here* (hither).

Hence, however, is still used in two other senses: to mean *from this time* (*You mark my words, six months hence there'll be trouble*) and to mean *therefore* (*You've signed the document, hence you must honor its undertaking*).

The words also survive in *henceforward* (*henceforward, we shall have to work harder*), *hitherto* (*hitherto we were prepared to overlook the matter, but this cannot continue*), and in the idiom *hither and thither*.

herb. One of the English words for which the Americans have retained an older English pronunciation — in this case *erb*. Americans have been known to protest vigorously at the Australian (and English) pronunciation *herb*, with the *h* sounded, but for once we are more up-to-date than they are.

hermaphrodite. See **androgynous/epicene/hermaphrodite.**

herself/himself. The use of these words in such contexts as *She herself opened the door* is quite unnecessary, and should be avoided, except where emphasis — it was *she*, not her husband, who opened the door — is intended.

hiccough/hiccup. Prefer *hiccup*, which in any case is the earlier form. Note *hiccupped, hiccupping.*

high/tall. *High* goes with *low* and *tall* with *short*. Therefore buildings are *high* rather than *tall*, though *tall* may be used for chimneys and poles.

Himalayas. The English pronunciation of this great mountain range is *HIM-a-layas*, the Hindi pronunciation — also heard in English — being *him-ARL-ias*.

himself. See **herself/himself.**

historian. For pronunciation, see *an historian/an hotel.*

historic/historical. *Historic* means *having an assured place in history*, as in *This is an historic occasion*. *Historical* means *concerned with history: an historical conference, an historical society.*

historic present. See **tense**, paragraph 4.

hither. See **hence/hither.**

hoeing. It is *a hard row* to hoe, not a hard *road*. The allusion is to growing things.

hoi polloi are ancient Greek words meaning *the many*, from which they have come to mean *the masses, the people at large*, often in a somewhat derogatory sense.

There is a tendency for *hoi polloi* to be used by some to mean *important people*, precisely the opposite of its real meaning, presumably because it sounds important.

Hoi means *the*, so strictly speaking to say *the hoi polloi* is to say *the the masses*, just as to say *Lake Victoria Nyanza* is to say *Lake Victoria Lake*. The *h* in *hoi* is not sounded.

hoist with his own petard. It may be said that when Dr Guillotin was guillotined he was, metaphorically, *hoist with his own petard*. A *petard* is a bomb — not, as many believe, a flag. Thus, literally, to be hoist with your own petard is to be blown up by your own bomb. Shakespeare, in *Hamlet* (act III, scene IV) writes:

> Let it work;
> For 'tis the sport, to have the engineer
> Hoist with his own petard . . .

holistic is quite a new word. Strictly speaking it means *related to holism, the philosophical idea that the whole is greater than the sum of the parts*. In practice it tends to be used more simply, to mean *looking at phenomena as a whole*. In this it has tended to replace *synoptic*, which means *taking a general view, bringing things together*.

Holistic, then, is something of a fashionable word. So fashionable that it is frequently spelt *wholistic*: "Wholistic Massage Diploma Courses," says an advertisement in the press. This is *wrong*. *Holism* and *holistic* come from the ancient Greek, *holos, whole*. Our word *whole* comes from quite a different source, in fact from an old Germanic word related to *hale*, as in *healthy*.

holocaust. Originally the word *holocaust* meant *a burnt offering*. It then came to mean *a great act of destruction or loss of life* (especially by fire). This use of the word has been popularised by the genocidal acts of the Nazi regime in Germany before and during the second world war directed against the Jewish people, which has come to be referred to widely as *the Holocaust*, with a capital *H*.

This last and special meaning has tended to drive the more general meaning, *a great act of destruction*, not so much out of use but into an embarrassing position, if a word can be in an embarrassing position. It is now impossible to use the word *holocaust* in any context without there being a referral in hearers' minds to the *Holocaust* with a capital *H*.

This cannot be helped, though it will make sensitive users of the language reluctant to use the word in its more general sense.

Whether it is desirable to be able to sum up such an act as that of the Nazis by a simple word such as *Holocaust* is, in our view, debatable. To use such a word, almost as shorthand, is to deprive the acts themselves of their true and terrible meaning and ambience. It enables a quick, almost cursory nod in the direction of what was perhaps mankind's greatest single act of evil. This may even become a form of easy dismissal.

We can use words to help us forget, as well as to remember.

home/house. In Australian and British English the use of the word *home* has been a defensive one. It is a domestic word, used in a domestic context, and to many "Will you visit my home?" sounds affected and pretentious.

Home is best kept for such uses as *Home at last!, I feel at home by the sea, I will be at home. You have a lovely house* is preferred to *You have a lovely home*, unless the intention is to suggest that it is the total domestic 'feel' of the house and the life within it that is meant.

Advertisers try to foist the word *home* on us because they think it sounds more intimate and attractive than *house*, and *home* for *house* is gaining ground because of the real-estate salesmen and because of the inroads of American English, where it is winning.

homed in/honed in. *To home in* on something is *to make for it as though for a target*. The imagery is that of the horse with its head turned for home. Many Australians believe that the phrase is not *homed in* but *honed in*. You can't *hone in* on anything. *To hone* is *to sharpen, to put an edge on a cutting implement*. You hone a scythe or a razor, for instance.

home is the sailor. Robert Louis Stevenson's famous line from his poem "Requiem" will be found on his tomb:

> Home is the sailor, home from sea,
> And the hunter home from the hill.

This is almost always misquoted as *home from the sea*. It was even misquoted on Stevenson's tomb, until an Australian Governor paid for it to be put right.

homogeneity. For pronunciation, see **deity**.

homogeneous/homogenous. *Homogeneous* means *composed of identical parts, uniform*: *The population of Ruritania is remarkably homogeneous, sharing the same language and origins*.

The *-geneous* part of the word is pronounced as the word *genius*.

Homogenous is used to mean the same as *homogeneous*, but should be avoided. It is best left to its specific biological meaning, which is to describe *organisms which share a common ancestry*.

homosexual. A *homosexual* is a person sexually attracted only by others of the same sex. Strictly speaking it should apply equally to both men and women, but there seems a general aversion to speaking of homosexual women as *homosexuals*, and the word **lesbian** is normally used instead.

The *homo* in *homosexual* derives from the Greek word for *the same* and not from the Latin word for *man*. Many are confused about this and, since they believe the word for *man* should be pronounced *home-o*, argue that homosexual should be pronounced *home-o-sexual*. The use of the abbreviation *homo* for a homosexual, which is always pronounced *home-o*, has been an additional influence towards the pronunciation *home-o-sexual*.

The pronunciation *hommo-sexual* is nevertheless preferred, not so much because the pronunciation of *homo* in both Greek and Latin is *hommo* not *home-o* (compare *homogeneous*), but because the abbreviation *homo* has a derogatory way of being used, and it is desirable to get away from that in the pronunciation of the longer word.

honor'd in the breach. The phrase is from *Hamlet*, act I, scene iv:

> It is a custom
> More honor'd in the breach than the observance.

Although this is always taken to mean *something that ought to be done but is more often not done*, and nothing much can be done about this, in fact taken in context the meaning is *a foolish action* [drinking to excess, in fact] *which it is more honorable to evade than perform.*

honorifics. The whole question of honorifics — that is, of titles accorded to people, and used before their names — is a difficult one for a democrat. Robert Burns said that the rank is but the guinea's stamp. In an egalitarian society people should not need handles to their names.

The trouble is that, whether or not everyone loves a lord, university teachers with doctorates are often as proud of the title *Dr* before their name as they are scornful of someone else's *Sir*. One of the frailties of the human species is the search for distinguishing marks.

Specialist works will inform readers about the correct way to address an archbishop formally, or the correct title of the wife of the younger son of a marquess. Here we merely note some common solecisms.

The wife of Lord Trend is *not* Lady Edna Trend, nor is the wife of Sir Archibald Adamite called Lady Jane Adamite. Their correct titles are *Lady Trend* and *Lady Adamite*. If there are two Lady Trends around, and it is desired to distinguish one form of lady from the other, then our Lady Trend may be referred to informally as Jane, Lady Trend, though strictly speaking this usage is reserved for the widow or divorced wife of a peer or baronet. To call someone Lady Jane Trend is to suggest she is the daughter of a duke, marquess or earl. To call her Lady (Jane) Trend is to imply that she is the divorced wife of a knight. The correct form, if it is desirable to distinguish between the wives of Sir John Trend and Sir Richard Trend, is Lady (John) Trend and Lady (Richard) Trend.

Sir Archibald Adamite is never referred to as *Sir Adamite*, but either by his full name or as *Sir Archibald*. To call him "Sir Archibald" is not a familiarity. The Reverend Gordon Chasuble is *never* referred to as *the Reverend Chasuble*, either in writing or speech. In speech he will be referred to as *Mr Chasuble*, in writing as *the Reverend Gordon Chasuble* or *the Reverend Mr Chasuble*. The exception is Catholic clergy, who are referred to as *Father* informally, *the Reverend Father* formally.

Note that surgeons, who as medical practitioners are entitled to the courtesy title of "Dr," in a convoluted form of inverse snobbery prefer to stick to the title of "Mr." This is not for democratic reasons, but rather to make the point that they are not like other (medical) doctors.

Note that "Mr" and "Dr" do not take the full stop after the abbreviation, the rule being that the full stop is omitted where the abbreviation ends with the same letter as the full word does. For this reason a full stop *is* necessary after the abbreviation "Rev.".

See also **doctor; political vanities; (the) Mr/Mrs/Ms problem; the reverends**.

honour/honorary. The word *honour*, like the word *honourable*, may be spelt with or without the *u*: we prefer *honor*, the so-called 'American' spelling.

The words *honorarium*, *honorary* and *honorific* must, however be spelt that way.

hoof. Pronounce with long *oo*, as in *zoo*, not with short *oo*, as in *hood*. The plural may be either *hoofs* or *hooves*, but normally prefer *hoofs*.

hopeful. "The manufacturers gear everything to a hopeful market overseas." Oh, no they don't. They gear everything to a *hoped-for* market overseas. This is a new variant on the sad story of *hopefully*. It is an attempt to change the meaning of a word. *Hopeful* means *full of hope*: *I was hopeful that my father would recover from his illness*. It does not mean *to be hoped for*, which is what the author of the above words was trying to wrench its meaning towards.

See also the following entry.

hopefully. "Hopefully, I will win the lottery next week." In a use like this, *hopefully* means *if all goes well*. This use of the word *hopefully* was unknown in English until recent decades; it seems to have come *via* American English and relates back to a direct translation into English of the German word *hoffentlich*, which means *I hope that* . . .

In traditional English *hopefully* means one thing only, and that is *full of hope*:

It is better to travel hopefully than to arrive.

The more recent use is now more widespread than the traditional use. Nothing can be done about this, and perhaps nothing should be done about it, but its use in the new sense will grate on many who prefer to hasten slowly when it comes to shifts in word meaning like this. To be discouraged.

Note that, probably by analogy with the new use of *hopefully*, other words are falling victim to the same process. For instance, *thankfully*, which means *full of thanks* ("He accepted the glass of water thankfully") is now being used to mean *it is a matter for gratitude that ...*, as in the sentence "Thankfully, the fire brigade arrived on time." In the case of *mercifully* the confusion of the two usages has now gone so far as to be irretrievable. Thus the original use ("The conquerors behaved *mercifully* to their enemies") now co-exists with "*Mercifully*, it didn't rain until after the match was over." In this latter case *mercifully* stands in for *It was a mercy that ...*

One rule-of-thumb to help avoid such misusages is not to use such words as the first word in a sentence.

horrendous has been in the language at least since the seventeenth century. Forgotten until recent years, it has been revived and popularised. It means *terrifying* or *frightening;* in its origins it meant that your hair was standing on end.

It has been suggested that the word's present popularity stems from the way it associates *horror* and *tremendous* in its sound. However much the word may be frowned upon as colloquial, in fact it is a legitimate revival of a traditional word.

hospitalise/hospitalisation. Prefer *send to hospital.*

hotel. For pronunciation, see **an historian/an hotel**.

housewife. Apart from the standard meaning of this word, it is also used in Australia, especially in the defence forces, to mean *a pocket kit containing mending materials.* In this sense the word is pronouced *hussif,* and its plural is *housewifes* (not *housewives*), pronounced *hussifs.*

hover. To rhyme with *lover*, with *over* or with the *hov* rhyming with the *sov* in *sovereign?* Pronounce to rhyme with *sov.*

how/however. Beware of the little word *how*. Like other little things, such as seeds in socks, it intrudes where it is not wanted; or it attaches an unnecessary *about* to itself.

Not *They told us about how they crossed the lake*, but *They told us how they crossed the lake.*

Not *They went into raptures about how magnificent the singing was*; prefer *They went into raptures about the magnificent singing.*

However is always written as one word, except with the interrogative "How ever did she manage that?", where the *ever* is simply being used to emphasise the *how*. It should never be used in conjunction with *but*, as in *But the rain, however, still held off.* Here either *but* or *however* is unnecessary.

However has been called "one of the misused words in the language." It can be used to mean *nevertheless, yet, on the other hand, by whatever means, no matter how* and as an emphatic form of *how*. ("However did that happen?"). But it is easy to use inelegantly, as in:

The books were returned, however their covers were torn.

Here *however,* is being used as a replacement for *but*, in other words as a conjunction or sentence-connector. This is illiterate, and the following examples are preferable:

The books were returned; their covers were, however, torn.

The books were returned. Their covers were, however, torn.

Although the books were returned, their covers were torn.

human being. The phrase *speaking as a human being* should be avoided. It invites the reply: "I come of a long line of human beings myself."

humanist/humanitarian. These words create much confusion.

A *humanist* is, broadly speaking, *someone educated in, or interested in, or working in the area of the liberal arts* — that is, classics, literature, history, philosophy and the like. In academic circles the word is sometimes used to distinguish someone working in the general area of the 'arts' from someone working in science or technology; which is not to say, of course, that a scientist can not have strong humanistic interests.

A *humanitarian* is *a person who has the interests of mankind at heart*, who wishes to do things for other people.

Humanitarians are not necessarily humanists, nor humanists humanitarians.

In barbarian nooks and crannies of Australian society *humanist* is used by political and religious fundamentalists as a synonym for *a godless one, an atheist seeking to destroy the moral basis of society*. This is presumably because some of those who reject non-material bases of belief and moral order call themselves *rationalists* or *humanists*. To abuse these people for seeking what they see as a more satisfactory philosophy of existence is to strike a blow at the concept of religious tolerance and spiritual enquiry in our community.

humour/humorist/humorous. *Humour* may be spelt either that way or *humor*, according to taste. (See **-or/-our.**)

Humorist and *humorous* must however be spelt that way.

There is again a choice with *humourful* and *humourless*.

hyper/hypo. These are prefixes — that is, they are used as the first part of words. They are both of Greek origin, and while the meanings slide around a bit, *hyper* has the general meaning of *above normal, excessive*, while *hypo* has the contrary meaning of *under*, or *less than*, or *beneath*.

These meanings emerge in such words as:

195

Hyperbole (pronounce the final *e*), an *exaggerated statement expected to be recognised as such*. Like the similar word *hyperbola* the literal sense is an *overthrow*. A *hyperbola* is a curve similar to that followed by a ball thrown into the air, although strictly speaking the curve followed by a ball or projectile is a *parabola*.

Hypersensitive, meaning *unduly sensitive.*

Hypercritical, meaning *unduly critical.*

Hypochondria, literally *what lies beneath the breast-bone,* means a morbid and unnecessary concern about one's health. To the medieval world the seat of melancholy was in one's chest.

Hypocrisy is from the Greek word *krites,* one who answers, expounds, orates. *Hypo* here has the sense of *less than, pretending to. Hypocrite* was, in a slightly different Greek form, the name for an actor, and referred to the actor's not believing what he or she said.

hyphens. Hyphens are used for many purposes, apart from the very useful one of making people's names sound grander.

1. The hyphen makes two words into one, where their relationship is so close that it would be misleading or uncomfortable not to have a hyphen:

A *black-out worker,* or a *black out-worker*? Only the hyphen can tell you.

She lost the election by 15-odd votes. Or were they *fifteen* odd *votes*? Again, the hyphen has to come to our assistance.

He was a near-contemporary, or *He was a near contemporary*? Two quite different meanings.

General Custer, the Indian fighter, or *General Custer, the Indian-fighter*?

A short story-writer, or a *short-story writer*?

An edible oil-refinery, or *an edible-oil refinery*?

Drive in fowl manure (sign) or *Drive-in fowl manure*?

The brown and white skua gulls or *the brown-and-white skua gulls*?

2. The hyphen turns phrases which are not adjectives into adjectives, so that:

You will find many members of the working class in Footscray becomes *Footscray is a working-class area.*

California has a system of junior colleges becomes *There is a junior-college system in California.*

3. However, it is desirable not to over-hyphenate adjectives and adverbs when the meaning is perfectly clear without the hyphen:

This is a beautifully built building is preferable to *This is a beautifully-built building.*

4. Note the special rules for *ill, well, better, best, worse* and *worst*:

This was an ill-found ship, but *This ship was ill found.*

This was the best-known of the opera singers, but *This opera singer was the best known.*

5. Some nouns are hyphenated, some are not: *rock-wallaby* but *lyrebird, homespun* but *home unit.* There are no rules, except that the more common the word the more likely to be spelt as one word, without a hyphen. *Tax payer, tax-payer* and *taxpayer* are, for instance, all acceptable forms. If concerned about 'correctness', find a dictionary you like and consult it.

6. Adjectives formed from verbs with prepositions, such as *to knock down, to drag out,* take a hyphen: *a knock-down, drag-out fight.*

7. The hyphen may be used to assist pronunciation. Words such as *co-operation, re-educate* and *re-establish* have a hyphen solely to show how they are pronounced. An alternative way of doing this is to use a *diaeresis,* thus: *coöperation, reëducate.* The diaeresis is, however, seldom found, except in a few traditional uses: *the Brontë sisters, Citroën,* sometimes the word *naïve.*

8. Hyphens are usual with *ex-, non-* and *self-: ex-serviceman, non-discriminatory, self-obsessed.*

9. Hyphens are normally not used with *anti-, co-, counter-, re-, neo-, pan-, pre-, un-,* unless the word following starts with a capital letter *or* there is likely to be confusion. Thus: *coreligionist, counterproductive, preoccupy, relocate,* but *pan-American, re-creation* (because of the word *recreation*), *re-form* (because of *reform*), *neo-Nazi.* Some words, like *counter-revolutionary,* take a hyphen because otherwise the spelling would look awkward.

10. The hyphen is used when a word is 'broken' at the end of a line of type, as in:

> Victoria is contesting the Com-
> monwealth's powers over the roy-
> alties in the Federal Court and a
> preliminary hearing is due on
> Friday.

The words *Commonwealth's* and *royalties* are 'broken'.

Care should be taken as to where the hyphen in a 'broken' word is placed. Any editor or teacher sees many 'breaks' like *governme-nts, revolutiona-ry, neede-d.* These are not so much wrong as plain bloody stupid. The main rule is to use your head. The following guidelines, however, are offered:

(a) Never 'break' single-syllable words.

(b) If a word is already hyphenated, break it at the hyphen.

(c) Never 'break' a word within one letter of the beginning of the word, and preferably not within two letters of the end.

(d) Take advantage of 'natural' sound-breaks in words:

plat-form	danger-ous	con-tinuous
apart-ment	nat-ional	struc-ture

(e) Beware of creating distracting combinations of part-words when 'breaking', such as *bed-raggled, disc-omfort, co-athanger, beg-rudged, proper-tied, anal-ogy, wee-knight.*

For further discussion of this problem see the Australian Government

Publishing Service's *Style Manual*.

11. The hyphen is a topic which can be discussed and refined almost indefinitely, and those with a taste for this are referred to the first and second editions of the classic *Modern English Usage*.

12. Lastly, the most important general rule is that words should not be hyphenated unless the sense and the sound demand it. The sentence *The ill-effects of the spring-rain upon the working-conditions in the country-side* has four unnecessary hyphens.

See also **dashes**.

I

ibid. See **referencing.**

-ics. *Politics, mathematics, ethics* and the other words ending in *-ics*. Are they plural (*His politics stink*) or singular (*politics is a dirty game*)?

The short answer is to consider these words singular when they refer strictly to the name of a science or area of activity, plural when used to describe a bundle of characteristics relating to something or someone. The above examples follow this. So do:

> Athletics is found in most schools.
> The company's ethics are open to question.
> The acoustics of the concert hall are faulty.
> Acoustics is studied at the university.

The matter is not quite as simple as this, however. Words such as *heroics* and *hysterics* which relate to behavior appear quite naturally to take the plural at all times: *Heroics are off the agenda in this performance.* And when a singular noun follows an *-ics* word it seems to require the *-ics* word to take the singular: *For her, mathematics is a passion.*

The best advice of all is the familiar one: say or write it the way it sounds best to you.

identify. The verb *to identify* is used correctly in these sentences:

> He identified the criminal.
> She identified the species to which the animal belongs.
> I identified my problems with his.

Identify should not, however, be used loosely to mean *to take a pronounced interest in.* Sentences such as

> She identified herself with the Country Women's Association,
> They were identified with the peace movement,

should be avoided. Strictly speaking, a person identified with the Country Women's Association would be in a position where it was not possible to say which was the person and which was the Country Women's Association.

identity. To most of the English-speaking world the word *identity* has only one broad meaning, *the combination of characteristics which identifies a person or thing as different from other persons or things.*

The word has, however, another meaning in Australia and New Zealand. (It is probably of New Zealand origin.) Here it also means *a well-known person,*

199

especially one identified with a certain place over a long period. We have all heard the phrase *She's a local identity.*

The word has been criticised because in this use it is distinctively antipodean and not accepted elsewhere. It has also been criticised because it wrenches away the original meaning of the word, as the use of **personality** to mean a *well-known person* is similarly criticised.

Identity in its Australian and New Zealand meaning has a long and honorable history, is closely identified with settlement and social patterns, and performs a needed function. It is to be welcomed and supported.

It is worth noting that the word *character*, which is first recorded in 1647 as meaning much the same as *identity* in the sense of the qualities making a person, had by 1773 also become a word for an unusual *kind* of person.

See also **personality**.

ideology. An *ideology* is *a set of ideas. One person's ideology is another person's ratbaggery.* Because of the close association of the word *idea* with the word *ideology*, the latter is too often spelt *idealogy*, which is *wrong*. The *Age* refers (22 April 1987) to Sidney Nolan as being "singularly devoid of idealogical motivation." This too is *wrong*. Read *ideological*.

Pronounce *EYE-deology*, not *IDD-eology*.

idiotic reversals. The seemingly inexhaustible resources of the English language are apparently not enough for many Australian advertising agents and public relations people. We are now being subject to such titles as *Bank Commonwealth* (that is, the *Commonwealth Bank*) and, from the ABC, "Worship Sunday" (that is *Sunday Worship*). This is, in the first place, supposed to be clever and trendy. Behind such transformations is also a brainwash motive: *Bank Commonwealth* and *Worship Sunday* transform a noun into the imperative form of the verb and seek to instruct us what to do. The perpetrators should be told to *off muck.*

idyll/idyllic. An *idyll* is *a scene or incident or occasion of simple, often rustic, charm.* Henry Lawson describes an idyllic occasion in his "Reedy River:"

Ten miles down Reedy River
  One Sunday afternoon,
I rode with Mary Campbell
  To that broad bright lagoon;
We left our horses grazing,
  Till shadows climbed the peak,
And strolled beneath the sheoaks
  On the banks of Rocky Creek.

The word *idyll* is also used to describe a piece of writing — as with Lawson's — describing something *idyllic*.

The British pronunciation is *iddle*, the American *EYE-dil*, as in the word *idle*. Australians use both pronunciations, with a bias towards the American. You have to make up your mind, if you choose to say *iddle* in order to show you know the 'proper' pronunciation, whether those listening to you will understand what you are saying.

i.e. This abbreviation stands for *id est* (*that is*), and should not be confused with *e.g.*, short for *exempli gratia*, meaning *for example*. See the entry under **e.g.**

-ie/-y. See **footie or footy?**

if/if not. *If*, when it is used to mean *although*, is a word to be handled with caution. It can lead to ambiguity. To say that *Her statement was inappropriate, if honest* can mean *either If her statement was honest, it was inappropriate* or it can mean *Her statement was honest but it was also inappropriate*.

The phrase *if not* is even more likely to lead to misunderstandings. Take this sentence:

> Theoretically it would be desirable, if not essential, for technical colleges to have the most up-to-date equipment.

Does this mean that it *is* essential, or does it mean that while it is desirable it is *not* essential? An ambiguity hangs over the sentence, which should read either:

> Theoretically it would be desirable, even if not essential, for technical colleges to have the most up-to-date equipment,

or should read:

> Theoretically it would be desirable, indeed essential, for technical colleges to have the most up-to-date equipment.

if/whether. Should we say *I wonder if she'll come to work* or *I wonder whether she'll come to work*?

The answer, strictly speaking, is the second example — *whether*. And this is why.

The proper title for *if* is *an adverbial conjunction of condition*. The title doesn't matter, but the word *condition* does. Some hold that *if* is used where there is actually a *condition* in the statement, an *if-not-then-not* sense:

> I will go to the shops if I may have the car.
> They will come tomorrow if the weather holds.

Whether is a more general word, a *that-or-that-not* word:

> You will have to make up your mind whether they understand.
> But I want to know whether they will come.

There are no conditions attached to these last two statements.

In practice, however, the words tend to be used interchangeably, and there can no longer be any objection to this.

Note that *Let me know if you'll be coming* is different in meaning from *Let me know whether you'll be coming*. In the first case you only have to let your friend know *if* you *are* coming (you don't have to let her know if you are not coming); in the second case your friend wants to know your decision, whatever it is.

See also **if/if not**.

ilk. *The William Charles Wentworth of Governor Macquarie's time was the first of that ilk.* Here *of that ilk* is being used somewhat facetiously to mean *of that family*, and it is in that sense that the term most often crops up. H. W. Fowler argued that this use is wrong, and that the phrase means only *of the same place*, that *John Knocklofty of that ilk* means *John Knocklofty of Knocklofty*. Fowler was both right and wrong. The use of which he disapproves is well established and acceptable.

illicit. See **elicit/illicit**.

ill/sick. *Ill* and *sick* should mean much the same thing: *out of health, unwell, suffering from some disorder or disease*. To be *sea-sick* doesn't necessarily mean that you are vomiting; it means that you don't feel well.

However, in the same way that *lavatory* became *water-closet*, and *water-closet* became *toilet*, because they 'sounded nicer,' so we have come to replace the verb *to vomit* with the verb *to be sick*. This means that the word *sick* now conjures up the image of *vomit*, and so is avoided as much as possible by 'nice' people. It is true that *I am sick* has a different meaning from *I am being sick*, but the phrases are close enough to make many people avoid saying *I am sick*.

All one can say is that people will go on avoiding the word *sick* when they can, but that is no reason we shouldn't use it if we want to.

We still use *sick* in such formations as *sick headache, sick-room, sick-bed, sick-pay,* and apparently have no self-consciousness about this.

If you are *ill* or *sick,* do you become *more ill* or *more sick* or *iller* or *sicker?* If possible you avoid all those comparatives, and simply become *worse*.

illusion. See **delusion**.

imbecile. Pronounce *IM-be-seel*.

imbroglio. As in many Italian words, the *g* is not pronounced, and so (in English) it is pronounced *imbrolyo*, with the *o* sound long. (The Italian pronunciation is slightly different.) The plural is *imbroglios*. The word means *a confused situation*.

immanent/imminent. *Immanent* means *contained within*. When used in a religious sense referring to God, it means *present throughout Creation*. In the non-religious sense it will be found in such a phrase as *the immanent power of words*, which is used in the Introduction to this book. There it is intended to mean *the power of persuasion that words have locked up within themselves, waiting to be set loose by a craftsman or demagogue*.

Imminent, from the Latin word for *overhanging*, means *about to happen soon*, as in *The train's arrival was imminent*.

impact/impacted.
1. *Impact* is a *noun*, as in the sentence *The impact of the blow was considerable*.
2. *Impacted* is an *adjective*, and is familiar in sentences like *He had an impacted wisdom tooth*.
3. However, *impact* is *not* fully accepted as a *verb*. It is questionable to write or to say *The full force of the situation at last impacted upon him* or, as the Melbourne *Sun* printed on its front page on 18 March 1986, *An adjustment this large will impact heavily on Japan's export industries*.
4. The use of *impact* as a verb is now acceptable in the United States and will undoubtedly spread in Australia, where many will continue to regard it as an **offensive intruder**.

See also **noun to verb: is change decay?**

impasse. The pronunciation of *impasse* as a French word (*am-pahs*) is no longer desirable. Pronounce *im-pass*.

imperial weights and measures. Although officially superseded by the metric system of weights and measures, the former, or "imperial" or "British" system, is still in wide informal use, sometimes to the despair of the improvers of society.

Babies are still most frequently referred to as being, shall we say, of *six and a half pounds*, properties are more frequently referred to as of *two acres* or *two thousand acres* than in their hectare equivalent, and policemen find it more productive to describe a wanted person as being *six feet* tall rather than *1828.8 millimetres*.

Since the 'old' measures have been driven out of the schools (it was for a time illegal to import one-foot rulers), and since a great deal of our literature uses these measures, let us put them on record.

implicit

LENGTH

12 inches (in) = 1 foot (ft)
3 feet = 1 yard (yd)
6 feet = 1 fathom (fm)
100 links (lk) = 1 chain (ch)
66 feet = 1 chain
22 yards = 1 chain
10 chains = 1 furlong (fur)
8 furlongs = 1 mile
5280 feet = 1 mile
80 chains = 1 mile
1760 yards = 1 mile

AREA

43,560 square feet (ft^2) = 1 acre (ac)
4840 square yards (yd^2) = 1 acre
10 square chains (ch^2) = 1 acre
640 acres = 1 square mile (mile^2)

WEIGHT

16 ounces (oz) = 1 pound (lb)
14 pounds = 1 stone
28 pounds = 1 quarter (qr)
112 pounds = 1 hundredweight (cwt)
4 quarters = 1 hundredweight
2240 pounds = 1 ton
20 hundredweights = 1 ton

VOLUME

20 fluid ounces (fl oz) = 1 pint (pt)
2 pints = 1 quart (qt)
4 quarts = 1 gallon (gal)
1 bushel (bus) = 8 gallons

See also **fathom; knot; metrication; nautical mile**.

implicit. See **explicit/implicit**.

imply/infer. A tricky couple, often misused. As in the following:

His constant addiction to the bottle inferred that he was a less than reliable surgeon.

What is meant here is *implied*. To *imply* is *to signify, to suggest, to hint*. A correct

204

usage is: *In her speech the Senator implied that she was going to take action on the matter.*

Infer means *to draw a conclusion from: I inferred from the Senator's statement that she was about to take action on the matter.*

Disapproval at the confusion of these words is relatively recent. Both Shakespeare and Jane Austen used *infer* to convey the meaning of *imply*. But this is no longer acceptable.

impracticable/unpractical. See **practicable/practical.**

imprecation/invocation. An *imprecation* is *a curse.* An *invocation* is *the act of calling for a response* — see **evoke/invoke.**

impression. See **edition/impression.**

imprimatur. Strictly speaking, an *imprimatur* is *a licence of some kind allowing something to be printed,* and especially the approval issued by a bishop in the Catholic Church for publication. More loosely, *imprimatur* can mean both a *stamp of approval* (*Her leave plans received my imprimatur*) or a *characteristic mark* (*Every word bore his imprimatur*), though this last use is a dubious one.

Pronounce *im-prim-AH-tur,* and certainly not as a French word, for it is Latin.

in abeyance. "Pending the appearance of the main star," we are told on television, "the audience is waiting in abeyance."

Surely not *in abeyance*? *In suspense,* perhaps, or *in expectation.* But *in abeyance* means that *something has been put aside for the time being.* It's not a phrase which is applied to people in any case, but to issues, sometimes legal issues. To put an audience into abeyance conjures up the image of the whole auditorium bodily transported into cold storage.

in about. Note the distinction between *in about three weeks,* a perfectly proper phrase which means what it says, and *in about 1970,* which is wrong. It is wrong because, in the latter case, whatever it was happened either *in 1970* or *about 1970,* and either the *in* or the *about* is unnecessary.

inarticulate. See **articulate/inarticulate.**

including. Be careful of the word *including* in such a sentence as

> There were all sorts of goodies in the basket, including chocolates, toffees, biscuits and so on.

Including in such a sentence implies that the writer is making a *selection* illustrating the point. To then add *and so on* implies, not selection, but completeness. *And so on* jars against the sense of the word *including* and renders it meaningless.

The sentence should read *either*

> There were all sorts of goodies in the basket: chocolates, toffees, biscuits and so on.

or it should read

> There were all sorts of goodies in the basket, including chocolates, toffees and biscuits.

incredible/incredulous. The scientist Ephraim Fischbach has discovered a fifth fundamental physical force, the *Age* informed us in May 1987. "And day by day Fischbach's incredulous idea is gaining credibility."

The idea was not *incredulous*; it was *incredible*, or so the writer meant.

If something is *incredible* it is *unbelievable: I find it incredible that Australians should allow the Queensland rainforests to be destroyed.* Note that (as in this example) we often use *incredible* when we mean, not so much *beyond belief,* but *beyond rational understanding.*

Incredible is also used informally to mean *Splendid!*

Incredulous means *not prepared or willing to believe,* as in *When told that their house would be destroyed for a freeway they were incredulous* – that is, they could not accept the reality of what was being put to them.

People, in other words, may be *incredulous* of something, and may find something *incredible,* but people are not in themselves *incredible.* You cannot say *I am incredible of that possibility,* though you can say *I find that possibility incredible,* or *I am incredulous of that possibility.*

Things, including people's actions, may be *incredible,* but they can not be *incredulous.*

inculcate originally stems from the Latin word meaning *heel.* To *inculcate* a belief or doctrine or attitude is *to ram it down,* as though you were treading down grapes with your foot.

You cannot inculcate a person *with* something. You *inculcate* something *in* or *into* or *upon* someone else. Not *The soldiers were inculcated with the killing instinct,* but *The killing instinct was inculcated into the soldiers.*

index. The plural is now more commonly *indexes* than *indices. Indexes* is recommended, except for scientific and mathematical use, where the plural remains *indices.*

indicate. *I indicated to the Minister that this may not be the right approach.* The verb *to indicate* is under something of a cloud, especially when used as a pretentious substitute for *pointed out, advised* and for the general action of conveying information from one person to another.

The point to remember is in fact the act of *pointing*. In its raw meaning *to indicate* means to point to something to show where it is: hence the *index* finger. So, in the bush, you may *indicate* the right track to someone who is lost. The verb may be used without criticism where it means *to be, or to give, a sign*: *shivering indicates a fever, aggressive behavior indicates insecurity, the speedometer indicated 100 kilometres an hour, I indicated by hand signal that I was turning. Indicate* may also be used when it means *to state briefly*: *She indicated her feelings in a few words.*

The trouble comes when *indicate* is used as a synonym for *say* and is followed by *that*. There are numerous words which are less self-conscious: *hint, suggest, say, propose, advocate, declare*, to name only a few.

Indicate, usually in the passive voice, also means *recommend* or *require*: *physiotherapy appears to be indicated for this complaint*. The extension of this usage to *a whisky is indicated* or *a few words of thanks are indicated* has been called "parlor slang".

Indicate should never be used to mean *discovered* or *suspected*: *before antibiotics were indicated, tuberculosis was a major threat.*

Indicator words. Australia is a democratic country and, fortunately, there's little attention paid here to what the English call "U and Non-U" usage – that is, to the way the upper classes, so-called, use items of vocabulary as a put-down for the 'rest'. Saying *table-napkin* instead of *serviette*, and that kind of thing.

Indeed Murray Sayle, writing in *Encounter* in May 1960, said of Australia that "hardly another country in the world has a working class so free of inferiority feelings ... so impervious to the subjugating tricks of accent, style and spurious patriotism used by practically every ruling class in the world."

Our philosophy in this book is that people may use what words they wish, and pronounce them the way they wish, provided they do not offend common sense or some useful criterion. Certainly slovenly English is not confined to any particular social class, far from it. At the same time we must recognise that all of us make mental notations, often unconsciously, on words we read and conversations in which we take part. No doubt these notations are usually mere prejudices, with little logic behind them, but prejudices are also part of real life, and an employer could well be put off by a job applicant who pronounces the word *advertisement* as *adver-TISE-ment*, and regard it as reflecting lack of sophistication or an unsatisfactory schooling.

Examples of word use which can arouse comment include:

The pronunciation of the letter H as *haitch* (see **aitch/haitch**).

The use of *lolly* or *lollies* instead of *sweet* or *sweets*. (The word lolly is said to have originated in Melbourne.)

The pronunciation of *anything* as *anythink*, or of *something* as *somethink*.

Ta-ta as a farewell.

The pronunciation of such place-names as *Cheltenham* and *Sandringham* as *CheltenHAM* and *SandringHAM* instead of swallowing the last syllable.

Similarly, the pronunciation of *Saint,* in such names as *Saint Kilda,* as *saint* rather than as an under-emphasised *Sint.*

The use of **book** for what is a *magazine.*

The word **advertisement** when pronounced *ad-ver-TISE-ment.*

Forehead when pronounced as spelt rather than as *forrid.*

Saying *Pleased to meet you* when introduced.

Describing the evening meal as *tea* (see **dinner/lunch/supper/tea**).

Pronouncing the word **clique** as *click.*

Making any other answer to the greeting *How do you do* than a simple repetition of that greeting.

The use of *than what* and *as what* rather than *than* and *as* (see **(the) wandering what**).

The pronunciation of *Tuesday* as *choose-day.*

Using *good night* instead of *good evening* as a greeting (see **good evening/good night**).

individual. People should not be referred to as *individuals* unless you are making a comparison with a *group,* as in *There was one individual in the vast rally who kept on shouting abuse.*

Individual should not be used as a handy synonym for *person.* Do not say, for instance, *There were too many individuals on the beach.*

inestimable. "The press has played an inestimable role in the Murphy affair" (radio broadcast).

The speaker meant that the role of the press in the legal process involving Mr Justice Murphy was so considerable that it could not be measured. Well, one may ask, how would one measure such a role, whether large or small? In fact, if one wanted to be difficult it could be argued that *inestimable* here could just as easily mean *very small* as *very large.*

Inestimable is more usually seen or heard in such phrases as *her inestimable services* or *a diamond of inestimable value,* phrases which we have heard so often that we instantly accept the word as meaning, roughly, *more than we can put our minds to.*

See also **invaluable.**

infectious. See **contagious/infectious.**

infer follows normal rules (see **doubling up**) in making *inferred, inferring,* but is anomalous in making *inferable.*

For its meaning, see **imply/infer.**

inflammable. See **flammable/inflammable**.

inflict. See **afflict/inflict**.

infra. See **referencing**.

infringe. The traditional transitive use of this verb (*She infringed the parking by-laws*) presents no problems, but there are still some who regard its intransitive use (*The fence infringed on my property*) as regrettable.

If you want to be sure, use *encroach* or *trespass* rather than *infringe on*, or *onto*, or *into*.

ingenious/ingenuous. *Ingenious* means *clever, especially in a manipulative way.*

Ingenuous means *naive, innocent to a fault, ignorant in a simple-minded kind of way: It was ingenuous of him not to realise the workers were going to strike over those grievances.*

ingenuous/disingenuous. *Ingenuous* means *naive, artless, innocent to a fault, a bit simple-minded:*

> Anyone who believes the statement "I'm from the government and I'm here to help you" is more than a little ingenuous.

Disingenuous, though, is a bit tricky. It doesn't mean *the opposite of ingenuous*, which would be something like *sophisticated*. Rather it means *pretending to be ingenuous, insincere, putting on a false front of innocence*:

> It was disingenuous of the man to say that he was climbing through the window with a jemmy in his hand in order to get out of the rain.

The word *disingenious*, seen as an error for *disingenuous*, does not exist, though it has been suggested that it would be a valuable addition to the political vocabulary, as a polite way of saying *dim*.

Ingénue means *an artless or inexperienced woman*, especially one portrayed as such on the stage.

inhuman/inhumane. To be *inhuman* is to lack the qualities of a human being. It is a word which applies to persons or actions which are totally repugnant. To be *inhumane*, however, is to be *lacking in compassion in some important respect*. A doctor, or even a hospital, may be *inhumane* in dealings with patients, though one might not go so far as to say the doctor or hospital was *inhuman*.

in place. "There is not yet in place an effective program to promote field collection of folklore." The author means *We do not yet have an effective program*. This is a good example of bureaucratese and of **puffery**.

inquiry. See **enquiry/inquiry**.

in respect of is a phrase much used by Mr R. J. L. Hawke. This phrase, together with *in respect to*, is not wrong so much as clumsy and inelegant, and should be avoided wherever possible. The word *about* can often be used instead, or the sentence restructured.

inside of. See **outside of/inside of.**

insofar/in so far. The Australian tendency is towards one word.

instil. *Instil* or *instill* (both are correct) means *to introduce something gradually*, and must be followed by *into*.

Thus a sentence such as *He instilled the spectators with the meaning of the occasion* is wrong, and should read *He instilled into the spectators the meaning of the occasion.*

On the other hand it would be correct to say that *He imbued* or *He inspired* the spectators.

integral. The pronunciation *in-TEG-ral*, though common in Australia, has support from no dictionary we have consulted. Prefer *INT-e-gral.*

intense(ly)/intensive(ly). *Intensive* and *intensively* are, except in certain specialised usages, inflated ways of saying *intense* and *intensely*.

In such phrases as *intensive application, intensive care, intensive bombardment, intensive thinker* and *intensive excitement, intense* is the better word.

inter alia is a useful Latin phrase meaning *among other things*. The poet Peter Porter has written:

> In Australia,
> *Inter alia,*
> Mediocrities
> Think they're Socrates.

It is usually printed in italics.

Amongst other people is, in Latin, *inter alios*, except where women only are being referred to, when the form is *inter alias.*

interesting. Pronounce *IN-trist-ing* or *IN-ter-ist-ing*. The pronunciation *in-ter-EST-ing* has no support.

interface. E. M. Forster's famous phrase was "Only connect!" Translated into contemporary jargon that would now read *Only interface!*

Interface is properly a noun with some specific scientific and technological meanings: *a boundary between two bodies, a kind of electrical circuit*. Its development as a verb to mean *connect* or *co-operate* is quite recent. In this sense it is often used as a **bully word** to impress and to convey a spurious air of competence.

inter-/intra-. *Inter-* as part of a longer word means *between*, as in *international, interstate.*

Intra- as part of a larger word means *within*. Thus, if the Treasurer of Queensland is arguing with the Treasurer of Australia about getting more money from Canberra, and the Australian Treasurer says "In my view that is an intrastate matter," he (or she) means that it is a matter that Queensland should consider its own problem and settle for itself.

interjections are one of the eight **parts of speech** in traditional grammar. The word means *thrown in* (in Latin) and interjections are words thrown in to a sentence to express an emotion or to attract the attention of the person addressed. Examples of interjections are *Ho, Hurrah, Alas, Hullo, Coo-ee.*

There is not much more to be said about interjections than that, but the following notes may be of interest.

1. The interjection is often said to be distinctive because it stands apart from the rest of a sentence grammatically and does not affect its sense. This is, however, not necessarily the case, as may be seen from such a sentence as *O for a horseshoe nail!* Here the *O* is in effect a shortened form of *O [I wish].*

2. Interjections are single words, some grammarians insist. An exclamation such as *Bless her heart!* is said by these grammarians to be in fact not an interjection but a shortened form of a normal sentence, *[May the Lord] bless her heart!* The argument may be left to the grammarians, though grammar has moved on since the days when this kind of argument was popular.

3. The common interjection *Alas!* is a shortened form of the Old French *Ha las!*, *I am weary.*

4. It is not necessary to use an exclamation mark after all interjections. Indeed, it is positively undesirable to use one after such an inoffensive word as *hullo*, unless there is some reason for giving it special emphasis.

5. Some modern grammarians classify single-word statements such as *Yes* and *Definitely* as *sentence substitutes*, that is as single words making a 'meaningful utterance' despite their isolation. The definition *interjection* is then reserved for ejaculations such as *Ow.*

interment/internment. An *interment* is *a burial*. An *internment* is suffered by those who are *interned*, that is, *placed in confinement for reasons other than offences against the law.* Enemy civilians in wartime are sometimes *interned*, as are combatants who appear in neutral countries.

interpersonal. "Her interpersonal relations with her staff were excellent." Why not just her *relations* or, if you insist, her *personal relations?* Interpersonal is a **poseur word**.

interpretative/interpretive. These adjectives mean the same thing: *providing an explanation. You won't be able to understand that painting until you read Smith's interpretative article.* Of the two words, prefer *interpretative*, as being closer to the normal formation of such words. The stress is on the second syllable. In the United States both forms are acceptable, but in Australia *interpretative* is the desirable form.

interviewee. *Employer*, the one who does something, *employee*, the one to whom it is done. *Legator*, the person who leaves something in a will, *legatee*, the person to whom it is left. The *-ee* ending, then, normally represents the *passive* or *receiving* or *secondary* partner in a transaction, although in such words as *refugee* and *escapee* (why not *escaper?*) the ending refers to an active agent. (In fact the Melbourne *Age* in 1988 adopted *escaper* for *escapee*.)

So far, fine, but there are limits, and the *-ee* ending should not be rapturously attached to any noun that crosses the mind. While it is true that there seems to be a law which says that languages will find ways of shortening bits and pieces of themselves if they can, it is also open to anyone who wishes to object if they don't like it. *Interviewee*, like *retiree* and similar coinages, is a lazy (if convenient) form. It is still an ugly word, not fully accepted, and should be avoided.

in the wake of. "Destruction on a massive scale followed in the wake of World War Two." The speaker here meant that destruction followed *in the wake of the outbreak of World War Two. In the wake of* is an idiom derived from the *wake* a ship leaves behind it, and means *something that follows on.* If the destruction followed *in the wake of World War Two* it would have happened *after* that war was over.

in to/into. These two expressions are sometimes treated as though they were interchangeable, as it may be agreed that **all right** and **alright** are interchangeable. In fact it is not always so.

Into implies motion or direction to a point *within* something:
> He drove his car into the garage.
> She threw the letter into the fire.

In to, however, rather suggests that the motion or direction stops at the point of penetration, or even before it:
> The chair was moved in to the fire (closer to the fire).
> He drove his car in to the city (to the city, but not necessarily into the city streets).

intention/intentions. Frequently misspelt *intension, intensions.*

intravenous. An *intravenous* injection is one that is injected *into a vein,* in contrast to an *intramuscular* injection. Do not pronounce *intravenious.*

intrigue. The use of the verb *to intrigue,* when it means *to arouse the curiosity of,* is sometimes attacked. The argument is that to say *I was intrigued with his facility at poker* or *She found the visit to the exhibition intriguing* is to use a somewhat pretentious word of French origin where standard English words would be better: *I was fascinated by his facility at poker* or *She found the visit to the exhibition interesting.* The verb *intrigue* in this sense is best used sparingly, and to convey the sense of *something to be unravelled*: *Many were intrigued with the bizarre ramifications of the Dreyfus affair.* You may be *intrigued* by the plot of a mystery story or by an unexplained announcement.

in-/un-. The following are the most common problem words forming the negative with *in-* rather than *un-*.

inconsolable	inexcusable	insoluble
indescribable	inexpensive	insupportable
indistinguishable	inexplicable	insurmountable
inedible	infrequent	insusceptible
ineffaceable		

invalid, when it means a person who is ill, may be pronounced *IN-val-eed* or *IN-val-id.* Prefer *IN-val-id.*
   This word, when it means *not valid,* is pronounced *in-VAL-id.*

invaluable. *Invaluable* should, it would seem, mean *not valuable, valueless,* as *insincere* means *without sincerity.* Yet we all know it means *of the highest value.* Why?
   The answer is that *invaluable* does indeed mean *without value.* It means that *something is so precious that there is no point in trying to put a value on it.* It is perhaps an odd way of saying it, but the same paradox also crops up with the word *priceless,* which means that *no price can be placed on this object because it is so valuable that there is nothing it can be compared with.*
   The opposite to *invaluable* and *priceless* is *worthless.*

inveigle. To *inveigle* is *to persuade someone to do something by cleverness or trickery: He inveigled me into signing the document.* It may be pronounced either *inveegle* or *invaygle.*

inverted commas. See **quote/unquote.**

invoke. See **evoke/invoke.**

irascible. To be *irascible* is to be *irritable.* The word is pronounced as though the *c* were not present: *ir-AS-ible.* The pronunciation *ir-AS-kible,* sometimes heard, is incorrect.

ironic/sarcastic/sardonic/satiric.
IRONY

An *ironic* remark produces its effect by saying the opposite of what the remark is meant to convey. The word *irony* originates from a Greek word meaning *deceit,* and the tone is one of amused mockery, directed against oneself or others. *Irony* is a subtle form of comment in its pure form, though it can also be a part of sarcastic, sardonic or satiric remarks.

Irony can be an over-subtle form of humor or comment, exemplified in the story of the judge addressing the jury who said "If you believe that this man was passing this house, badly needed to know the time, took his shoes off and entered the window in order to find a clock without awakening the persons in the house, and then absent-mindedly put these spoons in his pocket before leaving, you will acquit him." The jury, of course, acquitted.

One commentator, referring to a widely publicised dispute in 1986 between the American writers Gore Vidal and Norman Podhoretz, a dispute which in large part turned on whether or not Vidal was using words ironically, has suggested (ironically) that there should be a special typeface invented in which ironic remarks can be printed.

When Henry Lawson's character Mitchell says "If I hadn't wasted all my time and energy working and looking for work I might have been an independent man today," he is speaking ironically.

When Barry Humphries says that the word "Moomba" is "an old Aboriginal word meaning 'Let's get together and have fun,' " and that "They gave us the word because they had no further need for it," he is speaking ironically.

And so was the nineteenth-century Polish visitor Seweryn Korzelinski, when he wrote:

> Such a pleasant life in Australia. One has the choice of being shot by someone who intends to do so, or by someone who has no intention of doing so.

There is also a literary form known as *tragic irony,* where hidden forces and events disclose to the reader or observer the vanity of human hope and achievement. In real life an example of tragic irony is the finding of the bodies of Captain Scott and his comrades after they had been beaten to the South Pole by the Norwegians in 1912. The bodies were found by a relief party including the one Norwegian member of Scott's expedition, who used Scott's skis to complete what would have been Scott's journey back to base.

In literature tragic irony is a staple device, as when Duncan, in *Macbeth*, exclaims of Macbeth's castle that:

> This castle hath a pleasant seat; the air
> Nimbly and sweetly recommends itself
> Unto our gentle senses,

not knowing that he is to be murdered there that night.

Some hold that the word *ironical* should not be used simply to mean *paradoxical* or *perversely amusing*, as in:

> It is ironical that American oil wells off the coast of Angola are guarded by Cuban troops.

This usage is, however, well established.

SARCASM

A *sarcastic* remark is one of ridicule, often meant to be cruel. Sarcasm was a prime weapon, together with the cane, of the (old-fashioned?) schoolmaster. It comes from words meaning *to bite one's lips* in rage and resentment. A simple example would be to say to the person last in a race "The great victor!"

When Arthur Calwell said to Arthur Fadden (who at one time had been Prime Minister for a few weeks) "I well recall the time when, for forty days and forty nights, you held the destiny of Australia in the hollow of your head," he was being sarcastic.

And so was the poet Bruce Dawe when he wrote of a politician who was being awarded an honorary degree, "Was ever man so naked though well-dressed?"

SATIRE

Satire has, as its prime purpose, not to comment or wound so much as to *reform*. It seeks to mock, or invert, or exaggerate with the intention that, by so doing, idiocies may be corrected. Some of the greatest literature has been satirical in intent, one outstanding example being Jonathan Swift's *Gulliver's Travels*.

Satire, indeed, was very much an eighteenth-century literary form. One notable exponent was Alexander Pope, and it is no coincidence that one of Pope's admirers, the Australian poet Alec Hope, has been one of our most successful satirists. He has, perhaps, one eye on academic life when he writes:

> The City of God is built like other cities:
> Judas negotiates the loans you float;
> You will meet Caiaphas upon committees;
> You will be glad of Pilate's casting vote.

When the singer Margret Roadknight coined the slogan "Land rights for gay whales" she was satirising the trendy political enthusiasms of various community pressure groups.

And when Ned Kelly wrote that "it is not the place of the Police to convict guilty men as it is by them they get their living" he was being satiric as well as expressing a deeply held personal conviction.

215

THE SARDONIC

This word is related to *Sardinia*, the Italian island, where there was said to grow a plant which produced facial grimaces resembling horrible laughter. *Sardonic* remarks are pessimistic, often directed against oneself, seeking relief from a problem.

Much Australian humor is said to be sardonic, an attempt to make the best of things by joking about them.

Perhaps the most famous joke of the grim Depression years of the 1930s was the one about the policeman who grabbed an unemployed man with six hungry children just as he was about to jump over the Gap at Sydney Heads. "Let's have a talk about things," the policeman said. Well, they did; and then they both went over the Gap together.

A clever, sardonic remark was once made by the cricketer Arthur Mailey. A friend commiserated with him on his inability to take wickets in an important match. "You can't get any wickets if the catches are not taken," Mailey remarked. The friend said that he had not seen any catches dropped. Mailey replied: "There's a chap in the Outer dropped Ryder twice already off me."

And then there is Henry Lawson's remark: "A man doesn't shoot himself when he's going to be made a lawful father for the first time, unless he can see a long way into the future."

Irony, sarcasm, satire and the sardonic are often confused and, as we have said, the boundaries between them overlap. It is not difficult, however, to grasp the essential differences.

irredeemable/irremediable. Two words sometimes confused. *Irredeemable* means *not able to be reformed or regained*. *Irremediable* means *not able to be remedied*. The meanings are obviously close, and sometimes overlap, but *irredeemable* tends to apply to patterns of human behavior or human actions, while *irremediable* tends to apply to concrete situations. Compare *He is so far gone in iniquity that he appears irredeemable* and *The railway system is so run down that it is irremediable*. Paul Theroux writes of someone as *irredeemably Teutonic*.

irregardless/regardless. *Regardless* is an adjective, as in *She was regardless of the peril of the step*. Here it means *heedless, uncaring*. *Regardless* is also an adverb meaning *in spite of everything*. *She carried on regardless*. Despite a widespread impression to the contrary, especially among the young in Australia, there is no word *irregardless*.

-ise/-ize. Many verbs, such as *authorise* and *agonise*, can also be spelt *authorize* and *agonize*. So what are the rules?

The simplest way around the problem is to spell them all with the *-ise* ending. This will not be incorrect, though it will be frowned on by some. It is the solution adopted by the French, by most printers and by newspapers. It is opposed by the Americans, the *Oxford English Dictionary*, the scholarly presses and the London *Times*. The reason it is opposed is that the majority of such verbs come from Greek and Latin roots which contain the *z*, and that *-ize* is closer to the correct pronunciation. The Americans, in fact, are in a fair way to standardising on *-ize*. It seems a great pity that we cannot all agree to accept either an *-ise* or an *-ize* ending.

We recommend, however, the *-ise* ending as the simple solution. Among other reasons, there are far more words which *must* take *-ise* only (see below) than there are words which *must* take *-ize* only. (The most common such verbs are *capsize, prize, seize* and *size*.) The *-ise* ending is the tendency, some excellent authorities support it and, if you are willing to accept it, read no further.

If you wish to use *-ize* when it is traditionally proper, note the following:
1. The *-ize* ending will not be used where there is a noun in existence which is the same as the verb you wish to use, for instance *exercise, disguise, surprise*.
2. The *-ize* ending does not apply to verbs which cannot be traced back to the Greek. The following *must* take *-ise:*

advertise	disguise	premise
advise	enfranchise	prise
apprise	enterprise	promise
arise	excise	raise
chastise	exercise	revise
circumcise	improvise	rise
comprise	incise	supervise
demise	merchandise	surmise
despise	poise	surprise
devise	praise	televise
disfranchise		

3. The *-ize* ending may only be used where the main part of the word is recognisable by itself and where the *-ize* ending adds the meaning of *act in that way:* thus *familiarize, dogmatize*. Exceptions include *aggrandize, appetize, baptize, recognize* and *capsize*, where the main part of the word (or *stem*) is not immediately recognisable (or recognizable).

Note that whether *-ise* or *-ize* is used it is important to be consistent. If you start with *recognize*, stay with the *z* through *recognizable*, and so on. More than this: if you decide to use *-ize* throughout (except for those words that may *not* take it), use *-ize* for *all* such words, not just for some.

See also **-lyse/-lyze; spelling reform in Australia.**

217

Italian. Although *Iti*, pronounced *eye-tye*, is an affectionate Australian nick-name for an Italian, to pronounce the word *Italian* as *eye-talian* is ignorant and offensive. We do not pronounce *Italy* as *eye-tally*.

italics. Italic letters are used in writing in two ways: for *emphasis*, and for *formal distinctions*. Italic letters cannot be rendered in handwriting or most forms of typing, and the convention here is to indicate italics by underlining the word or words affected.

EMPHASIS

Queen Victoria was famous for her determined heavy underlinings in her letters, attempting to force her personality through the words she used on paper. Translated into print, these underlinings became italics, and here is an example of Queen Victoria's:

> I *never*, NEVER spent such an evening!! My *dearest* DEAREST DEAR Albert sat on a footstool by my side ... How can I ever ever be thankful enough to have such a *Husband!*

This kind of enthusiasm with italics and emphases is now regarded as a confession of failure to get a message across by the proper use of words. Effective writers organise their words so that the emphasis falls where it is wanted.

There are, of course, many occasions on which the use of italics to emphasise a word is necessary and desirable:

> I asked you to search *above* the door, not beneath it.

FORMAL USE

Italics are used for *the titles of published books* (but not for manuscripts, even manuscripts of book length). They are also usually employed for the names of magazines and newspapers and of ships. They are used where *foreign words and phrases* are incorporated into a text. Queen Victoria again:

> They, of course, like an *entente cordiale* with us at the expense of Austria.

Italics should not be used for the names of houses and institutions (which do not normally need quotation marks) nor for the titles of chapters of books or unpublished manuscripts (use quotation marks instead).

Do not place a phrase already in italics, such as the title of a book, into quotation marks as well.

If a word or phrase which would normally appear in italics appears within a passage already in italics, it should be set in roman type.

A fierce controversy rages among copy editors as to whether (for instance) one should print

> the *Queen Mary's* crew

or

> the *Queen Mary*'s crew.

The argument on the part of the sticklers for correctness is that properly only *Queen Mary* should be italicised, and that therefore the '*s* should be in roman rather than italic type. This bitter dispute can only be compared to the war described by Jonathan Swift between those who believed that boiled eggs should be opened at the blunt end and those who believed they should be opened at the sharp end. To rule on this risks life-long friendships, but it would seem reasonable to recommend that for most normal purposes convenience suggests that the form be *Queen Mary's*. It is not the only typographical area where we have to make concessions to common sense (see **quote/unquote**, section 5). Those engaged in scholarly and fine printing may continue to use the more 'correct' form.

See also **titles.**

iterate/reiterate. "Ms Johnson iterates that the play is not simply about reconciliation."

There is internal evidence here that the writer thinks that, because *reiterates* means *saying something again*, *iterates* must mean *saying something*.

In fact both *iterate* and *reiterate* mean the same thing — *to say something again* — and we could well dispense with one or the other in the English language. *Reiterate* is so well established that *iterate* is the better candidate for retirement.

To use *iterates* as a synonym for *says*, as above, is not only wrong but a nasty piece of pretension in the use of words.

it is I/it is me? Similarly, *It is he* or *it is him, It is she* or *it is her, It is we* or *it is us, It is they* or *it is them?*

Since the verb *to be* is followed by the subjective (nominative) case, the *correct* answer is *I, he, she, we, they.*

In writing, and especially with careful writing striving for correctitude, these forms should be used.

In normal speech and in informal writing *It is me* (*him, her etc.*) will be used more frequently than *It is I* (*he, she etc.*). This is to be expected and it is no longer considered incorrect or a solecism.

See **case.**

its/it's. One of the most common of confusions, and one of the most easily avoided.

Where the word is a shortened form of *it is* it takes the apostrophe, thus: *it's.* Otherwise it must be written as *its.*

J

jackaroo/jackeroo. Prefer the spelling *jackeroo*. The word is said to have been coined from the man's name plus -*aroo* from *kangaroo*, but the traditional spelling has long been *jackeroo*.

A *jackeroo* is an apprentice hand on a country property, often a son of the employing class who is learning his trade. The newer word *jilleroo*, a female jackeroo, is presumably now regarded as sexist, and to be abandoned.

The Holden car is spelt *Jackaroo*.

jargon. Jargon is different from **slang**. Slang is language experimentation on a large scale. Slang, to be understood and accepted at all, has to be widely used. Jargon is the slang of a small group, usually an occupational one. It is the code-language of the initiated. When an astronomer talks about a *black hole*, or a horse-doctor about the *strangles,* they are using quick-reference words which their colleagues at least will understand. It can be very useful, even essential.

In the law, for instance, the aim of professional jargon is clarity and exactitude. Words such as *covenant, tort, fee simple*, even *trespass* and *eaves-dropping*, have special legal meanings which have to be learnt, and without which legal communication is impossible. Phrases such as *hash function* (computers), *biotic potential* (biology) and *positive feedback* (electronics, moving into general use) are all *communication worthy*, if we may ourselves invent a piece of jargon. "Technical language," wrote Kenneth Hudson in his *The Jargon of the Professions* (1978), "is not, in itself, jargon, and it is not a criminal or moral offence to write or speak in a way which is not immediately understood by the man in the street."

However, by its nature there is an air of mystique about jargon. It excludes people. It is one of the ways in which words can be used to dominate and control, and we therefore often find jargon taken from its proper, professional setting to be used for put-down purposes or, at the very least, to create an impression of spurious professionalism. After giving a list of names to an administrator at the University of Melbourne recently, I was asked "And do you have the contact points?" It turned out that I was being asked for the addresses. An American general once said: "We were not micromanaging Grenada intelligencewise until about that timeframe." A politician in Tasmania refers to *visual impact management* (in other words, doing something about ugliness), and some Tasmanian road signs warn of *vertical curves*, in other words dips and humps in the road. The Pentagon calls tents *frame-supported tension structures*.

Among many examples given by Kenneth Hudson in the book named above is *the amount of wilderness recreation consumed;* he believes it would be difficult to think of any piece of jargon "more dreadful" than this. In his splendid book *Psychobabble* (1975) R. D. Rosen analyses the jargon of fringe psychiatry: the danger is not so much in the absurd words and phrases as in the whole mechanism of manipulation by language. But words are of course part of this: *primal therapy, engrams, the Count of Complete Consciousness, co-counselling* and all the rest of them. Nearer home, none of us are far away from *housing stock* (buildings), *clarification of goals, needs identification, significa-tion, foregrounding* and the like. The arts are a fruitful source of pretentious verbalising: *the* mise en scene *posits another horrible circularity* was recently heard. So too, on an ABC news commentary, was *defence aerospace technology*, meaning *building warplanes*. Note also *not time-specific* (anytime), *time slip-page* (delay) and *position statement* (description).

There is a useful discussion of jargon in chapter three of Philip Howard's *The State of the Language* (1984).

See also **academic English; artspeak; bully words; bureauspeak; Hawke-speak; technobabble.**

jejune strictly speaking means (or used to mean) *scanty, lacking nourishment, barren*. It comes from a Latin word meaning *hungry*, or *empty*. The word has come to be used, however, mainly to refer to someone's *half-baked, puerile or over-simple ideas*, as in *His arguments and, indeed, his whole approach, were jejune*.

The word is pronounced *j'-JOON*.

jerrican/jerry can. A *jerrican* or *jerry can* is the familiar pressed-steel petrol container, holding twenty litres and ingeniously designed to be carried by two persons or one.

For some extraordinary reason all the dictionaries we have consulted give the supposed origin of this name as *jeroboam*, a name for a large bottle.

The slightest acquaintance with worldly affairs on the part of dictionary-makers would have suggested the real origin of the name. In North Africa, during the second world war, General Auchinleck is said to have complained that one-third of his supplies were lost owing to the poor design of the standard army petrol container. Thus the German army container was copied by the allied forces. In 1942 a plant was set up by the British at a cost of more than 1.5 million pounds to manufacture an article which was named after its originators, the Germans or "Jerries", thus adding a new word to the English language.

Jervis Bay is a considerable embayment on the south coast of New South Wales. It is not commonly realised that the township of Jervis Bay, with seventy-three square kilometres of land around it, is Commonwealth territory. The Seat of Government Act of 1908 required access to the sea from the Australian Capital Territory, and this was provided in the Seat of Government Acceptance Act of

1909, which created a separate and legally distinct Jervis Bay Territory, which is not part of the Australian Capital Territory. ACT laws apply, however, in the Jervis Bay Territory insofar as they are applicable, and in practice this Territory is administered as though it were part of the ACT.

The preferred pronunciation of Jervis Bay is *Jarvis Bay*. The Australian Broadcasting Corporation has recently adopted the pronunciation *Jurvis Bay*, but we do not agree and neither would the Earl of St Vincent, after whom it was named.

The ABC likes to adopt a pronunciation based on what it believes to be local usage. Even if this were so in this case, we do not accept the principle. The way locals pronounce their place names is always of interest and, in the case of small places, may be accepted as standard. In the case of larger places other factors intrude. These include the pronunciation of the name in the wider Australian community, and in that wider community *Jarvis Bay* is a common and accepted pronunciation, and has the additional advantage of being historically correct.

jetsam. See **flotsam, jetsam and ligan**.

jewellery. Pronounce this word as *jewel-ry*, not as *joo-ler-y*.

Jew/Jewess. The word *Jewess* is no longer in approved use. If it is necessary to distinguish between male and female, use *Jewish woman*. The tendency to avoid the word *Jews* and speak instead of *Jewish persons* should be opposed, especially within the Jewish community.

There is no *Jewish* language. The ritual language of the religion of the Jews is *Hebrew*, and this is also the language of modern Israel — in the latter case a remarkable instance of the revival of a 'dead' language. Many Jews, especially those of central European and eastern European origins, speak *Yiddish*, a language which once had many affinities to medieval German, which contains many Hebrew words, and which is written with Hebrew characters.

To speak of a Jew as a *Hebrew* is undesirable.

jibe. See **gibe/gybe/jibe**.

Jospeak. Sir Johannes Bjelke-Petersen, long-serving Premier of Queensland, was notable for his tangled syntax, which may be compared with **Hawkespeak**. Here is an example, from the Melbourne *Sun* of 17 June 1987 (Sir Johannes is denouncing the Labor Party slogan "Let's Stick Together"):

> Who wants to stick together with them and get your stick feet, you know, if you get, stick foot on sticky paper, you get both of them on, you fall over and Mr Hawke asks us to stick with him. You put your foot on sticky paper with him, he's, and Keating, his government's got their feet on sticky paper, my word they have.

judgement/judgment. Either spelling is correct. Although the *Macquarie Dictionary* prefers *judgment*, and *judgment* is common newspaper style in Australia, we prefer *judgement* (a) because it has a closer resemblance to the root word *judge*, (b) because it adheres to the general rule that the *e* is kept before a suffix beginning with a consonant, and (c) it is favored by most standard works.

See **(the) silent 'e'**.

judicial/judicious. Something that is *judicial* relates to matters of the law. Something that is *judicious* need have nothing to do with the law. The word is used to describe an action that is *well-balanced, thoughtful, wise*.

junta. A *junta* as commonly used means *a body of self-appointed leaders*, and is normally used to describe authoritarian governments, especially in Latin America, where instead of one dictator there is a small group of dictators working together to rule a country.

This is a Spanish and Portuguese word and unfortunately smart commentators and trendies have recently cottoned on to this fact and have taken to pronouncing the word *HOONta*. The English word is *junta*, to rhyme with *punter*.

just. The pronunciation of this word as *jest* or *jist*, though common, is to be avoided.

just growed like Topsy. This phrase, especially familiar in the United States of America, but also heard in Australia, refers to the famous statement by Topsy in Harriet Beecher Stowe's *Uncle Tom's Cabin*: "I 'spect I growed. Don' think nobody never made me."

K

karri/kauri. Two trees often confused. The *karri* is the giant eucalyptus of Western Australia (*E. diversifolia*). The *kauri* is a pine of the *Agathis* family, found in Queensland and in New Zealand.

kerb. See **curb/kerb.**

keyboarding, keystrokes, keystroking. The replacement of typewriters by word processors and computers has called for new words. This is understandable. A typewriter produces a permanent imprint of type at a certain position on a piece of paper. A word processor or computer produces an electronic type-image which may be displaced or replaced by a flick of the finger. *Typing*, then, has in computerese become *keyboarding*, hardly an elegant word, but an appropriate one. The alternative to keyboarding, *keystroking*, will probably not last, but *key-strokes* is an obvious replacement for *typing strokes*.

kilometre. *Kilometre* should be pronounced *KIL-o-meter*, not *kil-OM-eter*. This is for at least two reasons. The first is that it is made up of two separate words, the *kilo* part meaning *a thousand*. The second is that *millimetre, centimetre* and so on are pronounced *milli-metre, centi-metre* and not *millim-etre, centim-etre*, and *kilometre* should follow suit.

If a further argument be required, then we may note that *units of measurement*, not only *millimetre* and *centimetre* but *kilogram, kilotonne, kilohertz, kilowatt* and so on are all stressed on the first syllable, while the *measuring devices* (*odometer, speedometer, tachometer* etc.) are stressed on the second. An exception here was *altimeter*, but even that is now being pronounced *alt-IM-eter*.

The abbreviation for *kilometres an hour* is *km/h*.

In Australia *kilometres* are referred to informally as *k's. K* is also becoming a common expression, especially in business circles, for *thousands of dollars*.

kind. The use of *kind* as a noun involves several not-so-obvious problems.
1. *Kind* is singular, therefore *those kind of oranges* or *these kind of oranges* is incorrect. One should say *this kind of orange* or *these kinds of orange*. Still, as Fowler points out, Shakespeare says *these kind of knaves*, and the 'incorrect' form may scrape by as an idiomatic usage.
2. *She was kind of in love*. Again, grammatically indefensible, but love laughs at grammarians and the idiom will stay. Not, of course, to be used in formal written English.

3. *He's a queer kind of a fellow. I'm a kind of a rebel.* Since a *kind* is a *class*, and *a* stands for *one*, can you have *a queer class of one fellow*? Of course not. So the *a* has to drop out, in correct English, and one should say and write *a queer kind of fellow.*

See also **collective nouns.**

kindergarten is the word, not *kindergarden. Kindergarten* is the German for *children's garden.* Its replacement in Australia by the word *pre-school* is ugly and unfortunate. It is not due to chauvinism and the desire to remove foreign words from our language, but to social climbing on the part of those who teach in kindergartens, which seemed too simple and unimpressive a word to be associated with 'professional teachers'. The change in name from the Melbourne *Kindergarten Training College* to the *Institute of Early Childhood Development* is a splendid example of academic inflation and pomposity.

King Canute was not so daffy as to try to stop the tide advancing on the royal toes at Bosham. He was a wise ruler and he put on the act to demonstrate to his courtiers, who had been flattering him about his limitless power, that he was but a mortal and subject to the rules of Nature and of God. The poor man has been subject to a great deal of derision, when he should have been praised.

So, if we use the story metaphorically, it should be used correctly.

King Charles's head. "This is his King Charles's head" means that *This is his little obsession.* We all recognise our friends' King Charles's heads, but are not so quick to identify our own. Mr Dick, the amiable eccentric in Dicken's *David Copperfield,* was trying to write a historical work which "never made the least progress, however hard he laboured, for King Charles the First always strayed into it, sooner or later, and then it was thrown aside, and another one begun."

kiwi fruit is a marketing name, invented by the ingenious New Zealanders, for the fruit which the more conservative of us will wish to continue to call the *Chinese gooseberry.*

kneeled/knelt. Prefer *knelt.*

knot. The *knot* is the measure of speed or velocity used at sea and in the air, and also for the description of wind speeds. Although it is not a metric measurement, as a term that is standard internationally it will remain in approved and legal use in Australia.

One *knot* is a speed of one nautical mile (1852 m or 6076.1 feet) an hour. Note that the speed is always in *knots*, and never in *knots per hour.* The term comes from the old method of measuring a ship's speed by the time it took for a certain number of knots in a rope to run out over the ship's stern.

See also **metrication; nautical mile.**

knowledge. For pronunciation, see **fortune.**

koala. The existence of an Aboriginal word, *koolah*, for the koala was noted as early as 1813, and by 1849 the naturalist John Gould was referring to the animal as the *koala*. For all that, the common word for the koala for most of Austalia's post-1788 history has been *native bear*, a usage that only began to die out between the two world wars, as did *laughing jackass* for *kookaburra*.

Koolah or *koala* is said to mean *a big animal.* The term *koala bear* should be avoided, if only because the koala is not a bear.

Koori/Koories. The way many Australian Aboriginals now prefer to refer to themselves. James Miller, in his book *Koori* (Sydney, 1985), writes:

> The term Aboriginal is a Latin-derived English word which was originally used to refer to any native people of any part of the world. The term Aboriginal did not give my people a separate identity. Furthermore, Aboriginal has always had derogatory connotations... The word Koori, however, is a generic term that was used by my ancestors and other peoples of the central coast of New South Wales to identify themselves.

And Miller explains that, although there are many other words in other Aboriginal languages that mean the same, it was the tribes of the central east coast that first felt the full impact of white settlement, and the word may be used as a mark of respect for their memories.

See also **Murri; Nunga.**

Kosciusko/Kosciuszko. Australia's highest mountain, some would say hardly more than a glorified hill, is Mount *Kosciusko*. It was named after the Polish patriot Tadeusz *Kosciuszko* (1746–1817) by Paul Edmund de Strzelecki. The mountain reminded Strzelecki of the mound over Kosciuszko's tomb in Cracow, Poland, so that "although in a foreign country, on foreign ground, but amongst a free people, who appreciate freedom and its votaries, I could not refrain from giving it the name of Mount Kosciusko."

The Australian Broadcasting Corporation's approved pronunciation for the name of the mountain is *koz-ee-OS-ko.*

Kriol, or *Aboriginal English.* See **Pidgin.**

kudos is a word from ancient Greek which we use to mean *fame, acclaim, recognition, prestige.* It may be pronounced *koo-dos* or *kew-dos.*

L

labor. *Labor* must be spelt that way, and not *Labour*, in the title of the *Australian Labor Party*. It is that party's official spelling. See **-or/-our**.

labor/Labor Party/labor movement. See **political terminology in Australia**.

lady/woman. *Lady* is an overdone word, particularly unfortunate in such unctuous phrases as *your good lady*. A woman is a woman, and presumably is as happy to be one as a man is to be a man. Unless there is a good reason for refer-ring to a *woman* as a *lady*, the word *woman* should be preferred.

Of course there are circumstances where *lady* is more appropriate than *woman:* in the phrase *Ladies and gentlemen!* for example. Where *gentleman* seems necessary or appropriate, then obviously *lady* will have to accompany it. These will usually be formal situations. Otherwise, let us try to stick with *women's tickets*, *women's lavatories* and *women's hairdressing*. The desire to prettify language being what it is, we are not likely to succeed. But that is no reason not to try.

Many will feel that in such usages as *She was a very fine woman* the impact is cheapened and weakened by the substitution of the word *lady*. We are told in Proverbs xxxi. 10 that the price of "a virtuous woman" is far above rubies. The price of a virtuous *lady* can be measured in paste.

Larc. A *Larc* is *an amphibious vehicle* (*that is, both a boat and a truck*) *used by the Australian army, in flood relief, in Australian Antarctica and elsewhere.* The word is an **acronym** for *lighter amphibious resupply cargo.* It is sometimes spelt with a small initial *l.* The word, though common enough, does not appear in any dictionary we have consulted.

lascivious. This word means *inclining to lust, naughty in the sexual sense.* Clive James is under the impression that it is pronounced *las-KIV-ious.* The rest of us will do well to stick with *las-SIV-ious.*

laser is an **acronym** standing for *light amplification by stimulated emission of radiation.*

last but not least. Avoid this tedious and overworked phrase.

last/latest. "Yes, I read that item in the last issue of the *Sydney Morning Herald.*"

the late

If the *Sydney Morning Herald* has indeed closed down, and you read about the matter in the *last* issue that ever appeared, then the word is correct.

If, however, you simply read it in Saturday's *Sydney Morning Herald*, and if there is every reason to suppose that there will be another issue of the newspaper on Monday, you did *not* read the item in the *last* issue of the paper, but in the *latest*.

See also **copy/issue**.

the late. The use of *the late* in such phrases as *the late Amelia Goodenough, my late husband,* is to be avoided. The only excuse for the use of this ugly and overworked form is when it is necessary to make it clear that someone is dead. Even so, it should be avoided if possible, and another way of saying the same thing preferred.

Nor should the phrase be used to mean *the former,* as in *the late Prime Minister, Mr Gorton.*

Latin America. See **America/United States**.

latitude. Note that, contrary to the logic of the map, latitudes get *higher* as one moves from the equator towards the South Pole, not lower. The highest latitude one can reach is that of the South Pole itself, 90° South.

La Trobe, Charles Joseph. C. J. La Trobe (1801–1875) was Superintendent of the Port Phillip District of the colony of New South Wales from 1839 to 1851, and Lieutenant-Governor of the colony of Victoria from 1851 until 1854.

Until recently the name has been spelt *Latrobe;* the street in Melbourne, the river in Victoria and the town in Tasmania are still spelt that way. La Trobe, however, spelt his own name *La Trobe*, and the La Trobe Library in Melbourne (properly the La Trobe Collection, State Library of Victoria) and La Trobe University have adopted that form.

lavatory. See **(the) smallest room**.

lawyer. Any qualified member of the legal profession is a *lawyer*. This includes judges, and university teachers so qualified, but the word applies mainly to *barristers* (advocates who plead a case in court) and *solicitors* (who run a legal office and handle the legal affairs of the public).

lay/lie. Some traps here for young players.
1. *To lie*, meaning *to repose.*
    I *lie* down.
    I *lay* down [past tense].
    I had *lain* down.

2. *To lie,* meaning *to utter an untruth.*
    I *lie* occasionally.
    I *lied* to him.
    He has *lied* to me.
3. *To lay,* with such meanings as:
    I *lay* him to rest.
    I *lay* a course for the harbor.
    I *lay* the ghost.
    I *lay* my hand on yours.
    I *lay* him under an obligation.
    I *lay* a charge against him.
    I *lay* the table.
    I cannot *lay* an egg.
In these cases *I lay* becomes *I laid* and *I have laid.*

leaders. For *leaders* in the sense of the punctuation mark (. . .), see **dots.**

leading question. "Now that's a leading question!" This is a phrase we often hear.

In television discussions and the like, what people usually mean when they say this is that it is an *important* question, a *central* question, a question that bears *immediately* on the matter being discussed.

In fact they are quite wrong.

A *leading question* is a question which tries to put into the mouth of the person being questioned the answer that the person asking the question wants.

"It was this man in the dock that you saw climbing out of the window, wasn't it?" is a leading question. It would be disallowed in a court of law because it is trying to influence the answer. Counsel should rather say: "Can you identify the man you saw climbing out of the window?" and, if the answer is "Yes", may then ask: "Who was he?".

lead on, Macduff. Actually this should be *Lay on, Macduff:* from *Macbeth,* act v, scene vii.

leaned/leant. Both are permissible, but prefer *leaned.*

leaped/leapt. Prefer *leapt.* Either may be pronounced to rhyme either with *steeped* or *stepped.*

learned/learnt. Either, but prefer *learnt,* partly because things are going that way in any case, and partly because the adjective *learned* (pronounce as *learn-ed*) exists, and there is no harm in distinguishing between the two words.

lectern/podium. A speaker *reads from* a lectern and *stands* on a podium, which is a raised platform.

lend/loan. In correct, traditional English *loan* is a noun (*I obtained a loan from my bank manager*) and *lend* is a verb (*Will you lend me the spanner?*)

In colloquial use, however, this is often reversed: *Will you loan me that book? Can I have a lend of the hammer?*

The use of *lend* as a noun has little support among those who choose to comment on language use, but the creation of a new verb from the noun *loan*, the verb *to loan*, does have some acceptance.

The use of *loan* as a verb can be traced back some five hundred years, and it survived as such in the United States, although not in England. In Australia the phrase *She loaned me the book* is probably at least as common as *She lent me the book*. So the use of *loan* as a verb has considerable support.

Nevertheless, those seeking for a traditional correctness in their speaking or writing will avoid it.

lesbian. The common word for a homosexual woman. Sappho, a Greek lyric poet who was a woman, lived on the island of Lesbos in the Aegean Sea about the middle of the seventh century B.C. She was apparently married with a daughter, and in legend committed suicide over a man's rejection of her love, so it is something of a mystery why she inspired the word *lesbian* (and the words *Sapphic* and *Sapphism*) in their homosexual meaning. She did, however, form a group of women around her for literary or religious observances. An old student song regrets the innocent days when "Lesbos was an island off the Smyrna coast."

See also **dyke; homosexual.**

less. See **fewer/less.**

let. "Let he who wishes follow me;" "Let he who is without sin cast the first stone." Such constructions are wrong.

Let is a verb, and is followed by an object, which must be in the objective (or accusative) case. The objective case of *he* is *him*. Thus, for *he* in the above sentences read *him*.

letter writing. See **yours faithfully/yours sincerely.**

liaise. "The Melbourne City Council liaised with the Victorian Government on planning problems."

Two comments. One is that the verb *to liaise*, which has been used above, is an illegitimate verb which has been formed by what is called 'back-formation' from the perfectly proper noun *liaison*. It is still not fully accepted and should be avoided. There are plenty of alternatives: *consulted the Victorian government*, for instance.

The second comment is that *liaise* is something of a **bully word**. As we have said, it relates to the word *liaison*, which is primarily a military word (except when referring to an 'improper' association between the sexes). To use either is to suggest to the audience a superior connection or competence, even if in rather a subtle way.

liaison. Australian politicians have a great deal of trouble with this word. One pronunciation heard in parliament is *lie-as-on*. The word is properly pronounced *lee-AY-son*, with the *AY* as in the word *pay*.

liberal education. Broadly speaking, this term means *an education in the humanities as distinct from the sciences and the technologies*. This used to be viewed, as the word *liberal* implies, as the only form of education suitable for a *free man*, or gentleman. The acceptance of this view among the governing classes in Britain, and to a lesser extent in Australia, is one of the reasons for the present economic difficulties of those countries.

In the middle ages the accepted 'liberal' studies were Grammar, Dialectic, Rhetoric, Music, Arithmetic, Geometry and Astronomy. In Britain in the nineteenth century a 'liberal education' came to mean almost exclusively the study of Greek and Latin and the classical authors.

A new meaning to the term was imparted by Cardinal John Henry Newman in his writings on the idea of the educated person, published around the middle of last century. Newman defined a liberal education as "the process of training by which the intellect, instead of being formed or sacrificed to some particular or accidental purpose, some specific trade or profession, or study or science, is disciplined for its own sake, for the perception of its own proper object, and for its own highest culture."

Newman's vision of a true liberal education is one to which lip-service is readily paid today, but which is overlooked when educational administrators actually move into action.

liberal/Liberal Party. See **political terminology in Australia**.

licence/license. The word *licence* is a noun, meaning *a permit, freedom of action* etc. It can not be used as a verb.

The word *license* is a verb, meaning *to allow something to be done, to issue a permit*, etc. From it come *licenser* and *licensee*.

The spelling of *licence* and *license* is often confused. The following is correct:
> The postmaster is *licensed* to issue *licences* to fish.

The Americans use the spelling *license* for both noun and verb. This is not acceptable in Australia.

The use of the *-ice* ending for the noun, and the *-ise* ending for the verb, is common in English, as witness *device/devise, practice/practise, advice/advise* and (also with the *c/s* switch) *prophecy/prophesy*.

lichen. A *lichen* is an unusual form of plant life, a symbiotic association of an alga and a fungus. It may be pronounced in the same way as the word *liken*, or it may be pronounced *litshen*.

lieutenant. In the Royal Australian Navy the word is pronounced *l'TEN-ant*. In the Army and Air Force it is pronounced *lef-TEN-ant*.

A naval lieutenant is equivalent in rank to an Army captain and an Air Force flight lieutenant. See **ranks in the armed forces**.

life-style. The life-styles of many have been diminished by the invention of the word *life-style*. This is an attempt to give a pretentious significance and authority to the phrase *way of life*. If words can become pests, this word has become one. Fortunately it has got to the point where people using the word *life-style*, except in a satirical way, are starting to be laughed at.

ligan. See **flotsam, jetsam and ligan**.

like.
1. *Like* is a preposition, which means that it can only introduce a noun (or noun equivalent), not a clause. So:

>She can sing *like* an angel

but

>She wished she could sing *as* the angels can.

As is a conjunction, and should be used when a new clause is being linked to a preceding one.

Therefore one should not say *Like the Duke of Wellington said, they frighten me more than the enemy*, because *Like the Duke of Wellington said* is a clause (that is, it has a verb). The correct opening is *As the Duke of Wellington said...* Of course it would have been correct to say *When I say they frighten me more than the enemy, I speak like the Duke of Wellington*.

Note that there are plenty of idioms in which *like*, though formally wrong, nevertheless sounds far better than *as* or *as if*.

>They went through the work like a knife [going] through butter.
>It looks like rain [is coming].
>You always drive too fast, like George [does].

2. Note the difference in meaning between such statements as *She sang like an angel* and *She sang as an angel* (in the first case she sang beautifully, but in the

second case she was dressed as an angel). Or between *She spoke as a politician* and *She spoke like a politician* (in the first case she was a politician, in the second she only sounded like one).

3. Since *like* is a preposition, it is followed by the accusative or objective case: *like me*, not *like I, like her*, not *like she*.

See also **unlike**.

like as if. *She walks like as if she is in a hurry.* You often hear this kind of thing but it is illiterate. The word *like* is an intrusion, and the sentence should read *She walks as if she is in a hurry.*

A similar illiteracy is to say *She walks like she is in a hurry.* The word *like* has other jobs to perform in the language; this is not one. Use *as if* instead.

Like has often been used as a conjunction by even the best writers but this use is frowned upon. The examples above show *like* being used in this way. *We hope that petrol in Australia does not become extremely expensive like in France* is another example. *As* is the word that should be used here, not *like.*

Those who want to follow other frowned-upon uses of *like* may refer to the major authorities, but the debate need not concern us here. It can get very involved, and fear of the word *like* can lead to some ridiculous alternatives.

limited edition. The production of a *limited edition* of anything, be it book or motor-car, obliges the producer to state the number of examples it is intended to produce, and to guarantee that no more will appear.

Any limited edition offer which does not include these safeguards is not a true 'limited edition' offer.

The ethics of limited edition publishing are often queried, but for certain goods it is the only practicable method of production.

NOTE

1. It has not been unknown for an Australian publisher, having published a 'limited edition' of a book which has sold unexpectedly well, to make some minor cosmetic changes to the book and then sell it as a 'trade' (i.e. non-limited) edition.

2. The expense of a limited edition does not guarantee subsequent rarity value. Limited editions tend to be preserved more carefully than other books, some of which, originally published in small, disregarded editions, appreciate more rapidly than many limited editions.

lingerie. The pronunciation of this inoffensive word, with its slight air of naughtiness, has caused broken friendships. It means, of course, *ladies' underwear*, and it comes, far back, from the Latin word for *linen*. The (almost) invariable Australian pronunciation is *LON-dza-ray* or *LONG-dzeray*, the *dz* here standing for the *s* sound in *treasure*. This is a bizarre version of the French pronunciation, of course, and even of the approved British pronunciation, which is *LON-dzerie*. The Americans tend to say *LARN-dzeray*, or *LARN-dzerie*. We are as much entitled to our version of the word as anyone else.

literal/littoral. *Literal* is an adjective meaning *in exact accordance*. If you give someone a *literal* account of what someone else says, you give them a *word for word* account. In printing it is used as a noun, meaning *a misspelling in a printed word*.

Littoral means *the shores of a sea or lake, or even of a continent*. It may be used as a noun (*They travelled along the littoral*) or as an adjective (*The littoral birds are few*).

literally. "A still from this advertisement was displayed on a huge bill-board. The woman's pelvic region literally hit you in the face as you walked down the street." (From a letter in the *Age*, 27 May 1985.)

This fine image was drawn to our attention by Mr Arthur Phillips prior to his death in 1985. "What a sad indignity," was his comment. He then added a very funny but unprintable few words.

Literally means *this is exactly what happened*. If you transcribe a page of a book *literally* you copy down every letter exactly as it first appeared. If someone *literally expires* when they hear a joke, then they actually die. The person who wrote the letter to the *Age* is complaining about *actually* being hit by the woman's pelvic region.

Literally does *not* mean *metaphorically*. It does *not* mean *I'm telling it this way but of course I'm exaggerating*.

literature. Pronounce the last syllable of this word as you would *nature*, not as you would *mature*. In other words, do not place any kind of a stress on it. The word should be pronounced *LIT-rit-cher*.

litterateur. A *litterateur* is a person who, while not necessarily a writer, is interested and engaged in the literary scene. The word is now anglicised to the extent that it need not take the accent it has in French, be pronounced as a French word or take a different form for the feminine gender. All the same, the stress remains on the final syllable. Note the spelling: a double *t*, unlike the single *t* in *literature*.

livid/lurid. *Livid* means *of a dull bluish color*, discolored like a bruise. It is often used in the sense of *livid with anger* (compare "He went blue in the face").

Lurid, which comes from a Latin word meaning *yellowish*, broadly means *ghastly, unnatural, terrible in appearance*. Its main meaning relates to color, but it is often extended to mean *sensational*, as in *lurid details*.

236

-l/-ll. On the doubling of the letter *l* before adding a suffix, see **doubling up**, sub-heading "Expanded Guide", paragraph 5.

loan. see **lend.**

loath/loth. In phrases such as *I am loath to do so* the preferred spelling is *loath*, though *loth* is not wrong.

Note the different spelling again of the verb *to loathe*. From this verb we get *he is loathly, it is loathsome.*

Loath/loth is *not* pronounced the same way as the verb *to loathe*, though many Australians think it is. *Loath/loth* is pronounced with the *th* as in *thin*, to rhyme with *oath*. *To loathe* is pronounced with the *th* as in *then*.

lobster. See **crayfish.**

locate. Many will hold that *to locate* something is not *to find* it but *to establish it as being in a place.* Thus a new refinery may be *located* in the Melbourne suburb of Altona, which does not mean that someone has *found* it there but that a decision was made to put it there and that it went there.

Thus Adelaide is *located* in South Australia. If you want to *find* it, consult a map.

The use of *to locate* to mean *to find* (*She located the missing bracelet*) is now in the dictionaries and no amount of scolding will stop its being used that way. A pity, though. It weakens the precision of a useful word. Perhaps the fate of *to locate* will give us strength to resist a similar attack on another word.

loc. cit. See **referencing.**

longevity is pronounced with the soft *g*, that is, with the *g* sounding like the letter *j*. It is often and incorrectly pronounced with the hard *g*.

longitude, longitudinal. The letter *g* in these words is soft. In other words, the *long* part of the words is not pronounced like the familiar word *long* but to rhyme with the *mange* part of the word *blancmange*.

the long s. In the seventeenth and eighteenth centuries English printing used an extra letter, one which we do not come across nowadays, and which is called the *long s*. Dr Johnson's famous dictionary, for instance, has *mechanifm* (mechanism), *paffed* (passed) and *fkin* (skin), amongst thousands of other examples.

While in the above examples we use *f* to represent the *long s*, and it is widely believed that that is what Dr Johnson's printer and many others did, in fact the letter was *not* an *f*, but a different letter, formed like the *f* but without the small cross-line on the right-hand side.

The common practice was to use *S* as a capital at the beginning of words and *s* to end words, but to use the *long s* for *s* elsewhere. There was also an attempt to get agreement on using s for a *z* sound (*easily*) and the *long s* for an *s* sound (*verſes*).

The convention stemmed, of course, from manuscript writing. It is still found in German printing, where the *double s* at the end of words looks rather like *fs*. In English one very occasionally comes across the *double s* in handwriting with the word *Miſs* (Miss) in addresses, where it is used because of its elegant appearance.

long-sighted. See **short-sighted.**

Lord Mayor/mayor/mayoress. The only *Lord Mayors* in Australia are those of Sydney, Melbourne, Adelaide, Perth, Brisbane, Hobart, Newcastle, Wollongong and Darwin. The Lord Mayors of the capital cities are styled *the Right Honorable*, those of the other three cities *the Right Worshipful*.

A *mayoress* is *the wife of a mayor*. A woman who happens to be a *mayor* is so called. There is as yet no term for the husband of a female *mayor*, the style thus being, for example, *Madame Mayor and Mr Smith*.

lost singulars. The decay of the classics in the Australian educational system, justified on the mistaken grounds that Greek and Latin are not 'relevant' to our present concerns, has led to a widespread confusion about the singular forms of words most commonly seen or heard in the plural. The singulars, however, should be fought for, in the interests of meaning. Common errors include:

"Her *criteria* was . . .", for which use "her *criterion* was.."

"He discovered a new *specie* . . .". *Specie* means coin as opposed to paper money. The singular of *species* is also *species*.

"She displayed a whole *spectra* of interests . . ." *Spectra* is the plural of *spectrum*, which should be used in this case.

"They drilled to the oil-bearing *strata* . . ." If only one is meant, the word should be *stratum*.

"It was an interesting *phenomena*." *Phenomena* is the plural. The singular, often overlooked, is *phenomenon*.

"The disease is caused by a *bacteria*." One such organism is a *bacterium*.

"ABC television is a *media* which comes in for much criticism." *Media* is plural. The word used here should be *medium*.

loth. See **loath/loth.**

lots of are/lots of is. See **half.**

lower case. See **upper case/lower case.**

lubra. This word was used in the past for an Aboriginal girl or woman. It is no longer acceptable. Use *Aboriginal woman.*

lucerne. *Lucerne*, or *lucerne hay*, is Australian for the leguminous plant the Americans call *alfalfa*. It is pronounced *loosen*. The Swiss city is pronounced *loose-SERN.*

lugubrious means *dismal, mournful*, with a sense of the ridiculous added. The *g* is hard, as in *get.*

lunch. See **dinner/lunch/supper/tea.**

lured, in the sense of *He was lured by false promises*, is pronounced to rhyme with *gourd* and not, as it is sometimes heard, to rhyme with *bird.*

lurks and perks. Good Australian words, the former more so – though *lurk* is certainly Australian, it appears to be of quite recent invention. The first recorded use is in *The Songs of a Sentimental Bloke* (1915):

> I found 'er lurk
> Was pastin' labels in a pickle joint.

But, like so much slang we think of as authentically Australian, the word goes back to English origins. Eric Partridge, in his great dictionary of slang, dates it, in the general sense of *begging dishonestly*, from the mid-nineteenth century.

In Australian usage today it means, of course, *a way of beating the system on the side*, and conveys a tone of illicitness and of admiration: "My word, you're on to a good lurk!"

Perk comes from the word *perquisite* and is not distinctively Australian except in the phrase *lurks and perks*. A *perquisite* is an extra benefit obtained by virtue of holding a certain job, such as free telephone calls for some Telecom employees. The word *perk* has, very understandably, a certain cynical ring about it.

luxuriant/luxurious. *Luxuriant* means *prolific, lush, free-growing: luxuriant grass covered the once-clear pathway*. *Luxurious* means *characterised by richly comfortable surroundings and circumstances.*

-lyse/-lyze. Should we spell *analyze* or *analyse, paralyse* or *paralyze*?

The standard English and Australian form is *analyse*, though the American is *analyze*. There is a certain logic in the English and Australian use, in that the relevant nouns are *always* spelt with the *s: analysis, paralysis.*

M

Macarthur. The name of John *Macarthur*, one of the founders of the Australian wool industry, and of his descendants, is spelt with a small *a*. The name of General Douglas *MacArthur*, the US commander in the Pacific in the second world war, takes a capital *A*.

machination. A *machination* is *a sordid plot or intrigue*. It is a word beloved of politicians, especially in Queensland. The fall of Premier Johannes Bjelke-Petersen, according to the incoming Premier Michael Ahern, was "surrounded by machinations."

The approved pronunciation of this word, in Britain, America and Australia, is *makkination*. The alternative pronunciation *mashination* has, however, such a firm hold in Australia that the *Macquarie Dictionary* actually gives it priority. Since dictionary makers these days say they don't give advice but only record usage, this means that the *Macquarie Dictionary* thinks that *mashination* is a more common pronunciation in Australia than is *makkination*. Other Australian dictionaries do not, however, agree. While *mashination* cannot be called wrong, stick with *makkination*.

The *mashination* pronunciation is probably influenced by the word *machine*, which is in fact related to *machination*.

machismo/macho. *Machismo* is a Mexican Spanish word, from the Spanish *macho*, a male.

Machismo is a noun meaning *exaggerated masculinity: He displays a lot of machismo*. In its abbreviated and fashionable form, *macho*, it can be either a noun, meaning this time *a man who displays machismo*, or an adjective: *It was a macho performance*.

The words may be pronounced either *makismo/mako* or *matchismo/matcho*.

macrocosm/microcosm. A *macrocosm* (from the Greek, *great world*) is a *total, overreaching, unified system*. The universe is the ultimate macrocosm. A *macrocosmic view* of any system attemps to see it in its entirety, disregarding the parts. We may take a *macrocosmic* view of the future, for instance, of the Queensland transport system. Here we would look at the total picture of how all the various aspects of Queensland transport relate to each other and work as a system. If they do.

A *microcosm* (*little world*) also conveys the sense of a system, but of *a system in miniature*, a system which is part of a number of systems which make up a macrocosm. In relation to the study of the Queensland transport system as a whole, an examination of, say, the Rockhampton transport system would be *microcosmic*.

These useful, conceptual words are in danger of being taken over as 'puff' words designed to impress the unsophisticated, as when the television magnate Kerry Stokes says (August 1987) that "It worries me when we get down to the microcosms of it." What Mr Stokes meant was that he was worried about the *details*.

madam/madame. *Madam* is the English form of the word. A letter may be addressed *Dear Madam*. The plural would be *Dear Ladies*.

Madam is also used to denote *a woman who runs a brothel*. The plural here is *madams*.

Madame is a title attached to a name, the equivalent in French of *Mrs* (though also used for women whose married status is not known). It is used in English in certain specialised contexts (*Madame Melba*, *Madame Lash*) and as a title for some foreign women (*Madame Mao*).

The plural of *Madame* is *Mesdames*.

madding crowd. See **far from the madding crowd.**

magazine. See **book.**

Mahomet/Muhammad, etc. Much controversy rages. Fowler's *Modern English Usage* claims that the traditional and most-used terms are *Mahomet* and *Mahometans*. The *Concise Oxford Dictionary* seems to favor *Muhammed* and either *Muhammadan* or *Mohammedan*. The *Collins English Dictionary* says *Mohammed* or *Muhammad*. Fowler says the first of these is for historians and the second for pedants. The author of this work, if left to himself without reference books, would have spelt the Prophet's name *Mohamed* or perhaps *Mohammed*, and the religion *Mohammedanism*.

Clearly there can be no prescription. *Mahomet* is at least simple, easily remembered and, they say, in general use. *Mahometan* and *Mahometanism* would follow.

However, for the adjective, and the name of the religion, there are escape routes. Instead of *Mohammedan* or whatever, the word *Muslim* (or *Moslem!*), or the word *Islamic*, may be used. For the word for the religion use *Islam*.

Remember, though, that *Islam* also means *all the people called Muslim* and *the countries which are predominantly Muslim*.

Mahony. The title of the great Australian trilogy by Henry Handel Richardson is *The Fortunes of Richard Mahony*, not *The Fortunes of Richard Mahoney*. Even those who should know better frequently get this wrong.

majority/minority. A *majority/minority is*, or a *majority/minority are*?

It depends on the sense in which these words are being used. One would say *The government's majority* is *threatened*, but *The majority of the voters present* are *hostile*. Where the emphasis is on the *majority/minority* as a bloc, the singular will be used. Where the emphasis is on the *majority/minority* as a group of individual people or things, the plural will normally follow.

NOTE

1. While one may say *The Left had a greater majority of votes than four years ago*, one may not say *The greater majority of delegates wore red ties*. If it is a majority, of course it is greater.

2. Do not use *majority/minority* when referring to only one entity. *The majority of the ship was damaged by fire* is wrong. The sentence should read *The greater part of the ship was damaged by fire*. On the other hand *The majority of the ships present were Italian* is correct, for a number of separate items are involved.

malapropism. At its simplest a *malapropism* is *mistaking for a correct word one of somewhat similar sound*. In this sense this book is full of words liable to be confused with one another: *definite/definitive*, *precede/proceed*, *empirical/imperial* and so on. A more precise definition of a malapropism, however, would ask that there should be more than a simple confusion of words: that the confusion should lead to *a euphonious, ridiculous (and frequently funny) outcome*. Malapropisms have a useful side to them: they emphasise the pleasures of word-play, the resources of the language and, sometimes, the psychological 'associationism' which lies at its heart. In the hands of James Joyce, for instance, deliberate, contrived malapropisms and similar word-plays have greatly expanded our understanding and enjoyment of our language. In *Finnegan's Wake*, for instance, Joyce turns *Celtic twilight* into *cultic toilette:* "admirable criticism," says Anthony Burgess.

Mrs Malaprop (*mal apropos*) is a character in Richard Brinsley Sheridan's famous play "The Rivals" (1775). Fowler calls her "the matron saint of all those who go wordfowling with a blunderbuss"—in other words, such persons are likely to bring down more out of the skies than they expect. Mrs Malaprop asked that *no delusions to the past* should be made; she said that someone was *as headstrong as an allegory on the banks of the Nile*; perhaps her most famous phrase was *a nice derangement of epitaphs* (a nice arrangement of epithets). Sheridan's derangement of language in creating malapropism is an old theatrical trick, used by Shakespeare and no doubt long before him.

A cousin to the malapropism is the *spoonerism*, named after the Warden of New College, Oxford (1903–1924), William Spooner. With the spoonerism the confusion is not based on ignorance but on the association of sounds. No doubt spoonerisms are attributed to Spooner which he did not make, but it is claimed that he was responsible for announcing a hymn as *Kinquering Kongs their Tikles Tate* ("Conquering Kings their Titles Take"), *You have tasted a whole worm*,

You have hissed my mystery lectures, You will leave by the town drain, A well boiled icicle, and *Which of us has not found in his heart a half-warmed fish?* Also claimed for the unfortunate Spooner are *It is now kisstomary to cuss the bride, The Lord is indeed a shoving leopard* and, referring to Queen Victoria, *our queer old dean.*

One American authority has written of "the great frequency of malaprops among educated people who write and speak extensively in the course of their professional work." Certainly social mobility and the spread of mass education has meant that the need to use, and impress by, words has outrun ability to handle them deftly and accurately. Some of Sir William McMahon's pronouncements as Prime Minister had a strong spooneristic flavor: *We will honor all our promises on the problems we have made.*

Modern malapropisms include *the threat of nuclear war is the ultimate detergent, languishing praise on his friends, he challenged the credulity of the witness, I resent you insinuendos, I am speaking for the edification and hallucination of the councillors,* a *shrewd awakening, the Democratic majority will run slipshod over the Republican majority.*

The adjective is *malapropian.*

Malay/Malaysian. A *Malay* is *a member of the Malay people.* He or she is also a *Malaysian,* a citizen of the country called *Malaysia.* This country includes large groups of Chinese and Indian origin, who may properly be called *Malaysians* also.

mall. A mall is *a public place, often a shopping precinct, designed for pedestrians.*

With the increasing popularity of *malls* in Australian cities has come argument about the pronunciation of the word.

In favor of the *mal* (to rhyme with *pal*) pronunciation are the two most famous uses of the word. *Pall Mall* and *The Mall,* in London, are so pronounced.

In favor of the word's rhyming with *maul* is the fact that it derives from a *maul* or *mallet,* used in playing the game *pall-mall.* In Australia it is the most common pronunciation.

Use either, but *maul* is preferred.

manageress is one of those female forms which may well be dispensed with. As with *poetess* and *authoress,* is has increasingly become a put-down word, and it is common in Australia. The word *manager* should be used to include both men and women.

See **(the) female critique.**

manifested. "Thousands of years ago," a film-maker assured us on his documentary, "a great period of human development manifested in India."

The verb *to manifest*, when it means *to reveal* or *to display*, is a transitive verb. That is, it must be followed by an object. There is no object of the verb in the above sentence. The speaker should have said *manifested itself*.

Manila. *Manila* is the capital of the Republic of the Philippines. *Manila paper*, *manila files*, *manila rope* are best so spelt, though *manilla* is an alternative. The capital *M* is not necessary. The town in New South Wales is *Manilla*.

mankind. *Mankind* as a word is under fire from those who see the *man* in the word as suggesting that *men* are the most important component in mankind.

There is no historical or linguistic justification for this view, which can best be termed a gut-feeling. It is the three letters *m*, *a*, *n*, in that order, which arouse the resentment. In other words, it is not the concept behind the word, but the symbol it contains, that arouses ire.

There are analogies between this kind of attitude and the opinion once heard by the author expressed at a left-wing meeting, where a speaker stated that those present should not speak of "capitalising" on certain events, because *capital* was a capitalist term.

For all that, people die for symbols perhaps even more readily than for logical ideas. If *man* in *mankind* is offensive to many, then where possible sensitive people will try to find a substitute, such as *humanity*.

mannequin/mannikin. A *mannequin* is *a dressmaker's model*, and may be made out of human flesh and blood or out of plastic. Sometimes it is hard to tell the difference.

A *mannikin* (or *manikin*) is *a little man, a dwarf or a child*. A *mannikin* may also be a small, anatomical model.

Despite beliefs to the contrary, the two words are pronounced the same. The pronunciation of *mannequin* as *manikwin* is not acccptcd in British and American dictionaries, nor in two out of three dictionaries which pay attention to Australian usage. Even the third only gives it as a secondary pronunciation.

manoeuvre. Prefer *manoeuvring* to *manoeuvering*.

manpower. There is a case for changing some words, such as **chairman** when applied to a woman, as unnecessarily offensive. In other cases the desire to achieve a unisex language can impede sane communications.

Manpower is a word that has surely lost any specific sex significance, if it ever had any. It would need an ingenious argument to establish that its use harms female interests. In many cases, it is true, alternatives are available and should, if possible, be used: *labor, staff, people, personnel*. In other cases it is not easy to suggest a suitable alternative:

Manpower planning presents an intractable problem for all industrialised nations. Use alternatives where possible.

See also **(the) female critique.**

manuscripts. The abbreviation for one manuscript is *MS.*, for two or more *MSS.*

margarine. Pronounce with a soft *g*, as in *general*. The stress may be on either the first or the last syllable: *MAR-jar-ine, mag-jar-INE.*

marginalise. A 1984 report to the Minister for Education and Youth Affairs in Canberra, on the subject of education in the arts, refers to the need to equalise the provision of arts education "particularly . . . to those groups whose cultural expression has been marginalised, such as Aboriginals . . ."

No dictionary we have consulted lists the verb *to marginalise*, which seems to mean *pushed to one side, reduced in importance*. It seems perversely amusing that a word of doubtful standing should be used in a report to the Minister for Education.

The process of a noun (*margin*) becoming an adjective (*marginal*) and then a verb (*to marginalise*) is not uncommon in language formation. The noun-turned-verb is an old target of those who take a conservative attitude to language change. *To engineer, to gun down, to axe, to motor* are among hundreds that have followed this path.

Perhaps all of these sounded as ugly when they first started coming into use as *marginalise* does to us today. And perhaps the people who pointed this out, and believed it their right to oppose such changes, were not wrong. Language change will always involve some kind of an interchange between 'conservative' and 'progressive' forces.

So *marginalise*, at this stage in its development at any rate, is an unpleasant, unnecessary word, a lazy word and a bureaucratic one. It does not have the justification that it fills a need not otherwise met. In the quotation above, the words *suppressed, inhibited, reduced* — and many others — could have been used in place of *marginalised*.

See **noun to verb: is change decay?**

marijuana. The plant itself is *Cannabis sativa* or *Indian hemp*. *Marijuana* is the dried leaves, flowers and stem of the plant which, when smoked, induce a narcotic state. *Hashish* (from which comes the word *assassin*) or *hash* is produced from the concentrated resin of the plant. *Marijuana* is popularly (and sometimes affectionately) referred to as *grass, pot* or *dope*. Cigarettes made from marijuana are called *joints, tokes* or *reefers.*

mass/weight

mark/marque. The Lee Enfield .303 rifle, Mark III, was the standard infantry weapon of the Australian army in the second world war.

Mark III meant that there had been two previous versions of the same weapon.

This use of the word *mark* is widespread, and not only in the armed forces. It presumably originated from industry's practice of placing the series number somewhere on products.

The word *marque* is similar in meaning, indeed frequently identical, and is especially prevalent in the automobile industry. Someone enquiring as to the *marque* of, say, a Holden car would expect to be told that it was an *EJ* model, or something of that nature: this would distinguish its *marque*. *Marque* is however sometimes used in a more extended sense: *What marque of car?* can mean, not *What model?* but *What make?*

The two words may be regarded as identical, the *marque* spelling being a somewhat pretentious one.

maroon. *Maroon* is a purplish-red colour; the word comes from the French for a chestnut, *marone*. The 'proper' pronunciation of *maroon* is as it is spelt. Somehow or other a variant pronunciation, *marown*, rhyming with *bone*, has become established in Australia, where it is recognised in Australian dictionaries. The Melbourne football team of Fitzroy, however, is known by the nickname of "The Maroons," which in this case at least is pronounced as spelt.

marshal/marshall. There is no such word as *marshall*, except as a person's name.

Note the following:

> He held the rank of *Field Marshal.*
> The general *marshals* his troops (though the troops are *marshalled* in English and Australian usage, *marshaled* in American usage).
> Will you please *marshal* your thoughts?

masochist. Masochists are people who enjoy the infliction of physical or mental pain on themselves. The word is pronounced with the *ch* as *k*, not as *sh*: *masokist*, not *masoshist*.

A *sadist* has been defined as *one who is kind to masochists.*

mass/weight. Most of us think we are entitled to talk about the *weight* of an object, but sententious scientists tell us we are wrong, and that we should speak of the *mass*. Attempts are being made to push this word on the public, an ungrateful public which shows no signs of responding.

Scientists are usually very bad at expressing themselves in simple terms owing to the deficiencies of scientific education, but in fairness to them let us see

247

what they mean.

Weight, to physicists, is an imprecise word. You may think you weigh fifty kilograms, but the scientists say that you only weigh fifty kilograms at a certain place at a certain time, and that if you were on the moon you would only weigh about eight kilograms. There would indeed be some variation in your weight, other things being equal, if you could be weighed at sea level and on the top of Mount Everest. For *weight* is the measurement of the pull of the force of gravity on you, and gravity varies.

What is the same at all places, even in outer space, is your *mass*. It is defined as *the measure of a body's resistance to changes in velocity*. In other words, how hard do you have to push it to make it move faster or slower? That will give you the measurement of mass. It is a question of *force* rather than, as we innocents think of it, of *heaviness*. One of the troubles, however, with this definition is that *mass* changes with *velocity*, just as *weight* changes with *gravity*. To an outsider it looks as though we are not any further forward.

There is no reason why terms which are entirely of sectional interest and application should be imposed on a general public which is interested in establishing the *weight* of its post-office parcel rather than its *mass*. The rot sets in downwards as government bodies, composed of or influenced by the more inbred kind of scientist, first of all compose policies in their own languages and then, at a later stage, carry the language as well as the policy through to the people. Or try to.

massive. This word is best avoided, except in architectural contexts.

materialise has some special meanings, but when used in the sense of *to actually happen* (*The cruise did not materialise*) it is best avoided.

Occur, happen, take place, come about are preferable.

material/materiel. *Material* is, well, *material*, but *materiel* is a special kind of *material*.

Materiel is a word often used to describe *the equipment and supplies of an organisation*:

> The shortcomings of the expedition on the materiel side were immense.

Needless to say, the word often gets changed back to *material* by typesetters unfamiliar with the word *materiel*.

Materiel may be written with the French accent, thus: *matériel*. If so, it may be placed in italics, but that is no longer necessary.

May Day/mayday. *May Day* is the first day of May, traditionally (in the northern hemisphere) marking the beginning of spring, and also in many countries the annual holiday of Labor.

The word *Mayday* is an anglicised version of the French *m'aider* ("help me") and is an international distress call used on radio transmissions.

may/might.

1. *May* is the verb. *Might* is the past tense of that verb. As a general rule *may* should not be used for events that happened in the past, and *might* should not be used for present and future events.

Thus, when Victoria's Premier John Cain states in a speech (*Age*, 6 May 1986):

> If young people cannot spell or compose sentences to the satisfaction of employers and tertiary teachers it might be because advertising agencies don't spell or compose sentences. If they murder the language it might be because the media — and politicians and bureaucrats — lost their sensibilities to plain English some time ago,

he twice uses the word *might* where the word *may* is called for, thus justifying his own remarks. For the same reason, the following are also incorrect:

> But for the Coral Sea Battle of 1942, Australia *may* have been invaded.
>
> Without your help the refugees *may* never have received the relief supplies.
>
> But for his deafness Beethoven *may* have written several more symphonies.

In all these cases, since they refer to the past, *might* is the proper word.

Similarly one should say *It* may *happen* and not *It* might *happen*, since we are referring to the present (or, to be precise, a present possibility concerning the future).

2. So much for the general rule, but it is a general rule which may be broken.

3. So far as the *present-tense* use of *may* is concerned, the general rule is overridden by another attribute of these two words, that *may* is a stronger word than *might* and in certain circumstances gives way to it. *She* may *be coming* is more positive than *She* might *be coming*; that is, it suggests that she is more likely to be coming than *She* might *be coming* does.

Similarly "I *may* be dead by this time next year" is a more alarming statement than "I *might* be dead by this time next year," and "*May* I have it?" is a more forthright way of asking for something than "*Might* I have it?"

So — *might* is allowable in the present tense if it is being used to express a greater uncertainty than *may*.

4. Note also a special use of *may* and *might*:

> You *may* tell the Newtons [if you wish to].
>
> You *might* tell the Newtons [if you would be so kind].

5. Now for the past tense, in which — as we have seen — the general rule is to use the word *might*.

There is a past construction, called the *perfect infinitive*, of which *to have stayed* is an example.

Depending on the sense, it will sometimes be necessary to use the word *may* instead of *might* in such a phrase. For example:

> He *might* have stayed longer than a week (had it not rained).
>
> He *may* have stayed longer than a week (but I do not know whether or not he did so).

Similarly:

> There *might* have been a civil war in Equador (but for the land reform).
>
> There *may* have been a civil war in Equador (but I don't know whether there actually was one).

In other words, if the event being referred to definitely did *not* occur, use *might*: otherwise use *may*. It's a matter of common sense and feeling for words, really, and most of us would use these constructions automatically. Note that here there is not really an exception to the general rule given above. We use *might* when the sentence is genuinely and without dispute in the past; we use *may* when there is an uncertainty which persists into the present.

See also **can/could**.

mayor/mayoress. See **Lord Mayor/mayor/mayoress**.

mean. See **average/mean**.

mechanics' institute/school of arts. These two terms are interchangeable in Australia, together with others less familiar, such as *lyceum* and *atheneum*.

The *mechanics' institute* was first developed by Dr George Birkbeck in Glasgow in 1802, when Birkbeck delivered a popular lecture series to working men. The movement developed rapidly from the establishment of the London Mechanics' Institute in 1823. The first Australian foundation was the Hobart Town Mechanics' Institution (1827), followed by the Sydney Mechanics' School of Arts (1833) and the Melbourne Mechanics' Institution (1839).

The idea was to improve both the moral and the educational levels of the community by encouraging mutual discussion and study, especially of the principles underlying various trades and callings. The mechanics' institutes became more popular and widespread in Australia than they ever did in Britain, but their educational activities became less important than their social activities, and in many cases were lost sight of. For all that, mechanics' institutes were precursors of present-day technical education.

Note that there is an important difference between a *school of arts* and a *school of art*. A *school of art* taught art, chiefly drawing and painting. A *school of arts* was a broadly based institution with many aims, of which the study of *art* may or may not have been a part.

In Victoria the normal term for these institutions was *mechanics' institute*, in New South Wales and Queensland *school of arts*.

The word *mechanic*, like the word *artisan*, meant to our forefathers *an industrious working-man, with some skills, and with a responsible attitude to his place in society.* The mechanic was always a cut above the unskilled laborer or rural hand.

Although mechanics' institutes were supposed to be for the upper working classes, in many cases they became identified with patronage and patronisers from above, so much so that in some cases working-class members rebelled and set up their own, rival institutions.

media. In Australia "we do have a free media", says Prime Minister Hawke in the *Australian* on 25 April 1986.

Well, we don't. We may have *a free medium.* Or we may have *free media.* But no-one, anywhere, can have *a free media*, any more than they can have *a red flags.*

One of the meanings of the word *medium* is *the means by which something is communicated.* Thus the *Sydney Morning Herald*, for instance, is a *medium* for the conveyance of news, ideas and opinions. Channel Two on the television is also a *medium.*

Because we so often refer to the press and/or the radio and television as *the media*, which is correct when we talk about them collectively, there has been a tendency to forget the singular form, especially in such constructions as *She regularly appears on this media.* This is wrong. It should be *on this medium.* See **lost singulars.**

There are two uses in which the plural of *medium* is *mediums* rather than *media.* In the case of an artist who works in (say) watercolor, oil and clay, we will often hear *She works in several mediums*; and *mediums* conduct seances.

See also **(the) electronic media.**

mediate/mitigate. *To mediate* is to play a conciliatory role in a dispute, as in *Mr Malcolm Fraser was a member of a group which attempted to mediate between the White and Black communities in South Africa.*

To mitigate is *to make something less harsh*, as in *The penalty of six months' suspension was mitigated by the tribunal to one of two months' suspension.*

medicine. People who like to think they are speaking 'correct' English often pronounce this word as *medsin* rather than *medisin.* Either way is permissible.

mega-. See **billion.**

Melanesia/Micronesia/Polynesia. These are terms (a) for ethnic divisions between peoples of the Pacific region (b) for the groups of islands on which they live. The words, together with *Malaysian*, were coined by the French explorer Dumont d'Urville during his voyage of 1826–1829.

Melanesia comprises most of the islands of the southwest Pacific, including Fiji, New Caledonia, Vanuatu, Solomon Islands and the New Guinea part of Papua New Guinea. Most of the people inhabiting these areas are of dark coloration, and the term means *the black islands*.

Micronesia encompasses islands in the west central Pacific, including the Mariana, Caroline, Marshall and Gilbert island groups, with Nauru. The term means *small islands*. The people are physically more Polynesian than Melanesian, but with some southeast Asian characteristics.

Polynesia means *many islands* and includes those who live on the islands of the central and south Pacific, including the Society Islands (Tahiti), Samoa, the Marquesas, the Tuamotu islands and Tonga. The peoples generally have light skins and hair less tightly curled than that of the Melanesians. The Maori people of New Zealand are Polynesian in origin, as are the Papuans of Papua New Guinea.

Melbourne. It is sometimes argued, for instance by Max Harris, that the original and 'correct' pronunciation of *Melbourne* is *mel-BORN*. William Lamb, second Viscount Melbourne, after whom the city of Melbourne is named, lived at Melbourne Hall in Derbyshire. Viscount Melbourne's kinsman, the Marquess of Lothian, who now lives at Melbourne Hall, has stated that the word has traditionally been pronounced as Australians pronounce it.

Melburnian. Of all Australian capital cities, only Melbourne has a 'describing' word which stands by itself, and that word is traditionally *Melburnian*, not *Melbournian*. Thus the Old Boys of Melbourne Grammar School call themselves *Old Melburnians*, and the following sentences also show the use of the word:

> That was a very Melburnian thing to say.
> He considered himself a Melburnian through and through.

Such words as *Sydneyite, Sydneian, Adelaideian, Canberran, Brisbaneite* (or *Brisbanite*) are sometimes heard, but they sound awkward, and normally a way round the matter is found: *She was an Adelaide woman*, for instance.

memorandum. The plural of *memorandum* is *memoranda*.

menu is pronounced *men-you*, not *meen-you*.

metallurgy. Stress this word on the second syllable, *met-AL-urgy*.

metaphor. A *metaphor* is *a word or phrase seeking to convey a meaning by an unrelated image*.

If we talk of a camel as *a ship of the desert* we are using a metaphor, albeit a tired one. Other familiar metaphors are: *burning the candle at both ends, playing second fiddle, skating on thin ice.*

Metaphors and *similes* are closely related. Perhaps the main distinction is that the *simile* proclaims its purpose, while the *metaphor* assumes it implicitly. In other words, the *simile* commences with *like* or *as*, while the *metaphor* lifts an alien image and assumes the hearer or reader understands.

See **metaphorical mischief; moribund metaphors and similes.**

metaphorical mischief. A *metaphor* is a figure of speech. We use them all the time and the language would not only be poorer without them, but would hardly exist. We would have to do without such phrases as *a bed of roses, nipped in the bud, hot potatoes, a cold fish,* and thousands more.

Beware, however, of an inappropriate metaphor which 'sounds all right at the time' but which actually is rather ridiculous. Such as:

at the height of the depression

on the eve of a new day

to draw the net wider (nets are drawn *closer*)

pregnant with virgin opportunity.

Beware also of the *mixed metaphor*, where two separate metaphorical ideas are in disharmony. Frank Sinatra once said that the inaugural he organised for President Reagan "jelled like clockwork." Ava Gardner is famous for the remark: "Deep down I'm extremely superficial." Note also:

she has a fluent grasp of the language

they marched into fresh fields but soon had to abandon the lifeboat

they saddled themselves with a white elephant

a torrent of marching feet.

it was a watershed turning the tide in politics (John Elliott, president of the Liberal Party, 1988)

a five-point package of proposals

a red herring that has been let loose (Julian Beale, shadow minister for tourism, 1987)

he split the beans and opened a can of worms.

See also **moribund metaphors and similes; simile.**

metric abbreviations. Approved abbreviations for the major units used in metric measurements are:

Length		Area	
millimetre	mm	square millimetre	mm^2
centimetre	cm	square centimetre	cm^2
metre	m	square metre	m^2
kilometre	km	hectare	h (10,000 m^2)

Electricity		Energy, work, quantity of heat	
ampere	A	joule	J
volt	V	**Temperature**	
watt	W	degrees Celsius	°C
kilowatt	kW		
kilowatt hour	kWh	**Volume**	
ohm	Ω	millilitre	mL
		litre	L
Frequency		kilolitre	kL (1000 L, or
hertz	Hz		1m³)
		megalitre	ML (1,000,000
Mass			L, or 1000 m³)
gram	g	gigalitre	GL
kilogram	kg		(1,000,000 m³)
tonne	t (1000 kg)		
kilotonne	kt (1,000,000 kg)	**Time**	
		second	s
Luminous intensity		minute	min
candela	cd	hour	h
		day	d
Thermodynamic temperature			
kelvin	K	**Angles and navigational calculations**	
		second	”
Speed		minute	’
metres per second	m/s	degree	°
kilometres per hour	km/h		

NOTE

1. Full stops are not used after these abbreviations, which strictly speaking are not abbreviations but "mathematical representation of units".

2. For this reason they remain the same in the plural. To write *kgs* for *kilograms* is wrong.

3. Separate the abbreviations from numbers by a space, thus: *134 mm, except* in the cases of *angular degrees, minutes* and *seconds (37° 40' 12")*, and *degrees Celsius (44°C).*

4. The word *per* is officially preferred for such terms as *kilometres per hour.*

5. Any unit may have its power increased by the addition of the appropriate index, as *m²* (square metre), *m³* (cubic metre).

6. Do not mix units. Choose the appropriate measurement and write, say, *1.234 m* or *1234 mm* but *not 1 m 234 mm.* Or so the bureaucrats say. Europeans, however, who have lived with the metric system for far longer than Australians, find no difficulty in referring to *1 metre, 62 centimetres,* rather than *162 centimetres.*

See also **imperial weights and measures; knot; metrication; nautical mile.**

metrication. The metrication of Australian weights and measures was foisted on the Australian public by the Metric Conversion Act of 1970. A large part of the case for adopting metric measurements was that Britain and the United States were 'going metric'. This has not happened. We not only lost our traditional units, but also an important part of our real and metaphorical language, a point that meant nothing to the politicians, bureaucrats and 'improvers' concerned.

For all that, the old imperial units remain at the time of writing (1986) still legal in Australia. It was expected that they would disappear, but their resurgence in the mid-1980s in public use and in the schools led to moves in 1985 to declare them illegal. A National Standards Commission spokesman stated in October 1985 that "I can understand teachers instructing in the old units. After all, their pupils live in a real world."

It is likely that in the near future most of the old imperial units will cease to be "Australian legal units". There will, however, be exceptions. In land dealings, for instance, titles already written in the old measures will remain legal, and traditional units will be retained with legal protection within certain industries and activities, including the import-export trade.

Non-metric units which will remain indefinitely in legal use in Australia include the *inch* (in) (in precision engineering), the *knot* (kn) and the *nautical mile* (n mile) in maritime use and in aviation, the *kilocalorie* (k cal) in food science, *horsepower* (hp) in defence and aviation, the *troy ounce* (troy oz) in bullion dealings and the *foot* (ft) for vertical height and separation in aviation, and for the depth of submarines. Some of these, such as the knot, the nautical mile and the foot, have to be retained because they are part of the standard international nomenclature.

See also **imperial weights and measures; metric abbreviations.**

Micronesia. See **Melanesia/Micronesia/Polynesia.**

midday. See **noon.**

middle class. See **working class.**

Middle East. See **Far East.**

midnight. The correct description of midnight is *12 p.m.*: that is, twelve hours *post meridiem* or *after midday.*

Since, however, many are going to assume that *12 p.m.* means *12 noon,* wisdom suggests that midnight be designated *12 midnight.*

One minute past midnight is *12.01 a.m.*

See also **noon.**

might. See **may/might.**

migrant. See **emigrant/immigrant.**

milage/mileage. Prefer the spelling *mileage. Mileage* is now moving from meaning *a measurement involving miles* to a *general measure of distance:*
> What mileage has this car done?
> Over 60,000 kilometres.

There can be no objection to this movement, especially as *kilometrage* is a word that, fortunately, does not exist.

mile. See **nautical mile.**

militate/mitigate. To *militate* for or against something is *to have an influence or effect: The fall in the value of the dollar militated against our taking an overseas trip.*

To *mitigate* is to make something less harsh: *The sentence of death was mitigated to one of life imprisonment.* You cannot *mitigate against* anything.

minimal is the adjective from *minimum* and means *the least possible,* as in *the minimal rations on which it is possible to survive.*

Nothing, then, can be "very minimal", though the phrase may be heard on the Australian airwaves. It is either *minimal* or *not minimal.*

Degrees of approach to the condition of being *minimal* may be qualified (*these were almost minimal conditions*), but the condition itself can not be qualified.

See **unique.**

minimise. See **diminish/minimise.**

minuscule is often misspelt *miniscule.* In ordinary use it means *very small,* though in printing terminology it means *small (lower-case) letters,* the antonym being *majuscule.*

minutia. This word is most often found in the plural, *minutiae,* meaning *small or trifling details.* The singular is pronounced *mine-YU-she-a* or *min-YU-she-a,* the plural *min-YU-she-ee* or *mine-YU-she-ee.*

mischievous is not spelt *mischievious!*

misinformation. See **disinformation/misinformation.**

misogyny/misandry/misanthropy. *Misogyny*, of course, means a *dislike of women*. Less well known but equally useful these days is the word for *dislike of men*, which is *misandry*.

Misanthropy means, not *hatred of men*, but *hatred of all humans*, men and women together.

misquotations. See under:
    abandon hope, all ye who enter here;
    alas, poor Yorick;
    all that glistens is not gold;
    a poor thing, but mine own;
    blood, sweat and tears;
    by the skin of my teeth;
    cloud no bigger than a man's hand;
    devil quoting scripture;
    gilding the lily;
    home is the sailor;
    honor'd in the breach;
    just growed like Topsy;
    money is the root of all evil;
    once more into the breach, dear friends;
    one small step for man;
    one touch of nature makes the whole world kin;
    power corrupts;
    "The best-laid plans of mice and men / Gang aft a-gley;"
    the writing on the wall;
    they shall not grow old;
    weighed in the balance;
    when Greek meets Greek.

Miss. See (the) **Mr/Mrs/Ms problem**.

missile. Australians say *miss-isle*, with the *isle* as in *island*. Americans say *missle*, to rhyme with *whistle*; in fact many Americans, victims perhaps of their education system, now *spell* the word *missle*.

mistake. This word makes *mistakable* or *mistakeable*, *mistakably* or *mistakeably*. The final *e*, however, has to be dropped with *mistaking*, *mistakingly*.

Mister. See (the) **Mr/Mrs/Ms problem**

modifiers. *Debbie is a slow swimmer.* We can all recognise *slow* as an adjective modifying the meaning of the noun *swimmer*. But nouns can modify the meaning of nouns, just as adjectives do: *a transport holdup, a non-meat day, the century mark, a business executive, a court-room lawyer, a brick building, highway code, community centre, alarm clock* and so on.

How should we describe the function of these nouns that modify the meaning of other nouns? They are *nouns acting as adjectives,* but are usually referred to as *modifiers,* or *modifying nouns.* They have slipped out of the traditional **parts of speech** categories, and remind us that traditional grammar can be a **procrustean** way of attempting to define language functions.

With modifiers, there are two storm warnings. (1) Do not use modifying nouns if you can use an appropriate adjective: *lunar research,* not *moon research; military base,* not *army base; literary studies,* not *literature studies.* (2) Beware the *headline disease.* PRIMARY SCHOOL SHORTAGE may be acceptable in a newspaper headline, but in an expanded text *the shortage of primary schools* is much to be preferred. Similarly, instead of *Farmers are pleased about their fine wool income figures* write *Farmers are pleased about their income from the sales of fine wool.*

See also **determiners.**

momentarily. *Momentarily* is an adverb which means *for a moment* (*She momentarily displaced the chess piece*). It is pronounced *MOM-ent-arily* or *MOM-entrily.*

Americans use this word to mean *very soon* (*I'll be back momentarily*) and pronounce it *moment-AIR-ily.* This seems an unnecessary import to Australia. See **offensive intruders.**

Monaro. The Monaro region of southeastern New South Wales is variously pronounced. Perhaps we should let Sir Keith Hancock have his say:

> Nor can we feel sure that the white men, when they pronounced the word *Mon-air-uh,* as old-timers of the district still pronounce it, were faithfully repeating the aboriginal sounds. Yet what a pity it would be if the salesmen of our busy times, who are doing all they can to make the second syllable of the word rhyme with *bar,* were to destroy at long last the traditional, beautiful pronunciation. (*Discovering Monaro* ... (Cambridge, 1972), p. 6.)

The recommended pronunciation then is *Mon-air-uh* or *Mon-air-o,* with the accent on the second syllable.

Monash. Geoffrey Serle, on p. xv of his *John Monash* (Melbourne, 1982), has this to say:

> The name Monash (Monasch) probably derives from Manesseh, one of the twelve tribes of Israel.

The normal German pronunciation is MOHnaash; occasionally it is MohNAASH. At some stage the Australian family adopted MOHnash. The natural popular Australian pronunciation has been MONash. Sir John Monash does not seem to have made a point of correcting mispronunciation, but his sister Mathilde was very particular. Most of those who knew Monash, especially military men, used MOHnash; however, the children and grand-children of some of his close associates are certain that they said MONash. In the 1930s, after Monash's death, his daughter Bertha Bennett and her husband decided to accept MONash. When consulted at the time of the foundation of Monash University, she and her children confirmed this pronunciation.

money is the root of all evil. Not so. The quotation is "For the love of money is the root of all evil," from the Bible, 1 Timothy vi. 10.

mongrel. English English for *a plant or animal, especially a dog, of unknown breeding*; Australian English for *a contemptible type of man* (rarely a woman). Pronounce, whether speaking of dog or man, *mungrel*, and not with the *o* as in *sorry*.

monotechnic/polytechnic. The word *polytechnic* is little used in Australia, though it is common in England, where it means *a technical college where many different technologies and allied subjects are taught.*

The word *monotechnic* does, however, occasionally occur in Australian education. It means a technical college where only one area of skills is taught. Examples are the Melbourne College of Printing and Graphic Arts and the Melbourne College of Decoration.

mood. Verbs may be used in four different ways, or so traditional grammarians hold. These four ways or *moods* are:
IMPERATIVE
This expresses a command. *Go to bed!*
INDICATIVE
This states a fact or asks a question: *She has gone to market. Has she gone to market?*
INFINITIVE
The simplest form of the verb. *To know, to travel.*
SUBJUNCTIVE
See **(the) subjunctive: is it still alive?**

moot point. *Moot* is an old Anglo-Saxon word meaning *a local assembly.* A *moot point*, then, is *a point which is worth discussing*, or *discussing further.* It often suggests a theoretical or hypothetical debate, as in *moot courts* held as an exercise by law students.

A *moot point* is *not* simply a dubious point, one to which exception may be taken. It is *an issue which is worth arguing.*

Rodney Fisher, writing an article in the *Sydney Morning Herald* (5 April 1986), states that Harley Granville-Barker's scheme to found a national theatre in England "was rendered moot by the outbreak of war in 1914." This is meaningless, for *moot* simply does not mean *ineffective,* which is perhaps what Rodney Fisher thought it meant. Presumably he assumed that *moot point* meant something like *a meaningless point,* and that therefore *moot* meant *meaningless* or *useless* or *ineffective.* As we have seen it does not.

The verb *to moot* means *to bring up for debate,* as in this comment of Christine Cremen's on the Sydney Film Festival (*Australian,* 2 May 1986):

> It has been mooted by the cynical that this audience suffers cold feet, missed or hasty meals and lack of sleep, and endures the woes of the rest of the world on celluloid as a bourgeois ritual of atonement.

more than one. The phrase *more than one* is considered a singular phrase, hence *More than one of the fish has* (not *have*) *turned bad.*

moribund metaphors and similes. That most distinguished Australian critic, A. A. Phillips, has told us that it is not the **cliché** that we should beware of in speech and writing, but the "dead metaphor", the worn-out figures of speech.

"A newly invented metaphor," George Orwell wrote, "assists thought by evoking a visual image." The first time someone said or wrote *riding roughshod over* or *no axe to grind* must have been a delight to the audience. Three hundred thousand times later nothing but a great glumness descends upon those hearing such phrases. Language is an attempt to convey from one mind to another the infinitely complex and sensitive nuances of thought in that first mind. Until we devise an instantaneous electronic link-up there is no other way. It is therefore important that the receiving mind be not deadened by stale signals.

Examples of dead metaphors offered by Orwell, in his essay on "Politics and the English Language", include:

ring the changes	swan song
take up the cudgels	Achilles' heel
play into the hands of	

It takes only a few seconds to think of more:

ride the waves	a curate's egg
a false heaven	a pillar of society

Or, with similes, and in Australian English:

silly as a two-bob watch	flat out like a lizard drinking
to go through like a packet of salts	beyond the Black Stump

In other words, there are thousands of tired images in our daily language.

Perhaps they do not always diminish that language. Perhaps they may be defended as clichés are defended. But, in general and on balance, they may be considered to represent laziness and inefficiency in language.

Orwell pointed out that it is possible to ridicule some expressions out of use, thus denying the arguments of those who say language has to be left alone to take its own form. He claimed that *explore every avenue* and *leave no stone unturned* have been killed by jeers.

the Mr/Mrs/Ms problem. It used to be simple, and to some people it still is. If you were Ann White and you married James Brown you became *Mrs James Brown* in formal communication. You and your husband together were addressed as *Mr and Mrs James Brown*. If you became a widow you continued to be *Mrs James Brown*. If you were divorced you became *Mrs Ann Brown*.

Many will still hold to this, but a great many will not. For a start, the feminist movement generally holds that, if a title be needed at all, it should be one that does not distinguish between the married and unmarried woman; and further, that the woman should retain her own name. Thus *Mrs James Brown* becomes *Ms Ann White*. There is a fall-back position here: (a) that the couple hyphenate their names, and (b) that the woman never be referred to by her husband's name. Thus *Mr James White-Brown* (or *Brown-White) and Ms Ann White-Brown* (or *Brown-White*).

(This raises problems, of course, in the next generation, when two persons with hyphenated names marry each other.)

Are you still with us?

There is another solution, and perhaps the most workable. That is, if the woman has no objection to taking the husband's surname in the traditional manner (or, for that matter, the husband's taking the wife's, which sometimes happens), then they should be formally known as *Mr James and Mrs Ann Brown*. It would not have done for our grandmothers, to whom the phrase *Mrs Ann Brown* would have indicated a divorced woman, but it will probably have to do for us. Traditionalists will have to concede that, not only should a wife not be a chattel of the husband's, but that she should not appear to be one.

Turning now to the word *Ms*, pronounced "Miz", we may first note that it is not an abbreviation but a word in itself. To many it sounds ugly, but we will get used to it. Most married women will cling to their *Mrs*, but *Ms* will make inroads. It *is* convenient, where the marital status of a woman is unknown; it *is* an equaliser, in the sense that it gives to women the right not to proclaim their marital status, a right that men have always had.

Many unmarried women will prefer to remain addressed as *Miss*, but in general the word *Miss*, like the word *Master*, is best used to refer only to children.

One simple solution, at least so far as the addressing of letters is concerned, is to ignore all honorifics and simply to use the unadorned name of the person to whom the letter is being sent. This sensible practice is increasingly being adopted in the United States, and seems worthy of emulation.

multi-. The use of the prefix *multi-* has become fashionable in Australia (see **multiculturalism**). In a single issue of the *Bulletin* (1 April 1986) we read of Brisbane as *a multi-functional metropolitan-wide local government* and of the *multifaceted genius of Shakespeare.* The *Australian* talks of *multi-role, frigate-type vessels.* The performers in Circus Oz are referred to on television as *multi-talented.* (There is a perfectly suitable standard word meaning *multi-talented*, and that word is *versatile.*) When you hear the prefix *multi-* in use, look for a lazy speaker of English, or a pretentious one, or perhaps one who is both.

multiculturalism. This is apparently an Australian coinage. *Multicultural* is now thought to be a 'nicer' word than **ethnic**. Since the new word is already leading to those of foreign extraction in our midst being termed *multis*, and since *multis* is already acquiring a disparaging ring, in due course the word *multicultural* will itself fall out of favor.

This decline in the status of a word is common in a living language. The only way to prevent it is by going back to an 'original' word, say in this case the word *foreigner*, and so educating and informing people that that word loses all its unpleasant nuances. Then, value-free, it will stay as an approved word.

Unfortunately this doesn't happen in real life or in real languages.

Multicultural is not a pleasant word: it is ponderous and patronising. (The point, however, is to think of a better.)

Australia has come late to the experience of being a country with diverse components derived from many overseas sources. The accelerated migrant intake since the second world war has coincided with the growth of 'welfarism' and government intervention on behalf of minorities. Where once migrants were left to find their own way into a new society, there is now argument about whether they ought to be encouraged to 'integrate' at all and, if so, to what extent. We have seen Greek schoolgirls in Australia, anxious to become lawyers and doctors, denied the use of an English dictionary. Sir Paul Hasluck has pointed out that it is desirable that multiculturalism lead to diversity, but undesirable that it lead to division.

Multiculturalism, both the word and the concept, should be opposed if it leads to the creation of cultural ghettos in Australia and hence the protection of the privileges of (a) established, 'main-line' Australians and (b) the officials and bureaucrats who stand to benefit from this process. It should be supported if it means respect for the baggage everyone has brought with them to Australia, an acceptance of the fact that we all stand in a continually changing relationship to our personal backgrounds, that Australia is both a *congeries* of cultures and at the same time something more than that.

Murri. The term used by Aboriginals in Queensland to distinguish themselves. See also **Koori**; **Nunga**.

mutual. To say to someone that *Diana is our mutual friend* has traditionally been considered wrong. If we mean that we both share friendship for Diana, then Diana is our *common* friend. *Mutual* means *between you and me and me and you*, or *between him and her and her and him*. It does not mean *between me and her and you and her* or *between him and her and you and her*. There must be a sense of a reciprocal relationship. Thus *Diana and I have a mutual friendship* (that is, *a friendship with each other*) is correct. *Japan and Australia share a mutual interest in better economic relations* is correct. *Australia and New Zealand have a mutual distaste for French atomic tests in the Pacific* is wrong. They have a *common* distaste.

For all that, the 'wrong' use of *mutual* is now well established and no doubt irreversible.

Mutual is often used in unnecessary repetition, as in *They put their heads together and mutually decided which house they wanted to buy. Mutually* in such cases is unnecessary and a doubling-up.

myself.
> My wife and myself (said the Prince of Wales at the Melbourne Cup).
> It was a year ago that myself and the Leader of the Opposition discussed the matter (said a Queensland politician on television).

The rule is *do not use the word* myself *when you can use the word* I.

To use *myself* instead of *I* in the examples above suggests (a) a sense of insecurity in the person speaking, as though they wanted to escape from facing up to themselves (b) a feeling that *myself* is more genteel and 'polite' than *I*.

Myself should be used (a) when the use is reflexive, as in *I have injured myself*, and (b) when the use is emphatic, as in *I drove the tractor myself*.

N

naive/naiveté. To be *naive* is *to be simple and unsophisticated in outlook*. It is the feminine form of a French word (the male form being *naif*) but we now use *naive* for both male and female purposes.

Naive is pronounced *nay-EVE* or *nye-EVE*. It has two syllables, as was shown when it was commonly printed with a dieresis: *naïve*. This is no longer necessary.

The most usual noun form is *naiveté*, which is direct from the French. An English version, *naivety*, is less common.

These words need not go into italics; they are effectively anglicised.

native. A person who is *native* to a country is a person born in that country.

The English in India and the Australians in New Guinea called the local people *natives*, and the word took on a condescending or demeaning character. In the post-colonial world the word has fallen into disfavor and has been replaced by such a word as *indigene*, also a Latin word, in this case meaning *begotten in*.

Spike Milligan, when asked "What are you doing here?" answered, "Everyone's got to be somewhere!" Everyone in fact has to be a *native* of somewhere.

Although the word *native* to most people still conjures up the concept of a 'colored' person, irrespective of his or her place of birth, the original and proper meaning is retained, for instance, in the title *Australian Natives' Association*. This is not an Aboriginal organisation but an association for those *born in Australia*.

In this sense the word remains a useful part of the language. Otherwise avoid it.

naturalist/naturist. A *naturalist* chases butterflies with a net. A *naturist* may also do so, but he or she does so without any clothes on. A *naturist* practises *nudism*, sometimes called *naturism*.

naught/nought. Use *naught* when the meaning is *nothing*, as in *All their efforts were brought to naught*.

Use *nought* when the figure *0* is meant.

nauseous. Properly speaking, something that is *nauseous* is something that *causes nausea* (that is, the feeling that you want to vomit): *This spaghetti is nauseous; I cannot eat it*.

That is the 'proper' use. However these days, when someone says "I am nauseous", they don't mean that they cause other people to feel like vomiting, but that they themselves feel like vomiting.

What they *should* say is "I am nauseated" or "I am bilious".

The changed meaning of *nauseous* has, however, such wide acceptance that little more can be done than point out that we have lost a word from the language.

Nausea comes from the Greek word meaning *sea-sickness* (*naus* is a ship) and is related, not only to *nautical* and *navy* but also to the word *noise*. It is hard to be sea-sick quietly.

nautical mile. The *nautical mile* is the measure of distance used at sea and in aviation. Although not a metric measurement it is, and will remain, a legal measurement in Australia.

In theory a nautical mile is defined as *the distance on the earth's surface subtended by one minute of latitude at the earth's centre.* If the earth were perfectly round a nautical mile would measure an arc of one minute at all places, but since the earth flattens out at the poles this in fact varies, and an average has been struck. This average is 1852 m (6076.1 feet) for the *international nautical mile*, to which Australia adheres. The traditional British figure for the nautical or geographical mile is 6080 feet (1853.18 m). This has now been superseded by the international nautical mile.

The nautical mile is thus considerably longer than the British, Australian and American land statute mile (5280 feet).

See also **metrication**.

navy. For naval ranks see **ranks in the armed forces.**

near by. The writing of this word as *nearby* (one word) was, until recently, regarded as incorrect, as with *alright* for **all right.**

Near North. See **Far East**.

necessity/need. *Necessity of* or *for* something, but *need to.* Thus:

There is no necessity for awakening him.

There is no need to awaken him.

Do not, in other words, say *There is no necessity to awaken him.*

This is not so much a matter of grammar as of idiom.

negotiate. *To negotiate*, in the sense of *working towards an agreement*, is the original and the preferred sense of this verb.

To negotiate, in the sense of *to surmount an obstacle*, is still frowned upon. This use originated, apparently, in jocular use on the hunting field: 'negotiating' a difficult piece of ground. It is now familiar in such phrases as *we negotiated the overhanging section of rock*, *we negotiated the check-point*, *we negotiated the sharp corner*. In these usages the word does have a sense of picking one's way delicately, and may perhaps be allowed its passage.

The word is pronounced *ne-GO-she-ate*, not *ne-GO-see-ate*.

Negro/Negress. The word *Negress* is no longer acceptable. When it is necessary to distinguish between a male and a female Negro, use *Negro woman*. *Negro* should always be spelt with a capital letter. Note that many American Negroes prefer to be called *Blacks*.

neither is always followed by a singular verb. In a sentence such as *Neither of the two young men has any manners*, the *neither* in fact stands for *neither one*, and hence has to be followed by the singular verb.

Neither of the two young men have any manners is, then, wrong.

Pronounce as *nye-ther* or *neether*. The latter tends to be the American pronunciation.

See also **either; neither/nor; nor.**

neither/nor.
1. Basically, this matter is quite simple. *Neither* is always followed by *nor*, *either* by *or*. Thus:

> *Neither* he *nor* his sister was present.
> *Either* we go today *or* we do not go at all.

2. It is sometimes said that *neither ... nor* should not be used where there are more than two alternatives. But Kipling thought otherwise:

> We can neither love nor pity nor forgive.
> ("The Secret of the Machines")

And so did Garibaldi, when he offered his followers "neither pay, nor quarters, nor provisions; but hunger, thirst, forced marches, battles, and death."

3. Some confusion can arise when the negative that starts the sentence is simply *no* or *not*, rather than *neither*. Take this example:

> The sailors did not think that the ship would sink, nor that the accident would cause any serious difficulties.

Strictly speaking, *nor* in this context suggests a double negative, and could be interpreted as meaning "they didn't think it wouldn't cause any serious difficulties." But *nor* in such a setting is so firmly entrenched as an idiom that it may be accepted as correct. *Or*, however, is preferable.

4. When *neither ... nor* or *either ... or* is used between singular subjects, the verb remains singular:

> *Either* he *or* his wife *drives* the children to school.
> It is unclear whether *either* job *has* been done.

See also **either; neither; nor.**

nem. con./unanimous. A *unanimous* vote is *a vote in which everyone present agrees*. It is a word often misused to describe a vote *where there are no dissentients*. This is wrong. A meeting where ten people vote for a motion and two abstain from voting is *not* unanimous. It is a meeting where the motion was passed *nem. con.*

    Nem. con. is an abbreviation of the Latin words *nemine contradicente*, meaning *with no-one opposing*.

né/née. These French words identify the name someone was born with. The feminine form *née* is more familiar, since it is women who by custom have most often relinquished their birth names. *Katharine Susannah Throssell*, née *Prichard* means that this woman was born a Prichard, was given the names Katharine Susannah, and acquired (in this case, by marriage) the name Throssell.

    In the case of a man the word is *né: The Duke of Wellington*, né *Wellesley*.

nephew. The Americans say *NEF-yoo*. The British say *NEV-yoo* (they borrowed the word from the French). Australians tend to *NEF-yoo*.

nepotism. "It is a pity that Australian farmers practise nepotism in handing down their farms to their sons rather than their daughters, for women are often more successful than men in running rural properties" (newspaper article).

    Originally *nepos* was the Roman word for a male grandchild, and *neptis* the word for a female grandchild. Later they became the words for *nephew* and *niece*. In Renaissance times *nepotism* became the agreed word for *arranging a job for a relative through influence*. This was no doubt helped by the practice of prominent figures in the Church organising agreeable positions for their bastard sons ("nephews").

    Nepotism today has no particular reference to males. It is used as a general term for the favoring of relatives or close friends by those in positions of power. It is quite wrong to use it in the sense quoted above. For a start, a daughter is as close a relation as a son. Secondly, while it may be undesirable to favor sons over daughters, it is not *sly and underhand*, which nepotism by definition is.

    The writer of the article could have been searching for the word *primogeniture*, which means *the right of an eldest son to succeed to an estate*. If the writer meant that sons in general are favored, she would have done better to write *favor their sons* rather than *practise nepotism*.

neurotic. See **paranoid/neurotic/psychotic/psychopathic.**

New Australian. Popular in the years after the second world war as a general term for the increasing numbers of migrants, particularly those from non-

English speaking countries, *New Australian* has now passed out of use and should not be revived.

Like many such terms, it became subject to the laws of debasement. Intended to be a kindly and helpful term, it acquired dismissive overtones, and in any case outlived its usefulness as *New Australians* came to think of themselves as *Australians*. See **ethnic**.

New Holland was the name given to the continent of Australia by the early Dutch explorers. It remained in use until well into the nineteenth century. An alternative to *New Holland* as the name for the fifth continent was *Terra Australis*, meaning "the land of the south". Matthew Flinders called his famous work, published in 1814, *A Voyage to Terra Australis*, though he would have preferred to call it *A Voyage to Australia* and was talked out of it by Sir Joseph Banks. See **Australia**.

A variant on this meaning of *New Holland* was the usage of early governors, who sometimes distinguished between *New South Wales* (under the governors' jurisdiction and extending from the coast to 135 degrees of east longitude, now about half-way across South Australia) and the rest of the continent, which they called *New Holland*.

It should be noted that neither *New Holland* nor *Terra Australis* encompassed the island we now know as Tasmania, and indeed until Federation in 1901 even the word *Australia* as often as not excluded Tasmania; thus frequent references in nineteenth-century literature to *Australia and Tasmania*.

In one sense this was a convenience, for we do not now have a word to describe *Australia without Tasmania*, and sometimes it is necessary to do so, particularly in scientific writing. *Continental Australia* is one possibility, but *New Holland* is still occasionally used in historical and anthropological writing. An example is: *The Aboriginal populations on the Bass Strait islands in the nineteenth century consisted partly of New Holland and partly of Van Diemen's Land* [or *Tasmanian*] *components*.

New South Wales/New South Welsh. Should we speak of the *New South Wales* government or the *New South Welsh* government? What, in other words, is the adjective from the proper noun *New South Wales*?

Either is correct, but *New South Welsh* has come to sound affected, and should be allowed to fall into disuse.

newspapers and magazines usually have their titles printed in italics, as of course do books. In typescript or in handwriting they should be underlined, which is in effect an instruction to the printer to set that word or words in italics.

Note, however, that the word *the* which precedes the titles of newspapers and magazines is never italicised or printed or written with a capital *t*. The following are correct:

It is an odd feature of Australian life that the *Australian Women's Weekly* appears once a month.

He was able to find the article he wanted in a February issue of the *Sydney Morning Herald.*

In Britain, for traditional reasons, it has always been customary to make an exception to these rules by referring to the London *Times* as *The Times.* An amiable courtesy, some may say, but there seems to be no reason why Australians should adopt this eccentricity.

Do not refer to a *magazine* as a *book.*

New World. The New World is the Americas, hence Dvořak's New World symphony, inspired by a visit to the United States. Occasionally the phrase is applied to the new discoveries in the Pacific in the eighteenth century, but if so is qualified by some such form as *the New World of the Pacific.* D. H. Lawrence, in chapter one of *The Boy in the Bush*, says of the Australian convict system that "the first thing that the old world had to ship to the new world was its sins," so the phrase is, at least occasionally, extended to Australia.

nice. The use of the word *nice* to mean *amiable, pleasant, attractive* and so on is pussyfooting and tiresome, so much so that is frequently undermines the impression it is intended to convey. To exclaim *That's a nice blouse* or *She lives in a nice house* carries a faint suggestion that *it's all right for her but I have somewhat higher standards.* If a compliment is to be paid at all, it's worth sparing a few words to make it a *precise* compliment. Most of us would prefer to be told that we live in a *beautiful* or *elegant* or *friendly* house rather than in a *nice* one. There is a separate entry in this book on the tedious and insincere *have a nice day.*

Jane Austen in *Northanger Abbey* has Catherine mentioning a *nice book*, to which Henry replies "and this is a very nice day, and we are taking a very nice walk; and you are two very nice young ladies. Oh! it is a very nice word indeed! It does for everything." Henry sounds a little superior, but he is making a nice point.

A *nice point*? Yes. *Nice* also has another meaning, which is *subtle, discerning, well-put, neat, close-fitting.* The Duke of Wellington said that the Battle of Waterloo was "a damned nice thing," by which he meant that its outcome was touch-and-go. Thus we can have *a nice distinction, a nice point, a nice fitting.*

Nice makes *nicish.* A *nicety* is not a *pleasantry* but *a subtle point*, as in *In preparing the wedding the niceties, such as bouquets for the bridesmaids, were not overlooked.*

niche. Should this be pronounced *nitsh* or *neesh*? Both are correct, but in Australia the usage tends towards *nitsh.*

nihilism means *the total rejection of accepted beliefs*. It may be pronounced either *NEE-il-ism* or *NYE-il-ism*. The *h* is not sounded.

Niue Island. Niue Island, in the south Pacific, is said to be the most naturally radioactive land on Earth. Pronounce *NYOO-ay.*

no. The word *no.* as an abbreviation for *number* is an abbreviation of the Latin word *numero*, meaning *with the number.*

Attempts to replace *no.* in Australia with the American symbol # should be opposed, if only because most of the population hasn't the faintest idea what # stands for.

Nobel. The name of Alfred Bernhard Nobel, Swedish founder of the Nobel Prizes, is pronounced *no-BEL* and not like the English word *noble*. Media announcers please note.

noisome/noisy. *Noisome* has nothing whatsoever to do with the word *noise*. It means *smelling bad* or, in Australian, *on the nose*. A *noisome welcome* is not a welcome with a brass band, but one at which rotten eggs are thrown. *Noisome* is related to the word *annoy.*

nom de guerre/nom de plume/pen-name/pseudonym. The phrase the French use for a name used by an author which is not his or her own is *nom de guerre*, literally *war-name*. It will be used in English writing by those who want to make it clear that they know what the proper French phrase is.

Nom de plume literally means *pen-name*. The French do not use the phrase, but it is common in English.

Pen-name is of course a direct translation of *nom de plume*. It is a useful English word and, of these four, is the one recommended for use.

Pseudonym is open to the objection that it has a general meaning rather than a literary one: *The Prince of Wales travelled under the pseudonym of Mr Charles Windsor*. It is best left for general use.

nominal. A *nominal* charge, a *nominal* payment, a *nominal* commitment: these mean *in name only;* in another word, *token.*

Nominal should not be used to describe a payment or charge which, while small, was reasonable for what was done or given. *Nominal* does not simply mean *low* or *small.*

non- as a prefix, as in such a word as *non-controversial* (prefer uncontroversial) or *non-essential* (prefer *inessential*) is under a cloud. It too easily becomes a lazy and boring way of making a word negative.

271

nonchalant

There are many useful *non-* words which are indispensable, words such as *non-combatant, non-aggression* and *nonconformist*. And in some cases there are useful distinctions between *non-* and *un-*, as with *non-professional* and *unprofessional*. But the random use of *non-* should be discouraged.

nonchalant means to be *casually unconcerned, indifferent*. It comes from words meaning *without warmth*. Pronounce *NON-shal-ent, NON-shil-int*.

none has/none have. Many assume that, because the word *none* is claimed, not altogether correctly, to be a contraction of *no one* or *not one*, it must be followed by a singular verb: *none has*. In fact the plural construction is more common: *none have*. Both are correct. It really is a matter of whether you have in mind, in writing the phrase, whether *none* in the context means *not one* or *not any*. In the latter case, of course, you will use *none have*.

noon. The correct designation for the time at noon is *12 noon* or *12 midday*. It cannot be 12 a.m. (which means *before noon*) or 12 p.m. (which means *after noon*).
One minute after noon is *12.01 p.m.*
See also **midnight**.

no-one/no one. Although H. W. Fowler in 1926 recommended the form *no-one*, on the ground that it was a sensible compromise between *noone* (which might be pronounced *noon*) and *no one* (which would make it the odd-one-out in the *anyone, everyone* league), Gowers in 1965 capitulated to the more widespread use of *no one*.
No-one is well established in Australian use and the advantages are the same today as they seemed to Fowler in 1926. *No-one* is recommended.

nor.
1. *Nor* follows *neither* in such constructions as *Neither the cat nor the dog had been seen for some days.*
2. Does, however, *nor* necessarily follow *not, never, no*, in such sentences as the following?
> Care should be taken not to identify a publisher as a printer, nor a printer as a publisher.
> He could not make rhyme nor reason out of the order.
> She must never come again, nor write to me.
In all of these cases *or* is probably preferable to *nor*. The argument is that the original *not* or *never* or *no* remains in force throughout the rest of the sentence, and does not need reinforcing with *nor*.
3. *Nor* can stand on its own, without a preceding negative, when it follows a

phrase with a negative resonance: "The world will little note nor long remember what we say here," said Abraham Lincoln at Gettysburg.

4. Note however that of course *nor* is essential when the force of the original negative does not carry over into another part of the sentence:

> She did not get in touch for six months, nor did her sister.

See also **neither/nor**.

normalcy/normality. *Back to normalcy* was a phrase made famous by the American President Warren G. Harding. An Englishman or Australian, or indeed a 'well brought-up' American, would say *back to normality. Normalcy* is a recognised word and Harding was entitled to use it. For all that, Australians should stick with *normality*.

normally. The most common use of *normally* is to mean *usually*, as in *We normally have breakfast at eight*. It is worth remembering, however, that *normally* comes from the Latin word for a carpenter's square and strictly speaking does not mean *usually* but *conforming to an expected pattern of response, relating to an established standard*. It was for this reason that two or three generations back teachers' training schools were called *normal schools*.

nostalgia is, strictly speaking, *homesickness*, and pedants will sometimes insist on this. However the word has been used for so long and so widely to mean *a longing for something experienced in the past* that to insist on a narrower meaning is useless and silly.

nothing is always followed by a singular verb. *Nothing but a few planks was to be seen*, not *Nothing but a few planks were to be seen*.

not only . . . but also. Watch for a booby-trap hidden here.

This sentence is correct:

> They passed the supplies not only to the officials but also to the general public.

This sentence is wrong:

> They not only passed the relief supplies to the officials but also to the general public.

The reason the second sentence is incorrect is more easily seen if we set it out this way:

> They not only passed the relief supplies to the officials but also [distributed mail?] to the general public.

In other words, by writing *not only passed* the meaning of *but also* is that they then did something else too. If *not only* is followed by a verb, then *but also* must also be followed by a verb.

The moral is, watch where you place your *not onlys*.

273

not un-.
> It is not unlikely that it will be hot tomorrow.
> It is not unfair to suggest he is wrong.
> It is not unkind to tell him to stop drinking.

The *not un-* formations are well calculated to send those who love the language into fits of anger and desperation. They are in almost all cases a timid, lily-livered, pussyfooting way of avoiding a simple and direct statement.

George Orwell has suggested that those who wish to be cured of the *not un-* disease should memorise:

> A not unblack dog was chasing a not unsmall rabbit across a not ungreen field.

nought. See **naught**.

nouns. The *noun* is one of the eight **parts of speech** in traditional grammar. Nouns *name a person, thing or quality.*

Nouns can be divided up into various 'types'. Here are some.

PROPER NOUNS: *Norman, Brisbane, Africa, Murray River, Ayers Rock, New Zealand, Festival Hall.* These name a particular person or thing. They start with capital letters.

COMMON NOUNS, which name classes of things: *door, street, radio, knife, finger.*

ABSTRACT NOUNS: *falsehood, loveliness, height, distance, repulsiveness.*

COLLECTIVE NOUNS: *congregation, crew, audience, troop.*

MASS NOUNS (which cannot take an *a* or *an* before them): *rice, coffee,* he had *egg* on his face.

Note that other parts of speech may from time to time function as nouns. Here are some examples:

PRONOUN: *He* then gave *it* to *me.*

PREPOSITION: I do not understand the *ins* and *outs* of this case.

VERB: Her aim was *to succeed; Succeeding* is pleasant.

In addition *noun clauses* and *noun phrases* (the clause has a finite verb and the phrase doesn't) contain different parts of speech but function as nouns:

> I thanked him for *what he did.*
> *Going to bathe* proved a difficult exercise.

For compound nouns, see **trades unions or trade unions?**

See also **modifiers**.

noun to verb: is change decay? Carpenters don't like seeing chisels used as screwdrivers, and people sensitive to language often voice strong disapproval at words with one familiar grammatical function being shanghaied for use in another.

A common target here is the change of nouns to verbs, as in the sentence *In this issue the Prime Minister is profiled by Joe Blow.* The word *profile* is a noun, with the journalistic sense of *an article surveying the personal life and career of someone.* But in the example given it is being used as a verb. Many would regard its use in this way as improper.

Max Harris, in the *Australian* (26 April 1986), calls this kind of thing a "slob writing reflex." He lists a number of nouns which are twisted to form verbs, and from his list we can construct such sentences as:

> This article has to be taken away and properly sourced.
>
> The matter has been actioned.
>
> The issue will be progressed through detailed assessment.

And he goes on to suggest some coming delights:

> Judith Wright poeted her feelings ...
>
> David Dallwitz tromboned ...
>
> The Sydney Symphony Orchestra auralised Mozart's *Jupiter* last night.

A few days later Max Harris was counter-attacked by a correspondent to the *Australian* who wrote that "The transmogrification from noun to verb is about the oldest step in language growth and is the source of half the rich store of verbs in the English language." He gave as examples:

To *tune* an engine	To *floor* an opponent
To *feather* a propeller	To *ladder* a stocking
To *buttonhole* a client	To *monkey* with the rules

He could have added *to house, to harbor, to mushroom, to target, to scapegoat, to access, to auspice, to glove* ("The keeper should have gloved this one") and many more.

There are two comments to be made.

1. Both Max Harris and his critic, Malcolm Ronan, are correct. The process of adapting and adopting words, of varying their function, is a part, and a proper part, of a living language. The first time it is done, in each case, will no doubt outrage many. Gradually the new usage comes to be seen as quite natural.

On the other hand the examples Max Harris gives are offensive to many, though *actioned* and *sourced* are certainly 'coming in', and *progressed* is a quite familiar and acceptable verb (*We then progressed further*), and it is the idiom in this case that Mr Harris is objecting to. People sensitive to words will tend to be cowards when it comes to using old words in new ways, and will wait, like most of the rest of mankind when placed in a difficult position, and like penguins on the edge of an ice-floe, until someone else does it first.

The following are among many examples which could be given of noun-to-verb or adjective-to-verb changes which still sound unpleasant to many ears, although the first one given here can be dated back to 1727:

> He *personalised* his stationery.
>
> Sales *plateaued* at this point in the campaign.
>
> The celebration *climaxed* with fireworks.
>
> She *authored* the play.
>
> You will find the Great Fire of London *diarised* in Samuel Pepys.
>
> The prima donna *vocalised* beautifully.

> This happening was *facsimiled* the following day.
> The matter has been *prioritised.*
> The ruckman *springboarded* Carlton's attacks.

2. As we see above it is not only the noun-to-verb transformation that occurs. When someone writes in the *Age* about education in Victoria, and refers to "the current ramshackled system", he is turning an adjective into a verb, even though he is the assistant secretary of the Victorian Secondary Teachers' Association. The noun *fall* reversed the process Max Harris objects to, and was created from the verb *to fall* seven hundred years ago. The verb *to stride* has become an Australian word for *trousers, strides.* When we talk about a newspaper being *a daily* we are using a noun that was once no more than an adjective or adverb. A *verbal* statement, as taken down by the police in an interview, has now become a verb, as in "I was verballed." Examples are endless.

See **marginalise**.

nth degree. The letter *n*, in numerical notation, stands for *any number.* In specific cases it can be minus 1 or ten million. To say therefore that *John's room is untidy, but Sarah's untidy to the nth degree*, is meaningless in arithmetical terms. This will not stop people using the term to mean *very much more so.*

nubile. Strictly speaking *nubile* (*a nubile young woman*) means *ready for marriage*, not *sexually attractive*, and therefore to talk of *a nubile bride* verges on a **pleonasm**. This sense of the word, however, has long been overtaken by *sexually alluring*, and to use the word only in its 'proper' sense would be pedantic.

nuclear is pronounced as written. A common mispronunciation in American English is *NOO-kew-ler*, in Australia (including ABC announcers) *NYOO-kew-ler.*

Nullarbor. The *Nullarbor Plain* is so spelt, not as *Nullabor.* The name comes from Latin words meaning *no tree.*

number.
1. In sentences such as *The first indication of the raid was the sirens* should the verb be *was* (singular, to agree with *indication*) or *were* (plural, to agree with *sirens*)?

The general rule here is to follow the number of the subject. The subject here is *indication*, so the correct form of the verb is *was.*

Conversely, if the sentence read *The sirens were the first indication of the raid*, then *were* (plural, agreeing with *sirens*) would be correct.

Note that in such a sentence as *Three years is the time normally allowed for the completion of a doctoral thesis* or *Some weeks has been put aside for this purpose* a singular verb is used because the sense is singular — that is, we silently assume the words *A period of* before *three years* and *some weeks*.

2. Where there is more than one subject in a sentence the verb following should be in the plural, whether or not the subjects are of different numbers: *One man and his dogs go to mow a meadow.* (But see **as well as.**)

3. The position is more complex where there are two subjects in a sentence, different in number, as can occur with the use of the word *or: Either the men or the manager is/are right.*

There are really only two solutions here. The first is to turn the sentence round: *Either the men are right, or the manager is.* The second, and less satisfactory, is to have the verb agree with the noun nearest to it: *Either the men or the manager is right.*

4. **Collective nouns**, such as *committee, group, team*, may take either a singular or a plural verb. Which you choose to use will sometimes depend on the context. An example is the word *number*, itself a collective noun. Here the recommendation is to link *the number* with the singular, *a number* with the plural, as in:

> The number of cartons *is* too many for the truck.
>
> A number of those present *are* drunk.
>
> There *have* been a growing number of complaints

Similarly, *a quarter of the rooms are occupied*, rather than *a quarter of the rooms is occupied*.

Note that in such a phrase as *a number of aspects are relevant, a number* stands for *numerous* or *many*, in other words is an adjectival phrase relating to the noun *aspects*, and the verb must agree with *aspects* by being plural.

5. *There's some people on the beach.* Since *people* is plural, the verb should agree, and the sentence should read *There are some people on the beach.* The incorrect use is, however, a common one, perhaps because of the difficulty of saying *There're some people on the beach.* Henry Lawson tells us that:

> There was short, plump girls, there was tall, slim girls
>> and the handsomest ever seen —
> They was four-foot-five, they was six-foot high, and every
>> height between.

numbers.

1. In writing, express the numbers from one to one hundred in words, but after that in figures.

Exceptions to this are:

(a) Words above a hundred should be spelt out if they can be written in one or two words: *299*, but *three hundred; Man arrived on the Australian continent at least some thirty thousand years ago, having somehow managed to cross the water barriers from Asia.*

(b) Large numbers over one million may, if reasonably short, be spelt out (*twelve million*) or, if more complicated, be expressed in figures *and* numbers, as *17.54 million* (which is 17,540,000).

(c) Where there is a list of quantities, they should be expressed in figures, for instance: *Included in the two shipments were 13 camels, 3 zebras and 24 pigs.*

(d) Where two numbers come together, one should be written in numbers, one in figures: *He had two 115-horsepower motors on the back of his boat.*

(e) Where there are two sets of numbers involved in the same statement, it is helpful to place one set in figures, one in words: *Of the sixteen trees in the park, eight had 2 pairs of birds nesting in them, four had 3 pairs and four had 5 pairs.*

(f) In journalism and technical writing it is usually accepted that *numbers above ten* should be in figures. In the case of related numbers, some above ten and some below, adopt one form or the other, but not both (*ages ranged from seven to sixteen*, or *ages ranged from 7 to 16*).

2. Money, times, weights and measures, degrees of temperature, percentages and the like should be expressed in figures at all times, thus: *42 per cent, 230 millimetres, 10.30 a.m., $45.87.*

3. Never use a number for the opening of a sentence. If you can't switch the words around then spell out the numbers: *One hundred and forty-seven of the 315 persons involved in the accident survived.* Similarly a sentence should not start with a date. *1985 was a bad year for frosts* should be avoided. *The worst year for frosts for some time was 1985* would be preferable.

4. *Between four and six million*, not *between four to six million.*

5. In the punctuation of numbers, commas are used to separate these numbers into groups of three; for instance: *23,467,211.*

When there are only four numbers, however, commas are optional. One may write *3456* or *3,456.*

Commas are not used in the numbers of years, houses or rooms.

There is now a tendency to use a space instead of a comma in measurements given in the metric system: for instance, *16 344 metres*, not *16,344 metres.* This is because in many countries the comma is used instead of a decimal point in metric measuring, so that what in the USA, Britain and Australia is 16,344 metres is in France or Germany 16 metres and a bit. To retain the comma in large numbers could lead to serious misunderstandings. And note that numbers less than unity in the decimal system take a zero before the decimal point: *0.05*, not *.05.*

See also **billion; roman numerals**.

Nunga. Many Aboriginals, especially in South Australia, prefer to be referred to as *Nungas*. See also **Koori** and **Murri**.

O

O! For *O!* as an exclamation, see **O!/Oh!**

obligate/obligatory/oblige.
1. Let us simplify the matter by taking *obligatory* first. This means that something is *compulsory*, not voluntary. This is confusing to some because of the association with the word *oblige*, which suggests a certain voluntariness. But if someone says to you *It is obligatory that you take this seat*, it means that you have to. It should be pronounced with the accent on the second syllable, thus: *ob-LIG-at-ory*.
2. However, just because it is a perfectly useful adjective does not mean that *obligate* is necessarily the equivalent verb. *Obligate* means *to be formally bound by law or duty to do something*, as in *All parents are obligated to register their children's births*. Even so, it is an awkward word, which can almost always be adequately expressed by *obliged*, and is best left to legal language.
3. *Oblige* has the same legal meaning as *obligate* and is normally to be preferred. But *oblige* is more often seen or heard in such settings as *I am much obliged to you for your kindness, I think you are obliged to answer this letter*. To use *obligated* instead of *obliged* in such cases is a clumsy solecism which should be avoided.
4. In other words, in normal discourse avoid the word *obligate*.

oblique stroke. This punctuation mark, often occurring in the term *and/or*, is also called a *solidus, slant, slash mark, stroke, bar, virgule* or *diagonal*.
1. When the oblique stroke is used in an ordinary text it means *either/or*, as in:
> Everyone must seek the result he/she desires.
>
> We will need courage and/or luck to win through.

Such short-cut ways of expression are, however, best reserved for technical, official and informal contexts.
2. Note that the oblique stroke does *not* have the same function as a hyphen. To write of a *radio/cassette* when a *radio-cassette* is meant is both sloppy and wrong.
3. The oblique stroke is also used:
    (a) To present an alternative form of a word, as in *Examine the sentence to see if you can identify the verb/s*.
    (b) To separate dates, especially when they are consecutive: *3/4 March*, or *1886/87*. Or to write dates: *3/3/1986*.
    (c) To write fractions such as 1/3, though a horizontal line is also used here.

(d) To serve instead of the word *per*, as in *km/h, kilometres per hour*.

(e) To indicate subsections of documents, identifications of files, as in *CSO 2/34/1234*.

(f) In some abbreviations, such as *a/c* (*account*) and *c/o* (*care of*).

(g) To indicate lines of poetry, when that poetry is not being set as poetry: "I think that I shall never see / A poem lovely as a tree."

oblivious. Strictly speaking *oblivious* means (or used to mean) *forgetful* rather than *unaware*, but we need not worry about that. We may, however, bear in mind that *oblivious* may be followed by either *of* or *to*, and that *of* has rather more approval than *to*.

obtuse. See **abstruse/obtuse.**

Occam's Razor is sometimes referred to in print. William of Occam was an astute medieval English philosopher. He is remembered for his precept: *Essentia non multiplicanda sunt praeter necessitatem*.

Literally translated, this means *Don't employ more categories than are necessary*. More informally, it means *If there's a simple answer, consider that one first*. In other words, if your telephone is out of order, don't rush to the conclusion that there's been a Soviet nuclear strike on your nearest capital city.

It sounds obvious enough, but in these paranoid days William's words are often worth bearing in mind.

occupant/occupier. An *occupant* is *a person who happens at the moment to be in occupation of a seat, compartment or room*.

An *occupier* is *a person who lives in a house or other premises on a continuing basis*.

Oceania. See **Australasia.**

oculist/ophthalmologist/optician/optometrist. An *ophthalmologist* is a qualified medical practitioner who specialises in diseases of the eye. He (or she) used to be called an *oculist*, but the word didn't sound grand enough and, in any case, *oculists* were confused with *opticians*. *Oculist* is passing out of use in Australia.

Until about the second world war the usual name in Australia for a person who made lenses and fitted spectacles was *optician*. This word also has been subject to social climbing. As registration examinations for opticians were introduced over a period in all Australian States, the term *optician* was replaced by the grander-sounding *optometrist*, imported from the United States. The word *optician* is accordingly also in the discard.

-œ-. The letter *œ*, a combination of the letters *o* and *e*, is what is called a *digraph:* two letters representing a single sound. It is seldom now that we actually see the letters attached, or ligatured into, each other, but they are familiar in such words as *oesophagus*, *foetus*, *oecumenical* (and, in earlier times, *oeconomical*).

As with the similar digraph *ae*, the tendency today, especially in American English, is to discard the *o* and keep the *e*, which represents the pronunciation. Hence *fetus*, *ecumenical*.

Although touted as a desirable spelling reform, there is one major objection to this development. This is that the digraph *oe* represents the sound *ee*. To remove it from a word such as *foetus*, and spell the word *fetus*, opens the way to that word being pronounced to rhyme with *bet us*, which it doesn't.

We have seen the process at work with such words as *economic* and *ecumenical*, now often pronounced *ekumenical* and *ekonomic* rather than *eecumenical* and *eeconomic*.

It is clearly a process that is under way. But the argument for it is not clear-cut. Words that seem especially resistant to the change include *amoeba*, *manoeuvre*, *Oedipus*, *foetus* and *diarrhoea*.

See also -æ-.

offensive intruders. It is silly to be too parochial about one's language, especially when it's English, the language perhaps above all others which hasn't cared a damn about borrowings. The New Zealand writer Laurie Edmond has said of English:

> It never minds how much it's in the red,
>
> Pinching from other tongues, not paying fees;
>
> This language is the world's, the world has said.

At the same time Australians don't particularly like seeing their mines and industries passing under foreign control. Sometimes this is for emotional and even irrational reasons, but it's very understandable, and does relate to the feeling that it would be a dull world indeed if we had nothing we could call our own. As Vance Palmer once said, "The unity of man is based on his infinite diversity."

Outside words have often entered Australian English and will continue to do so. Many are inevitable and welcome: *videotape*, *hassle*, *star wars*, *stagflation*, *brainwash*, *payola*, *hi-fi*, *smorgasbord*. They are needed. Others however are like introduced plants and animals which drive out the native species. They thus diminish an Australian language-pool which, as Max Harris has frequently pointed out, is already diminishing rapidly enough through immigration.

So — unless a new word or pronunciation serves a useful purpose we should have a bias towards sticking to the old. If you agree, we will:

> Not say *zee* when we mean the letter *Z*.
>
> Not say *gotten* when we mean *got*.

Not say *cookies* when we mean *biscuits*.

Not say *jump rope* when we mean *skipping rope*.

Not say *plimsolls* or *sneakers* when we mean *sandshoes* or *runners*.

Not say *off limits* when we mean *out of bounds*.

Not say *for real* when we mean *really,* or *actually.*

Not say *five through ten* (even worse, write *five thru ten*) or *1974 through 1979* when we mean *five to ten* or *1974 to 1979.*

Not say *named after* when we mean *named for.*

Not use the symbol # to mean *number* when we already have a perfectly acceptable abbreviation in *no.*

Not say *Have a nice day!* as a sales gimmick.

Not say *getting past first base* when we mean *getting past the first obstacle.*

Not say *I'll take a raincheck* when we mean *I'll defer that.*

Not say *guy* when we mean *chap* or *bloke* or *fellow.*

Not say *I'll fix myself a drink* when we mean *I'll make myself a drink.*

Not say *fresh out of* when we mean *just out of.*

Not say *cool it* when we mean *take it easy* or *steady on.*

Not say *check it out* when we mean *look at it, check it* or *investigate it.*

Not say *drapes* when we mean *curtains.*

Not say *period* when we mean *full stop* or *point.*

Not say *take a shower* when we mean *have a shower.*

Not say *run for office* when we mean *stand for office.*

Not say *meet (up) with* or *visit with* when we mean *meet, visit.*

Not say *I'll call you* when we mean *I'll ring you, I'll telephone you.*

Not spell *sceptic* as *skeptic.*

Not say *surely!* when we mean *certainly!*

Not say *for free* when we mean *free.*

Not say *trail* when we mean *track.*

Not say *movie* when we mean *film.*

Not say *casket* when we mean *coffin.*

Not say *Hi!* for *Hullo.*

Not say *momentarily* when we mean *very soon.*

Not say *trash-cans* when we mean *dust-bins* or *rubbish-bins.*

Not say *cans of beans* when we mean *tins of beans.*

Not say *freight train* when we mean *goods train.*

Not say *steer* when we mean *bullock.*

Not say *herds of cattle* when we mean *mobs of cattle.*

Not say a *stampede of cattle* when we mean a *rush of cattle.*

Not say *rodeo* when we mean a *buckjump show.*

Not say *veterans* when we mean *returned servicemen.*

Not say *talk with* when we mean *talk to.*

Not say *that's for sure* when we mean *that's certain.*

And so on.

offsider. *Offsider* is a word that has nothing to do with football. It has entered the Australian language, where it is now a 'proper' word, from bullock-drivers' slang. Here the *off-sider* walked on the off side of the team while the senior man walked on the near side, thus enabling all bullocks in their linked yokes to be kept under control. The word now means *an assistant of any kind*.

often. An inoffensive word, but one with the dignity of being able to be pronounced four ways, all of them correct: *off-ten, off-en, orf-ten, orf-en*. Educated usage favored *orf-en* (hence the *orphan/often* joke in "The Pirates of Penzance"), but the *t* has come back into the word under the influence of the 'speak as you spell' tendency. The Prince of Wales says *off-ten*, if that helps. Take your pick.

of the order of. See **orders of magnitude**.

oh! For *Oh!* as an exclamation, see **O!/Oh!**

older/oldest. See **elder/eldest and older/oldest**.

Once more into the breach, dear friends. The actual words are *Once more unto the breach, dear friends.* Shakespeare's *Henry V*, act III, scene i.

one/one's.
1. The use of the word *one* as a pronoun in English is not as simple as it may seem. A phrase such as *One does not go to the zoo*, perfectly acceptable in French, does not sit easily in the English language, though it is not incorrect. The trouble is that, having started with *One*, you can get into trouble later:
   One does not go to the zoo, does one? Or does one ignore such a stupid rule?
2. For, if you do start with *One*, the use must be consistent through the following sentence. To say *One cannot walk on water, even if you do think you are God* is wrong, though Americans would accept *One cannot walk on water, even if he thinks he is God*. In approved Australian English the correct construction is *One cannot walk on water, even if one does think one is God*. James Thurber said that the chief objection to "a consistent, or 'cross-country' use of 'one' is that it tends to make a sentence sound like a trombone solo."
3. In constructions such as *One of the girls is missing* the verb must (as here) agree with *One*, that is be singular, rather than with *girls*. *One of the girls are missing* is wrong.
4. Beware of such a construction as *This was one of the best, if not the best, autobiographies of recent years*. At first sight or hearing it may sound all right, but if you look at it more closely you will see that, while *one of the best ... autobiographies* is fine, you cannot have *if not the best ... autobiographies* when in fact you mean *if not the best ... autobiography*. The plural doesn't work.

Write or say rather *This is one of the best autobiographies of recent years, if not the best.*

5. Note that *One of the best cricketers who has ever stepped on the field* is wrong. The verb *has* should agree with *who*, which stands for *cricketers*, and should therefore be *have*.

6. Note that *one* is the only personal pronoun that takes an apostrophe and the *s* in the possessive: *one's, anyone's, everyone's.*

7. An argument for the use of *one* is that it is 'gender-neutral', that is, that it avoids the equally clumsy *he/she* problem we often end up with. See **(the) female critique**, paragraph 4.

one small step for man. Neil Armstrong's actual words as he landed on the moon on 21 July 1969 were, "That's one small step for a man, one giant leap for mankind."

one 't' or two. *Regretable* or *regrettable*? See **doubling up.**

one touch of nature makes the whole world kin. This Shakespearian quotation is from *Troilus and Cressida*, act III, scene iii. *Nature* here does not mean the natural world about us, but *human nature*. That, at least, is what is often claimed. John Silverlight, however, writing in the London *Observer*, has pointed out that a close reading of Shakespeare's lines discloses that the quality Shakespeare is talking about — or, more correctly, that his cynical character Ulysses is talking about — is fickleness.

ongoing. We read of "an ongoing campaign to make Australian exports more cost-effective," and this faddish word is so widely used that it may be heard or read many times daily in newspapers, on radio and television and in discussions.

Ongoing, in the sense of *continuing*, can be traced in the language as far back as 1877. Until about 1960 it remained an unusual word; since then it has swamped us.

There is little to be said about the word except that it is pretentious and officious, and *continuing* should be used in its place.

only. The main problem with this innocent-looking word is its protean quality, its versatility, its ability to change the meaning of a sentence by darting around that sentence. For example, note the different meanings of these sentences:

1. Only Belinda flew by Qantas as far as Hong Kong. (The others were already there, or travelled by some other means.)

2. Belinda only travelled by Qantas as far as Hong Kong. (She did nothing else.)

3. Belinda travelled only by Qantas as far as Hong Kong. (She did not switch to Cathay Pacific at Manila.)

4. Belinda travelled by Qantas only as far as Hong Kong. (Ambiguous: means either 3 or 5.)

5. Belinda travelled by Qantas as far only as Hong Kong. (She travelled further by other means.)

6. Belinda travelled by Qantas as far as Hong Kong only. (She did not go to Peking; or see 5.)

It is dogmatic to insist that the word *only* should be placed in front of the word it modifies, and nowhere else. Other things being equal, it should be placed where the speaker or writer feels it best fits. But, amongst the 'other things' should be a close look at the meaning.

on the nose. In Australian English this means *it stinks.* In American English it means *precisely, exactly, on the dot.*

on to/onto. The (incorrect) tendency is to run these words together at all times, perhaps by confusion with the word *into.*

1. Note first an important difference in meaning between:

> We walked onto the Sydney Harbor Bridge.

and

> We walked on to the Sydney Harbor bridge.

In the first instance you actually stepped onto the bridge. In the second you may have at that moment been at Hunters Hill, but decided to continue walking in the direction of the Sydney Harbor Bridge. Note that a comma could be placed after the second *on*, but not after the first.

2. *On to* in such cases as the following is an unnecessary doubling-up:

> He forced his opinions on to the company.

> An unfair burden of taxation is being forced on to the working class.

In both cases the word *to* is unnecessary.

3. Where *onto* is a preposition related directly to a following noun, as in *He fell onto the spikes, He swung onto the train*, it should be written as one word.

4. Otherwise stick with *on to*, as in such sentences as *The package was passed on to the correct recipient, We must fight on to the end.* Note again, a comma could, without doing violence to the sentence, be placed after the *on* in both these sentences; and that in neither example is the *on* really necessary.

O!/Oh! When members of parliament are aroused from their slumbers by an unusually scandalous remark, they shout (so Hansard tells us) *Oh!* ("Cries of Oh!").

When they fall on their knees to seek comfort by communing with their Maker they say *O God.*

When Sir Walter Scott was (perhaps) thinking of politicians, he wrote:

> O what a tangled web we weave,
> When first we practise to deceive!

O these days tends to be reserved for invocations (*O Lord, O ye sinners*) and for use in somewhat poetic contexts, as Sir Walter uses it above. Otherwise, used as an interjection or mark of surprise, it is spelt *oh*.

oo or yoo? Should the word *suit* be pronounced to rhyme with *hoot* or should it be pronounced *syoot* to rhyme with *beaut?* Should we say *soo-preme* or *syoo-preme?* Should we say *soo-perb* or *syoo-perb?* Should we say *interlood* (to rhyme with *prude*) or *interlyood?* The short answer is that the English like the *yoo* sound, but that Americans and Australians don't. Sir Humphrey Appleby, in the television program "Yes, Minister", pronounces *issue* as *issyoo*.

The longer answer is that no-one likes the *yoo* sound after *ch, j, r* and *sh*, which is why we say *rude, shoe, juice* and *chute* with the *oo* sound and not the *yoo* — all of us.

At the same time *everyone* likes the *yoo* sound after other consonants (with exceptions which are noted below): *abuse, huge, putative, fuse, duplicity, nude, demure*.

There are two exceptions to this.
1. The Americans (but not necessarily the Canadians) prefer the *oo* sound after *d, n, s* and *t*: *dooty, doo, dooly* (*duly*), *noosance* (*nuisance*), *noomerical, ensoo* (*ensue*), *stoodent, toomult, toomur*. (Even so, American dictionaries show the *yoo* pronunciation as an alternative, and some Americans use it.)
2. The *yoo* sound after *s* and *l*, which is where the problem we raised in the first paragraph above comes in.

All that anyone can say is that *yoo* in such usages is giving way to the simpler *oo*, but in certain words, and for no apparent reason, *yoo* after *l* seems to be hanging on quite easily: *dilute* and *prelude* are examples.

We do not accept the *Macquarie Dictionary's* point of view that in Australia the pronunciation of such words as *interlude* is overwhelmingly *interlood*. *Interlyood* is still alive and well, as are other pronunciations such as *delyooded* (*deluded*), *dilyoot* (*dilute*), *nyood* (*nude*), *lyoor* (*lure*) and *resolyoot* (*resolute*).

See also **ensue; suit/suitable/suite**.

op. cit. See **referencing**.

operative, in the sense of *This is the operative clause of the contract*, does not mean *This is the most important clause of the contract*. It means *This is the clause of the contract which relates to the carrying out of the contract*.

Operative as a noun is increasingly replacing the word *operator*, as in *keyboard operative*. Agreed, it appears in the dictionaries in this meaning, but in many ways is a pretentious word, even a **bully word**. If people got paid more for being *operatives* than *operators* we might diminish our objections. But we doubt that they do.

ophthamologist. See **oculist.**

optician. See **oculist.**

optometrist. See **oculist.**

oral. See **aural/oral/visual.**

Order of Australia. Strictly speaking, no-one receives the Order of Australia. The Order of Australia is not a piece of insignia or a medal, but "an Australian society of honor for the purpose of according recognition to Australian citizens and other persons for achievement or for meritorious service."

A person honored does not, then, *receive* the Order of Australia, but *becomes a part of it.*

A person may be appointed to the order at several levels: Companion, Officer or Member. There is also a Medal of the Order.

Correctly speaking, then, reference should not be made to a person's holding the Order of Australia, but rather to his or her having been made, or being, a Companion, Officer or Member of the Order of Australia.

Abbreviations are AC, AO and AM. A holder of the Medal of the Order is OAM. Holders of the OAM are not members of the Order of Australia.

In 1976 the Fraser government added to the distinctions within the Order of Australia knighthoods (AK) and damehoods (AD). The Hawke government in 1986 repealed this section of the Act. In all twelve knights and two dames were appointed to the Order.

orders of magnitude. The term *orders of magnitude* is in fact a mathematical term, but is commonly heard in general discourse these days. *We spent more on the arts than they did by whole orders of magnitude* usually means nothing more than *We spent a lot more than they did.*

But *order of magnitude* has a precise meaning, which is *a quantity expressed as a power of ten.* A figure which differs by an order of magnitude from another figure is either *ten times as much* or *ten times less.* The Earth's mass and that of the sun vary by five orders of magnitude: the former is 10^{22} tons and the latter 10^{27} tons. To outspend someone by an order of magnitude is to spend ten times as much.

See also **quantum leap.**

ordinance/ordnance. An *ordinance* is *an officially promulgated regulation.* *Ordnance* (a 'mass' noun which cannot have *a* or *an* in front of it) means *artillery, munitions* or *military supplies.*

orgy means *a wild party, often with suggestions of 'liberated' behavior.*

The pronunciation of this word is *OR-djee*. For some reason, quite a few Australians appear to believe that the word is pronounced with a hard *g*, as in *get*.

orient, orientate. *Orientate* in particular has become something of an 'in' word. "We must orientate our sales campaign," meaning "We must select our targets," conveys an impression — or at least many business people hope it does — of scientific competence. *Orientate* in any case is an undesirable usage, probably what is called back-formation from the word *orientation*, and may be termed an *illegitimate verb*. The real verb is *orient*. Strictly speaking it means, of course, to place something (e.g. a church) so that it faces east; more generally it means to take one's bearings.

The sales manager should have said: "We must *orient* our sales campaign." Or, even better, might have searched for a less pretentious way of putting it.

-or/-our. Should *labour* be spelt *labor*, *succour* be spelt *succor*, *honour* be spelt *honor*, and so on? The issue has become confused because of emotional anti-Americanism in Australia, and the belief that to use the *-or* ending somehow endorses the policies of the Pentagon. In fact, as with many American usages, the *-or* ending harks back to an earlier form of the English language. The *-our* ending is a genteelism which can be traced to an eighteenth- and nineteenth-century cultural cringe towards French forms and to the influence of Samuel Johnson's dictionary (1755). It is seldom found in early Australian documents and despatches, but has crept into common use in the last hundred years or so. Even so, many Australian newspapers and school systems have favored the simple *-or* ending. In mid-1985, of eleven major Australian newspapers, six used the *-or* ending. Their circulations were double those of newspapers which used *-our*.

The *-our* ending has a spurious dignity about it, best exemplified in the ruling of the Melbourne *Age* to its reporters that the spelling of such words as *labor* shall not have the *u*, except the word *savior* when it refers to Jesus Christ, in which case it shall be spelt *Saviour*.

There are, in any case, more words in British English which have dropped the *-our*, or never had it, than there are words which retain it: *actor*, *author*, *error*, *terror* and so on.

The *-or* ending is always to be preferred, except with such cases as the British *Labour Party*, where the spelling is part of a formal title. Note that *Australian Labor Party* and *Pearl Harbor* should always be so spelled, for the same reason.

The above discussion does not apply, of course, to words which, although they end in *-our*, give that ending a different sound to that of the words mentioned above. Thus words such as *contour*, *devour* and *pour* retain at all times their *-our* ending.

The *-our* ending is gradually dropping out even of English English. The following words, though spelt in English English with the *-our*, drop the *u* before the suffixes *-ous*, *-ate*, *-ation*, *-ary* and *-ise/-ize*:

clamour *but* clamorous
clangour *but* clangorous
glamour *but* glamorous, glamorise
honour *but* honorary
humour *but* humorous
labour *but* laborious
odour *but* odorless, odorous, deodorize
rigour *but* rigorous
valour *but* valorous
vapour *but* vaporise, vaporous
vigour *but* vigorous, invigorate

See also **spelling reform in Australia**.

O.S. Australian youngspeak, an abbreviation for *overseas* which became widely used in the 1960s and later: *I'll be O.S. for two years*. The New Zealanders have a similar term, *O.E.*, meaning *overseas experience*: *Got your O.E. yet then?* The New Zealand author Keith Ovenden, introducing his novel *O.E.* (Auckland, 1956), calls the term "that most rare of concepts, an abstract consumer durable."

otherwise is a word which the English language could often do without. It seldom performs a useful function, and it should be handled with care.
1. Note that in such a sentence as *There are many sub-standard houses in the township, old and otherwise*, *other* is preferable to *otherwise*, but *old and new* would be better than either.
2. In a sentence such as *The government is concerned with the possibility, or otherwise, of coming to terms with the European Economic Community*, the words *or otherwise* perform no function except that of wasting ink.

In a sentence such as *Hurry up and get ready, otherwise we'll be late*, the word *otherwise* is acting as a conjunction joining two sentences, and may be replaced by *or* or *or else*. Some hold, however, that *otherwise* in this case is a stronger word than the alternatives.

There is no argument about the use of *otherwise* where it is used to mean *different*, *differently* or *different in outcome*, and can be seen as a form of *otherways*:

The facts of this matter are in fact *otherwise*.
I wouldn't have thought *otherwise*.

Otherwise is also acceptable in the sense of *in other respects* in such contexts as:

> This was an *otherwise* sensible solution.
>
> We had failed to consider the possibility of a flood; *otherwise* the plan was perfect.

ours. Not *our's*.

outside of/inside of. "Until we were elected leader and deputy leader [of the Liberal Party] in March 1983, John Howard and I never had a conversation outside of the Parliament." So said Andrew Peacock, quoted in the *Age*, 7 September 1985.

Outside of is an illiteracy, as is *inside of* in such a phrase as *it all happened inside of ten minutes*. The *of* has no place and is unnecessary. The phrases should be *outside the Parliament* and *inside ten minutes*.

In the same way avoid phrases such as *outside of the established guidelines*. Say or write *outside the established guidelines*.

over is over-worked. It is a preposition used loosely to do the work other prepositions can do better. It is desirable to remember that it means *above*, and in particular it should not be used as another way of saying *about*.

In these examples the preferred preposition is in brackets:

> The unionists were angry over (*about*) the decision.
>
> There was much anxiety over (*about, concerning*) the patient.
>
> An improvement over (*on*) last month's results.
>
> He was questioned over (*about*) an offence.
>
> They were criticised over (*for*) the poor arrangements.

overflowed/overflown. *Overflowed* is the past participle of the verb *to overflow: The river has overflowed its banks.*

Overflown is the past participle of the verb *to overfly: The base was overflown several times daily by spy satellites.*

oversee/overseer/oversight. *To oversee* means to superintend, and an *overseer* is a person who does this.

A lot of people have difficulty with these words, particularly the verb. One does not say, for instance, *He overseed the job*, or *The job was overseed*. The important thing to remember is that the core of the expressions is the verb *to see*, and that the words themselves follow this.

Thus *He oversaw the job, the job was overseen.*

The word *oversight* has no relation to those above. It means *something that has been accidentally omitted.*

owing to. See **due to/owing to.**

P

pace. Discussing "The Gillies Report", a reviewer in the *Sydney Morning Herald* (14 December 1985) writes that "Cook's cartoons and columns, and Clarke's and Gillies's monologues, are essentially expressions of their individual senses of humour, and observations of man's insanity to man (pacé feminists)."

Pace is pronounced *pacy* in English and *parkay* in Latin. Its literal meaning is *with peace* [*to*]. It is used when you want to make a quick, throw-away apology (or mock apology) to someone who may be offended by what you are saying. Examples:

> *Pace* Winston Churchill, the British withdrawal from India was both desirable and necessary. [Churchill opposed that withdrawal.]
>
> It is my view, *pace* Mr Robin Grey, that the Premier of Tasmania's fight to dam the Franklin River was politically ill-judged.

The reviewer we quote above is therefore using the word in the right sense. He is in fact saying that he apologises to feminists for using the word *man* to mean *human beings*. The only error is the acute accent on the *e* of *pace;* presumably he is under the impression that it is a French word which, of course, it is not.

Fowler's *Modern English Usage* holds that the word "is one that we could very well do without in English," partly because it is often not understood, partly because it is sometimes wrongly used to mean *according to* or *notwithstanding*.

The word, however, is quite common and will continue to be used in literary and political contexts. It is therefore necessary to understand it.

Pakistan should be pronounced with both *a*'s long, as in *park* rather than in *pack*. The name was coined in 1933 by Choudhary Rahmat Ali, a Muslim student at Emmanuel College, Cambridge, to signify the claims to national status of those portions of India that were predominantly Muslim. The *P* stands for the Punjab, the *a* for the North-West Frontier Province (also known as the Afghan Province), the *k* for Kashmir, the *s* for Sind and the *stan* for Baluchistan. The word may also be read as *the land of the pure* (*pak* meaning *pure*), but scholarly sources deny this intention.

palindrome. A *palindrome* is a word or sentence which can be read either way. The first palindrome was *Madam, I'm Adam*. One of the most famous is the supposed statement by Napoleon: *Able was I ere I saw Elba*. Another is *Sums are not set as a test on Erasmus*. James Thurber's is *He goddam mad dog, eh?*, while an anonymous genius devised *Naomi, sex at noon taxes, I moan*. The most polished is held by many to be *A man, a plan, a canal, Panama!*

See also **anagram**.

panacea. Many words starting with *pan-* have the meaning of *universal* about them, such as *pandemic* (a disease which manifests itself everywhere) and *panorama* (an unbroken view).

Panacea, then, means a *universal remedy*, from the Greek words meaning *all healing*.

Panacea should not be used to mean *a partial solution*. To say "One panacea to the housing problem is to build more public housing" is incorrect. A solution that is a *panacea* is *a complete cure*.

papaw/pawpaw. Prefer the spelling *pawpaw*, which is the pronunciation of the word in Australia and the South Pacific. *Papaw* is the American term.

Papua New Guinea. Properly speaking *New Guinea* is the name of the whole island, now comprising the nation state of Papua New Guinea and the Indonesian province of West Irian, formerly Dutch New Guinea.

That section of New Guinea now known as Papua New Guinea was, prior to the first world war, divided between two colonial powers. The northern section was *German New Guinea*, the southern the Australian colony of *Papua*, properly pronounced *Pah-poo-a*. After the first world war German New Guinea became an Australian mandate under the League of Nations. In practice both the mandate and Papua were administered as one territory.

There are considerable ethnic divisions within what is now known as Papua New Guinea, and especially between the inhabitants of what was the 'mandated territory' and those of Papua. These were accentuated by the disparate history of the two areas while under European administration. As a result, in 1971 the name of the *Territory of Papua and New Guinea* was changed to *Papua New Guinea*, this becoming the name of the new nation on independence in 1972. It was politically impossible to call the whole new nation *New Guinea*. (It would also have been geographically inappropriate.) The Papuans do not regard themselves as New Guineans.

While some efforts were made to find a quite new name for the new nation which would satisfy everyone this proved a thankless task, and the decision was made to call the new state *Papua New Guinea*.

Like most compromises, this was not a very happy or euphonious solution.

In the name there is no hyphen between *Papua* and *New Guinea*. Citizens are called *Papua New Guineans*. Within *Papua New Guinea* Papuans, in particular, continue to refer to themselves as such. In Papua New Guinea citizens who are born in the country are called *nationals*.

Papua/Papuan. *Papua* is the southern section of Papua New Guinea. Although the *Macquarie Dictionary* gives the pronunciation of Papua as *PAP-yoo-a*, and although this may be a common pronunciation among Australians, the correct pronunciation is *PAH-poo-a, PAH-poo-an.*

See also **Papua New Guinea**.

paradigm means *an example, a pattern, a model: The evacuation of Gallipoli in 1915 was a paradigm of successful military deception.*

It is frequently heard in the phrase *a paradigm case*, which is a **pleonasm** — that is, a phrase which says the same thing twice.

Paradigm is pronounced with the *digm* sounding as *dime*.

paradisiacal means *resembling paradise.* There is no such word as *paradisial.* Alternative forms are *paradisiac* and *paradisaical.*

Paradisiacal is pronounced *parra-dice-EYE-ikl.*

paragon/parergon. *Paragon*, once a favored name for Greek cafes in Australian country towns, means *a model of excellence.* The word comes originally from the ancient Greek for a sharpening stone. One talks of *a paragon of virtue.*

Parergon is a noun meaning *work that is not one's main employment.* If you have *a job on the side*, if you are *moonlighting*, you have a *parergon*. The emphasis is on the second syllable. It comes from two Greek words meaning *alongside work.*

paragraphs. Trendiness has overtaken the publishing and printing industry in Australia and elsewhere, as it has invaded food. The trend is the same: the consumer becomes a victim of the self-esteem of the producers.

In printing and publishing, where once the major aim was to facilitate easy communication between author and reader, an aim to which the best designers and editors still adhere, we now have the developing intrusion of innovation for its own sake.

There are many examples, the worst probably being the over-printing of text on graphic work, so that the reader can neither see what the picture is about nor readily follow the words. The abandonment of the double quotation mark is common in Australia and has diminished our ability to interpret the text presented to us (see **quote/unquote**). Another is the new habit of printing paragraphs without an indented first line (the first lines of all these paragraphs are indented, apart from the first). This means that, if the spacing between paragraphs is inadequate, the author's intention of declaring a break may easily be lost.

The indentation of the first line of paragraphs is a time-honored device enabling us rapidly to identify a break or development in whatever argument is being presented to us. If there were a consumer's association for the readers of books and magazines, this should be one of the issues for it to fight.

parameter/perimeter. *Parameter* has a specific mathematical meaning, and from this has developed a subsidiary meaning of *a limiting factor*. The word has now become vogueish and is in increasing use, especially in bureaucratic areas, as a 'power' word and as an 'Aren't I clever?' word.

The word does not mean, as many seem to believe, something like *fixed boundaries* in a geographical sense. It means a *fixed constant within an otherwise fluid problem*, as in:

> Whatever the desirable direction of Australian development, a major parameter is the absence of water.

The word *perimeter*, however, does mean *the limits of something, a boundary*.

paranoid/neurotic/psychotic/psychopathic. "I get so paranoid about doing a good job when I'm speaking." (Allan Border, Australian XI captain, on an ABC interview, 1 May 1985.)

The psychologists and psychiatrists have a lot to answer for. The words they have brought into the language are seldom understood or used properly. No doubt they would say that that is not their fault.

There's a famous old medical joke which says that "Neurotics build castles in the air, psychotics live in them, and psychiatrists collect the rent."

Well, that's a start. *Paranoid* means that one has an abnormal and deranged tendency to suspect and mistrust others. Psychiatrists are now wary of definitions of *neurotic* and *psychotic*, and of attempting to draw a clear border between these states, but for our purposes there are general definitions which will suffice. *Neurotic* relates to a person's inability to take a rational view of life and its problems; in common parlance it is sometimes used as a synonym for 'nerves'. Such people are normally aware of their problem. *Psychotics*, however, have a severe mental derangement involving the whole personality and producing abnormal and often bizarre behavior. They normally are not fully aware of their condition.

A *psychopath*, on the other hand, appears a normal person, but may be seen as socially rather than medically ill. He or she exhibits anti-social behavior but has no guilt or anxiety about it. There is no association with any other mental disorder. The gaols are full of psychopaths. They are sometimes called *sociopaths*.

Allan Border would have been better advised to have said that he gets *neurotic* about speaking engagements, and better advised still to have said simply that he gets *nervous*.

parenthesis. See **brackets**.

parlay/parley. *To parlay* means *to double up your winnings on the next bet*, to make your winnings from one bet into your stake on the next. The verb has been used for a hundred years in American horse racing, and is now used in a general sense: *to build on an initial small investment* (*he parlayed his charm and sense of timing into the managing directorship*). The word originated in the eighteenth-century card game faro, and is probably from the Italian *parole*, meaning *promises. Parlay* is both a noun and a verb.

Parley also is both a noun and a verb. A *parley* is *a discussion, especially between enemies, traditionally in order to arrange some form of truce*. It is from the French *parler, to talk*.

parliament. It is an affectation, and incorrect, to pronounce the *i* in this word. The word is pronounced *parlament*.

parsimonious/penurious. "Governor Arthur may have been parsimonious, but he was certainly never penurious" (from a book review). *Parsimonious* means to be careful with money, even stingy. *Penurious* means to be poor. The words are sometimes confused.

participles are formed from verbs. There are two kinds of participle. The *present participle* always ends in *-ing: diving, driving, gardening*. The *past participle* usually adds *-ed* or *-d* or *-t*, but may be formed in a number of ways. Thus:

Infinitive	Present participle	Past tense	Past participle
to break	breaking	broke	broken
to burn	burning	burned	burned, burnt
to cut	cutting	cut	cut
to dive	diving	dived (US dove)	dived
to enter	entering	entered	entered
to fight	fighting	fought	fought
to run	running	ran	run

NOTE

1. The problem of **hanging participles.**
2. Do not habitually begin sentences with participles. This becomes wearisome to the reader:

> *Climbing to the top of the mountain,* we were overcome by thirst. *Startled by a clap of thunder,* we took shelter in a hut. *Singing to keep our spirits up,* we spent the night there.

3. The question of the gerund. Is the proper expression *She loved his singing* or *She loved him singing*? What this amounts to is whether *singing* in this case is a kind of adjective or a kind of noun. *See* **to gerund or not to gerund.**

partly/partially. It is not always easy to distinguish the different roles of these two prepositions, but the short answer is that *partly* means *in part*, while *partially* means *to a limited degree*.

We may thus write of a car *partly made of fibre-glass*, or of a person being *partly to blame for the accident*.

It would however be more appropriate to write of one's grandfather as *partially blind*, or of an appeal in a law court being *partially upheld*.

Generally, use *partly* (a) for physical objects, and (b) for an isolated part of a whole. Use *partially* (a) when a general condition or state is under consideration, and (b) when a *whole* rather than a part is being discussed.

Consider the distinction between *a partly disappointing campaign* (most of it was good but some of it was bad) and *a partially disappointing campaign* (the whole campaign was not up to much).

parts of speech. There are in traditional grammar eight parts of speech, which are discussed separately in this book under the headings **adjectives; adverbs; conjunctions; interjections; nouns; prepositions; pronouns** and **verbs**.

Words are not born tidily labelled *noun, verb* and so on. Any such labels are merely our inventions. We place words in little boxes, and write *nouns* on one box and *verbs* on another, in an attempt to understand better how language functions. As with all theoretical constructs in any field — and grammar is nothing if not a theoretical construct — the quest for truth and understanding can easily be forgotten in the excitement of the quest for categories.

For this, and other, reasons, modern grammatical scholarship has moved into quite different paths from those of the traditional grammarians. There, no doubt, the new grammarians are also deforming the quest for truth as they seek to advance it. We shall not follow them.

We believe that, for the writer and speaker of English who is interested in the language as a working instrument, traditional grammar is still of value; that indeed, for such people, there is nothing else. That is why we have not ignored it in this book.

For instance, the same word may be used in a number of different ways. The word *age* can be noun, verb and adjective, and so can hundreds more. And words are changing their grammatical function in the sentence all the time: it is part of the growth of language. This book frequently comments on such changes. So long as we realise that *any* grammatical definitions are artificial constructs, and that the language has always outwitted the grammar that has been imposed on it, we may find them useful in understanding how words work.

An admirable discussion of the use and abuse of grammar, as well as of many other matters connected with the study of language, will be found in Anthony Burgess's *Language Made Plain* (Flamingo/Fontana, 1984).

parvenu. A *parvenu* is *an upstart, an arriviste*, a man who has risen rapidly in the world and shows it. The female is a *parvenue*, though *parvenu* will do for both male and female. The plural is *parvenus*, and the word is pronounced *PAR-ven-yoo*.

passim. See **referencing.**

passive voice. A simple sentence may read as follows:
> The dog bit the toad.

Here the verb is in the *active voice*, because the action is performed by the subject of the sentence, *The dog*. But when the subject *suffers* the action we say that the verb is in the passive voice:
> The dog was bitten by the toad.

It is even possible to forget the toad altogether:
> The dog was bitten.

The passive is a valuable weapon in the hands of the bureaucracies and all who wish to appear as faceless men and women:
> It is deeply regretted that your husband died in preventive detention last month.

By couching the statement this way the need to intrude an embarrassing *I* or *we* into the words is avoided, and the power of anonymity is emphasised.

Similarly the Transport Regulation Board in Victoria, by announcing "Seatbelts must be worn" rather than "You must wear your seatbelt", adds a minatory inevitability to its statement.

patent. Pronounce with the first syllable as in *pate*, though the pronunciation *pattent* is sometimes heard when the word is used in the sense of the *patent* on an invention, as when referring to the *Patent Office*.

Paterson, "Banjo". The Australian poet Andrew Barton Paterson ("The Banjo") has his name so spelt. Although the most popular of Australian poets, as often as not his name is misspelt as *Patterson*.

pathetic. It has been suggested that *You were truly pathetic as King Lear* is a lovely example of (perhaps deliberate) ambiguity.

This does remind us that *pathetic* means two things: it can mean *expressing pity* or *evoking pity* (as King Lear at his best does), or in informal and slangy usage it can mean *quite worthless*.

In the latter sense it has been overdone and the word is now a rather weak cliché.

patina. A *patina* is *a fine layer or sheen on some object, usually one denoting great age or much handling*. A green *patina* caused by oxidation is often found on objects of copper or bronze. The word is pronounced *PAT-inna*, not *pat-EEN-a*.

patio

patio is a Spanish word which we use to describe *an open courtyard within a building* or *a similar space adjoining a house.*

The Spanish pronunciation is *part-yo.* There are two accepted pronunciations in English, one to rhyme with *ratio* and the one more favored in Australia, which is *patt-io.* The latter is to be preferred, not only as the common pronunciation in Australia but also because it is closer to the original.

patriot may be pronounced with the first syllable rhyming either with *pat* or *pate.*

pedant. A *pedant* is a person who advises others on how to pronounce words. In other words, a *pedant* is a *stickler for detail,* a *nitpicker. Pedant* rhymes with *head ant* and not with *heed ant.*

pedlar/peddler/pedaller. A *pedlar* is *someone who hawks, or peddles, goods in the street or from house to house.* The term comes from a word for a basket. *Pedlar* is the approved British and Australian spelling, though *peddler* (or *pedler*), the American form, is making some progress. A person who *pedals* a bicycle is a *pedaller.*

penalise. Pronounce *PEEN-alise* and not *PENN-alise,* as some ABC sports reporters do.

peninsula/peninsular. These words give a lot of trouble.
Peninsula is the noun:
The family took their holidays on the Mornington Peninsula.
Peninsular is the adjective:
The Peninsular Ambulance Service covers the Mornington Peninsula.

pen-name. See **nom de guerre.**

penultimate. See **ultimate/penultimate/antepenultimate.**

people. "There is nearly a hundred people who work on 'A Country Practice'," we were told on Channel Ten on 26 April 1985.

People is in almost all circumstances a plural noun, thus this statement should start *There are,* not *There is.*

We say *The people of India live for the most part in a hot country,* not *The people of India lives ...*

The only occasion when *people* is singular is when the word refers to the people of a country as a metaphorical collective, as in *The people is a stronger concept than is government.* This usage is relatively rare.

per. "Sixty *per* year." "Forty-seven *per* term." The use of the word *per* in such cases is intended to give an aura of competence and expertise. In fact it suggests the opposite: a sense of unease and a desire to posture.

"Sixty a year" and "Forty-seven each term" are forms greatly to be preferred.

Per annum is a phrase best discarded in most cases, and replaced with *a year*.

Per capita, widely believed to mean *per head*, does not in fact mean this (it means *per heads*), and is again best avoided in any case. Use *a head*.

Percentage is a word to be used with caution, and *never* in a phrase such as *a percentage of the population were stricken with the disease*. What percentage? Ninety-nine per cent? One per cent?

Per cent, short for *per centum* in such a phrase as *Forty per cent of the class were absent*, should theoretically have a full stop after the *cent* to indicate that it is an abbreviation. This is, however, so common a phrase that the modern trend is to drop the full stop. Nor, since the phrase is naturalised, is there any need to italicise the words.

Forty per cent was or (as we have written above) *Forty per cent were*? The latter is correct, as will be realised if we expand *Forty per cent* to *Forty students out of every hundred in the class were absent*.

per annum. Prefer *$20,000 a year* to *$20,000* per annum.

per capita. Prefer *This will cost five dollars a head* to *This will cost five dollars* per capita.

percentages. If the price of butter, say, increases from 4 per cent of the average household budget to 5 per cent, *it has not increased by 1 per cent but by 25 per cent*.

It has, however, increased by *one percentage point*.

pergola. A *pergola* is a *horizontal framework, extending from a house or over a path, on which climbing plants are usually found*. The 'correct' pronunciation is *PER-ger-la*, though a variant pronunciation, apparently found only in Australia, is *per-GOLE-a*.

period. For *period* meaning the punctuation mark *full stop*, see **full stop**.

perpetual calendar. Using the table on page 300 it is possible to identify on what day of the week any date fell or falls between 1 January 1801 and 31 December 2000. Karl Marx was born on 5 May 1818. What day of the week?

Go to the year-list for 1801–1900. Find 18. Read across the columns to the column for May under the month-list. The code-number is 5. Add to this the day of the month (5), making 10. By reference to the day-list we find that 10 represents *Tuesday*.

Years

1801–1900	1901–2000
01 29 57 85	25 53 81
02 30 58 86	26 54 82
03 31 59 87	27 55 83
04 32 60 88	28 56 84
05 33 61 89	01 29 57 85
06 34 62 90	02 30 58 86
07 35 63 91	03 31 59 87
08 36 64 92	04 32 60 88
09 37 65 93	05 33 61 89
10 38 66 94	06 34 62 90
11 39 67 95	07 35 63 91
12 40 68 96	08 36 64 92
13 41 69 97	09 37 65 93
14 42 70 98	10 38 66 94
15 43 71 99	11 39 67 95
16 44 72	12 40 68 96
17 45 73	13 41 69 97
18 46 74	14 42 70 98
19 47 75	15 43 71 99
20 48 76	16 44 72 00
21 49 77 00	17 45 73
22 50 78	18 46 74
23 51 79	19 47 75
24 52 80	20 48 76
25 53 81	21 49 77
26 54 82	22 50 78
27 55 83	23 51 79
28 56 84	24 52 80

Months

J	F	M	A	M	J	J	A	S	O	N	D
4	0	0	3	5	1	3	6	2	4	0	2
5	1	1	4	6	2	4	0	3	5	1	3
6	2	2	5	0	3	5	1	4	6	2	4
0	3	4	0	2	5	0	3	6	1	4	6
2	5	5	1	3	6	1	4	0	2	5	0
3	6	6	2	4	0	2	5	1	3	6	1
4	0	0	3	5	1	3	6	2	4	0	2
5	1	2	5	0	3	5	1	4	6	2	4
0	3	3	6	1	4	6	2	5	0	3	5
1	4	4	0	2	5	0	3	6	1	4	6
2	5	5	1	3	6	1	4	0	2	5	0
3	6	0	3	5	1	3	6	2	4	0	2
5	1	1	4	6	2	4	0	3	5	1	3
6	2	2	5	0	3	5	1	4	6	2	4
0	3	3	6	1	4	6	2	5	0	3	5
1	4	5	1	3	6	1	4	0	2	5	0
3	6	6	2	4	0	2	5	1	3	6	1
4	0	0	3	5	1	3	6	2	4	0	2
5	1	1	4	6	2	4	0	3	5	1	3
6	2	3	6	1	4	6	2	5	0	3	5
1	4	4	0	2	5	0	3	6	1	4	6
2	5	5	1	3	6	1	4	0	2	5	0
3	6	6	2	4	0	2	5	1	3	6	1
4	0	1	4	6	2	4	0	3	5	1	3
6	2	2	5	0	3	5	1	4	6	2	4
0	3	3	6	1	4	6	2	5	0	3	5
1	4	4	0	2	5	0	3	6	1	4	6
2	5	6	2	4	0	2	5	1	3	6	1

Days of the week

S	1	8	15	22	29	36
M	2	9	16	23	30	37
T	3	10	17	24	31	
W	4	11	18	25	32	
T	5	12	19	26	33	
F	6	13	20	27	34	
S	7	14	21	28	35	

per se. *Per se* is a Latin phrase meaning *in itself.* It has a slightly affected ring to it, but for all that it can be useful. It is used to emphasise the fact that something is being looked at on its own account, and not in association with other matters:

> Looked at *per se,* we might agree, but when looked at in relation to the other issues, I suggest we should not.

> I cannot agree with you that this painting, *per se,* should be included in the exhibition, though if it were hung with other examples of the painter's work it might pass muster.

The meaning is similar to the meaning of **qua**, though grammatically they are used differently.

persimmon. The name of this tree is invariably pronounced *PERS-immon* in Australia, though British and American dictionaries admit no pronunciation other than *per-SIMM-on.*

personality. Keith Dunstan in the Melbourne *Age* (6 May 1986):

> You may have noticed there has been a well-publicised war among Melbourne's radio personalities. Interesting that, you don't have people in radio, you have personalities.

There is a traditional use of the word *personality* which is well known. It means *the distinctive characteristics of persons which make them identifiable individuals.* We may speak of a person's *happy personality.* We sometimes expand the definition a little by saying *she'll need a lot of personality for that job,* meaning that *she'll have to have qualities which make an impression on people.* But, in all these senses, a person's personality is within them.

But the use of the word in Keith Dunstan's sense is quite different. Here the word means something like *celebrity*, perhaps a *failed celebrity:* the relationship is with the outside world, not the inner one. The word, in this sense, is in the dictionaries. But it is still not fully accepted, and the discriminating will avoid it in both speech and writing.

Here, of course, Keith Dunstan is using the word ironically.

See also **identity**.

personal/personalised. An ABC announce advised us that a documentary we were about to see was "a very personalised view of this Indian festival."

Why *personalised*? Why not *a very personal view*? Only because *personalised* sounded more impressive, might make our attitude to the documentary more respectful.

If the word *personalise* is to be used at all, it should be reserved for the action of marking clothes, stationery and so on with name or initials of the owner.

perspicacity/perspicuity. Let's start with the adjective *perspicacious*, which means *having the ability to see or understand clearly, perceptive, discerning: It* *was perspicacious of her to see that those plans were going to fail.* The word comes from the Latin for *to see through, to look at closely.* The noun is *perspicacity: Her perspicacity in this matter was remarkable.*

The adjective *perspicuous* means *easily grasped, easily understood: My itinerary is more perspicuous than yours, I'm afraid.* The noun is *perspicuity: I admire the perspicuity of your itinerary.*

To generalise: people are *perspicacious,* things are *perspicuous.*

persuade. See **convince/persuade.**

petard. See **hoist with his own petard.**

pharisee/pharisaic. The Pharisees were an ancient Jewish sect, referred to in the Old Testament, renowned for their strict religious observance and their 'holier than thou' behavior.

The word *pharisee* (with or without a capital letter) means in English a Most Superior Person who looks down his or her nose disapprovingly at the behavior of others. This is a bit unfair to the Pharisees, who believed in working among the people as scholars and teachers instead of adopting the stand-off attitude of the Sadducees, but the way we use words is often unfair.

The adjective *pharisaic* is preferred to *pharisaical.*

pharmacist. See **chemist/pharmacist.**

phase. See **faze/phase.**

phenomenon/phenomena. "This new phenomena" (Senator Gietzelt, in the Senate, 25 February 1985). *Phenomena* is plural, and so Senator Gietzelt should have said *phenomenon,* the singular form of the word. See **lost singulars.**

-phile/-phobe. The ending *-phile* attached to a word means *lover of.* Thus a *Francophile* is someone who is fond of France or the French, an *Anglophile* someone fond of the English. There is a tendency, not yet standard, to drop the *e* from the ending of these words and to pronounce it as *-fill* rather than as *-fyal.*

The *-phobe* ending means the opposite, a dislike or loathing for something. Thus *Sinophobe,* someone who has a dislike of China or the Chinese.

the Philippines. The Philippines were 'discovered' in 1521 by Magellan, and subsequently named after Philip II of Spain. The name of the republic is *The Philippines.* The name of a male citizen is a *Filipino,* of a female *Filipina,* of a number, *Filipinos.* The adjective is *Philippine,* as in *the Philippine navy.* Pronounce *Philippines* to rhyme with *scenes,* not with *lines.*

philistine/philistinism. The *Philistines* were an aggressive, active people, known for their maritime trading activities, who inhabited ancient Palestine — hence the name.

Those who envied them dismissed them as uncultured barbarians, dead to the finer things in life while they bartered and sold their dyes and their cloths. The word, with the associated word *philistinism,* may be applied by any pleased with themselves to those they think of inferior quality, especially in the appreciation of the arts.

phobia. We heard a distinguished Australian knight say the other day, apropos the growing of geraniums, that "It's a phobia of mine."

He meant, of course, that it was an *enthusiasm* of his. He was stretching for the right word and he got the wrong one. And it can happen to us all.

A *phobia* is something you dislike, or have a morbid fear of.

See also **-phile/-phobe.**

phoney/phony. This word is spelt *phoney* (*phoneys, phoneyness*) in Britain, *phony* (*phonies, phoniness*) in America. Australian use favors the British, though the American use is found in both Britain and Australia.

The word is said to come from the Irish *fainne,* a ring, used in a confidence trick.

phrase. The word *phrase* may be used in a number of different senses.
1. In the broadest and most general use it may simply mean *a group of words which is part of a sentence but not a full sentence.* If a writer wishes to discuss, for instance, the words *inferiority complex,* he or she cannot say *the word 'inferiority complex',* for it is more than one word. The alternative is then to say *the words 'inferiority complex'* or *the phrase 'inferiority complex.'*
2. A more formal definition is that a *phrase* is a group of words in a sentence which (a) does not make complete sense by itself, (b) relates to other parts of the sentence as noun, adjective, preposition or adverb, (c) contains no verb, or only a non-finite verb-form (*to see, seeing, saw*).
Examples:

> *Going to hell* with good intentions is no comfort. (This phrase performs the function of a noun, and is thus a *noun phrase.*)
> Dr Walter Richardson, *father of Henry Handel Richardson,* lies in the Koroit cemetery. (Noun phrase.)
> *Fast and beautiful,* there was never any doubt about Phar Lap's appeal. (Adjectival phrase.)
> *By means of the ladder,* he reached the top of the wall. (Prepositional phrase.)
> *His wife being absent,* he was unable to come to dinner. (Adverbial phrase.)
> They found it *very much harder* by the second route. (Adverbial phrase.)

3. New-fangled grammarians, rather than traditional ones, are tending to expand the definition of *phrase* so that it means any group of words whatsoever in a sentence, except the subject of the sentence.

picnic. The use of this word to mean *a disorganised event* — "It was all a bit of a picnic" — is an Australian contribution to the English language. But, whatever meaning is given to the word, note the spelling of *picnicked, picnicking*.

picture. Pronounce the *ct* in this word, and avoid the pronunciation *pitcher*, which is common.

Pidgin. *Pidgin*, with a capital *P*, and not *Pidgin English*.

A *pidgin* is a language constructed from elements of other languages. While in a sense this probably applies to all languages, in special circumstances political and geographic events can greatly accelerate the formation of 'compromise' languages. The English we speak today was originally a pidgin, containing elements of Anglo-Saxon, Old Norse and Norman French vocabulary and grammar. Like other pidgins, English dropped genders and inflections and other complexities in the interests of simplified communication.

The rise of pidgins or 'New Englishes' in Africa, India, the Caribbean and the Pacific is perhaps the most dramatic event in the history of the language since it first evolved. It has been claimed by some language specialists that the true world English of today is not Anglo-American English, but the local variants springing up and gaining sophistication around the world. It has been calculated that, while the speakers of 'standard' English as a mother tongue number about 350 million, those using the language for communication now number some 1000 million.

Pidgin English was the original term for the speech that simplified intercourse between native English speakers and the colonial subjects they wished to communicate with. The word *pidgin* is a corruption of *business*. The term originated either in southeast Asia or in Africa, both homelands of Pidgin. Pidgins go by various names: *Krio* in West Africa, *Creole* in the Caribbean. The forms of most interest to Australians are *Melanesian Pidgin* (which is also called *Neo-Melanesian* or *Tok Pisin*), a *lingua franca* of Papua New Guinea, and *Kriol*, a form of Australian Aboriginal English.

Melanesian Pidgin is spoken, with local divergences, not only in Papua New Guinea but also in Solomon Islands, Vanuatu (where it is called *Bislama*) and other Melanesian areas. Although disapproved of by well-meaning academics, and by English-speaking indigenes themselves, the language has survived and flourishes. It is an official language of the Papua New Guinea parliament and serves, of course, as an invaluable medium of communication between the speakers of the many different languages within Papua New Guinea itself.

Melanesian Pidgin is far from being merely a corrupt form of English. It has its own grammatical structure and draws on a vocabulary from many languages. It has developed to the stage where it is the mother tongue of many, hence a true *creole*, subject to rapid change and development, and is now accorded the status of a language in its own right.

The so-called "broken English" of the Aboriginals of the Northern Territory and parts of Queensland is now developing rapidly in the same direction, so much so that serious work is now being directed towards the translation of English texts into what is called *Kriol*, or *Aboriginal English*. Kriol has, like Melanesian Pidgin, its own grammatical structures, related to those of Aboriginal languages, and has also reached the point of 'take-off', in the sense that it is now the mother-tongue of many. Kriol, as spoken among Aboriginals (and such Whites as are familiar with it) is not fully understandable by normal English speakers, any more than Melanesian Pidgin is.

Aboriginal English is termed *Kriol* by linguists (a) because it is in linguistic terms a *creole* language, that is a language born of other languages which has become the primary speech of a linguistic community, and (b) because it was felt desirable to distinguish Aboriginal English from the creole languages (related to French and Spanish) of Louisiana and the West Indies.

Here are three versions of the same extract from the Bible, verse 8 of chapter I of Revelation:

The King James version
I am Alpha and Omega, the beginning and the ending, saith the Lord, which is, and which was, and which is to come, the Almighty.

From Nupela Testamen (The New Testament) *in Papua New Guinea Pidgin:*
Bikpela, God I Gat Olgeta Strong em i tok olsem: "Mi tasol mi paslain tru na mi las tru." Em dispela God tasol, nau em i stap, na bipo tru em i stap, na bihain bai cm i kam.

From Holi Baibul *in Kriol (North Australia):*
God im strongbala en im brabli haibala. Wal im na bin tok, "Mi na dei kolum mi Basdamwan en Binijimapwan. Longtaim aibin sidan basdam, en mi stil sidan tidei, en mi garra stil sidan bambai du. Mi na brabliwan."

pique. *Piqued by my request, the librarian soon located the portraits.* The verb *to pique*, from the French *piquer* (*to sting*), can have two meanings. It can mean, as here, *to interest or excite.* More frequently, though, it means *to irritate*: *She cut me in the street, and I felt piqued.* The noun *pique* means only one thing: *a feeling of irritation or resentment.*

pissant. "The favourite word in Parliament House, Canberra, is 'pissant' — surrounded and amplified by traditional expletives it bounces off the wall in the non-members bar and ricochets down the corridors of power. Its most commonly accepted meaning is that you don't matter; that you don't have the ear of the powerful."

So a writer in the *Sydney Morning Herald* of 26 April 1986.

Firstly, we are surprised that this useful word does not appear, as such, in S. J. Baker's book *The Australian Language*, the *Macquarie Dictionary*, or G. A. Wilke's *A Dictionary of Australian Colloquialisms*. True, these sources quote the verb *to pissant around* and the phrases *as game as a pissant* and *as drunk as a pissant*, but nowhere is the word *pissant* itself listed or defined.

Secondly, we are surprised that the earliest date, even for these references, is for the mentions in Baker's book (1945), though of course Baker was drawing on older material. In our own experience *pissant* was in common use in the 1930s. In the course of a court case in Sydney in 1809 between William Wall and Samuel Terry, the "Botany Bay Rothschild", Terry called Wall an "Old Piss Ant, Rogue and Rascal."

Thirdly, the meaning of *pissant*. Our use and understanding of the word is that there is a species of (Australian?) ant which is small, aggressive and, even more than most ants, smells like urine when crushed. Thus a human who is called a *pissant* is regarded as *small and unimportant but noisy and aggressive* (and possibly able to leave a smell behind when crushed?).

This definition agrees in part with the Parliament House use as quoted above. But the Canberra definition leaves out an important component of ours: that a pissant may be unimportant but that he or she is busy and noticeable.

To pissant around follows clearly enough. So does *brave as a pissant*. But *drunk as a pissant* is not so clear. Perhaps the aggressive behavior of pissants is reminiscent of drunks waving their arms about on the streets.

Pissant is very much an Australian word, though it is also known and used in the United States. In 1941 the US Secretary of State, Cordell Hull, called the Japanese diplomats in Washington, whose task it was to deceive him about Pearl Harbor, "scoundrels and pissants." An American dictionary of slang defines it as meaning *an insignificant wretch*. There is only one reference to the word in the *Oxford English Dictionary*, and that is for 1662 ("a multitude of pissants and vermins"). *Pissmyre*, also an ant, has been more widely used in traditional English, and in much the same way as we use *pissant*. Chaucer writes of someone as being *as angry as a pissmyre*.

A *pisswhacker*, according to the *Macquarie Dictionary*, is *a female cicada which makes no noise but squirts a noisome fluid when disturbed*. The word is occasionally applied to women.

pistol/revolver. A *pistol* is *a handgun in which the rounds are contained in an internal magazine*, often inside the butt or handgrip. A *revolver* is also a handgun, but in this case *the rounds are contained in a circular magazine,* visible to the observer, which rotates as each round is fired. Pistols and revolvers should not be confused.

See also **gun/rifle.**

place names. Presumably all Australians know that Melbourne is pronounced something like *MELBin* or *MELB'n*, that Brisbane is pronounced something like *BRISbin* or *BRISb'n*, and that Canberra is pronounced *CANbra*, though this news has yet to get through to the English and the Americans. There are, however, many other place names which can give trouble to those not personally familiar with them. Here are recommended pronunciations for some of the more important or difficult:

Albany (W.A.)	The *Al* is pronounced to rhyme with *pal* rather than with *awl*, though some older Albany families use the latter.
Ballan (Vic.)	*Blan*
Barcaldine (Q.)	*BarCAWLden*
Beaudesert (Q.)	*BoDEZet*
Biloela (Q.)	*Bill-o-WEEL-a*
Bombala (N.S.W.)	*Bom-BAH-la*
Bowral (N.S.W.)	*BOUGH-ral*
Brewarrina (N.S.W.)	*Brew-WORR-inna*
Bribie Island (Q.)	*BRY-bee*
Bruny Island (Tas.)	*BROON-y*
Buderim (Q.)	*BUDD-erim*
Cairns (Q.)	Both as spelt and as *Cans*
Calboolture (Q.)	*Ca-BULL-tcher*
Candelo (N.S.W.)	*Candle-o*
Canowindra (N.S.W.)	*Ca-NOWN-dra*
Castlemaine (Vic.)	*CASS-elmaine*
Ceduna (S.A.)	*Se-DEW-na*
Chullora (N.S.W.)	*Chu-LORR-a*, with the *ch* as in *chat*
Cockburn (S.A., N.S.W., W.A.)	The *cock* is pronounced as *coe*.
Cohuna (Vic.)	*Co-HOON-a, C'HOON-a*
Condobolin (N.S.W.)	*Con-DOE-blin*
Coogee (N.S.W.)	*Cu-JEE*, with the *u* as in *pull*
Coorparoo (Q.)	*Coop-a-ROO*
Corowa (N.S.W.)	*CORR-o-wah*
Creswick (Vic.)	*CREZ-wick*
Dalby (Q.)	*DOLL-bee*
Derby (W.A. and Tas.)	As spelt, not *Darby*
Dumaresq (N.S.W.)	*Doo-MERR-ick*
Elliminyt (Vic.)	*El-IM-in-ite*
Eurobodalla (N.S.W.)	*You-ro-bo-DALLa*

place names

Fingal (Tas.)	*Fing-GAWL*
Fremantle (W.A.)	*Free-MAN-tl* or *Fr-MAN-tl*. The common Eastern States pronunciation of *FREE-man-tl* is not always approved locally.
Gympie (Q.)	*GIM-py* (hard *g*, not *jimpy*)
Glenorchy (Tas.)	*Gle-NAW-kee*
Goondiwindi (N.S.W. and Q.)	*Gun-de-WIN-dee*
Guildford (W.A.)	*GILf'd*
Gulargambone (N.S.W.)	*Gu-LAR-gam-bone*
Gumeracha (S.A.)	*Gumma-RACKa*
Jervis Bay (A.C.T.)	see separate entry
Jimbour (Q.)	*JIM-ba*
Jugiong (N.S.W.)	*JEW-gee-ong* (*g* as in *get*)
Kaniva (Vic.)	*Ka-NY-va*
Kingaroy (Q.)	*King-a-ROY*
Kyeamba (N.S.W.)	*Ky-AM-ba*
Lachlan (Tas. and N.S.W.)	*LOCK-l'n*
Launceston (Tas.)	*LON-ses-ton* (*LON* to rhyme with *don; not LAWN-ses-ton*)
Maatsuyker (Tas.)	*Mat-SIGH-ka* or *Mat-SOO-ka*
Mackay (Q.)	*Ma-KYE* (with some local support for *Ma-KAY*)
Maria Island (Tas.)	*Mar-EYE-a*
Meningie (S.A.)	*Men-NINGE-ee*
Merbein (N.S.W.)	*Mer-BEEN*
Michelago (N.S.W.)	*Mick-e-LAY-go*
Moe (Vic.)	*Mo-ee*
Moliagul (Vic.)	*Moll-EYE-a-gull*
Monaro (N.S.W.)	see separate entry
Monash (Vic.)	see separate entry
Mooloolaba (Q.)	*Mo-LOO-la-bah*
Moorooduc (Vic.)	*MOO-ru-duck*
Moree (N.S.W.)	*Maw-REE*
Moulamein (N.S.W.)	*MOO-la-min*
Murwillumbah (N.S.W.)	*Mur-WILLim-bah.*
Muswellbrook (N.S.W.)	*MUSSel-brook*
Nambour (Q.)	*NAM-ba*
Naracoorte (S.A.)	*NARRa-kort*
Nimmitabel (N.S.W.)	*Nimmi-tee-BEL*
Nullagine (W.A.)	*NULL-a-gyne* (with *g* as in *go*)
Ouyen (Vic.)	*O-yen*
Prahran (Vic.)	*p'RAN*
Pyrmont (N.S.W.)	*PEE-a-mont*

Queanbeyan (N.S.W.)	*QUEEN-be-an*
Ravenshoe (Q.)	*RAVE-ns-hoe*
Reservoir (Vic.)	*REZ-avore*
Sans Souci (N.S.W.)	*San-SOO-see*, also *San-SUZ-ie*
Sofala (N.S.W.)	*So-FAH-la*
Strzelecki (Vic.)	*Strez-LECK-ee*
Subiaco (W.A.)	*Soo-be-ACK-o*
Suggan Buggan (Vic.)	*SOOGG'n BOOGG'n*
Tallangatta (Vic.)	*Ta-LANG-ga-ta*
Toowong (Q.)	*Too-WONG*
Toowoomba (Q.)	*Tu-WUM-ba (u* as in *pull)*
Waaia (Vic.)	*WAY-eye*
Wagga Wagga (N.S.W.)	*WOGGa WOGGa*
Waikerie (S.A.)	*WAY-ke-ree*
Wakool (N.S.W.)	*WAW-kool*
Wangaratta (Vic.)	*WANG-ar-atta (wang* rhymes with *bang)*
Wangi Wangi (N.S.W.)	*WONN-jee WONN-jee*
Wauchope (N.S.W.)	*WAW-hope*
Wauchope (N.T.)	*WALK-up*
Weetangera (N.S.W.)	*Wee-TANJ-era*
Wollongong (N.S.W.)	*WOOL-on-gong*
Woolloomooloo (N.S.W.)	*WOOL-oo-mool-oo*
Wycheproof (Vic.)	*WITCH-ee-proof*

The above pronunciations, not being rendered in phonetics, are only approximate.

See also **Melbourne; Melburnian**.

plaque most commonly means *an inscribed tablet*. The word also has medical and dental meanings. Queen Elizabeth II caused some comment while in Australia in 1986 by pronouncing this word as *plak*, to rhyme with *back*. The most usual pronunciation is *plark*, to rhyme with *dark*. The Queen, however, was correct. Either pronunciation is permissible.

platonic love. *Platonic love, platonic affection* and the like: we all know what it means. It means a purely spiritual love for another, normally assumed to be another of the opposite sex.

That's fine, and there is no reason why the term should not be used this way. Occasionally, however, one catches a clever aside to the effect that this is not actually what Plato meant.

Well, what did Plato mean?

Plato's view was that one should never feel love for persons of either sex, that love should be applied only to such qualities as virtue, knowledge and so forth *in* people, but not *to* people themselves. Thus the ancient Greeks would have found Christianity very odd indeed — a faith which said you had to love bad people, your enemies, the diseased.

It doesn't matter very much but, as our grandmothers used to say, it's no weight to carry.

platypus. The plural of *platypus* is *platypuses*.

The great Melbourne University classicist, Professor T. G. Tucker, was once asked by the woman sitting next to him at a dinner party whether the plural of *platypus* was *platypi* or *platypoi*. He answered, in one of the great Australian put-downs: "Madam, that argues an ignorance of three languages."

Why? While *platypus* with its *-us* ending looks like a Latin word, and if it were would take the plural *platypi*, it is in fact a Greek word, the *-pus* ending being the Greek word *pous* which takes the plural *podes*. (Some Greek words take the *-poi* ending, but not this one.)

It could thus be argued that *platypodes* is an acceptable plural for *platypus*, but that is too pedagogical by far. It is best to stick with a standard English plural, in other words *platypuses*.

In Professor Tucker's view, his unfortunate dinner companion showed ignorance of English, Latin and Greek.

It is true that the *Macquarie Dictionary* gives *platypi* as well as *platypuses* as an acceptable plural, but the only way this case could possibly be maintained would be by arguing a descent from the Greek into a Latin word. This, a distinguished classical scholar has informed us, can be no more than an "argument of desperation."

Scientists sometimes use *platypus* as the plural of *platypus*: *There were a number of platypus in the creek.*

plead/pleaded/pled. In British and Australian English one says *I plead in this case today; I pleaded yesterday also.* Americans frequently say *I pled yesterday*, and this form of the verb is becoming accepted in the United States.

See also **dived/dove.**

please/thank you. *Please* is used in the asking of a favor, *thank you* (not one word and not hyphenated) in the recognition of a favor granted.

It is a common informal error in Australia to use *thanks* or *thank you* when *please* is intended, as in *Can I have that cup, thanks?* It should be avoided.

Please, in the sense used here, does not enter the English language until about 1622, and hence is not found in Shakespeare. The word does appear in Shakespeare's time in such phrases as *if it pleases you* which, of course, is a use of the verb *to please*, which means *to give pleasure to*. The word *please* as we use it clearly is an abbreviation of *if it pleases you*.

Thank you kindly is an idiomatic phrase, and we all know what it means, but looked at closely it is rather absurd. We are not *thanking people kindly* but *thanking them for being kind.*

pleonasms. A *pleonasm* is a phrase which says the same thing twice. Pleonasms have been called "cotton-wool language". They are easily overlooked. Mr Gough Whitlam, discussing his book *The Whitlam Government* in the *Age* for 9 November 1985, said: "I am fairly pedantic. 'At 2 p.m. that afternoon' will not reappear in the second edition." At the 1987 Grand Final at the Melbourne Cricket Ground spectators were informed: "We'll be welcoming countries from other parts of the world."

To join together is a pleonasm, and so are:

interspersed among	final outcome
the general public	essential condition
right throughout	long period of time
new recruit	close proximity
never ever	they both shared
both of us (we)	revert back
the third consecutive year in a row (Paul Keating)	appear on the scene
	for me personally
different alternatives	completely fulfil
population numbers	first origins
a prefatory overture	in actual fact
sufficiently enough	more preferable
very unanimous	stemmed originally
personal opinion	universal panacea
new innovation	paradigm case
unauthorised trespassing	more especially
general consensus	including for example
ensemble group	shared similar views
huddle together	enclose herewith
serried rows	successfully refute
at this moment in time	a good redeeming feature
one minute of time	a small detail
more better	original source
no other alternative	violent explosion
a tiny little boy (Shakespeare)	weather conditions
languish away	an emotional feeling
completely full	integrated together
lonely hermit	

Pleonasms are not always to be looked down upon. To say *the colour of this book is red* or *the word* annual *is Latin in origin* may involve repetition, but this may be for such good reasons as emphasis or euphony. They will always have a place in the cadences of spoken English, in particular. But normally they should be avoided.

A pleonasm and a **tautology** have much in common, the difference being that a pleonasm uses unnecessary words within the one phrase, while the tautology says the same thing twice in different words.

plethora. A *plethora* is *an over-abundance*, as in Senator Janine Haines's statement on ABC television, *a plethora of public servants*. Unfortunately Senator Haines pronounces the word *pleth-OR-a*. The correct pronunciation is *PLETH-ora*.

plurals. The formation of plurals in English is quite simple, and the minor complexities not difficult to handle.

Plurals in English are formed by the addition of *-s* to the singular form. This is normally a straightforward matter, but note the following:

1. Nouns ending in sibilants (*s, sh, ch, z, x*) add *-es*, not *-s: matches, sexes, gases.*
2. Nouns ending in a consonant plus the letter *-y* change the *-y* to *-ies: fairies, ferries, rubies.* But proper names do not change: *Kellys.*
3. Nouns ending in a vowel plus *-y* follow the general rule: *storeys, journeys, valleys.*
4. Nouns ending in *-f* and *-fe* may or may not follow the general rule. See the following entry, **plurals of -f and -fe.**
5. Most words ending in *-o* add *-oes*, but see the entry, **plurals of -o.**
6. There are a few words which are the same in both singular and plural (*sheep, aircraft*); there are a few nouns with no singular form at all (*news, athletics, mathematics*), but note that these often take a singular verb *(the news is good);* and there are a few survivors from Old English which form the plural in an unusual way *(men, mice, feet, children).*
7. There are a number of foreign words which have become absorbed into the English language which keep their foreign plurals. These include *fungi, theses, nuclei, oases, bases* (plural of *basis*), *phenomena.*

plurals of -f and -fe. Some nouns ending in *-f* and *-fe* form their plural by adding *-s*, while some delete the *-fe* and add *-ves.*

There is no simple rule. Here are some of the most common examples.

1. Simply add *-s*:

griefs	roofs
handkerchiefs	safes
mischiefs	staffs (*in music,* staves)
proofs	strifes
reliefs	

2. Delete *-f* and add *-ves*:

calves	selves
elves	sheaves
halves	shelves
knives	thieves
leaves	wives
loaves	wolves

3. Either plural form is permissible with the following words:

beefs (kinds of beef)	oafs *or* oaves (*prefer* oafs)
beeves (oxen)	scarfs *or* scarves
dwarfs *or* dwarves	turfs *or* turves
hoofs *or* hooves	wharfs *or* wharves

plurals of -o. There are rules for the plurals of nouns ending in *-o*, but there are so many exceptions that the rules are not worth giving. Note the following:

1. End in *os:*

albinos	infernos
archipelagos	magnetos
banjos	manifestos
cameos	merinos
crescendos	patios
dittos	photos
dynamos	quangos
embryos	radios
Eskimos	stereos
espressos	stilettos
fiascos	studios
folios	trios

2. End in *-oes*:

cargoes	innuendoes
desperadoes	mosquitoes
dingoes	Negroes
dominoes	noes
echoes	potatoes
embargoes	tomatoes
goes	torpedoes
heroes	

3. End in either; the preferred is the version given:

buffaloes	halos
commandos	mangoes
frescoes	mottoes
ghettos	peccadilloes

porticoes	volcanoes
provisos	zeros
tobaccos	

Note also that all words ending in *-oo* take a simple *-s* plural (*kangaroos*), and that so do all proper names ending in *-o* (*Romeos*).

plus. "Chappell now had a cash flow from his business," Hugh Lunn wrote in the *Australian* (3 May 1986), "plus ... he started earning a lot more from cricket." A little later Lunn wrote that in Queensland Chappell invested with others in Brisbane property, "Plus they bought and restored several colonial houses in Queensland."

Plus is a preposition meaning *increased by the addition of,* or *with the addition of.* Some would no doubt wish to see the use of the word confined to mathematics, *two plus two equals four.* But there can be small objection to the use of the word in a broader sense, provided the meaning is not affected. Thus *When she retired she received a cash bonus, plus her long-service pay* may not be particularly elegant, but is not offensive.

Nor is it offensive to use *plus* and *minus* as nouns, a short way of saying an *advantage* or a *disadvantage,* as in:

> It is surely a plus, not a minus, on the part of literature to instal us in the past and to give us an intimate sense of cultural change.

But Lunn (and a great many others, including schoolchildren) are using *plus* in a different way. Lunn uses *plus* as a conjunction to mean *and in addition,* rather than in its proper prepositional sense of *with the addition of.* This *is* offensive to many.

Lunn could easily have avoided this solecism. Instead of writing:

> Chappell now had a cash flow from his business, plus ... he started earning a lot more from cricket,

Lunn could have written:

> Chappell now had a cash flow from his business, plus a lot more from cricket.

poet/poetess. The word *poetess* should no longer be used. See **(the) female critique**.

poignant. *Poignant* means *painful to the feelings,* often in a wistful kind of way. It may be pronounced *POIG-nant* or *POIN-yant.*

political terminology in Australia. Many years ago the historian Sir Keith Hancock suggested that, in Australian politics, the Labor Party was the *party of initiative* and the conservative parties were *parties of reaction.* In other words, new ideas came mainly from the Left, the ideas of the Right being mainly responses to the ideas of the Left.

This was an interesting idea. Today, with the growth of interventionist and 'radical' right-wing politics in both Britain and Australia, it is no doubt particularly disputable. The point we wish to make, however, is that, even with these few words above, we are in the middle of the problem of the use of descriptive words in politics.

This is an area where there will be much disagreement. In politics, above all areas, the meaning of words depends on the standpoint of the user. Here are some attempts at clarification:

TORY

Used in Britain (a) as a synonym for the Conservative Party or its members (b) to identify *conservative* conservatives. Little used in Australia, and when it is intended to be pejorative, that is, an insult. Not always used that way in Britain.

REACTIONARY

Broadly used to categorise right-wing conservatives (in Australia, normally members of the Liberal Party or the Country Party) or their policies. The sense is that such people not only oppose change, but actually fight to put the clock back.

CONSERVATIVE

Not an official political title in Australia, though most members of the Liberal Party, for instance, would be prepared to acknowledge that they are 'conservatives'. In the traditional British sense conservatives do *not* consider themselves to be *reactionary* or opposed to change, but argue that change should occur in the context of respect for precedent and tradition. But we should note Sir Keith Hancock's comment: *"Conservative* is a word which has no currency at all; in Australia it signifies *reactionary*. Similarly, if a politician declares he is *liberal*, his audience will understand that he is by nature *conservative*."* Although published as long ago as 1930 (*Australia*, pp. 227–228), the observation still holds good.

LIBERAL

A much-abused word, so much so that it is common in intellectual circles to distinguish, in conversation, whether one is talking about an "upper-case Liberal" or a "lower-case liberal" (in other words, between *Liberal* with a capital *L* or a small *l:* see **capital letters**). The original meaning of the word was *befitting a free man*. For its educational meaning see **liberal education**. In Britain it distinguishes the Liberal Party, which may be termed *a left-conservative party*, standing between the Conservative Party and the Labour Party, emphasising democratic reform and civil liberty. In Australia the word was seized on in 1945 by R. G. Menzies for what was, in effect, a cosmetic re-naming of the discredited United Australia Party. Thus, in Australia, the word *Liberal* was wrenched out of context to become a political synonym for *conservative*. It was a naughty deed for a man who professed to support the correct use of words.

Accordingly, in Australia one must pick up from context whether the word means (a) a member of or relating to the Liberal Party of Australia, or (b) a person who is neither a conservative nor a socialist but who is generally 'well-meaning', 'progressive', prepared to examine issues on their merits, concerned with civil liberties and individual freedoms. When used by the far-Left of the political spectrum, however, often in the phrase *bourgeois liberal*, it can mean politically indulgent, wishy-washy, escapist, trying to have the best of two worlds.

In economic and political theory the term *liberalism* retains the sense of a movement to maximise freedom in the context of the emergence from a pre-modern to a modern governmental regime. The classic nineteenth-century economic liberals, outstanding among them John Stuart Mill, did not consider themselves conservative *or* socialist, but argued against excessive state intervention in any area of life, including economics. Present-day political theorists such as F. A. von Hayek, while strong advocates of the free market, would not consider themselves *conservative*, but rather *anti-statist*. The same applies to Margaret Thatcher, at least in economic theory, where she and her supporters could be described as adhering to *classical liberalism*.

DEMOCRAT

The dictionary definition is *someone who advocates government by all the people*. In this sense, these days everyone is (or pretends to be) a democrat. In Australian political usage, and with a capital *D*, a member of the political party known as the Australian Democrats, a centre party broadly corresponding to the British Liberal Party. Democracy is not as simple a concept as it may appear. Alain Touraine has recently said that "nobody would define democracy as the rule of the majority but rather as the respect of minorities."

SOCIAL DEMOCRAT

Sometimes accepted as an abbreviation for *socialist democrat*, someone who believes in democratic socialism, but more commonly accepted as a definition of one who believes that democracy should be pushed beyond the goal of civil and political liberties into the area of social reform; in other words a democrat who believes in active intervention in the ills of society, but stops short of the advocacy of full-blooded socialism.

If one accepts the first of these definitions, that a *social democrat* believes in *democratic socialism*, it may be asked why, since socialism is believed in by its followers because it represents the apotheosis of democracy, it needs to be qualified by the words *democrat* or *democracy* at all. The answer here is that such social democrats are uneasily aware that there are many political movements that call themselves *socialist*, some of them — as time has shown — very far from 'democratic'.

Many members of the Labor Party have, in the sense that they consider themselves both *socialists* and democrats, accepted the term *social democrat*. The issue, however, has recently been confused by the formation in Britain of a Social Democratic Party which represents a breakaway to the Right from the

British Labour Party, and which has been in an alliance with the Liberal Party in that country. This is a repetition of the R. G. Menzies ploy with the word *liberal*, an attempt to steal a word out of context (*if* we agree that *social democratic* equates with *democratic socialism*). In any case, it may now be assumed that members of the Labour Party in Britain and of the Labor Party in Australia will seek to distance themselves from the term *social democrat*.

The issue is further confused by the distinction drawn by many between the traditional social democratic parties on the model of continental Europe and the 'laborist' parties of Britain, Australia and New Zealand, with strong trade-union bases. It is argued that the former *are* parties of democratic socialism, the latter rather different. The matter is discussed further under *Labor* below.

SOCIALIST/SOCIALISM

Socialism is a political theory which holds that the private ownership of investment capital is immoral and anti-social, and that the means of production, distribution and exchange should be in public hands.

If everything went by definitions, a Martian would assume that Mr R. J. L. Hawke of Australia and Mr Michael Gorbachov of the Soviet Union, both being socialists, were political bedfellows. Both Mr Hawke and Mr Gorbachov would agree that, alas, this is not so. Like Lenin, Mr Gorbachov would consider the Australian Labor Party a 'liberal-bourgeois party', not a socialist one. Mr Hawke is too politically astute to say what he thinks of Mr Gorbachov's party.

As with the word *liberal*, the word *socialist* is, however, a talismanic word, so vague as to be, at the same time, both meaningless and politically useful. In Australia it is useful to those in the Labor Party who seek to bind highly disparate components together. It is also useful to the Labor Party's opponents, and hence embarrassing to the Labor Party, as a scare-word. When conservative politicians wish to taunt the Labor government of Australia, they call it the "socialist" government.

The problem with this word for the Labor Party is beautifully demonstrated in an attack on the State government of Queensland by the Queensland Salvation Army leader, Major Graham Harris (*Australian*, 9 June 1986). Major Harris, who compared the Bjelke-Petersen government in Queensland to that of Marcos in the Philippines, criticised Mr Bjelke-Petersen for "labelling everything that is not of his persuasion as 'socialist'. " He added that "most members of the Christian church would find difficulty in, with an informed conscience, so labelling our federal political leaders".

The problem is, of course, that half the time our "federal political leaders" are *anxious* to be called "socialist," in order to beat off attacks from the left wing of the Labor Party. In this sense Major Harris is, innocently, playing into the hands of Messrs Hawke and Keating's enemies.

The other half of the time our "federal political leaders" would agree with Major Harris that it is nasty to call them "socialist."

political terminology in Australia

LABOR

As a noun, this word often means the *Australian Labor Party*. As an adjective, it can mean *associated with the Australian Labor Party, and its aims and objects* or, more simply, *generally to the Left in politics.*

What *is* a *labor party*? Some historians and political scientists will argue that a labor party, rather than being concerned with the application of theoretical socialism to government, expresses a broader and less coherent philosophy. This holds that those who *work* (using that word with great elasticity) have a common interest as against those who *profit*, and that the task of Labor is to promote public policies favorable to those who work.

The historian Stuart Macintyre has recently developed at some length a thesis outlining a development in Australia from what he terms *laborism* towards *social democracy*. ("The short history of Social Democracy in Australia," in Don Rawson (ed.), *Blast, Bludge or Bypass: Towards a Social Democratic Australia*, Department of Political Science, Australian National University, 1984.) Macintyre defines a *laborist* program as one of intervention in a semi-mature capitalist society, primarily concerned with the conditions of labor, the concept of males as breadwinners, the interests of the public as consumers and the belief that the business of the state was "to build the economy by methods that would best safeguard living standards and create employment." Since the second world war, he argues, the essential features of 'laborism', such as the regulation of the market rather than the expansion of the public sector, are still a distinctive mark of Australian politics when compared with any of the "developed welfare capitalist economies" of West Europe. Nevertheless the Whitlam government of 1972–1975 swung towards *social democracy* with its emphasis on welfare capitalism and a shift of resources into the public sector, creating a "new middle class" to administer that sector, and a "welfare class" which is — in theory at least — the beneficiary of support intended to compensate for the fact that no political system can any longer maintain a full-employment and equitable society by no more than touches on the political wheel.

In Macintyre's terms, then, *social democracy* is to be defined *not* so much as *democratic socialism* but as an interventionist political philosophy in its own right.

LABOR MOVEMENT

Generally, the Australian Labor Party, *plus* the trade-union movement, sometimes with the addition of supporters and sympathisers outside both. Parties to the left of the Labor Party also generally consider themselves part of the Labor Movement, and seek to identify themselves with broader elements on the Left by using the term.

COMMUNIST

Broadly, those who believe that the final social aim should not be just socialism ("from all according to their ability, to each according to his or her contribution") but communism ("from all according to their ability, to each according to

318

his or her needs"). Until about 1960, communism was represented by the Communist Party of Australia, which accepted the leadership and guidance of the Communist Party of the Soviet Union.

The last twenty-five years have seen a proliferation of communist parties, including the Communist Party of Australia (now unaligned), the Socialist Party of Australia (Moscow-oriented) and the Communist Party of Australia (Marxist-Leninist), which is Peking-oriented, though it got a shock when China's political 'line' changed in recent years. In addition there are many smaller far-Left groups ("a few red spots pretending to be a rash", they have been unkindly called) adhering to their views of Marxism. Apart from some traditional strengths in trade-union leadership, the communist movements in Australia have been politically unsuccessful. They have been useful to other parties as Aunt Sallies and for scare-mongering tactics. *Communist* as a term of abuse has usually meant *You stand to the Left of me, I don't agree with what you say and believe, and I think you're a menace.*

FELLOW-TRAVELLER

A 'cant' word once common in communist circles to describe someone who shared Communist Party objectives and worked in its interest, but who was not formally a member. This word is also used in the same sense by anti-communists.

PROGRESSIVE

An imprecise term meaning virtually anything those using it want it to mean. In the political language of the Left, including the far Left, the word has frequently meant *not one of us, but inclined to our way of thinking.*

RADICAL

Classically, one whose political and social beliefs go to the root (Latin, *radix*) of things. In Britain, historically, on the Left of the Liberal Party. In general usage a person (often working-class) who is politically conscious and informed, not conservative and not attached to a political party.

TROTSKYIST

In Communist Party circles, a term of abuse directed at those who accepted Marxism as a guide to political action but who refused (and refuse) to accept communist parties or the Soviet Union as models. Trotsky, a leading political figure in the early years of the Soviet Union, broke with Lenin and Stalin and went into exile. The chief theoretical dispute was over the question of 'socialism in one country'. The Trotskyists believe that revolution cannot be successful in one country standing aside from the major issues of world revolution. The Soviet government has argued that communism may be achieved, if necessary, within the borders of one country.

Although the distinction may appear somewhat academic to outsiders, Trotskyists and communists have devoted intense energies to fighting each other with the utmost bitterness. In the course of this Trotsky himself was murdered by Stalinists.

319

There are sundry small Trotskyist groupings in Australia.

ANARCHIST

The popular image propagated of anarchists was of political desperadoes addicted to bombs and dynamite. In fact most anarchists are rather gentle political idealists, who believe that the best form of government is no government, and the best form of organisation no organisation. It is thus difficult for anarchists to organise effective political action.

The stronghold of classical anarchist belief is in Spain. Anarchy as a concept has a small fringe following among Australian Left intellectuals.

See also **bourgeois; (the) Establishment; wet/dry; working class.**

political vanities. Politicians, like the rest of us but perhaps even more so, love their little distinguishing marks. If you want something from them, it is advisable to use the correct form of address.

Members of the Privy Council are entitled to the prefix "Right Honorable". (These days Labor politicians do not accept appointment to the Privy Council, though Arthur Calwell was a member and, of the roll of Australian Prime Ministers, only Deakin, Whitlam and Hawke have refrained. Mr Hawke is therefore not a "Right Honorable", though he is often distinguished as such.)

Holders of government ministries, State and federal, are entitled to the prefix "Honorable", as are members of upper houses, but not the Commonwealth Senate. The presiding officers of the upper and lower houses of all Australian parliaments are also "Honorables". Commonwealth ministers retain their titles for life. In other cases there are special rules governing retention.

Traditionally members of the House of Representatives have had the letters "M.H.R." after their names, members of a legislative assembly "M.L.A." (in Tasmania, "M.H.A."). Legislative Council members have traditionally been "M.L.C." Nowadays they *all* like to be called "M.P." — it sounds less provincial, more chic. The change is hardly worth opposing, though it does represent a cultural cringe towards the British House of Commons.

Polynesia. See **Melanesia/Micronesia/Polynesia.**

polytechnic. See **monotechnic/polytechnic.**

poppycock. It is pleasing to record that this useful word comes from the Dutch for (to put it as elegantly as possible) *soft dung.*

pore/pour. You *pore* over a document, but you *pour* a cup of tea.

porpoise. See **dolphin.**

portentous means *signifying something to come*, especially when it is of a calamitous nature: *Perhaps the most portentous event of the second world war was the dropping of the atom bomb on Hiroshima.* It is often pronounced and written as *portentious*, which is wrong.

portmanteau words. See **suburban nomenclature**.

Port Phillip. Melbourne stands on *Port Phillip*, not on *Port Phillip Bay*. Sydney does not stand on *Sydney Harbor Bay*. But use *the bay* when referring to the stretch of water informally: *the bay beaches.*

poseur words and phrases. Poseur words and pompous inflations seek to hide reality behind a smokescreen of 'gentility', 'refinement' and 'expertise'. They include the use of:

> interpersonal *for* personal
> a large number of *for* many
> affluent, wealthy *for* rich
> problematic *for* problem
> thematic *for* theme
> in that time frame *for* then
> floral tributes *for* flowers
> address *for* tackle, approach, pay attention to

See also **clichés; euphemisms.**

posit. *May we posit a suggestion?* is a phrase sometimes heard. The answer is a very firm *No*. Although the word in itself is a perfectly proper one, based on the Latin word for *place in position*, it has an impossibly affected ring about it and is best widely avoided. If anything, the noun (*I should like you to consider this posit*) is even worse than the verb.

the possessive and the 's' sound. We all know that you form a simple possessive by adding an apostrophe and an 's', thus:

> It was Richard's birthday.

The matter is not quite so simple when the name of the person referred to itself ends in an 's' sound. Here there is a choice:

> It was Charles' house.
> It was Charles's house.

Both forms are correct, though *Charles's* is the form preferred.

The chief exceptions, exceptions which do *not* take *'s*, are *Jesus'* and ancient and classical words, which traditionally follow the form *Moses'*, *Pericles'*, *Mars'*, *Venus'*. The *s* after the apostrophe is also dropped where there are two or more sibilant sounds before it (*Kansas' governor*, not *Kansas's governor*) and in certain expressions where the following word begins with *s*: *for conscience' sake, for goodness' sake.*

The above are all singular words. The position is a little more tricky where we have a proper noun which is plural, say in the case of two people, husband and wife, who live together and are both called Hughes. How do we identify their house? We can say *the Hughes house*, using *Hughes* as an adjective (or noun modifier) of *house*. Or we can say *the Hugheses' house*. Here *Hughes* (one person), *Hugheses* (two people). Since plural nouns ending in *s* can take only the apostrophe, and nothing more than the apostrophe, after the word (see **apostrophes**), we cannot have *the Hugheses's house.*

possum is not an Aboriginal word but, in its earlier form, comes from the North American Algonquin Indians. The word was adopted by settlers about 1610 as *apossoun*, becoming *opossum* by 1763. Although a marsupial, the American *opossum* is a quite distinct animal from the Australian *possum*, to which its name was transferred.

Australian *possums* should never be called *opossums*.

See also **goanna**.

post-. See **ante-/anti-.**

post-secondary education. All post-secondary or post-compulsory education in Australia is organised into three areas.

Two of these areas relate to training at the fully professional level. That is, on graduation the student will normally be qualified to join the relevant professional institute and to practise legally as a doctor, engineer, architect, teacher etc. (Very often a period of work experience is required before full entry to the profession.)

These two areas are *universities* and *colleges of advanced education.*

Colleges of advanced education comprise what used to be called *technical colleges* and *teachers' colleges.* Some colleges of advanced education are relatively new foundations which did not grow from technical or teachers' colleges and have established teaching interests and roles of their own.

The third sector of post-secondary education is the *technical and further education* sector, often abbreviated to TAFE. This large and diverse sector handles such areas as trade and technician training, hobby instruction and elements of adult education. The TAFE area is not, in the full sense, a 'professional' area of education.

Some confusion is possible because some institutions, such as the Royal Melbourne Institute of Technology, include under the one name both an *advanced college* (i.e. a *college of advanced education*) and a TAFE college.

See also **educational nomenclature.**

pounds, shillings and pence. Although these items are no longer in use in Australia the need to use the terms crops up in many kinds of writing, and it is offensive to refer to money in use before decimalisation (1966) in terms of today's dollars.

Six pounds, twelve shillings and fourpence may be written as £6/12/4 or as £6.12.4, but is best expressed as £6 12s 4d. If a 'pounds' sign (£) is not available, use an L, if possible with a stroke across it.

In the old currency there were twelve pence in a shilling and twenty shillings in a pound. The word *crown* was sometimes used to mean *a five-shilling piece*. A *guinea*, used in auction sales and professional fees, was £1 1s.

Note pronunciations: *HAY-pny* or *HAY-penny* for *halfpenny*: *tuppence* for *two pence*; *tuppeny* for *two-penny* (*a two-penny bus*); *thrippence* for *three pence*.

It is worth remembering that, until the decimalisation of the Australian currency, the word *dollar* in Australian usage meant *five shillings*. Subsequently, however, the dollar was declared to be the equivalent of *ten shillings*.

power corrupts. Lord Acton did *not* say "Power corrupts, and all power corrupts absolutely," but he *did* say "Power *tends* to corrupt, and absolute power corrupts absolutely."

practicable/practical. If something is *practicable* it is *capable of being put into practice*. If something or someone is *practical*, then it (or he, or she) *responds effectively to actual conditions*.

It is, for instance, *practicable*, in terms of current technology, to build a bridge across the entrance to Port Phillip Bay. If, however, you take into account all factors, including costs, it is certainly not *practical*.

The negative forms are *impracticable* and *unpractical* or *impractical*.

practically is an interesting word. Only a few generations ago it was taken to mean by those who heard it *for all practical purposes*, or *in practice*. For example, *Apprenticeship has thus been practically replaced in the professions by a more systematic course of training.*

The present use of *practically* is rather different. It now means *almost*, as in *He was practically at the finishing line.* Some will say that there is only a shade of difference in the two usages, and for most purposes that may be so. But there are times when it is helpful to remember the evolution of a word which still holds two meanings, even if one is moribund.

Indeed, ambiguity is now often close when the word *practically* is used by someone perhaps not entirely conversant with idiomatic English. When the Czech-Canadian writer Josef Skvorecky says on television that "Czechoslovakia is practically a Soviet colony," does he mean that Czechoslovakia is *almost* a Soviet colony, or that for all practical purposes, and despite the pretence of independence, it *is* a Soviet colony?

There is also a third meaning of *practically*, which means *in a practical manner*. An example is *He outlined the process theoretically, but he demonstrated it practically*.

practice/practise. *Practice* is a noun, as in *The doctor's practice was overextended*, or *Her trombone practice was offending the neighbors*.

Practise is a verb: *He practised medicine, She practised the trombone*.

The American usage is to use *practice* for both noun and verb, but this is not acceptable in Australia.

pragmatic. A *pragmatic* approach to an issue is an approach which is dictated more by practical considerations than by theory or dogma. It does *not* mean a *practical* approach. On the contrary, a *pragmatic* approach to a complex issue may be thoroughly unpractical.

precedent. Pronounce *press-ident*, not *prees-ident*.

precede/proceed. *Proceed* is a perfectly acceptable verb which means *to advance*. It is not, and should not be used as, a synonym for *to go*. *You will then proceed to the cashier's office* is a horrible misuse of a decent word. Furthermore, it is *minatory* — it is intended to give an impression of hidden force, beloved of officialdom. See **bully words**.

The verb *to precede* means *to go before: the brass band was preceded by the drum-major*.

precis. *Precis*, an abstract or condensation of a text, is now so much an English word that the absence of the French accent (*précis*) may be allowed. The plural is the same as the singular: one *precis*, two *precis*. And note *precised*, not *precissed*.

precocious has two meanings. In such a sentence as *She is a precocious child*, it can mean either (a) *She is spoilt, bad-mannered and too conscious of her own cleverness*, or (b) *She is unusually developed, mentally or physically, for her age*. The second sense, of course, has no pejorative meaning.

The word comes from the Latin *praecox, ripe before its time, premature*.

predicate. In traditional grammar, the *predicate* is the part of the sentence which tells you what happened to the subject. In:

The Melbourne trams stopped operating for over six weeks

everything after *The Melbourne trams* is the predicate of this sentence.

Predicates can come before the subject as well as after: in *Around the rugged rock the ragged rascal ran* the predicate is *Around the rugged rock . . . ran*.

In more general use the verb *to predicate* may mean *to declare* or *to imply* or *to base an argument upon*, as in:

> She predicated her opposition to church-going on her refusal to believe in the supernatural.

Except when used in a specialist sense by philosophers, the verb *to predicate* should be avoided as pretentious.

And *to predicate* does not mean *to predict*.

prefer/preferable/preferably. The word *prefer* becomes *preferred* in the past tense, but it drops back to a single *r* with *preferable*, which is unusual.

Preferable means *more to be desired.* To say *more preferable* is saying the same thing twice, and should be avoided.

Preferably may be pronounced *PREF-reb-ly* or *pre-FER-ably.* The former is recommended.

premier. The word *premier*, as in *the Premier of Queensland*, is pronounced with the *prem* rhyming with *hem*, not *heem*.

prepared to admit. If one is *prepared to admit* something one should then be prepared to *admit* it.

In other words: *I admit that you are right*, not *I am prepared to admit that you are right.*

prepositions. A *preposition* is used before (sometimes after) a noun (or equivalent) to relate it in time or space, or in some other way, to the rest of the sentence. It is one of the eight **parts of speech** in traditional grammar.

The words italicised here are prepositions: *alongside* the jetty; *in* a hurry; *notwithstanding* his presence; *in accordance with* your suggestions; *after* dinner; a book *of* mine; *in front of* the bureau; *behind* the times.

Prepositions are not as simple as they look. They are perhaps the most idiomatic of all parts of speech. The precise way they are tied to other words in individual cases may be simply a matter of custom rather than rule or logic, as with an interest *in* something rather than *for* it, indifference *to* something rather than *about* it, oblivious *of* rather than oblivious *to*, covered *in* spots rather than covered *with* them. *Possessed of* (owning) means something quite different from *possessed with* (controlled by). Why does one live *in* Sydney but *at* Port Fairy? How can a person be *beside herself*? Why do we agree *to* a thing, *with* a person, *on* a matter and *in* an opinion?

This is a brief list of recommended usages:

affinity between *or* with (*not* to *or* for)	brood on *or* over (*not* about)
alternative to	compare (see **compare/contrast**)
averse to *or* from	comply with

prepositions at the end

contrast (*verb*) with	identical to (*not* with)
contrast (*noun*) between	oblivious of (*not* to)
in contrast with	opposite to (*not* from)
derogatory to	substitute for (*not* with)
die of (*not* from)	sympathetic to
different from (*rather than* to)	sympathy with *or* for

prepositions at the end. The preposition in English may be placed wherever in the sentence it fits most naturally. To play around with a sentence such as *He was worth talking to* in order to remove the preposition from the end of the sentence is an offence to the English language, a most flexible instrument, and an equal offence to common sense.

The pernicious but widespread belief that prepositions should not be placed at the end of sentences stemmed from writers who were conscious of the rules of Latin. Even so, the greatest of writers in English have used a final preposition when they felt it appropriate.

Having said that, it must also be added that, just because so much has been said on this topic, there is a sensitivity to the issue which, in formal writing, authors may be wise to take into account, if only to avoid distracting a reader's attention. Thus in certain settings it may be desirable to write *He was the man with whom she went home* rather than *He was the man she went home with*.

The schoolteachers' famous example of the possibility of overdoing the 'preposition at the end' is that of the boy who says to his mother "What did you want to bring the book I didn't want to be read to out of up for?"

prerogative. A *prerogative* is a privilege or right which you have because of the office you hold. It is the *prerogative* of the Royal Marines to drink the Queen's toast while sitting, of a government Minister to be driven to work in a government car, of every citizen to fly the national flag. The word comes from two Latin words which mean *getting in first*, hence the *pre-* in the word. *Prerogative* should not be pronounced *perogative*, though it frequently is.

pre-school. See **kindergarten.**

prescribe/proscribe. *To prescribe* something is *to make a rule about it: The textbooks were prescribed* or *The announcement was prescriptive* (that is, it had to be done).

To proscribe is *to condemn, prohibit or outlaw: The taking of dogs onto the beach is proscribed.*

presently. "I shall do it presently" means, or should mean, "I shall do it in a short time, as soon as I can get round to it." It does not mean *immediately*,

326

though it used to, and this is an American and a Scottish usage which seems to be creeping into Australian speech.

Here are two examples of the use of the word *presently* to mean *soon, in a short time*, both from the writing of Peter Quennell:

> Although he presently recovered, he had had various later troubles.

> ... but the Hammonds I presently met and found an odd, endearing couple — old-fashioned Fabian Socialists, belonging to the same high-minded school as Beatrice and Sidney Webb.

The word **directly** is similar to *presently* in suggesting *soon* rather than *now*.

There is another meaning of *presently*, signifying *at present*. In a sentence such as *There are presently three million inhabitants of Melbourne* the word *presently* is admissible, though *at present* would, to our ears, sound better.

pressure/pressurise. If you *pressure* someone you bring forces to bear on them designed to change their opinions or actions.

If you *pressurise* (or *pressurize*) something you inflate it, as with a tyre, or otherwise raise its pressure, as with the air in a plane cabin.

prestigious. This is an overworked word which will normally be avoided by people sensitive to the nuances of spoken or written English. Originally derived from the Latin word for jugglers' tricks, it is only in recent decades that it has taken on itself the meaning of *generally esteemed*, of *having or giving prestige*. The word has just a slight air of inflation or puffery about it.

The word should be pronounced *pres-TIDGE-jus* and not, as is commonly heard on radio and television, *pres-TEEDGE-jus*.

presume. See **assume/presume.**

presumptive/presumptuous. If something is *presumptive* it is something that is *presumed to be true.* The *heir presumptive* to the throne is the person who, at any given time, is the *presumed* successor. Queen Elizabeth II, when a princess, was the *heir presumptive* to the British Crown because it was *presumed* she would become Queen. It was never certain, however, that she would do so while the possibility of a brother's being born remained. Should a boy have been born in her family he would have become the *heir apparent*, that is the *actual* heir.

Presumptive is used correctly in such a sentence as *This finding is based merely on presumptive evidence* — in other words, it is a matter of opinion.

Presumptuous means something quite different. It is a word applied to behavior that is *overweening, arrogant, presuming an authority which does not exist.* To write to the Pope offering to re-write the Bible would be *presumptuous* behavior.

priceless

The two words were at one time interchangeable, but now have strictly different (but often confused) meanings.

priceless. See **invaluable.**

Prichard, Katharine Susannah. The name of this well-known Australian writer is often, indeed usually, misspelt. There is an *a* in the *Katharine* and no *t* in the *Prichard.*

pride goeth before a fall. The actual quotation is "Pride goeth before destruction, and an haughty spirit before a fall," from the Bible, Proverbs xvi. 18.

prima facie. See **a priori/prima facie.**

primarily. The American pronunciation *pry-MARE-ily* is still regarded as affected in Australia. Nor is that pronunciation standard in the United States.

primer. The word *primer*, meaning a school-text in a primary school, is now pronounced with the first syllable rhyming with the word *prime* in Britain. The old pronunciation, *primmer*, continues to be used, however, in Australia, New Zealand and the United States.

principal/principle. A *principal* (with one exception) is a person, a *principle* is a thing.

We talk about the *principal* of a school, the *principals* of a company or, using the word as an adjective, the *principal* actor in the opera. *Principal* used as an adjective need not, of course, refer only to people. You can have the *principal* crop, for instance. The word means *first in order or rank.*

Principal is also used, as both a noun and an adjective, to apply to *capital* (in the financial sense) as opposed to *interest:* we thus talk of *a principal and interest account.*

A *principle* is *a personal belief held for moral reasons:*

> No man ever did anything foolish except for some strong principle.
> (Lord Melbourne)

It can also mean *a fundamental law of some kind in the scientific or philosophical sense:*

> It is a principle of physics that heat expands and cold contracts.

prior to. In such phrases as *prior to his death* prefer *before his death.*

pristine. Pristine does not mean *clean,* or *unsullied,* as in *the pristine snow, the pristine tablecloth. Pristine* means *ancient* (*a pristine era*), *old and unspoiled, pure and uncorrupted, in the original state.*

Thirty years failed to dim his pristine enjoyment, and at the end of his life a visit to the theatre with him was like accompanying a child who had never been before.

(Rupert Hart-Davis on Hugh Walpole)

privacy. The *priv-* in *privacy* may rhyme with either *hive* or with the *triv-* in *trivia*. The former is favored.

probe. This is a word beloved of sub-editors because it fits easily into headlines. Except in medical and technical senses, that is where the word should stay.

problem/problematic. A *problem* is *something that is difficult to deal with*, or *a question or puzzle that requires an answer.*

"What," asks an interviewer on the ABC of an English film-maker, "are the problematics of making films in foreign countries?"

There is no such accepted word as *problematic*, used in this sense, that is, as a noun.

What the interviewer should have asked was a question about the *problems* of making films in foreign countries.

Problematic is an adjective which means *having the appearance of a problem, questionable.* It is properly used in such a sentence as *Whether Australia will ever rely in large part on icebergs for its fresh water is problematic.* But the adjective *problematic* should not be used to mean *troublesome,* as in the Melbourne *Herald* (2 May 1988), referring to the wardrobe for a stage production: "One problematic Russian hat was redesigned over the phone," or "their problematic father," seen in a television review (*Sydney Morning Herald*, 30 April 1988).

A working party on cultural policy, sponsored by the Victorian government, issued a paper in January 1986 which states "The definition of culture is problematic, for it is a word that means many things to many people."

Government working parties on culture cannot be expected to have a very close understanding of good English. Even so, we would have hoped that even they might have realised that the first phrase would have been better expressed as "It is difficult to define the word 'culture'."

Looked at even more closely, it could be argued that what the cultural bureaucrats are trying to say is not that 'culture' is hard to define, but that it is hard to get agreement on the definitions. If so, the sentence might well have run: "It is hard to get agreement on the meaning of the word 'culture', for which there are many definitions."

A similar usage, also to be deplored, is **thematic.**

proceed. See **precede/proceed**.

process. Both the noun (*This was part of a continuing process*) and the verb (*We processed the information*) are pronounced *proe-sess*, not *prossess* — in other words the *pro* rhymes with *hoe*, not with *moss*. (*Prossess* is the American pronunciation.) While both the noun and the verb are stressed on the first syllable (*PRO-cess*), the verb when it means *to take place in a procession* is stressed on the second (*pro-CESS*).

procrastinate/prevaricate. We find it hard to believe, but are told that these two words are frequently confused. So, for the record:

> *Procrastinate* means *to delay, to put off doing something,* in Australian idiom *to drag the chain.* In Latin it means *to put off until tomorrow.*
>
> *Prevaricate* means *to fudge the truth, to skirt round issues in a misleading manner, to imply a lie, to quibble.* It comes from the Latin for *knock-kneed,* or *walking crookedly.*

Both words have this in common: they may cause us to reflect that Latin, far from being a 'useless' language, has a lot to do with our understanding of our own language. Perhaps it should go back on the school curriculum alongside "Human Relations."

procrustean/promethean/protean. All words from classical mythology often found in contemporary writing, but with very different meanings.

Procrustes was a robber who, having got innocent travellers into his bed, then stretched or chopped off their limbs in order to make them fit. If you say that something is procrustean (often with a capital *P*) you mean that it is something designed to make people fit rules, to produce conformity without regard to the means. An example of a procrustean statement: *Anyone who does not answer this question in* precisely *350 words will be deemed to have failed.*

Prometheus was the god who made mankind out of clay, stole fire for them from heaven, and taught them many skills. For these and other sins Zeus had Prometheus chained to a rock, where an eagle fed on his liver, the liver being renewed every night so that the torture was continuous. You will be glad to know that Prometheus was eventually rescued by Hercules. One may talk of a *Promethean punishment,* but the adjective normally means *daringly creative,* someone or something *enhancing life through action.* One may talk of *the Promethean art* of — say — Brett Whiteley or Fred Williams.

Proteus, in the *Odyssey,* is an ancient mariner who is a seal-keeper, knows all things, and can assume different forms to evade interrogation. If a person has *protean talents,* he or she is *extremely versatile, able to adopt convincingly different roles at will.* Many would, for instance, regard the talents of a Noel Coward — actor, director, composer, novelist, artist — as *protean.*

professor. Frequently misspelt *profesor* or, even worse, *profeser.* Even by university students.

profit margin. *The company had a profit margin of $126,000 dollars. The profit margin on this item is 20 per cent.* Why *profit margin?* Why not just *profit?*

Note the distinction between *margin* or *profit margin* (the percentage of the final selling price that is gross profit) and *mark-up* (the percentage of the cost price added to arrive at the selling price). A 100 per cent *mark-up* is only a 50 per cent *margin*.

program/programme. The spelling *program* is to be preferred, even if prejudice is unlikely to see it easily adopted in Australia, on the ground that it is "American". *Program* was the regular English spelling until last century, when the word fell victim to the embellishers, and in any case it is related to words such as *telegram* and *diagram*. *Program* has for many years been the official spelling of this word by the Australian Broadcasting Corporation.

progressive. See **political terminology in Australia.**

project. This word is both a noun and a verb. You can have a favorite *project*, and your thoughts can be *projected* into the future.

Firstly, note that the noun and the verb are stressed differently. The noun has the emphasis on the first syllable, the verb on the second.

Next, the vexed question of pronunciation. The British recognise only one pronunciation of the noun, which is *PROD-dzekt*. If you are concerned about the Queen's English, this is the way she pronounced the word in Australia in 1988. The more common Australian pronunciation, however, is *PRO-dzekt*, the *pro* rhyming with *foe*. Both are correct.

With the verb the first syllable is slurred, and the word sounds something like *pr'-DZEKT*.

proletariat. See **working class.**

promethean. See **procrustean/promethean/protean.**

promiscuous. "The theatre is more promiscuous in Sydney than in Melbourne." This sounds exciting, and conjures up visions of merry times behind the stage and after the shows, for *promiscuous* in its most common meaning conveys the sense of *indulging in casual and indiscriminate sexual relationships.*

The word does, however, have a secondary meaning, *a confused mixture,* and this is what the writer meant. This meaning emerges more often in phrases such as *Her choice was promiscuous.*

prone/supine. "It would be tragic if we all stand supine," says a correspondent in the *Age* (7 September 1985).

331

This is a startling statement because in fact the basic meaning of *supine* is *lying on one's back*. *Prone* means the opposite, that is *lying on one's stomach*.

Of course *supine* has another meaning as well, stemming from the first meaning: *indolent, lazy, lethargic*. This is what the letter-writer meant, but he expressed it rather unfortunately.

pronouns. The pronoun is one of eight **parts of speech** in traditional grammar. Pronouns are stand-ins for nouns: they save repeating the nouns. (In the previous sentence, *they* is a pronoun. Without pronouns, the sentence would have to have read *Pronouns are stand-ins for nouns: pronouns save repeating the nouns.*)

For convenience, pronouns are classified into the following:

PERSONAL PRONOUNS: *I, me, my, mine; we, us, our, ours; you, yours; he, him, his; she, her, hers; it, its; one, one's; they, them, their, theirs.* (And see also **thee/thine/thou** for earlier forms.)

DEMONSTRATIVE PRONOUNS: *this, that, these, those, such, the other, the same, so.* Example:

> *This* is the day that I intend to undertake *that*.

(See also **determiners**.)

RELATIVE PRONOUNS: *who, whom, whose, which, that, what, whoever, whatever, etc.* (On the **that/which** distinction, see under that heading.) The pronoun is *relative* because it *relates* to a noun or personal pronoun going before.

INTERROGATIVE PRONOUNS: *who? which? what? whom? whose?*

REFLEXIVE PRONOUNS: *myself, ourselves, yourself, yourselves, himself, herself, itself, oneself, themselves.*

RECIPROCAL PRONOUNS: *each other* and *one another*.

INDEFINITE PRONOUNS, referring to an unspecified number of persons or things: *any, anybody, anything, some, somebody, something, nobody, nothing, anyone, each, both, all, many, someone, none, no-one, everybody, everything, either, neither.* Examples:

> *No-one* could bring *anybody* to that pass.
> *Something* attempted, *something* done, has earned a night's repose.

pronunciation in Australia. While the vocabulary of Australian English is remarkably uniform throughout the country, and while *regional* differences in pronunciation are minor, there is a wide range in the nature of the pronunciation of Australian English generally considered. The existence of a distinctive Australian 'accent' was noted as early as the 1820s.

In extreme cases this accent can go so far as to make it difficult for Australians accustomed to one kind of pronunciation to recognise the same words when spoken by Australians using another kind.

The differences are not so great as in the United Kingdom or the United

States, where specific regional dialects can be baffling even to fellow citizens, but they do affect communication. In addition, there are prejudices in Australia relating to the 'class' nature of pronunciation which are absent from countries which have regional dialects.

The pronunciation of Australian English is often divided (for instance, by J. R. L. Bernard) into such groupings as *Broad* (the most extreme 'Australian' pronunciation), *General, Cultivated* and *Modified. (Modified* refers to attempts by Australians to speak English in a more English way than the English do.) *Broad, General* and *Cultivated* relate broadly to class or sociological distinctions, but with many exceptions. Many Australian university professors, for instance, will be found speaking *General*, or even *General* with touches of *Broad*, rather than *Cultivated*.

In any case, of course, there are no compartments into which we can sort Australian accents, and the divisions suggested above represent convenience rather than scientific exactitude. There is a continuum of pronunciation moving through from *Broad* to *Modified*.

The distinguishing features of the Australian pronunciation of English (as compared to the 'standard' or 'received' British pronunciation) include:

The pronunciation of *a* (as in *hay*) as *i*, so that *away* sounds something like *a-why,* *information* something like *inform-eye-shun, training* as *tryning.*

The tendency of *i* to slip towards *oy* in pronunciation, so that *die* sounds like *doy.*

Shifts of vowel sounds from *a* to *e* and from *e* to *i*, so that *had* moves towards *hed* and *bet* moves towards *bit.*

A tendency to suppress the *r* in words like *card*, so that the word tends to sound like *cad* or *cud.* (Americans preserve their *r* sounds.)

The suppression of the short *i* in unstressed syllables. (The short *i* is the *i* sound as in *hid.*) The example often given here is *boxes* and *boxers,* words often pronounced the same way in Australian English (*box-is*), where the British pronounce boxes as *box-is,* but sound the *r* in *boxers.*

A shift in the *ou* sound in such words as *counter, bounty* towards a short *a* sound: *canter, banty,* the *sand* of music.

A shift in the *oo* sound towards *ee*, so that a student saying "Where's Medina?" turns out to be asking where his *doona* is.

The tendency to pronounce such words as *worried* with the full *ee* sound on the last syllable (*wurr-eed*) where the British would say *wurr-id.*

A tendency, especially perhaps among the young, to adopt the American *fludder* (*flutter*), *studder* (*stutter*) sounding of the *t* between vowels.

There are also some differences in intonation, which can cause confusion or irritation, especially perhaps the 'down-up' shift on the last word in such questions as *Shall we go to town?* which the British use.

Is the Australian accent bad? Is the Australian accent ugly? Such questions are often heard. They are in many ways meaningless questions. For a start, there is

property

no one Australian accent. There are, as we have seen, said to be four. Others might say there are sixteen million. Secondly, we have each to make up our own minds as to what we find 'ugly' or 'bad' or, for that matter, 'incorrect'. Many factors will enter into this. It is commonplace in the political world, for instance, for those with left-wing and 'democratic' career ambitions to switch from middle-class accents learnt at privileged schools to demotic tones. This process sometimes has bizarre results.

The author of this book does not find Broad Australian particularly pleasant to listen to, especially on radio and television, where self-conscious efforts are now being made to promote it. The distinguished British commentator on Australia, John Douglas Pringle, has complained that many Australian women "speak with a strident, saw-like whine that is indescribable." Such individual judgements are of course subjective, but they are unavoidable and even desirable.

The problems of trying to stand *above* such conclusions, of attempting to adopt Olympian standards, may be seen from the *Macquarie Dictionary*, where on the one hand we are told that "a dictionary is not there to make recommendations", but "to report current practice," and within a few lines we are told that "It could hardly be expected that the editors of a general reference dictionary would feel the need to record the pronunciations of uncultivated or incompetent speakers ..."

In other words, 'if in my view you are uncultivated, your way of using language may be ignored.'

In *Right Words* we have not hesitated, from time to time, to recommend pronunciations we feel desirable, taking all circumstances into account. Generally these pronunciations will be in the area of Cultivated Australian, but occasionally recommendations dip towards General or even Broad. We remain sympathetic to H. W. Fowler's view that "the popular pronunciation of popular words" is a major consideration, while at the same time we recognise that a lot depends on what that first "popular" means. Fowler, we believe, did not mean by "popular" the pronunciation of East End London, but the pronunciation of a rather ill-defined 'man in the street'. We seek for those mythological creatures, the 'average Australians', but, even when we find them, we do not necessarily accept all they have to say.

See also **dance/darnce; indicator words; regionalism in Australian language**.

property. See **attribute/character/property/quality/trait**.

prophecy/prophesy. *Prophecy* is the noun: *The prophecy was unfavorable.*
Prophesy is the verb: *The parson prophesied ruin if we did not pray for rain.*

proprietary/propriety. *Proprietary* is an adjective meaning *related to property*, or *privately owned*. Thus the word is used as part of the title of many companies. It is also used in such a sense as *He takes a very proprietary interest in his fruit trees*, which means that he doesn't take kindly to people picking apples over the fence.

Propriety is a noun meaning *the quality of being appropriate, conforming to recognised standards in dress, speech and so on: Although under much provocation, she behaved with perfect propriety.* It is perhaps more common in the plural, where *proprieties* means *the standards of behavior viewed as correct: It was a dinner party at which all the proprieties were observed.*

propriety. See **proprietary/propriety.**

protagonist in its original and classical sense means *the actor who takes the main part in a play.* It has therefore frequently been argued that the word should be extended no further than to mean *the chief participant in an affair,* as in:

> The protagonist in the moves to buy the London *Times* was Mr Rupert Murdoch.
> The protagonist in Joseph Furphy's novel *Such is Life* is Tom Collins, the alleged author himself.

It has also been argued that there cannot be more than *one protagonist* in a situation: the *pro-* does not stand for *for* but for *first* (there was also a *deuteragonist*), and therefore *protagonist* is not the opposite of *antagonist.*

The supplement to the *Oxford English Dictionary* now accepts, however, that common usage has won and that *protagonist* can be used in the plural to mean the most important persons in a situation. The sense remains, however, of *a leading advocate* or *leading advocates,* rather than any advocate.

Protagonist is pronounced with a hard *g,* as in *get,* and not as *protadjonist.*

protean. See **procrustean/promethean/protean.**

protest. The verb *to protest* (*I protest at what you have done*) is pronounced with the second syllable stressed and the *o* indistinct, as *pr'TEST.*

The noun *protest* (*She led the protest*) has a long *o* (to rhyme with *stow*) and is accented on the first syllable: *PRO-test.*

To protest is an *intransitive* verb, which means that it cannot be followed by an object. You cannot, or at any rate should not, say *The government has protested them* (news report, ABC) or *They protested the visit of the American navy.* The Americans do use the verb *protest* this way (*Women protest discrimination*) but Australians do not.

Except in one usage. We do say *She protested her innocence, They protested their goodwill.* But here we are using the word in its rarer meaning, *to declare,* and not in its primary meaning of *to kick up a fuss about.*

Australian and British English use the verb *to protest* (in its *dissent* meaning) in an intransitive sense only when it is followed by the prepositions *at, about* or *against: They protested at the building of the freeway.* Since there is an ambiguity in the use of *at* here (did they protest on the site of the freeway, or did they protest against its construction?) *about* or *against* is preferred to *at*. So: protest *about* something, or *against* something.

provedore. This is an interesting example of a common English word — at least in Australian use — which simply does not appear in our dictionaries. This can only be because, in the first place, dictionary-makers copy from each other rather than listen to what people say and write; it doubtless is also evidence of the lack of interest of lexicographers in commercial and maritime affairs. *Provedore* (sometimes *providore*) is a 'non-word' which is in constant use, as may be seen from the Yellow Pages of Australian telephone directories.

A provedore is *a person or firm supplying consumable goods to ships*. Thus ships are *provedored* when supplies of food are placed aboard.

The full *Oxford English Dictionary* gives the word a mention, with one of its meanings a *purveyor* or *steward*, but with no indication of its modern meaning or use as a verb. It does not appear in the four dictionaries designed for Australian use, the *Macquarie*, the *Australian Pocket Oxford*, the *Australian Concise Oxford* and the *Heinemann Australian Dictionary*.

proved/proven. The normal past participle of the verb *to prove* is *proved*: *This matter has been proved beyond all doubt*. There is, however, an alternative past participle, *proven*, which may be used instead of *proved*. *Proven* crops up in the Scottish trial verdict of *not proven*, where a jury finds a case neither established nor disproved, and in the form of an adjective *proven*: *This is a proven method*. Pronounce *PROO-ven*.

the proverbial. Some Australian newspaper columnists are addicted to such phrases as *as bright as the proverbial button, as dead as the proverbial dodo*. H. W. Fowler, in his *Modern English Usage* (entry on *superiority*) advised such two-bob-each-way writers to decide whether they wished to be dignified or informal, to abandon efforts to "touch pitch and not be defiled." In other words, if you want to use informal language or old saws, have the confidence to do so without apologising for it.

provided that/providing that. Should we say "I shall come to the cricket provided that my car is mended", or "I shall come to the cricket providing that my car is mended"?

Both forms are acceptable, although *provided that* has more support. Usually, however, the simple *if* is preferable to either.

pseudonym. See **nom de guerre.**

psychopathic. See **paranoid/neurotic/psychotic/psychopathic.**

psychotic. See **paranoid/neurotic/psychotic/psychopathic**.

publicist. One Martin Dougherty, we were informed in the Melbourne *Age* of 3 October 1987, played a key role in the struggle for the Fairfax media empire at that time. He was described as "a journalist turned highly skilled publicist."

From the rest of the article it appeared that Mr Dougherty owned a large Sydney public relations firm.

The word *publicist* is primarily reserved, as the *Macquarie Dictionary* puts it, for *one who is expert in or writes on current public or political affairs*. In this primary and, in our view, classic sense of the word, it conjures up names such as those of Brian Fitzpatrick, historian and advocate of civil liberties, and B. A. Santamaria, the social and religious commentator. Such persons are often acting out of a sense of duty, rather than as paid agents.

It is true, however, and also noted by the *Macquarie Dictionary*, that the word *publicist* to denote what is normally called a *public relations agent* is creeping into Australian use. This is because of a certain shadow that lies over such phrases as *public relations agent* and *advertising agent*, and the desire of those engaged in these trades to enhance their own images as well as those of their clients.

This is undesirable, because it undermines the traditional and very useful sense of the word. Those who engage in public relations and advertising should not be ashamed to admit it, and certainly those who write about them should not be sucked in to prettification.

publishing/publication. These terms give rise to much confusion among those not familiar with the world of book production. The *publisher* of a book is the risk-taker, the entrepreneur, the one who stakes the money. He or she will, it is hoped, pay the printer (who normally is no more than a sub-contractor) and in due course distribute royalty payments to the author. To *publish* a book is, in broad terms, to display it for sale in a public place. Thus it is possible to have books which are printed and distributed without being published; and hence the term "Not Published" in some bibliographies.

Care should be taken not to identify the *publisher* of a book as its *printer*, or the printer as a publisher.

puffery often takes the form of redundant adverbs, intended to add strength to the word they relate to, but often so expected and so tired that they have the opposite effect. Examples are:

perfectly delightful	supremely inappropriate
gloriously unexpected	absolutely new

Such pufferies may be excused in informal conversation, which perhaps could hardly exist without them, but they have no place in the written language.

Other examples of puffery: the use of

categorise *instead of* classify	proceed *instead of* go
hospitalise *instead of* send to hospital	commence *instead* of start

See also **in place**.

punctuation. See separate entries on **apostrophes; brackets; colons; commas; dashes; dots; exclamation marks; full stop; hyphens; oblique stroke; question marks; quote/unquote; semicolons.**

purport. "Number 17 changed hands every few years until the late 1930s when the National Trust purports the last tenant shut the door behind him" (Jenny Brown, the *Age*, 2 December 1985).

Presumably the author of this article meant that the National Trust *reckons* or *believes* or *supposes* the last tenant left the house.

To *purport* means *to claim to be something or someone*, as in:

He purported to be the Lord High Executioner, but he had no axe.

The noun *purport* means *significance* or *intention*, as in:

The purport of the communication was that we should prepare to leave within a week.

As a verb, pronounce *pur-PORT*, as a noun *PER-port*.

purse. In Australia a *purse* is a small, closed bag in which money is kept and which resides in women's *handbags*. In most of the rest of the world a *purse* is a handbag.

Q

Qantas is an **acronym** standing for *Queensland and Northern Territory Aerial Services.*

qua. "I not only enjoyed the painting *qua* painting but I appreciate the affection that lay behind the gift."

Qua is a Latin word which in English means simply *as a.* It is not an affectation to use it in the right place. It does convey, economically, a special meaning: *looking at something just as it stands, without for the moment looking at the implications.*

quality. See **attribute/character/property/quality/trait.**

quandary. Despite the belief of many who should know better, to say *She was in a quandary* does *not* mean that she was in a position of hardship or danger, in other words that she was *in a plight.*

To be in a quandary is *to be in a predicament, a dilemma, to be worried about a course of action.*

quango. The word *quango* is an **acronym** (a word made up from the initial letters of other words). It stands for *quasi-autonomous non-government organisation.* Governments in recent decades, perhaps especially in Britain and Australia, have tended to decentralise government business by placing responsibility in the hands of organisations created for a specific purpose.

Originally a *quango*, in Britain, was a body which appeared to be independent of government, but which was in fact carrying out government policy and using government funds. The best-known examples were the Royal Society for the Prevention of Cruelty to Animals and the National Trust. Both in Britain and Australia the meaning of the term has been broadened.

In Australia *quangos* include such bodies as the Melbourne and Metropolitan Board of Works, the Gas and Fuel Corporation (Victoria) and the National Capital Development Commission (Canberra). There are hundreds more.

In Australia *quango* is still not a very familiar word, and such bodies are usually called *statutory authorities* or *semi-government instrumentalities.*

quantum leap. Politicians — and others — are fond of talking about *quantum leaps*, a term stolen from physics, and usually intended to mean *a big jump*: *There has been a quantum leap in this budget's allocation for defence spending.*

In physics a *quantum leap* or *quantum jump* is *an abrupt transition from one energy state to another in an atomic or molecular system*. A *quantum* is *an indivisible unit of energy*, and is Latin for *how great a thing*.

There is, then, about the term *quantum leap* a sense of *qualitative* change, not just *quantitative* change. There is no objection to stealing the term from physics and using it in a more general sense, but in doing so the sense of *a change in character* should be preserved.

A (Queensland) correspondent has suggested that if a policeman rises from being a bush constable to assistant commissioner in two years, that is a *quantum leap*; that if a company's profit rises 500 per cent in one year, that is not a *quantum leap*; but if that company were to progress from being a backyard company to a multinational giant in three years, then that would be a *quantum leap*.

See also **orders of magnitude**.

Queensland. Before June 1859 Queensland did not exist, and was referred to as *the northern squatting districts of New South Wales*, or sometimes *Moreton Bay*.

question marks. The sign *?* is used, of course, at the end of a question. In fact in origin it is a letter *Q*, standing for the Latin word *quaere*, meaning *inquire*.

There is only one point worth making about question marks, which are normally easy enough to handle. It should be noted that in a sentence such as

Will you, I wonder, place that poem in your new collection,

there is no question mark. The sentence is not a question to the poet, but a statement of attitude by the person writing the sentence. Of course if the two words *I wonder* were left out, it would be a question, and would need a question mark.

questionnaire. To pronounce this word as though it were French, that is with the first syllable sounding like *kest* rather than *quest*, is an affectation anywhere, but particularly in Australia.

Note that the word is spelt with two *n*'s.

quite is a deceptive word. We use it blithely and frequently but often fail to reflect that it has two meanings.

Consider this sentence:

His behavior was quite reprehensible.

In fact the statement is ambiguous. It could mean *either* "His behavior was *utterly* reprehensible" *or* it could mean "His behavior was *rather* reprehensible."

These two uses of the word *quite* can normally be sorted out easily enough, but there is an area, certainly in Australian usage, where misunderstanding can easily arise. In the statement:

Thank you, the present was quite nice,

the more educated hearer would assume that the speaker was saying that the present was only *rather* nice. In other words, the remark is a bit of a put-down. But in non-received or uneducated Australian use, and also, it is said, in American use, the remark can, and frequently does, mean that the present was *very* nice, and a compliment may be intended.

quixotic does *not* mean *absurd*. It means *idealistic, but in an impractical way*. To attempt to solve the world arms race by sending a peace convoy to Moscow would be an admirable, if quixotic, approach to the problem.

quote/quotation. Careful speakers and writers will avoid using *quote* as an abbreviated form of *quotation*, and will reserve the word for use as a verb: *I quote you often.*

quote/unquote.

1. Quotation marks are used for chapters of books, titles of articles and short stories, poems, names of paintings, often the names of houses and properties, radio and television programs and films.

Names of books and pamphlets, as well as names of ships, are normally set in **italics**.

Some names take neither quotation marks nor italics. This applies to works of art, books of the Bible (Ephesians, not "Ephesians" or *Ephesians*), railway engines (the Spirit of Progress) and, increasingly, names of houses ("He wrote at Wyewurk, Thirroul").

2. The more important use of quotation marks is in the identification of direct speech. While it is perfectly possible to print direct speech without quotation marks, and quite intelligibly, as the Bible and some modern publishers do, quotation marks are the normal way of indicating to a reader that what she or he is reading is a precise record of the original, whether that original be someone's actual speech or an extract from someone's writing.

This is of enormous importance to accuracy in the transmission of information and ideas. Quotation marks are therefore extremely important aids to understanding. Their correct use is vital to efficient communication.

Quotation marks ("quotes", for short) or *inverted commas* are of two kinds, single ('--') and double ("--").

The single quotation mark should be reserved for two purposes only: (a) where the writer is trying to convey to the reader that the word inside the single quotation marks is being used in a special, perhaps unexpected sense; (b) where there is a quotation within a quotation.

The double quotation mark indicates something that is actually being quoted, as

"Hell!" said the duchess.

The distinction between single and double quotation marks is not only a useful one which should be preserved. If we abandon this distinction and use single quotation marks only, we throw away one entire mark of punctuation, dismiss it from the written language, deprive ourselves of the flexibility it gives us, condemn the language to unnecessary confusion. It is significant that it is publishers, incorrectly looked upon as guardians of literary standards and preservers of the integrity of the language, who have led the way in the abandonment of the double quotation mark. It should also be noted that the people who have promoted this attack on the language's versatility are the first people who rush to insist on the importance of preserving the distinction between, for instance, *uninterested* and *disinterested*, because that distinction gives the language more scope.

Fortunately, the inane abandonment of the double quotation mark has been firmly opposed on some important sections of the battle-front, and there is yet hope that mindless Australian publishers will come to their senses. The double quote is used in newspapers in Australia; it is used in all the publications of the London *Times* group in Britain; and it is standard throughout North America.

As we have said, the double quotation mark indicates that something is actually being quoted.

The use of the single quotation mark to indicate words used in a special way is illustrated in these examples:

> They found that the corned beef was 'on the nose'.
> A 'word' can be a simple inherited sound-sequence.
> I saw the very last of the 'time-before' in New Guinea.
> The process of getting 'up there' in the Communist Party suppressed intelligence.
> The 'front' workers in the mass organisations were often middle-class intellectuals.

In the first case above *on the nose* is in single quotes because it is a slang phrase which is on a different literary level from the rest of the text. In the second case *word* is in single quotes because the author wishes to make it clear (as he does from the surrounding text) that here he is using the word in a special way. In the third case *time-before* is in single quotes because the author is signalling the reader that he is using an unusual phrase but has a reason for doing so (in this case, that it is the Pidgin word for the period before the second world war). In the fourth case *up there* is in single quotes because without them the reader would say to himself or herself, "Up where?". In the last case *front* is in single quotes because it is a common word being used in a specialised sense, and the author wishes to make this clear.

Note that in *none* of these cases is the word being *quoted* from any other source. In at least some of the cases, however, and unless there is a distinction retained between single and double quotes, the reader would be justified in assuming that the word is actually being quoted, in looking for the source and in wondering why the word *is* being quoted.

Let us look at a sentence from Geoffrey Serle's *The Rush to be Rich*, published by Melbourne University Press, which does not recognise the distinction between single and double quotation marks. Serle, talking of the 1880s, and the proliferation of banking institutions in Victoria, says:

> E. S. Parkes, the able and vigorous Superintendent of the Australasia, believed Victoria was 'overbanked' . . .

Now, is Serle quoting Parkes? Or is it a special word Serle has made up to meet the circumstances? There is no way of knowing unless we preserve the distinction between single and double quotation marks; and some time it will be very important to someone to know whether the word was Parkes's or Serle's.

Note the following text from a Railways of Australia poster (1984):

> A Luxury "Hotel" stretching from Sydney to Perth?
> Yes!
> Australia's own 'Indian Pacific'.

The word *hotel* is not being quoted here from any source. It is simply being used in a special sense, and should be in single quotation marks.

Note too the use of single quotation marks around the name of the train. In the first place, if the words *Indian Pacific* are to be put into quotes at all, they should be in double quotes, because the name is actually being *quoted*. In the second place there is no need for any quotation marks at all around such a name, but the random use of quotation marks in public notices has become a galloping disease, used by signwriters to embellish any word that takes their fancy.

RECOMMENDATIONS

1. Use double-quotes at all times, *except* (a) when quoting within a quote and (b) when using a word in a special way.

2. With lengthy quotations indent them in the text (as in the entry on **Monash**) but do *not* use quotation marks at all, except for quotations *within* the quotation.

3. If however a quotation in several paragraphs is being used, and it is not being indented, then there should be an opening quotation mark at the commencement of *each* paragraph, with a closing one at the very end of the quotation.

4. In a sentence like this:

> He then remarked, "This is useless."

where should the full stop go? Inside the end of the quotation marks, or outside them? Logically the full stop should be outside the quotation marks, like this:

> He then remarked, "This is useless".

However it is traditional printing practice, and one used by Australian newspapers, to print this sentence thus:

> He then remarked, "This is useless."

In other words, in this usage the full stop comes inside the quotation marks.

Quality publishers, and the *Style Manual* of the Australian Government Publishing Service reject the newspaper style and use and recommend the more logical:

He then remarked, "This is useless".

It clearly is a matter of taste which style one adopts. We support the newspaper style, on the grounds that it was used, even by quality publishers, until recently, and looks (to us) better. The important point is that, whichever style is adopted, it should be used consistently throughout a manuscript.

Note that if a whole sentence is quoted, then of course the quotation mark *has* to go outside the full stop:

"This is quite useless, and I will have none of it."

5. That logic does not always prevail, even with 'fine' printers, can be seen from the following.

There is no difficulty, of course, with this sentence:

Why do you say "You can go home now"?

But what about this sentence?

Why do you say "Can you go home now?"?

In this latter example the punctuation marks should logically follow the form we have given, but the fact that we then end up with no fewer than *three* successive punctuation marks is regarded as ungainly, and the final question mark should be omitted.

Notice, however, that this will not be possible when there is a mixture of three different marks:

Why do you say "Go home immediately!"?

In this case we just have to accept the traffic-jam of punctuation marks.

R

race/racial. Since Adolf Hitler, these words have been out of bounds. About the only way the word *race* can now be used without shame is in referring to the human race: *compared with the Martians the human race has* [or *have*] *only two ears.* Sections of the human race may no longer be referred to as *the Caucasian race, the Negro race* and so on. Nor, of course, do we talk of *the Jewish race.* Some other word or form of words has to be found by writers and speakers: *she is ethnically Caucasian,* for instance, or *the Aboriginal people.* We have lost what used to be a useful word, but few will mourn it.

Racism and *racist* will, however, remain in use as long as there is a need for them.

Australian Broadcasting Corporation announcers to the contrary, *racist* is not pronounced *rayshist.*

rack/wrack. *He was wracked with pain* or *he was racked with pain?* The latter is correct, although Shakespeare in the First Folio has "the wracke of this tough world" ("King Lear"). The origin is the rack as an instrument of torture.

radar is an **acronym** standing for *radio detecting and ranging.*

radical. See **political terminology in Australia.**

radius. The plural of *radius* is *radii.*

railway gauges in Australia. The following are the measurements of the standard State railway gauges in Australia, in imperial and metric measures. In certain cases, notably the transcontinental line from Sydney to Perth, the New South Wales gauge, sometimes called the *standard gauge,* has been carried through into other States.

State	Gauge		Distance
Queensland	3 ft 6 in	1066.8 mm	
New South Wales	4 ft 8½ in	1435.1 mm	
Victoria	5 ft 3 in	1600.2 mm	
Western Australia	3 ft 6 in	1066.8 mm	
South Australia	5 ft 3 in	1600.2 mm	1870 km
	4 ft 8½ in	1435.1 mm	3603 km
	3 ft 6 in	1066.8 mm	893 km
Tasmania	3 ft 6 in	1066.8 mm	

raincheck. In the United States of America a *raincheck* is a voucher given to those who have bought seats for a baseball game or sports meeting when that activity is cancelled because of bad weather. It entitles the bearer to attend on the same basis on a future occasion. We do not use the term in this way in Australia, presumably because on such occasions we expect a refund rather than a 'raincheck'.

The word however has spread into wider use in America, and increasingly in Australia, to mean *a deferment*:

"Can you come to our party on Tuesday?"

"I'll take a raincheck on that."

This means that the person invited cannot come to the party, but would like to be invited on another occasion. It is also used to mean that the person invited is not yet sure whether or not he or she can come, but will let the host know.

The word used in this sense is, perhaps, an **offensive intruder**. On the other hand it could be argued that it is a graphic piece of new language which meets a need and which is worth adopting into Australian use without argument.

There is now a third use of the word *raincheck* in wide use in the American retail trade and rapidly gaining currency in the Australian retail trade. Where a chain of retail stores issues a catalog it is now common to see under certain items the phrase *No rainchecks*. This means that when that item is sold out in the store in question it can not be placed on order for re-supply; in other words, that the store in question has only a certain number of that item, and when those are sold, that's it.

raise/rise. *Raise* is a verb: *we raised the window. Rise* is both a noun and a verb: *it was a steep climb up the rise* (noun) or *Rise and shine!* (verb).

Since *rise* is a noun you can say if you want to *I had a rise in my salary*. But you should not say *I had a raise in my salary* because *raise* is not a noun.

A confession: to be honest, *raise* does appear in the dictionaries as a noun, used in the sense above. It is edging its way in. But *rise* is still preferred.

ramifications. The word *ramifications* comes from the Latin *ramus*, a branch, and the sense is of something that *branches out*, as with a family tree, or an investigation into drug-smuggling. The word is often used as though it means the same as *repercussions*, but the two words are quite different in meaning. The *repercussions* of an event are *consequences that flow from it: The repercussions of the scandal included the resignation of the Prime Minister.*

ranks in the armed forces. The nomenclature for comparative officer ranks is as follows:

Navy	Army	Air Force
Admiral of the Fleet*	Field Marshal*	Marshal of the RAAF*
Admiral	General	Air Chief Marshal
Vice Admiral	Lieutenant General	Air Marshal
Rear Admiral	Major General	Air Vice Marshal
Commodore	Brigadier	Air Commodore
Captain	Colonel	Group Captain
Commander	Lieutenant Colonel	Wing Commander
Lieutenant Commander	Major	Squadron Leader
Lieutenant	Captain	Flight Lieutenant
Sub-Lieutenant	Lieutenant	Flying Officer
—	Second Lieutenant	Pilot Officer

*No serving or retired members of the Australian armed forces hold these positions, though the Duke of Edinburgh holds all three. The only serving Australian officer to hold rank at this level was Field Marshal Sir Thomas Blamey.

rap/rapt and wrap/wrapped.

1. *I'm wrapped* (or *wrapt*) *in Boy George* or *I'm rapt in Boy George*?

The answer is *either. Rapt* is a word which means *engrossed, spellbound*. You can be *rapt with wonder, rapt in thought, rapt with joy*. So you can, if you feel like it, be *rapt in* or *with* Boy George. The word originally meant *carried away, raped*.

There has undoubtedly been a strong influence in the relationship of *wrapped* and *rapt* because they sound the same, but a stronger influence has surely been the fact that they present two different images of absorption in another person or thing, contradictory in their way, but each suggesting handing oneself over. If you are *rapt* in someone or something you are *carried off your feet*, if *wrapped* you are *enveloped*. There seems little or no point in arguing the matter.

2. *He gave me a wrap-up* or *he gave me a wrap* are Australian ways of saying *He praised me*. The evolution of this would seem obvious enough — *to envelop someone in compliments* — but G. A. Wilkes, in his *A Dictionary of Australian Colloquialisms*, says the word is interchangeable with *rap, rap-up*, and gives many examples. The correct spelling, however, would seem to be *wrap, wrap-up*.

3. *He gave me a rap* means in Australia (and elsewhere) *he gave me a reprimand*, from *rap over the knuckles*, as well as the meaning in paragraph 2 above. *He gave me* the *rap* means, to this writer at any rate, *he tipped me off that it was going to happen*. We can find no dictionary reference to this meaning, but in American English one of the meanings of *rap* is *to speak to*.

4. The many uses of *rap*, often in idiomatic form, almost defy listing. They include *he took the rap, a burglary rap, I don't care a rap*.

rate/rating/rateable. The verb *to rate*, meaning *to appraise*, and best known to most of us by its use to mean *the assessment of local taxes*, becomes *rating, rated, rateable, rateability*.

rather. See **unique**.

ratio. Pronounce *RAY-shee-o*, not *RAY-see-o*.

rationalise. The verb *to rationalise* has two common usages.
(1) It can mean *to think up reasons for having done something*: *After taking a leading part in the family row John rationalised that it was really all for the best.* There is no objection to this way of using the verb. But *to rationalise* can (2) also mean *to sort things out, to order them efficiently*: *After rationalising the organisation of the office they were able to sack two typists.* In this sense the word is a nasty bureaucratic coinage. It carries something of the sinister overtones of *liquidate*. Prefer *Let's reorganise* (or *reform*) *our procedures* to *Let's rationalise them*.

reaction has several meanings. One is *the interaction of two or more ingredients*. Another is *political opposition to change* or *the desire to return to a former state* (Evelyn Waugh once said that the trouble with the Conservative Party in Britain was that it had never put the clock back a single second).
   The use of the word *reaction* simply to mean *response of any kind* ("His reaction to the proposal was favorable") has gone too far to oppose successfully. A small sigh of regret is permitted.

reactionary. See **political terminology in Australia**.

reafforestation/reforestation. The word, in either form, means *the re-establishment of trees on forest land*.
   Reforestation is the American form of the word, now accepted as the standard word by international agreement.
   Afforestation, a word that in general world usage means *the establishment of a forest where one does not exist*, in Australia and New Zealand means, more commonly, *the establishment of a plantation or forest of non-Australian trees*, especially the planting of softwoods.

real-estate terminology. See **apartments/condominiums/flats**.

reason.
   I do not love thee, Doctor Fell,
   The reason why I cannot tell,

> But this I know, and know full well,
>   I do not love thee, Doctor Fell.

1. We may pardon the poet because of the requirements of scansion. However, phrases such as *the reason why* and *the reason is because* are tautologous — that is, they say the same thing twice. It is *the reason* you cannot tell, not *the reason why*. In other words, prefer *The reason she could not attend is that she is ill* to *The reason she could not attend is because she is ill*.

2. *It was because of that reason that he did it.* Again, the fact of *cause* is mentioned twice here, where once is required. Read rather *It was for that reason that he did it*.

3. *The reason for the epidemic may be attributed to the lack of sanitation*. It is the *epidemic* that may be attributed, not the *reason*. The reason is the *lack of sanitation*.

receptionist. Not *receptioniste*.

recipient. In such phrases as *She was the recipient of congratulations* this word should be avoided. Say rather that *She was congratulated*.

reckon. To use *reckon* to mean *believe* is considered an Americanism, though in fact it goes a long way back in standard English. Today it is regarded as a vulgarism: "I reckon it'll be a big party tonight."

Reckon has, however, a perfectly proper place when used to mean *to calculate* ("I reckoned up the account and it came to $16") or *to come to a conclusion based on some form of calculation* ("I thought about it and I reckoned that she could not be less than seventy years old.")

See also **dead reckoning**.

recoup/recuperate. In the magazine *Good Weekend* of 17 July 1987 we are told that the Sheraton hotel group "wants to recuperate a participation of $10 million" from the wealthy Saudi Arabian Ama Khashoggi.

To recuperate as an intransitive verb (one that does not take an object) means *to recover from ill health or exhaustion*. The word is very seldom used in any other way. But, in fact, there is another use of the word, in this case as a transitive verb, in the sense in which it is used in the quotation above. Here it means *to recover losses*. The verb *recoup* is, however, much more common in this meaning.

recrimination/retribution. A reporter writing in the Melbourne *Sun* (30 May 1987) informs us that the train robber Ronald Biggs, living in Brazil as a fugitive from British justice, may be troubled "with fears of recrimination" in the after life.

It is unlikely that Biggs is troubled with thoughts of the after life, but if he is it will be *retribution* that he will be worried about, not *recrimination*.

Recrimination is, strictly speaking *a charge made against a person who is accusing you*: "It was you who broke the window, not me." More generally the word is used for any kind of accusation.

Retribution means *punishment for wrongdoing*, or *the act of punishing for wrongdoing*: "He suffered retribution for the assault." More loosely the word is used also to mean *recompense* or *compensation*, but this is undesirable.

recur/recurring. *Recur* is pronounced with the *ur* sound as in *burn*. *Recurring* may repeat the same sound, or may have the *ur* as in *hurry*. *Recurrent* has to have the *ur* sound as in *hurry*.

recurrence/reoccurrence. *Reoccurrence* is a common, but illiterate, form of the correct word, *recurrence*.

red-letter day. A *red-letter day* is a *special day*, a day to be recalled because of the pleasant memories it brings. The term stems from the tradition of printing saints' days and special holidays in red letters in calendars and almanacs.

refer follows normal rules (see **doubling up**) in making *referring, referred*, but is anomalous in making *referable*, though *referrable* is also acceptable.

referencing. With the increasing professionalisation of writing and publishing in Australia it is becoming common, and necessary, to have a 'reference apparatus' (sometimes called a 'critical apparatus') as part of any serious article or book.

What we are talking about is what most people would call *footnotes*.

Footnotes, however, is not an appropriate term, firstly because all reference notes now tend to be accumulated at the end of a chapter or a book, and seldom appear at the bottom of the page. More importantly, a distinction may be drawn between *footnotes* (expansive comments on the text by the author) and *source notes* (references to the source of the statement, opinion or quotation being given).

In older books *source notes* are uncommon and *footnotes* did tend to appear at the foot of the relevant page, often distinguished by devices such as the star or asterisk [*] or the dagger [†].

Today, owing to the increasing quest for economy in the publishing industry, it is common for *footnotes* and *source notes* to be lumped together in a simple numerical sequence of what are called *shoulder* (or *superior*) figures [1].

This is a basically straightforward system. The frequent use of the following terms within that system, designed to save much time and space, should be noted.

IBID.

Ibid. is short for the Latin word *ibidem* and means *in the same place.*

If, for instance, you have this reference:

[23]Francis Adams: *The Melbournians* ... (London and Sydney, 1892), p. 75.

and your next reference happens to be the same book, you need not write the whole thing out again, but can simply put:

[24]*Ibid.,* p. 76.

OP. CIT.

Op. cit. is an abbreviation for *in the work cited.* If, after reference 23 above, reference 24 was something quite different, but reference 25 returned to Francis Adams's *The Melbournians,* you would write:

[25]Adams, *op. cit.,* p. 76.

If among the previous references there were references to more than one book by Francis Adams, then you would have to make that clear:

[25]Adams, *The Melbournians* ..., p. 76.

Note that common sense is necessary in the use of *op. cit.,* as indeed in the use of all such abbreviations. *The essential thing to remember is that all reference notes are there to help the reader identify a source as quickly and easily as possible.* Consistency is desirable, but is less important than clarity. Do not, for instance, '*op. cit.*' a reference that last appeared four chapters earlier. In a book, start the whole procedure anew with each chapter.

Note that since *op. cit.* means *in the work cited,* it can only follow the author's name, not the name of the work: *The Melbournians, op. cit.* is nonsense.

LOC. CIT.

Loc. cit. means *in the place cited.* It seems to cause more trouble in use than any other such abbreviation, and is best avoided if possible. It is, in fact, seldom necessary. It is used in such a case as this:

[31]Humphrey McQueen: "Cultures and illiteracies", in *Australian Society,* vol. 5, no. 1, January 1986, p. 17.

If, some references further on, you want to refer back to the McQueen article, the abbreviation *op. cit.* is not appropriate (since neither the article nor the magazine is a 'work' in the sense of a book, but rather a location where a quotation appears). The reference should read:

[36]McQueen, *loc. cit.,* p. 19.

ET AL.

Et al. is short for *et alii,* which means *and other people.* Where you have a book or article by a number of authors, it is usually necessary only to mention the first to appear on the title page. The reference would then read:

[10]Kate McNeill *et al.:* "A new phase for equal pay", in *Australian Society,* vol. 5, no. 1, January 1986.

PASSIM

Passim is a Latin word meaning *throughout.* If, in a reference, you want to indicate that a work contains scattered references all relevant to your argument, you may, instead of page references, use *passim*:

> [33]W. G. Spence: *Australia's Awakening* ... (Sydney and Melbourne, 1909), *passim.*

ET SEQ.

Et seq., short for *et sequentes*, means *and what follows*, as in:

> [42]Eris O'Brien: *The Foundation of Australia* ... (Sydney, 1950), p. 51 et seq.

It is preferable to write (a) if possible, the actual page numbers, or (b) p. 51f. (meaning page 51 and the following page), or (c) p. 51ff. (meaning p. 51 and the following pages).

VIDE

Vide means *see*, as in:

> [17]*Vide* McQueen, *loc. cit.*, for confirmation of this point.

See, however, is preferable to *vide*. Vide is pronounced *vie-day* or *vie-dee*.

SUPRA *and* INFRA

These mean *above* and *below*, as in:

> Further confirmation will be found in the section of Margaret Kiddle's work quoted *supra.*

The reader would then expect to find the reference earlier in the same chapter or article. *Above* and *below* are, these days, preferred to *supra* and *infra*.

NOTE

1. Certain titles above are followed by dots, as with *Australia's Awakening* ... This is because the actual title on the title page is longer than that given: for the purpose of convenience it has been shortened. (If a bibliography is attached to the work the title will be given *in full* in that bibliography, as will the publisher, who is normally omitted in reference notes.)

2. In mentioning pages, dates etc., prefer *pp. 161–192* to *pp. 161–92*, and prefer *1934–1946* to *1934–46*.

3. Always copy the title of a book from the title page, *not* the jacket or the spine.
   See also **book titles**.

referenda. The formal, Latin plural of *referendum* is *referenda*. This form has, however, for some time been giving way to *referendums*, which should now be regarded as the appropriate word.

refute. "I refute your argument." Though increasingly used simply as a synonym for *deny*, in fact this usage is in error and is bringing a useful word to the edge of the precipice. *Refute* means *to oppose successfully with facts or argument, to disprove*. No other single word means this, and to use it as simply another word for *deny* is to lose an important word to slovenliness.

regardless. See **irregardless/regardless**.

regiment. The 'accepted' pronunciation of this word until quite recently has been *regm'nt*, with the *i* not being sounded. This is one of a number of words (*often* and *medicine* among them) whose 'received' pronunciations have been changed by the growth of general literacy and the tendency to pronounce words as they are spelt, just to be on the safe side.

regionalism in Australian language. Australia lacks distinctive regional accents. It would be a bold person who would seek to differentiate a Queenslander from a Western Australian on the ground of accent alone. There are different Australian accents, and they are distinctive from the accents of Britain, America, Canada and New Zealand, but they are not *regionally* different within Australia. J. R. L. Bernard has said that "the picture is of a widespread homogeneity stretching from Cairns to Hobart, from Sydney to Perth, a uniformity of pronunciation extending over a wider expanse than anywhere else in the world."

This has, at least, been the view until recently. It is challenged by Dr David Bradley of La Trobe University, who claims that his team, when trained, can convincingly identify the home State of speakers as often as 60 per cent of the time. Dr Bradley says that he has identified quite clear differences in pronunciation in about fifty words, and that there are many more subtle variations.

Given the increasing dominance of centralised communications in Australia, such regionalisms may well be diminishing. If so, this would be regrettable. In Britain and the United States regional accents add to the variety and pleasure of intercourse and are increasingly accepted as not only permissible but desirable.

But even with current research the most we can boast of in Australia are a few minor regional variations in vocabulary, pronunciation or sentence structure. The word *port* (*portmanteau*) for *suitcase* often identifies a Queenslander. So, sometimes, does the word *duchess* for a *chest of drawers*. The odd use of the word *but* at the end rather than the beginning of a sentence (*He didn't come to the party after all but*) is again largely a Queensland peculiarity, as is the reinforcing word *hey: We're not going to stand for it, are we, hey! Tissue* for cigarette paper is heard in Tasmania (and New Zealand), but not elsewhere. *Trough* is sometimes pronounced *trow* in Tasmania. Victorians are said to say *worry* (to rhyme with *lorry*) rather than *wurry*.

Recent research, reported in the *Age* (17 February 1986) and in the *Australian Journal of Linguistics*, has expanded this list. *Trombone*, for instance, is a word for *marrow* in South Australia. The word *spider* for *ice-cream soda* (now a vanished taste in any case) was stated in this research to be confined to Victoria though since the publication of the first edition of this book angry correspondents have declared that *spider* is also used in Tasmania, South Australia and Western Australia. *Cheerio* is a Queensland word for a *cocktail sausage*. In Western Australia a *pumpkin* is called a *gourd*, in Sydney *swimming togs* are called *swimmers* or *cozzies*, and a *scollop* is a potato-cake. There are no doubt a few score such words, but they amount to little in the generally uniform language picture. We ourselves have an entry on **deli** (*delicatessen*) as it is used in Australia.

The research worker mentioned above, Pauline Bryant, has suggested that there are four Australian language regions: (a) Queensland and New South Wales; (b) Victoria, Tasmania and the Riverina; (c) Western Australia; (d) South Australia. The fact that this proposed division is based on the nomenclature for only 32 items tells us what an early stage Australian language studies are in.

The long *a*, short *a* distinction in Australia in such words as *dance* and *castle* is discussed under **dance/darnce**.

See also **pronunciation in Australia**.

regrettably/regretfully. These words are frequently confused. *Regrettably* means *unfortunately*: *Regrettably, the plane arrived too late for the transfer of passengers. Regretfully* means *full of regret, with feelings of regret*: *The time had come for them regretfully to say farewell.*

regulatory. Pronounce *reg-u-LAT-ory* not, as often heard, *re-gul-at-OR-y*.

reiterate. See **iterate/reiterate**.

relaid/relayed. A path is *relaid*, a message *relayed*.

relate/relating.

> Don't forget the importance of relating to the audience.
> He related well to his mother-in-law.
> You must relate for all you're worth.
> Coming from the same background, she was able to relate.

To relate, properly speaking, means two things: (a) to tell a story, and (b) to establish an association between different things, or to have that association. Examples of the second meaning are:

> The thigh bone relates to the knee bone.
> She related the revised plans to the originals.
> A nut and a bolt are closely related mechanically.

To use the verb *to relate* to mean *to establish a close personal understanding with other people*, as in the examples with which this entry starts, is frowned upon by many. In this sense it is a piece of sociological jargon which is edging its way into general use and, like a cuckoo in the nest, is ousting other perfectly satisfactory phrases. *He got on well with his mother-in-law* is a far less pretentious way of putting the matter than *He related well to his mother-in-law.*

In short, *things* relate but *people* don't.

relatively. See **comparatively/relatively.**

relative pronouns. See **pronouns.**

relevant. Frequently misspelt *relevent.*

the religious. See **(the) reverends.**

remembrance. This word is *not* spelt *rememberance.*

remuneration. Your *remuneration* is the money you get for doing some work. It comes from the Latin for a *gift* or *reward,* an origin which crops up again in *munificent.* It is common in Australia to hear this word mispronounced *renumeration,* perhaps because *renumeration* sounds a more 'likely' word.

renege. *To renege* is *to back out of an obligation.* The original pronunciation rhymed with *league,* but in Britain it has gradually been overtaken by a pronunciation which rhymes with *plague.* The Australian pronunciation, however, rhymes with *peg.*
   The word is accented on the second syllable, and the *g* is hard, as in *get.*

repatriation. One's *patria* (in Latin) is one's *homeland. Repatriation* broadly means *the return of a person or persons to their homeland.* In Australia the use of the word has been affected by its adoption after the first world war to cover *the return and resettlement of Australian servicemen overseas to Australia.* Until recently the title of the federal department dealing with the affairs of ex-servicemen was the *Repatriation Department.*
   The word, as used in Australia, thus tends to have a special, even primary, sense of a military nature.

repel/repulse. An enemy may be *repelled* or *repulsed.* In both cases the sense is of *driving back.* But note that, while *repulsive* means *causing disgust* (*We found his behavior repulsive*), you cannot say *His behavior repulsed us.* Here the verb *to repel* must be used: *His behavior repelled us.*
   To repulse also has the metaphorical meaning of *to reject coldly: Our very friendly overtures were repulsed.*

repercussions. See **ramifications.**

replete. "A body of fiction replete with data about daily life in the schools."
   Replete means *stuffed full.* It is best used only in connection with a good meal. Its advertising connotations — *replete with every modern convenience* — have made it an unsuitable word for general use. The writer of the sentence we quote

above would have been better advised to say "A body of fiction full of information about daily life in the schools."

replica. See **copy/duplicate/facsimile/replica**.

reportage. No British or Australian dictionary we have consulted gives the primary meaning of this word as we understand it.

To us *reportage* means *a piece of factual writing, about a recent event or series of events, designed for newspaper or magazine publication in the first instance, and of a descriptive and literary nature.* In this sense, widely accepted we believe in America and Australia, the word is pronounced *rep-ort-AHZH.*

Dictionaries we have consulted define *reportage* as *the process of reporting news, a journalist's style of reporting, a journalistic story told through pictures,* or *a factual presentation in a book.*

We would regard *rep-ORT-idge* as the appropriate pronunciation for the word in the first two of these definitions, *rep-ort-AHZH* for the other two.

repulse. See **repel/repulse**.

reputable. A person that is *reputable* has *a good reputation*. The word is pronounced *REP-yoo-tibl,* not *rep-YOO-tibl.*

Why write (as above) *a person that* instead of *a person who*? See the entry on **that/which/who/whose**, paragraph 1.

research. The traditional and 'proper' way to pronounce *research* is *r'SEARCH,* the first syllable hardly sounded. There appears to be a movement away from this and towards *RE-search,* which some authorities say is the American pronunciation. But American dictionaries still favor the traditional pronunciation and, if *RE-search* is coming in, it would seem just as likely that it is because of the 'stress to the first syllable' tendency in English as any foreign plot.

The use of the verb *to research* — *I have to research the French Revolution for next week's lecture* — is sometimes frowned upon, but it is acceptable.

resin/rosin. *Resin* is a gummy exudation from trees. *Rosin* is obtained from the distillation of turpentine, and is a substance used on the bows of certain stringed musical instruments.

resister/resistor. A *resister* is a person who resists. A *resistor* is an electrical device.

respective/respectively. "My parents died within a short time of each other in their seventy-first and seventy-second years respectively." *Respectively* here means *in the order given*. Since there is no order given, such a sentence as this makes nonsense. It would *not* make nonsense if it read *My mother and father died within a short time of each other in their seventy-first and seventy-second years respectively,* for when it is put that way we know who comes first and who second.

The words *respective* and *respectively* are best avoided where possible; and it usually *is* possible. If they are to be used, they should be used with reason:

> The three fishing boats went to Portland, Port Fairy and Warrnambool respectively.

Without the *respectively*, which here means *separately*, it would be a likely assumption that *all* went to *each* of the three ports.

An example of the senseless use of the words is:

> Both the Tasmanian and the Victorian police forces have respectively deplored hazardous adventures which risk the lives of rescuers.

See also **former/latter**.

respite. A *respite* is *some kind of a pause for relief*. One talks of *working without respite*. The word may be pronounced *RES-pit* or *RES-pait*, to rhyme with the word *spite*. In either case the stress is on the first syllable.

restaurant/restaurateur. A *restaurant* is a public place where meals are served, and the *restaurateur* is the proprietor. He or she is *not* a *restauranteur*. Only about one in ten you hear speaking on television about food get this one right.

Restaurant may be pronounced (a) with the final *t* silent and the *n* sounded as in *sing;* (b) the same way but leaving out the central syllable; (c) with the last syllable rhyming with *want*.

restricted clauses. See **that/which/who/whom**.

rest room. See **(the) smallest room**.

retribution. See **recrimination/retribution**.

revaluate/re-evaluate. "... forcing BHP to re-evaluate their investment in South Africa" (Max Walsh, ABC-TV, 29 July 1985).

There is no such word as *re-evaluate*. The words are *revaluate* and *revalue*.

the reverends. A priest of the Catholic Church is formally addressed as the *Reverend Father* and informally as *Father*. If in charge of a parish he is known as the *parish priest*, and he lives in a *presbytery*.

Some Anglican (Church of England) ministers like to be known as the *Reverend Father* and *Father* also, and to be identifed as *priests*. This indicates a leaning to the High rather than the Low Church. Otherwise, and normally, *the Reverend* is the title, and *Mr* is used in normal conversation. An Anglican minister in charge of a parish is known as the *vicar* and he will live in a *vicarage*. (In some dioceses he is called the *rector*, and lives in a *rectory*.) Assistants to vicars and rectors are called *curates*.

In the Presbyterian and Uniting Churches the clergyman is called the *minister*. He lives in a *manse*. As with the Church of England, the formal title is *the Reverend* and, in addressing him or her directly, or talking about him or her, the correct usage is not "Reverend Smith" but "Mr Smith" (or Mrs, or Miss, or Ms, as the case may be).

Catholics often refer to *the Religious*, a rather odd phrase which means *a member of a religious Congregation or Order in the Catholic Church who has taken solemn or simple vows relating to chastity, poverty etc.* (A solemn vow is taken by a member of a religious Order, and encompasses poverty, chastity and obedience. A simple vow has more liberal rules in relation to poverty.) The Religious includes brothers and nuns and some priests, but does not include the normal parish, or 'secular', priest, who does not take vows.

revolver. See **pistol/revolver.**

rewarding. The use of this word in its fashionable sense, Eric Partridge has written, is "indefinably yet undeniably 'pseudo'."

riesling. The correct German pronunciation of this German word is *reece-ling*, not *rice-ling* or *reez-ling*. *Reez-ling* is however accepted as an alternative English pronunciation.

robot. This name for an automatic machine performing human functions is pronounced as it is spelt, and not as *ROB-o*. The word was coined by the Czech writer Karel Čapek in his play *R. U. R.*, and comes from the Czech *robota*, work.

The study or science of robots is called *robotics*, a term first used in a series of stories by Isaac Asimov.

robust meaning *strong, well-built*, may be pronounced *RO-bust* or *ro-BUST*. The former is more common.

romance. The preferred pronunciation of this word is with the stress on the second syllable, *ro-MANCE*. This applies to both noun and verb.

Romania. Prefer this spelling to *Rumania* or *Roumania*.

roman numerals. The most important of the Roman number-symbols are:

I	=	1	C = 100
V	=	5	D = 500
X	=	10	M = 1000
L	=	50	

The way the system works is through two simple rules:

(a) When a symbol is preceded by one of lesser value, subtract that value from the total to give the number. Thus IV equals 4.

(b) When the symbol is followed by another of less or equal value, add them together. Thus XXI equals 21.

Here are some other examples:

    XLVIII   =   48 (XL is 40, VIII is 8)
    LXXXI   =   81 (L is 50, XXXI is 31)
    CDI   =   401 (CD is 400)
    MCM   = 1900 (M is 1000, CM is 900)
    MCMLXXXVI = 1986 (MCM is 1900, LXXXVI is 86)

NOTE

1. The figure 4 is sometimes given as IIII, and 400 as CCCC.

2. Small as well as capital letters may be used.

3. In such a sentence as *Elizabeth II is the Queen of England*, do not follow the II with a full stop.

4. The symbol for *one* in Roman figures is *I*, not *1*. Therefore *World War II*, not, or not yet, *World War 11*.

romantic. See **classical/romantic.**

roof. Although some distinguished academic writers, as well as television journalists, apparently believe otherwise, the plural of *roof* is *roofs*, not *rooves*.

rort. A splendid Australian word, meaning, let us say, *a party with the lid off*. It comes from the English slang word *rorty* or *raughty* of the last century, meaning *first-rate*, *spirited*, *lively*. Australians have formed a noun from the English adjective and have given the word an extra sense of abandon.

Rort in Australian English can also mean *a bungled operation* (especially in soldiers' slang) and *being shoved around*, especially by officialdom. "They told us it was a dinkum raffle, but it was a rort."

Although not recorded as such in any reference books, the word now is becoming a verb. At the Royal Melbourne Show on 26 September 1985 the Premier, John Cain, was interviewed, and said (of the Australian taxation system) "The whole system is being rorted." By this Cain meant *taken advantage of*. And the State director of the Liberal Party in Queensland, Gary Neat, says that the Queensland government is responsible for the "rorting" of

State electoral boundaries (*Age*, 12 April 1986).

The word then clearly has two broad meanings: (a) a wild party, and (b) something suspect, something involving bad dealings.

roster. See **rota/roster**.

rota/roster. Both *rota* and *roster* mean *a list of names specifying the order in which persons perform certain duties*. *Rota* is the common British usage, *roster* the Australian.

Russia/Soviets/Soviet Union. The correct title for this country is the *Union of Soviet Socialist Republics*, normally abbreviated to *USSR* or *Soviet Union*.

Russia, prior to the revolution of 1917, was the name of the vast empire of the czars. Today the word may properly only be applied to the Russian Soviet Federated Socialist Republic, one of seven republics within the Soviet Union, though vastly the largest of them. Native speakers of Russian number about half the inhabitants of the Soviet Union.

A citizen of the Soviet Union should not formally be referred to as a *Russian*, unless perhaps he or she happens to be a member of the Russian ethnic group within the Soviet Union, and the word is intentionally being used that way.

Nor should a citizen of the Soviet Union be referred to as *a Soviet* (although *Soviet citizen* is acceptable). A *soviet* is a *council*, in Soviet usage a council of workers' and peasants' deputies. Thus *the Soviet government* (i.e. the government of the soviets) is correct, as is *The Soviet troops were smartly turned out*, but *The Soviets have a good sense of humor* is wrong. The word *Russian* can not simply be replaced with the word *Soviet*, and *Soviet* does not mean *Soviet citizen*.

Although it is strictly incorrect, there is no easy alternative, in fact, to the phrase *The Russians have a good sense of humor*, unless one wants to move to the rather labored *The Soviet citizens have a good sense of humor*. In informal use, then, *Russian* meaning *Soviet citizen* may be used, provided it does not give offence and the qualifications are understood.

The position is in some ways analogous to that of citizens of the United States of America. We do not say *The citizens of the United States of America are here* (as we should) but *The Americans are here*. (See **America/United States**.)

If referring to the period before 1917, when the name of the country we now know as the Soviet Union was *Russia*, then *Russian* is of course a correct description of a citizen at that time (though not necessarily, of course, an accurate ethnic description).

Soviet is pronounced, preferably, with the *o* as in the word *sober*.

S

s. For the old-fashioned *long s*, as in *miſs* (miss), see **(the) long s.**

-'s. For *-'s*, in the form of *my sister's child* as alternative to *the child of my sister*, see **double possessives**.

sail and steam. Sailing ships used to *sail*, and steam-ships used to *steam*. What do we do now, when most ships neither sail nor steam?

There is no acceptable word for describing how a motor-vessel or nuclear-powered vessel proceeds, unless you use as ugly and colorless a word as *proceeds*. So, "We sailed from Hobart for Antarctica on the motor-vessel *Icebird*" is a perfectly acceptable usage. "We came steaming into the Kent Group on the [diesel-powered] *Miranda Bay*" is also acceptable.

sailer/sailor. A *sailer* is a ship or boat, as in *I own a trailer-sailer* or *This boat's a good little sailer*. A *sailor* is a seaman.

salination/salinisation. *Salinisation* is a familiar word in Australian rural life. It refers to the rising salt levels in the soil which, especially in such places as the Murray River irrigation areas, constitutes a menace to agriculture. For all that the word does not appear in any of the three 'Australian' dictionaries; not does it appear in any other English dictionary we have consulted.

Salination is a rarer word. It too does not appear in any dictionary consulted. CSIRO advised that it is sometimes used to mean the *deliberate* subjection of, for instance, plants to high salt levels.

salubrious. A leading Australian publisher recently commented, to a gathering of several hundred literary people, that they were participating in a "salubrious event". Had these people been taking part in a bush walk across the Australian Alps they *might* have been taking part in a salubrious event, for *salubrious* means *conducive to good health*. Since the audience was in fact consuming large quantities of rich food and drink the occasion was hardly a *salubrious* one. The word, however, is increasingly used in Australia to convey the sense of *happy* or *pleasant* or *notable*. There is no justification whatever for this.

The opposite of *salubrious* is *insalubrious*, not *unsalubrious*.

sanction. Watch this word, especially when used as a verb. The trouble is that *a sanction* has (amongst others) two contradictory meanings. It can mean *an* *encouragement to do something* (*She gave her sanction to the extra expenditure*) or *a penalty for doing something* (*Sanctions are proposed against South Africa*). Thus such a sentence as *The people of the town were aware of the racist behavior of some of their number, but it was not sanctioned* can mean *either* that they did not approve of the behavior *or* that they did nothing about it.

sarcasm/sarcastic. See **ironic/sarcastic/sardonic/satiric.**

sardonic. See **ironic/sarcastic/sardonic/satiric.**

satire/satiric. See **ironic/sarcastic/sardonic/satiric.**

scam. This quite new word appears to have originated in the United States about the early 1960s, and to have moved on to Britain and Australia. Its derivation is uncertain, though it may be related to *scamp*, and it means *a lurk, a racket, a fraud*; it conveys the sense, at least in Australia, of *a course of action which may not be against the letter of the law but which is against its spirit, and which has been carefully devised.* We are informed that in this country it is very much a public-service word, which seems believeable.

scarf. The plural is either *scarfs* or *scarves.*

scenario. S. J. Perelman tells the story of the two vultures clinging to a crag outside Los Angeles. One says: "That sure was a delicious scenario writer. You'd have to go all the way to Beverly Hills for one like him." The other replies: "Listen, that bad I don't need *anything.*" A *scenario* is, properly, *the summary of the plot of a play or film.* It has now been taken over from the entertainment industry and is widely used as a vogue word meaning *the general prospect or prospects in a given situation,* as in, for instance, *This is the scenario for our next sales campaign.*

Many would hold that that sentence would be better expressed as *This is the plan for our next sales campaign* or *This is the outline of our next sales campaign. Scenario* in its recent sense is something of a 'smartarse' word, and should be avoided.

sceptic/skeptic. The Australian spelling is *sceptic* and *scepticism.* Either through ignorance or a desire to ape the Americans, *skeptic* and *skepticism* are increasingly being seen. These spellings should be discouraged.

The pronunciation of *sceptic* and *sceptical* as *septic/septical* sometimes has unintended humor about it, but is *wrong.*

schedule. The Australian pronunciation of this word is *SHED-yule,* but the

American *SKED-yule* is making some inroads. This is very largely due to the shortened form of the word, which is always pronounced *sked*.

schism. A *schism* is a noun which means either *the division of a group into opposing factions* or *a faction so formed*: *A schism developed in the Australian Labor Party when Dr Evatt attacked Catholic Action.* The word conveys the meaning of *a complete breakaway,* or at least *a serious division likely to lead to such a breakaway,* so it would be undesirable and inaccurate to refer, for instance, to the factions within the parliamentary Labor Party in Australia as *schisms.* The Protestant Reformation movement created a *schism* within the Catholic Church which led to a separation.

One who takes part in a *schism* is *a schismatic.* In Catholic eyes, Martin Luther was a *schismatic. Schismatic* is also an adjective: *a schismatic tendency.*

'Educated' opinion prefers the pronunciations *sizm, sizmatic.* But the alternative pronunciations *skizm, skizmatic* are probably more common in Australia. *Shizm, shizmatic* are unacceptable.

schnapper. See **snapper**.

schnorkel/snorkel. The word, now used mainly for a breathing device used by skin-divers, was originally the name used by German submariners for the ventilation and exhaust tube extended above the surface from a submerged submarine. Spelt *Schnorchel,* it is related to the German word meaning *to snore.*

The preferred English spelling is now *snorkel,* the verb *snorkelling.*

school of arts. See **mechanics' institute/school of arts**.

schools. Government schools in Australia are everywhere called *State schools,* except in New South Wales, where they are called *public schools.*

This is confusing, because (a) private schools in New South Wales are referred to as the Greater Public Schools and the Associated Public Schools, and (b) in Victoria, and to a lesser extent in other States, most major independent schools are called *public schools.*

Therefore when you say of someone in Victoria that he or she has had a *public school education* there is some indication of elitism, whereas the same phrase in New South Wales implies the reverse.

It is safe to call non-State schools *independent* or *private* schools in all States.

In South Australia independent schools are sometimes called *colleges,* and in Queensland there is a type of secondary school which is semi-independent and semi-government and is called a *grammar school.*

See also **educational nomenclature**.

sciencespeak. A distinguished physicist of our acquaintance has given us some examples of the mode of scientific explication today:

> It is thought that ... (i.e., *I thought*).
>
> A typical specimen ... (*the best we can find to establish the case*).
>
> ... was handled with great care ... (*was not dropped on the floor*).
>
> It is well known ... (*I'm not going to look it up*).

Our friend contrasts this with the way a nineteenth-century scientist would have opened his paper:

> On the way between King's Cross and Edinburgh I met Professor Brown, who informed me that he had found an interesting plant, subsequently named *Golfingia macintoshii*, while on the links at St Andrew's.

(*Golfingia macintoshii*, our friend further informs us, actually is the name of a plant.)

The justification for today's sciencespeak is that, while scientists are just as egotistical today as they ever were, it is now thought desirable to obscure the fact. The problem, however, with the 'objectivity' of sciencespeak is that, in abandoning the personal for the impersonal, it attempts to influence the reader's subconscious, for instance with the use of the passive voice (*It is thought that ...*, *It is well known*). Today's sciencespeak is also, of course, less honest and less interesting.

See **passive voice; tendentious**.

scientific nomenclature. Living organisms are classified scientifically by Latin names which specify (a) the *genus*, (b) the *species*, (c) sometimes the sub-species, (d) the name of the person who first described the organism in scientific literature.

The scientific name of the box jelly-fish (or **sea wasp**) of northern Australian waters is thus *Chironex fleckeri* (Southcott). In this case *Flecker* was the name of the medical practitioner who did much work on the creature.

Note that the genus and species (and, if present, sub-species) names are in **italics**, and note that the genus name has a capital letter but the others not. *Southcott*, in brackets, is the name of the *describer* and is not in italics.

A species of amoeba is, delightfully, known as *Chaos chaos*.

scientism. *Scientism* may be called 'the unacceptable face of science.' It means *the misuse of science*, arguments or actions claiming respectability from scientific achievement or the method of science in order to achieve non-scientific ends. It can also mean *the elevation of science to a position of absolute authority*. The word does not appear in *The Macquarie Dictionary*, which is a pity. Scientism is well and truly alive in Australia.

The adjective is *scientistic*.

Scotch/Scots/Scottish. The *Scots* do not like the word *Scotch*, which they regard as an English word, and prefer to be referred to as *Scots*, and things Scottish to be referred to as *Scottish* rather than *Scotch*.

The exception is *Scotch whisky*, which is always *Scotch* (or so we hope).

screen. One meaning of the verb *to screen* is *to shelter, to protect, to conceal*. Its use (though well advanced) to mean *to isolate people on the grounds of specific requirements* does injury to the primary sense of the word: people are seldom *screened* for their own comfort.

For this more sinister use of *screen* prefer *sift*.

seasonable/seasonal. *Seasonable* means *in keeping with the season: The weather is really very seasonable*. *Seasonal* means *happening at a particular season, relating to the seasons: The seasonal changes in Australia are not very marked*.

sea wasp. The feared *sea wasp* of northern Australian waters, responsible for many fatalities, is now known as the *box jellyfish*. The name was changed because many people were under the impression that it flew around in the air. The scientific name is *Chironex fleckeri*.

second world war. Prefer *Second World War* or *second world war* to *World War II*.

secretary. A common Australian pronunciation of *secretary* is *secetry*. It is wrong.

section. New Zealand English for *a block of land*.

semicolons. The *semicolon* (;) is a punctuation mark which, in 'stopping power,' lies between the comma and the colon. Here are some of the ways in which it is used:

BETWEEN CLAUSES WHICH COULD HAVE BEEN SEPARATE SENTENCES

> Camped again without water on the sandy bed of the creek, having been followed by a lot of natives who were desirous of our company; but as we preferred camping alone, we were compelled to move on until rather late, in order to get away from them.
>
> W. J. Wills

TO BRING ORDER INTO A SENTENCE WITH MANY COMMAS

> And so we, tired but happy, made our way home; while the others, equally exhausted, slept on the spot.

TO SEPARATE ANTITHETICAL PHRASES

> We had far to go; our time was running out.

365

BEFORE CLAUSES BEGINNING WITH CERTAIN ADVERBS
Such adverbs include *so, therefore, however, for instance:*

> You will meet with many difficulties in this calling you have chosen; therefore consider carefully how you will prepare yourself for it.

TO SEPARATE ITEMS WHERE COMMAS HAVE ALREADY BEEN USED

> Take the following with you: a large, red ball; two dozen eggs, all of them brown; one harrow, second-hand; and a spotted cravat.

TO SERVE AS A 'REST' STOP
This is especially useful in long sentences where the semicolon, used late, helps to sum up what has gone before:

> Because half-a-dozen grasshoppers under a fern make the field ring with their importunate chink, whilst thousands of great cattle, reposed beneath the shadow of the British oak, chew the cud and are silent, pray do not imagine that those who make the noise are the only inhabitants of the field; that of course they are many in number; or that, after all, they are other than the little shrivelled, meagre, hopping, though loud and troublesome insects of the hour.
>
> Edmund Burke

send her down, Hughie! There have been many arguments about the derivation of this Australian invocation of rain. A classical scholar has pointed out to us that *Huei* is the Greek for *It rains,* and that *stone the crows* is a literal translation of a similar expression in Aristophanes. For further evidence that Australian slang was invented by classical scholars and not by the "nomad tribe" (in Anthony Trollope's phrase), see **tall poppies.**

senile. This word may be pronounced *seen-ile* or *senn-ile.* The British and Americans prefer the former, the Australians the latter. In either case *senility* is pronounced *senn-ill-ity.*

sensibility/sensitivity/sensuality/sensuousness. A person of *sensibility* is *unusually influenced by emotional impressions.* In her novel title, *Sense and Sensibility,* Jane Austen contrasts reason and emotion. Yet *sensibility* does not mean overcharged emotions so much as delicacy of response to outside stimuli. To say that someone has a *pronounced sensibility to music* is rather to offer praise than criticism. *Sensitivity* is at the same time a coarser and a broader word. It means *capable of being affected by outside impressions.* It can be applied to photographic paper, to impressions of pain, to feelings of concern. It can be applied to someone who reacts badly to criticism, but here the word *sensitiveness* is often preferred.

Sensibility relates not to physical impressions, but to emotional or intellectual ones (see also next entry). *Sensitivity* may relate to either physical or emotional impressions.

But *sensuality* is firmly related to matters that can be heard, seen, felt, smelled or tasted. A *sensual* person is *a person concerned with the gratification of the senses. Sensuality* is the state of being *sensual.*

Sensuousness, like *sensuality*, means related to the five senses, but in a more refined and appreciative way than *sensuality.* To call someone sensual, or to refer to their *sensuality*, may suggest an element of coarseness or lack of discrimination. But a *sensuous* person is one who appreciates aesthetically the impressions gained from their senses.

sensible/sensibly. Most of the time, in using these words, we intend them to mean *wisely*, as in *During the crisis she behaved very sensibly.*

There is another, very different, use of these words. If you say that someone was *very sensibly affected by the news* it doesn't mean that he or she was very sensible about it. It means that the person was *clearly and obviously affected* by the news, that it had a big effect. The root word is the Latin *sentire, to feel.*

Another example, from that master of the English language Evelyn Waugh: "It had been an earthquake which, in the more sensible motion of the cab, had escaped our notice." Here the word *sensible* means *apparent to the senses, obvious, intrusive.* In other words, the cab was rattling around so much that those in it did not notice the earth-tremor. Physicists talk of *sensible heat*: heat that warms the air and that you can feel.

In writing the entry on **life-style** in this book we first wrote *The life-styles of many have been sensibly diminished by the invention of the word life-style.* By this we meant that *the life-styles of many have been perceptively diminished . . .* But then we removed the word *sensibly*, sensibly coming to the conclusion that, if left in, it might be thought by some readers to mean the opposite of what we intended.

The words *sensible* and *sensibly*, used in this second and special sense, are more familiar in the forms *insensible, insensibly.*

several. It is correct to write *Only a few people were there*, and it is correct to write *Several people were there.* But, since *several* already means *only a few*, it is incorrect to write *Only several people were there.*

Several can also, and perhaps confusingly, mean *separate*, as in *They went their several ways*, or in the legal phrase *jointly and severally*, which means *together and apart.*

sewage/sewerage. *Sewage* is a noun, and refers to the human waste products that have to be disposed of by organised communities. *Sewerage* is the means by which this is done. It is both a noun (*The sewerage is complete*) and an adjective (*The sewerage scheme is under way*). So *sewerage* refers to the pipes, *sewage* to what goes in them.

sexism in language. See (the) female critique.

shall/will.
1. Let us first take *shall* and *will* simply as words which make a statement about the future. Traditionally we have had:

I shall	We shall
You will	You will
He/she/it will	They will.

In this sense *will* is replacing *shall*, in Australia as elsewhere, and its victory, at least in the spoken language, is almost complete. The common use of the contractions *I'll* and *we'll* has assisted this process. If *I shall* and *we shall* mean precisely the same as *I will* and *we will*, as they usually do, there can be little or no objection to the replacement of one by the other.
2. While *shall* is slipping out of use in simple statements about the future, it retains its power and function when it is being used to express *determination* or to emphasise *prediction* — that something is bound to happen. Here *shall* is used with all the personal pronouns:

I shall	We shall
You shall	You shall
He/she/it shall	They shall.

Examples of the use of *shall* to emphasise determination and prediction are:

"I shall certainly do this," she said with passion.

We shall fight on the beaches.

You shall be free!

They shall come when they are told.

Or in "Song of the Western Men:"

A good sword and a trusty hand!

A merry heart and true!

King James's men shall understand

What Cornish lads can do.

3. *Shall* also retains a place in common speech in questions: *Shall I come? Shall we go home?* Note the difference between *Shall you come to the party?* (are you going to come to the party?) and *Will you come to the party?* (please do come to the party.) And between *What time will we arrive?* (simple question) and *What time shall we arrive?* (what is the best time for us to arrive?)
4. If in doubt, use *will*.

shambles. Originally a *shamble* was a *market stall*, perhaps one on which meat was displayed for sale. Later the word came to mean *a slaughterhouse or abattoirs*, and later still *a place where there had been much killing of any kind.*

The word has been watered down to mean, for instance, what the children's room looks like much of the time, or, indeed, any kind of heroic mess. It has also become singular.

We can't do anything about this but should remember that *shambles* is still sometimes used in its meaning of *slaughterhouse*.

shammy. See **chamois/shammy.**

sheikh. Pronounce to rhyme with *shake.*

shelf. The plural is *shelves.*

ship. See **boat or ship.**

shithouse. See **(the) smallest room.**

shoal. "Liberal leader Sir William Knox will readily advance that Sir Joh Bjelke-Petersen would never have shoaled on the Lindeman Island deal if the steadying Liberal influence had still been there" (*Bulletin*, 25 March 1986, shortened).
   A *shoal* (noun) is a patch of shallow water. (That witty man, Matthew Flinders, named the Troubridge Shoals in the Gulf of St Vincent, South Australia, after Sir Thomas Troubridge, who ran his ship aground at the opening of the Battle of the Nile in 1798 and participated in the battle as a spectator.)
   The word *shoal* may also be an adjective (*shoal water ahead*), or a verb meaning *to enter shallow water* (*we were shoaling as we entered the estuary*) or *to become shallow* (*the water then shoaled*).
   The verb *shoaled*, in the extract from the *Bulletin* above, appears to mean *grounded*, or *come to grief.* If so, it is incorrect. There is no such meaning, literal or metaphorical, of the verb *to shoal.*

shortfall. The use of this word to mean *a shortage* of any kind is a **cliché** of our times. *Shortfall* is best reserved to mean *the amount of a deficiency: There was a shortfall in the delivery of fourteen cases.*

short-sighted. A *short-sighted* person is not a person who has difficulty in reading without glasses. On the contrary, a short-sighted person often has excellent near-vision, and may be able to do without spectacles until late in life. What the short-sighted person suffers from is poor *long* vision, a difficulty in focusing on distant objects. For this such a person may need spectacles.
   Conversely, a *long-sighted* person has excellent and normal *long* vision, but will probably need spectacles for reading.

should of/would of. These phrases, as in *He should of done it*, are common illiteracies. The correct wording is, of course, *He should have done it*. Because *should have* and *would have* are so often abbreviated to *should've* and *would've*, and because *should've* and *would've* sound something like *should of* and *would of*, people think that is actually the way it should be.

should/would. The general rule is that the correct forms are *I should, we should,* but *you would, he would, she would, it would, they would.*

However *I would* and *we would* are common and acceptable:

I wondered whether we would ever reach home.

The word *should,* however, has other meanings, especially the meaning of *ought to.* Here *should* may be used not only with *I* and *we* but also with *you, he, she, it* and *they:*

The Russians should withdraw their troops from Afghanistan.

You should sign that document before it is too late.

It should be a fine day tomorrow.

shy. Note *shyer, shyly, shyness.*

sic. *Sic* is the Latin word for *thus.* When used in an English sentence it always appears within brackets and means *yes, this is what appears in what I am quoting, but it is a mistake or anyway very odd, and I'm just warning you that the responsibility for the statement is not mine.*

So *sic* can save a lot of words! Because it is a foreign word, it always appears in italics (i.e. underlined in typescript).

An example:

The brochure states that it is about a thousand metres *(sic)* between Melbourne and Sydney.

The *sic* in this example is drawing attention to the fact that the word should be *kilometres.*

significant. This word, used as a comment on, say, a picture or a book, has been called "an egregious example of very crafty question-begging."

the silent 'e'. Should we keep the *-e* at the end of words such as *acknowledge* when we add a suffix such as *-ly, -ing* or *-ment*?

With some words we may take our choice: for instance, *acknowledgement* or *acknowledgment,* **judgement** or **judgment,** *abridgement* or *abridgment.*

There is however a general rule, which is:

(a) Keep the *-e* before a suffix beginning with a consonant. (Thus keep it before *-ment, -ly.*)

(b) Get rid of the *-e* before a vowel. (Thus get rid of it before *-able, -ible, -ing.*)

Following this rule will then give us *judgement* but *judgable* and *judging, lovely* but *lovable, likely* but *likable* (although in fact *likeable* is also permitted), *movement* but *movable* (though *moveable* is also correct and is more common).

Apart from alternatives such as *likable/likeable* and *movable/moveable*, there are a few important exceptions to the rule. These are:

(a) Keep the *-e*, where it is necessary to distinguish a word from another with the same spelling: for instance, *holey* (holy), *singeing* (singing), *dyeing* (dying).

(b) Keep the *-e* where to drop it would mean, by the rules of pronunciation, that a preceding *c* or *g* would otherwise be pronounced hard: *changeable* not *changable, advantageous* not *advantagous, peaceable not peacable, noticeable* not *noticable*.

(c) Other exceptions include *rateable, mileage, duly, wholly, truly*.

See also **-able/-ible**.

simile. A *simile* is a figure of speech in which two *unlike* things are linked by reference to a common quality. The difference between a *simile* and a **metaphor** is that a metaphor directly identifies two things (*He is a cold fish*) while the simile *compares* them by using words such as *as, like* or *such*: *He behaves like a cold fish*.

See **metaphor; moribund metaphors and similes**.

simple/simplistic. Objection has been taken by some commentators to the word *simplistic*, on the grounds that there is nothing that *simplistic* can do that can not be done as well by the word *simple*, and that in any case the expansion of words to make them seem more profound, for instance *purist* into *puristic*, is an offence.

Simplistic, however, has been in the language since 1881 at least, though it must be admitted it is now a fashionable and over-used word. It has been called a "simple-minded word beloved of the half-sophisticated." The *Oxford English Dictionary* says that it means *of extreme simplicity*.

The reason why the word *simplistic* is needed is that it does a job that *simple* cannot do. To say that a friend's assumptions about a certain matter are *simple* may be to praise them (see **Occam's Razor**). To say that an argument is a *simple* one may, again, be to speak in its favor. But if we wish to criticise an argument or point of view as being of *too great simplicity*, then the word *simplistic* is needed.

simulate. "The Israelis have the capacity to simulate nuclear capability" said an American commentator on ABC television on 16 July 1985.

The American meant that the Israelis have *achieved* nuclear capability, in other words that they have the bomb. But by any normal rules this is not what he said. To *simulate* means to *pretend*, to *mimic*, to *feign*. Unless there is a quite new American use of the word *simulate* coming into the language, what he said was the opposite of what he meant.

since. See **ago.**

sinecure. A *sinecure* is *a job without duties,* such as harbor-master at Heard Island. Everyone dreams about sinecures at times. The word comes, quite simply, from two Latin words meaning *without cares.* The preferred pronunciation in Britain and the United States is with the first syllable pronounced as *sign.* In Australia preference is given to its being pronounced the same way as the word *sin.*

Singapore. A citizen of the country named *Singapore* is a *Singaporean.*

situations. *Situation* is a bullfrog word when used in such contexts as *in the classroom situation, in the waterfront situation, in a conflict situation.* Those saying or writing thus are trying to inflate their importance and give the impression of studied familiarity. Say or write *in the classroom, on the waterfront, in a conflict. Situations* are found in the classified advertisements of the newspapers.

sixth continent. See **fifth continent.**

sizable/sizeable. Prefer *sizeable.*

slang is unconventional English, and the origin of the word itself is unknown. *Slang* differs from *jargon* in that it does not have a particular occupational base, though there will of course be social and 'class' differences in the slang people use.

Slang is the incoming tide of a restless sea of language. Words are cast up on the shore. Some are drawn back by the next wave into the sea, and disappear for ever. Some remain, driven ever higher by the water, to sprout like coconuts on a Pacific island, and to become a fixed part of the linguistic environment. The word *mob,* for instance, was once merely slang.

What is slang depends on the viewpoint of the listener or reader. In Australian schools the word *chook,* used for *chicken,* would be regarded as slang. To many Australians, especially in rural areas, *chook* is standard Australian English. George Eliot once said that "Correct English is the slang of prigs who write history and essays."

The slang 'problem', if it is a problem, is self-correcting. Words of no more than passing fashion soon fade away. Words that a language community needs, either because they don't exist in the language at all, or because that language community has special characteristics which lead to the invention of new words, or the new use of old words, will survive. The Australian word *earbasher* was needed because the English word *bore* had gentlemen's club connotations that did not 'fit' in Australia. It will probably pass into standard Australian English, and perhaps in a century people will be astonished that it was ever regarded as slang. It may even pass into international English, as the words *whinge* and *whinger* are now doing. (Like much Australian slang, *whinge* will be found in English dictionaries, but it is Australians who adopted, adapted and popularised it.) The word *bludger*, another splendid Australian coinage, which has developed from its original meaning of a prostitute's pimp to fill a language gap, is probably a permanent part of the Australian language, and may, like *whinge*, be exportable.

A language without slang would be a dead language. In written and formal Australian English slang should be used circumspectly and with respect to the audience and the effect intended. It should be discouraged, like other language, when it becomes tired, repetitive and an excuse for not thinking about what we are saying. But, at its best, it is the yeast in the dough of words.

slash mark. For comments on this punctuation mark (/), see **oblique stroke**.

sleight, as in *sleight of hand*, is pronounced *slight*.

slough. Where this word means a marsh or bog, as in Bunyan's *the Slough of Despond*, pronounce to rhyme with *how*.

Where it is used as a verb, for instance in *the snake sloughed its skin*, pronounce *sluff*.

sly. Note *slyer, slyly*.

the smallest room is a **euphemism** for the place where human excretory functions are performed. Other words and phrases with the same meaning include *lavatory, toilet, shithouse, shouse, water closet* (or *WC*), *rest room, men's room, ladies' room, dunny, loo*.

The variety of evasions testifies to the unease, guilt and puritanical revulsion which a necessary and inescapable human function arouses.

As one new euphemism becomes too closely identified with the natural functions (itself a euphemism) it is replaced by another. Thus *WC* in polite usage was replaced by *lavatory* (strictly speaking a place where one washes rather than defecates), *lavatory* by *toilet*, and *toilet* by *rest room* or some other invention.

The colloquial words *shithouse* and *dunny* have alone proved resistant to change, partly because they are never used in polite circles in any case, and partly because they represent a deliberate reaction against mealy-mouthed talk.

Of all the words mentioned, *dunny* is the most traditionally Australian and the most affectionately regarded. It comes from the old British word *dunnaken* or *dunnakin*, meaning *a place of dung*. Although *dunny* may be used generally, its special and traditional meaning is the once-familiar backyard structure, first cousin to a sentry-box, from which the 'pans' were removed by the 'night-cart man' once or twice a week. A fisherman in Bass Strait once said to us that the sea was "as flat as a night-cart man's hat."

When the outside dunny, the pans and the night-cart man fell victims to social progress, much Australian folklore went with them.

Toilet is probably the most used and most approved of these words at the moment. Under the Law of Defecatory Declension it will before long be replaced by another.

See also **euphemisms**.

smelled/smelt. Both are permissible, but prefer *smelt*.

smoke-o/smoko. This is the traditional Australian bush term for a break in the day's work for tea and a smoke. The recommended spelling is *smoko*, not *smoke-o* or *smoke-oh*. The plural is *smokoes*.

snapper. Authorities prefer the name of this well-known fish of Australian and New Zealand waters to be spelt *snapper*, not *schnapper*. The historic spelling however, is *schnapper*, and there is no reason whatsoever why anyone who wants to spell it this way should not do so. Note that Schnapper Point, at Mornington, Victoria, remains spelt that way.

See also **fish**.

snoek. See **barracouta**.

snorkel. See **schnorkel/snorkel**.

snuck off. Sir Henry Bolte, long-serving Premier of Victoria, once forced the Legislative Assembly to sit for thirty-two hours, but himself "snuck off and played snooker." This distressing story was told to the *Age* by one of Sir Henry's victims.

Snuck off, of course, is a jocular form of *sneaked off*. There seems to be a tendency for *regular or weak* verbs to want to become *irregular or strong* verbs if they can, just as — it is said — all white wines would be red wines if they could. Sometimes verbs actually achieve this: Americans now quite accept *dove* for **dived** and *pled* for **pleaded**.

Snuck is not there yet, but one day it will be.

so. See **that**, paragraph 2.

sobriquet. A *sobriquet* is a *nickname* or epithet attached to someone's name. If, for instance, a politician is known as *the toecutter,* that is his *sobriquet.*

The first syllable of *sobriquet* is pronounced like the *sob-* in *sober.*

so-called. Just because very often, when we use the word *so-called,* we use it with something of a sneer, some people regard it as a term of abuse: *the so-called Bob Hawke, the so-called John McEnroe.*

This is stupid.

So-called has only one meaning, which is to question the accuracy of the following name or description:

The so-called ti-tree is in fact a tea-tree.

That so-called cricket ground is in fact used exclusively for football.

social democrat. See **political terminology in Australia.**

socialist/socialism. See **political terminology in Australia.**

social/socially. We use these words in several ways, and the distinction is not always obvious.

To say of someone that *She is very socially conscious* may mean either that *She is very aware of political issues, class-distinctions and the general problems of society,* or it may mean *She is very much an upper-crust lady, aware of what she imagines her position in society to be.*

To put it another way, if we talk of an issue as a *social* issue, we can mean either that *it relates to the whole of society* (as in the use *anti-social*) or we can mean that it relates to *'high society',* as in *It was a very social occasion.*

Social and *socially* therefore have two different (and sometimes almost opposite) meanings: (a) *relating to the whole of human affairs,* or (b) *relating to 'fashionable' society.*

Social also has a third meaning. Such a phrase as *a very social occasion,* which we use above, can mean *a very fashionable occasion.* It can also mean, however, depending on the context in which it is used, *a very friendly, communicative, 'mixing' kind of occasion.*

The words, then, have to be used with some caution, in the realisation that the meaning they will convey to the reader or listener will very much depend on the context.

sojourn. A *sojourn* is a *temporary stay* somewhere. It may be pronounced with the *o* sounding like the *o* in *sod,* or the *u* in *sud.* The American pronunciation is with the *o* sounding like the *o* in *sober.*

solace. Pronounce *SOLL-is.*

375

solidus. A solidus is an *oblique stroke* or *slash mark*, thus: /, in punctuation. The plural is *solidi*.

See **oblique stroke.**

Solomon Islands. The name of the new island state in the Pacific is *Solomon Islands*, not *the Solomon Islands*.

sophistical/sophisticated. Both these words stem from *the Sophists*, professional philosophers in ancient Greece. One may say that the Sophists, like the Jesuits (*jesuitical*) have had a bad press. A *sophist* has come to mean *someone who argues for the sake of argument, a person who makes an art of quibbling or cleverness.*

Sophistical (or *sophistic*) emerges from this meaning, as an adjective for someone who argues as the Sophists are supposed to have argued.

Sophisticated has two meanings, one of them very different from *sophistical*. Normally, if one talks of someone as *sophisticated*, one means that *they have developed and cultured tastes and habits*, that they know what is going on, not only in their own field but in others.

Sophisticated can, however, also mean *over-refined, pretentious* or *superficial*. If this is the meaning intended, it has to be picked up from context. Generally, *sophisticated* is regarded as a 'favorable' rather than an 'unfavorable' word.

sough. John Masefield wrote, in "Trade Winds":

> There is the red wine, the nutty Spanish ale,
> The shuffle of the dancers, the old salt's tale,
> The squeaking fiddle, and the soughing in the sail
>   Of the steady Trade Winds blowing.

Pronounce *sough* to rhyme either with *tough* or with *bough*.

Southeast Asia. Prefer the form *Southeast Asia* to *South East Asia, South-east Asia, southeast Asia* or *south-east Asia*, when referring to the area as a political or geographical unity.

If, however, you are referring to the area in a more generalised way, use *Weather patterns are variable over south-east Asia*, or *Most of the south-east part of Asia lies above the equator*.

See **compass points.**

southern hemisphere. In *The Divine Comedy*, Dante held that the Southern Hemisphere was where Satan landed when he fell from Heaven. In horror, all the land in the Southern Hemisphere migrated to the northern, leaving behind only Mount Purgatory, "a natural prison, with a vile floor, and very badly lit."

Those living under the Southern Cross, then, should beware of facile comparisons. To say proudly that the National Gallery of Victoria (say) has more Rembrandts than any other gallery in the southern hemisphere invites the rejoinder from a European that there are (let us say) three hundred Rembrandts in the northern hemisphere and three in the southern. Australians are insular enough as it is without trying to make a virtue of living below the equator.

Soviet Union. See **Russia.**

spasmodic/sporadic. *Spasmodic* describes *something that happens in sudden brief spells, in spasms: The radio only works spasmodically.*

Sporadic does not have the 'accidental' sense of *spasmodic.* If something is happening *sporadically* it is, as with spasmodically, happening intermittently, but with some purpose: *The firing was now only sporadic. Sporadic,* which is related to the word *spore,* has a geographical sense as well as a chronological one: *the weed infestation was not uniform through the property, but was sporadic.* A *sporadic* outbreak of disease may be one that occurs from time to time, or from place to place. The sense is usually the latter.

special pleading. Originally, in law, the preparation by a party to a law suit of a statement of the *precise* issues to be examined in a forthcoming case.

The proper legal use of the phrase has been extended, *via* the sense of legal quibbling, to mean *trying to avoid in argument anything that tends to undermine one's case,* in other words not admitting the validity of any argument that goes against one's own narrow interest in the matter.

This has been called "not indeed the highest, but at any rate the almost universal, argumentative procedure." Gower argues that the word *special* is now tautologous in this phrase, but our view is that it retains its force.

special/specially. See **especial(ly)/special(ly).**

species. A *species* of plant; many *species* of plants. The singular and the plural are the same. *Specie* means something different. See **lost singulars.**

specific/specifically. Australians often, and incorrectly, pronounce these words as *pacific, pacifically.*

spectacular. Something that is *spectacular* has to be something that can be *seen.* When ABC FM radio announces it will broadcast "a ballet music spectacular" it has delusions of being a television channel.

spectrum, spectra. The former is the singular. See **lost singulars.**

spelled/spelt. Either is correct. Prefer *spelt*.

spelling reform in Australia. Spelling reform is one of those ideas which sounds fine, and *is* fine in principle, but is far from simple to put into practice.

If, for instance, we say that English should be spelt as it is pronounced, that raises the question of whose pronunciation of (say) the word *today* we choose to standardise the spelling on. In words like *hark* we find no *r* sound in Standard English, but we do in many English dialects and in American English.

What then about the *cough/bough/tough* problem, the usual starting point for criticisms of English spelling? Even if we could get all those with a right to have a say to agree on reform here, we would still be creating new problems. Anthony Burgess, in a general discussion of these issues in his *Language Made Plain*, points out that if we change *night* to *nite* we are not only depriving the Scots of two letters they use, but will need agreement on some new device to show how the *i* is pronounced. He adds that to change *education* to *edyukeishun* is not going to be of much assistance to a foreigner who uses the word *educacion*.

Burgess, very sensibly, suggests we should sort out some minor irrationalities but leave the bulk of our spelling alone, as a link with Europe and a link with our past. We should not exaggerate the difficulties of English spelling, and in teaching it make sure that an adequate phonetic alphabet is available as an aid.

Australia has a large, self-contained printing and publishing industry and is in a good position to work towards some reforms or standardisations which would not cut us off from other users of English but which would make life a bit easier. Such reforms might include:

EASY

Agree on *-or* endings rather than *-our*. (See **-or/-our**.)

Agree on *-ise* endings rather than *-ize*. (See **-ise/-ize**.)

Agree that the digraphs *ae* and *oe* become *e*. (See **-æ** and **œ**.)

A BIT HARDER

Agree on *-er* rather than *-or* endings for words, so that we spell *advisor* as *adviser*. (See **-er/-or**.)

HARDER STILL

Agree on *-able* endings instead of *-ible*, so that *accessible* becomes *accessable*. (See **-able/-ible**.)

Drop *-e* from the root of all words (with some possible exceptions) before adding suffixes, to give us *blamable* instead of *blameable*, *namable* instead of *nameable*. (See **-able/-ible**; **(the) silent 'e'**.)

Agree that final consonants of words of more than one syllable not be doubled on adding suffixes, to give us *transfered* instead of *transferred*. If we cannot do this, let us at least agree that the letter *l* follow the same rule as other final consonants, so that we have *traveled* instead of *travelled*. (See **doubling up**, Expanded Guide.)

Agree that where *ei* or *ie* have the sound of *ee*, they will be spelt *ie*, to give us *sieze, wierd*. (See **ei and ie**.)

spilled/spilt. Both are correct, but prefer *spilt*.

spiritism/spiritualism. The more familiar word is *spiritualism* (*spiritualist, spiritualistic*), the belief that it is possible to communicate with the disembodied spirits of the dead. It has been in rivalry with the word *spiritism* (*spiritist, spiritistic*) since both words came into currency in the 1850s. Spiritualists, who once favored *spiritism*, are now said to prefer *spiritualism*, but both usages remain current. It would seem sensible to prefer *spiritualism* etc. for the world of mediums and seances, *spiritism* for ethnological use.

split infinitives. An infinitive is the form of a verb starting with the word *to*: *to run, to read, to protest*.

Since the verb in such cases is not *run, read, protest*, but *to run, to read, to protest*, grammarians and stylists have traditionally preferred that it should not be torn asunder. *The politician was moved to vehemently protest* is frowned upon. The argument is that the sentence should rather run *The politician was moved vehemently to protest*, or *The politician was moved to protest vehemently*.

The grammarians and stylists have a point. If it is possible to avoid a split infinitive without affecting the sound and sense of the sentence it is usually a good idea to do so, if only for the reason that many people become hypersensitive to split infinitives and there is no point in upsetting them unnecessarily.

In the above case the last example, *The politician was moved to protest vehemently*, seems the best way of putting it.

There will be many cases, however, where more harm is done to the good use of the English language by self-consciously avoiding a split infinitive than by using one. *To really understand this matter requires a lot of study* can hardly be put any other way, except perhaps by leaving out *really* altogether, for it adds little to what is being said.

On the whole, people who 'carry on' about the split infinitive should be told that "a little learning is a dangerous thing." The essential issue is that the sentence in question should make good sense in the least pretentious way. Raymond Chandler once wrote to the editor of the *Atlantic Monthly* about their proof-reader: "Tell him that when I split an infinitive, God damn it, I split it so it will stay split."

Note that in such sentences as *To be seaworthy this boat needs to be carefully repaired* the phrase *to be carefully repaired* is *not* a split infinitive. Nor does *Tertiary education was about to be totally reorganised* contain a split infinitive.

spoiled/spoilt. Either is correct. Prefer *spoilt*.

spokesperson. This ungainly word has been wrenched into life because of feminist objections to the use of the word *spokesman* in contexts where the *spokesman* may in fact be a woman.

The solution is not to use *spokesperson*, but to use *spokesman* or *spokeswoman* as the case may be, or even *speaker*.

See **(the) female critique**.

spontaneity. For pronunciation, see **deity**.

spoonerism. See **malapropism**.

sporadic. See **spasmodic/sporadic**.

spout/sprout. Water *spouts* from a tap, and words may *spout* from a speaker's mouth. Seeds in the garden *sprout*. It is common to hear of people *sprouting* nonsense. They can't, though they can *sprout* ideas, in the metaphorical sense of having an active mind.

spry. Note *spryly*.

square brackets. See **brackets**.

stalactite/stalagmite. The limestone columns descending from the roof of a cave (*stalactites*) or rising from its floor (*stalagmites*). The words come from the Greek for *to drip*. It is the *stalactites* that have to hold on *tight*.

stand/stance. *She takes a stand on abortion; she takes a stance on abortion.* There is an unfortunate tendency to regard *stance* as a more impressive word than *stand*, but as equivalent to it in meaning. If we look closely at the above sentences, however, we notice a difference in meaning. If you take a *stand* on something you are saying *this far and no further*; if you take a *stance* you are *expressing an opinion, taking an attitude*. This attitude need not represent a final *stand*.

stasis/statist/statistician. *Statis* is the condition of being *at rest*, the condition of *no change*. Nothing, of course, is in a position of pure stasis, unless perhaps it is nothing. The word, however, is normally used in opposition to *dynamic*, in such a sentence as *Compared with the dynamic condition of European capitalist societies in the nineteenth century, the cultural position of the peoples of Africa was relatively static* (or *in a position of stasis*).

Statist (pronounce *state-ist*) is quite a new word, emerging from the study of political science. It means *someone who believes in the concentration of power in the hands of the state, rather than in the hands of individuals or autonomous bodies.*

Statist (pronounce *stattist*) was also a word for *statistician*, though in this sense it has fallen out of use. A *statistician*, of course, is someone involved in the collection and study of statistics.

state. The word *state*, used in a governmental sense, has two meanings in Australia.

We use the word, as it is used anywhere, to refer to the generalised concept of authority and government, as in the phrase *the powers of the state.*

But we also use the word to refer to the components of our federal system: Victoria, New South Wales, Queensland, South Australia, Western Australia and Tasmania.

When we use the word to refer to one of these *States* it takes a capital letter. The main reason for this is to avoid confusions which can easily arise. If, instead of *the powers of the state* we wrote *the powers of the State*, we would have to be referring to one of the States of Australia, and the meaning could be very different.

In referring to what we now call the States of Australia before the year 1901, they should be called *colonies*, not *States.*

Note *interstate*, not *inter-State*. The *state* here takes a small *s* because there is no possibility of confusion.

state of the art. This unfortunate phrase has become smart jargon around the English-speaking world. When used by advertisers and others it is intended to convey that what is on offer is *the best of its kind.* In fact the phrase means the opposite. It comes from the field of patent law, where it is necessary, in applying for a patent for a new invention, to establish that it transcends the existing *state of the art.* The term means then, at least in its origins, *what is accepted as the standard, existing situation.*

stationary/stationery. Stationary means *standing still. Stationery* means *writing materials.* They have the same origins. A *stationer* was someone who had a fixed shop, rather than being an itinerant pedlar.

status. Pronounce *STAY-tus*, not *STATT-us.*

stevedore. In the United States the word *stevedore* means what in Australia is called *a waterside worker* or *wharfie.* In Australia the word *stevedore* means *a company (or its representative) engaged in the transmission of ships' cargoes*, and hence often in conflict with waterside workers.

stone the crows! See **send her down, Hughie!**

story/storey. A *story*, of course, is *a tale*. A *storey* is a floor in a building. Thus *a many-storied saga* but *a many-storeyed building*.

For everyday purposes, however, prefer *a five-storey building* to *a five-storeyed building*.

stratum, strata. The former is the singular. See **lost singulars**.

For *strata title*, *stratum title*, see **apartment/condominium/flat**.

stress. See **accent**.

strident. "Strident efforts are being made to achieve this" said the deputy premier of Victoria on the air in June 1988.

Mr Fordham meant that *strenuous* efforts were being made. *Strident* means *making a loud or harsh sound*. *Strident demands* are demands which are being *vociferously and publicly made*.

subconscious/unconscious. A *subconscious* action or motive is one in which one's full intellectual awareness is not involved. An *unconscious* action is the same, only perhaps more so: no intellectual awareness whatsoever is involved.

Neither word, however, means *unintentional*, though it is clear that, if intellectual awareness is not involved in subconscious and unconscious acts, then they will be, in one sense at least, unintentional.

But the frequent use of these words to mean *unintentional* is wrong. An unintentional act is *an act carried out with complete intellectual awareness but which has results which were not desired*. If you kill someone in a car accident it is *unintentional*, we hope, but not *unconscious* unless, without being aware of it, you were in a suicidal or murderous mood.

the subjunctive: is it still alive? Not really, but yes, is the answer to this question. In other words, there are a few areas in which the subjunctive hangs on, but only just. It will probably disappear from the language in time.

What in fact *is* the subjunctive? It is a different form of the verb, used to express an action or situation which is hypothetical or not actual. *if it* be *so, I wish I* were *in Dixie* are subjunctive forms, and quite correct as such: though it would be more common these days to read or hear *If it is so* or *I wish I was in Dixie*. These are, of course, not subjunctive forms of the verb, but what is called *indicative*. The author of this book prefers the former examples, because they sound more natural to him, but many with different backgrounds and interests will think the reverse.

Subjunctives are in fact used by us all every day, without our being conscious of the fact. They occur most frequently in idioms and catch-phrases:

> If need be.
>
> Convention be damned! (and similar usages)
>
> Come what may.
>
> Be that as it may.
>
> Come Christmas we shall go to Sydney.
>
> I move that another chairman be elected.

But in fact there is a good deal of shading off between accepted idiomatic use and general use. And indeed, as Sir Ernest Gowers has pointed out, there is one area in which the subjunctive has made something of a come-back. He claims American influence for its use after any words of command or desire:

> Public opinion demands that an enquiry be held.
>
> He is anxious that the truth be known.

Although it could presumably be argued that, rather than a true subjunctive, such usages are really an abbreviated form of *should be: Public opinion demands that an enquiry [should] be held.* This, though, is a grammarian's argument.

The subjunctive is still used in certain other connections. It is common with the phrases *as if* and *as though*, where doubt is being cast on an issue: *The Prime Minister spoke as though the issue were* [not *was*] *solved.* It is also used in certain sentences where what is being talked about is not a fact: *If he were here, I'd give him a good dressing down.*

Technically, the subjunctive has been defined as "the mood of imagination and command". In all verbs except the verb *to be* the subjunctive is the same as the indicative: for instance, *I come* is both subjunctive and indicative. The exception here is the third person singular of the present tense, where the subjunctive form is *he come, she go.*

The verb *to be* however declines the whole of the present tense in the subjunctive: *I be, you be, she be, we be, they be,* and in addition *I was* becomes *I were* and *she was* becomes *she were.* Thus *If she be here* is an outmoded way of saying *If she is here,* and *If he were here* does not mean *If he had been here,* but *If he was here now.*

The subjunctive terrifies many, once they have become aware of it at all, but it is an unnecessary terror. People should use it or not according to the way it sounds best to them, or according to whether they feel comfortable with it.

sublimate. *To sublimate,* used in the psychological sense, does not mean simply *to suppress an impulse.* It means to divert an impulse, especially a sexual one, elsewhere. Romantics may hold, for instance, that sublimated love may produce high art.

The verb may also mean *to make purer,* as when Samuel Johnson wrote that "The heat of Milton's mind may be said to sublimate his learning."

Chemically, *to sublimate* is *to change directly from a solid to a vapor or gas without first melting*, as with solid carbon dioxide (dry ice).

subliminal. In the *Age* on 10 June 1986 a writer describes house-moving as "an industry which has virtually become subliminal."

Subliminal? The word comes from two Latin words meaning *below the threshold*, and *subliminal* is a psychological term meaning *below the level of conscious awareness*. Thus *subliminal advertising* describes messages flashed on screens so briefly that they are not consciously 'received', but nevertheless do have an effect on the observer.

Subliminal as a word was dragged into common discourse on the coat-tails of television in the 1950s, when there was much discussion on the potential evils of the new medium.

What does the writer of the *Age* article mean by calling an industry *subliminal*? On reflection he would seem to mean that *it is very hard to find a firm prepared to shift a house*. Or does he mean that *that industry has now dropped out of public awareness*? In either case he would have done better to have spurned *subliminal* as trendy **jargon** and as a **bully word**, and to have used, say, *invisible*.

subscribe. See **ascribe/subscribe**.

subsidence. *Sub-SIDE-ence* is still the preferred pronunciation of this word, though *SUB-sid-ence* is making headway.

substantiate. Pronounce *sub-STAN-she-ate*.

substitute/replace.
1. *Substitute* does not mean the same as *replace*. If Professor Smith goes on leave, the university *substitutes* Dr Brown for him. Professor Smith is then *replaced* by Dr Brown.

This will be clearer if we say that *to substitute* is to *put in the place of*, to replace is *to take the place of*.

Jones does not *substitute* for White as opening bowler; he is *substituted* for White and he *replaces* him.
2. The two words take different prepositions: use *substitute for*; *replace by* or *with*.

suburban nomenclature. A *portmanteau word* is a new word coined from two existing words, such as *chortle*, coined by Lewis Carroll from *chuckle* and *snort*, and *smog*, a combination of *smoke* and *fog*.

Australians have exhibited a sad lack of creativity and imagination by adopting in recent years portmanteau words as placenames. Thus *Aldonga* came into some use as a description of the Albury-Wodonga area, and in the suburbs the idea, hitting municipal minds with the force of a vision, has been seized on enthusiastically: Ashwood (Ashburton-Burwood), Heathwood (Heathmont-Ringwood), Warranwood (Ringwood-Warrandyte) and the rest of the ghastly collection.

It is of course to be expected that unimaginative suburban development will be accompanied by unimaginative nomenclature, but the aspect of this which hurts most is that many people must think it *clever*.

Are the joint resources of the English language and the local-government mind really so incompatible?

And, as for the Aboriginals whose names, in many cases, we not only steal but corrupt — well, the poet David Martin made the best comment on this: "septic sewers and a ghost."

succinct. A *succinct* statement is *one that is marked by brevity and concision*. *Succinct* is pronounced *suk-SINKT*, not *SUS-inkt*.

such as. *It is not easy for novices such as I* or *It is not easy for novices such as me*?

Traditionally, it has been asumed that what the speaker is actually saying is *It is not easy for novices such as I* [*am*].

> I have never heard a singer such as she [is].
>
> It could never happen to such as we [are].

In such cases *such as* is regarded as a conjunction, but present-day arguments suggest that *such as* should be declared a preposition within the meaning of the Act, which would enable people who say *It is not easy for novices such as me* to claim that they were speaking grammatically.

Which all goes to show what asses grammar and grammarians are.

In fact people these days will probably say *such as me, such as her, such as us;* that is, if they don't prefer *like me, like her*. We can accept this as colloquial and idiomatic without trying to find specious arguments to support it.

suffragan. A *suffragan* is a bishop who has the task of assisting a senior bishop. The word is pronounced with the last syllable having a hard *g*, as in *began*.

suit/suitable/suite. The more gently-born of the English like to pronounce *suit* as *syoot* and *suitable* as *syootable*, but in Australia such a pronunciation is as affected as pronouncing *girl* as *gel*.

In fact the gently-born English went even further than this in the past and regarded the only permissible forms of *flute* as *flyoot*, *blue* as *blyoo*, *loo* as *lyoo* and even *glue* as *glyoo*.

Suite is the same word as *suit* in such usages as *a suite of rooms, a suite of retainers*, but is pronounced *sweet*.

See **oo or yoo?**

supersede, meaning *to replace* or *supplant*, is often misspelt *supercede*. The correct spelling may be memorised by thinking of the Latin origins of the word: *super*, *above*, and *sedere*, *to sit*.

supine. See **prone/supine**.

supper. See **dinner/lunch/supper/tea**.

supra. See **referencing**.

surely. "Will you fetch the pincushion for me?" "Surely."

Surely as a synonym for *certainly* is so well ensconced in American English that there would be no point in challenging its position. There are signs that it is creeping into Australian usage. In traditional English and Australian usage *surely* means (a) *done with thoroughness and certainty*, as in *He rowed surely on his course, despite the threatening waves*; (b) expressing probability, as in *Surely we have already met?*

Surely in its third meaning of *certainly* or *undoubtedly* is found in English dictionaries and is certainly not an incorrect usage. In Australian usage it still has an American sound to it, however, and may quite properly be discouraged; this is not because of prejudice but because we already have a word that does the job perfectly well, and because we should not lightly abandon traditional forms.

surprise/astonish. To *surprise* someone is *to take them unawares*, at least in its traditional meaning: *The burglar was surprised by the police as he was opening the safe.*

It is however common these days to say also *the burglar was surprised to see the police*, meaning that he was *astonished* to see them.

So there are two ways of using the word *surprise*, however regrettable this may be, and both ways are firmly ensconced in the language.

There is the well-known story of the pedantic grammarian who was caught by his wife in bed with the housemaid. "I am surprised," said his wife. "No, my dear," replied the grammarian. "*I* am surprised. *You* are astonished."

Surrey Hills/Surry Hills. The Melbourne suburb is *Surrey Hills*, the Sydney suburb *Surry Hills*.

surveillance. Pronounce the *ll* in this word: *sur-VEY-lance*, not sur-VEY-ance.

suspicious. Such a sentence as *He was a suspicious person* looks simple enough, but in fact it can have two very different meanings.

It can mean *He was the kind of person who always suspected something wrong,* or it can mean *He was the kind of person one should have suspicions about.*

In using the word *suspicious* it is necessary to make clear which meaning is intended.

swap/swop. *To swap* or *swop* is *to trade one thing for another.* The word probably comes from the sound made when two people strike each other's hand to signify a deal made. The gesture may still be seen among traders in New York streets.

Either spelling is correct, but prefer *swop*, as the more common Australian spelling in everyday use, and also because it more accurately indicates the pronunciation of the word.

sycophant. A sycophant is *a person who uses flattery to win favor, a toady*, in Australian English *a crawler.*

Schoolboys used to be amused at what was supposed to be a dictionary reference to the origin of this word: "See under the figleaf." The word comes from ancient Greek, and means *showing the fig.* To *show a fig* is to use the famous Mediterranean gesture of contempt, where the thumb (representing the penis) is pushed between the first two fingers of the hand. It means, quite simply, *Get fucked.* Dante refers to the gesture in his *Inferno.*

But how is this related to the meaning of *sycophant?* Some claim it is because the sign of the fig was a gesture used before a magistrate in ancient times to accuse a person of a misdeed, and hence to ingratiate oneself with the authorities. Others point out the the word *fig* signifies *vagina* in some Mediterranean languages (the impression created by a split-open fig?), and that this accounts for such expressions as *not worth a fig.* (Others opt for a more simple explanation: that a dried fig is a pretty worthless commodity.) The *vagina* school goes on to argue that *to show the fig* (that is, to be a *sycophant*) is to display one's anus or genitals in a form of submissive behavior, as some animals do, by bending over.

So a sycophant, as well as being an *arse-licker*, can also be an *arse-flasher.*

Incidentally, *sycophant* please, pronounced *SICK-o-fant*, not *psychophant*, which is the way it has been pronounced in parliaments. *Psychophant* is a pleasant word which does not exist, but which perhaps should. A proposed definition is *lost political souls who have found security at last in being told what to believe.*

Sydneysider. From the earliest days this term was used by those living in the general area known as Victoria to describe those living north of the Murray, or perhaps sometimes north of the Murrumbidgee. Until 1851 there was no separate colony of Victoria, the Port Phillip Settlement being part of New South Wales. As all living in the present area of New South Wales and Victoria were therefore New South Wales residents, a term was necessary to indicate those who owed informal allegiance to Sydney rather than to Melbourne. The term has remained in use, nowadays used rather to describe a resident of Sydney than *any* inhabitant of New South Wales.

sympathy. The word *sympathy* may be followed by either *with* or *for*. See also **empathy/sympathy**.

synoptic. See **holistic**.

T

t. For the use of one or two *t's* in such words as *regrettable*, see **doubling up**.

TAFE (technical and further education). See **post-secondary education**.

tall. See **high/tall**.

tall poppies. One of the fundamental characteristics of Australians is supposed to be their inexhaustible desire to *cut down tall poppies*, to undermine, not only self-importance, but any kind of egregious distinction or achievement (except, of course, in sport). The term is distinctively Australian, and its first appearance in print was in a pamphlet of 1902, *The Voice of the People*..., by H. L. Nielson. This was an argument for cutting down the costs of government: "The 'tall poppies' were the ones it was desired to retrench ..."

The original story is from Livy. Tarquinius Superbus was the last of the Roman tyrants of the old order. Tarquinius's son Sextus sought to displace his father, and sent a message to this end. The king made no reply, but walked into his garden: "There, walking up and down without a word, he is said to have struck off the heads of the tallest poppies with his stick."

Many more Australians read Livy in the nineteenth century than do today.

A discussion of the tall-poppy metaphor in Australian life, by Richard Ely, will be found in the issue of *Australian Cultural History* for 1985.

tandem. The term *in tandem* does not mean *side by side* or *together*. If two or more people are swimming or walking *in tandem*, the second is behind the first, the third behind the second and so on. Normally the phrase refers to two people only. The formation is what the navy calls *in line ahead*.

tangential. Something that is *tangential* has the nature of a *tangent: a line or curve or surface that touches another line or curve or surface but does not intersect it*.

The word is often used metaphorically: "His views were tangential to the main thrust of the discussion."

There is no such word as *tangental*.

tank. Tanks hold water, but there are two kinds of tanks to be found in the Australian countryside: the normal domestic tank and the large, dam-like structure excavated from, and constructed out of, earth and clay. Tank-sinkers were, perhaps still are, familiar figures in the Australian bush.

Although listed in G. A. Wilkes's *A Dictionary of Australian Colloquialisms* as an Australian expression, the word in fact occurs in Yule and Burnell's marvellous *Hobson-Jobson*, their glossary of Indian English, first published in 1886. They give the meanings as *an artificial pond, a domestic reservoir or cistern*, and trace the use of the word in English back to 1589. It is said to come from the Gujerati *tankh*.

This raises the interesting and little-examined issue of the migration of Indian words into Australian English. Familiar examples are *bungalow, gunny-bag, dekko* and *veranda*.

tantalise. "Libya rather than farms is what tantalises the media" at a press conference with Prime Minister Hawke in Washington, wrote Michelle Grattan in the *Age* (26 April 1986).

The verb *to tantalise* comes from the ancient Greek myth relating to the punishment of Tantalus in Hades. Tantalus was placed in a pool which always receded when he tried to drink from it, and under fruit trees whose branches were always blown aside when he tried to pick the fruit.

To *tantalise* (or *tantalize*) is, then, *to torment by apparently offering something which in fact turns out to be unattainable.* A *tantalus* is a container for decanters which allows the decanters, though visible, to be locked so that they cannot be unstoppered.

Was Michelle Grattan using the word *tantalises* correctly in the above quotation? If the suggestion in the story was that the journalists wanted to discuss Libya, were given the impression that they would be allowed to, but then found that Libya was not on the agenda, the use of the word would have been correct. From the context, however, we learn that Libya was discussed at the press conference. Perhaps a better word in the circumstances would have been *fascinates*. Better still, perhaps, would have been *interests*.

tarmac. Short for *tarmacadam*, tarmac describes *the mixture of crushed rock mixed with tar and bitumen* used for roads, runways etc., and also describes the surface so treated itself. Note the spelling *tarmacked*.

tart. "She's a bit of a tart" means, in today's Australian usage, *she plays around a bit, her sexual behavior is on the loose side.* From this we may assume that *tart*, at least to many, signifies *a prostitute*.

The word, in the way we use it in Australia (and also as it is used in Britain), has come down in the world a bit. Up to the 1920s or later there was no suggestion of moral turpitude about it. A man's *tart* was his *girlfriend*. The amusing poet W. T. Goodge wrote in 1899:

> And his lady-love's his 'donah'
> Or his 'clinah' or his 'tart'.

And in his 1916 pantomime song "Billo" (which became a Melbourne favorite) Percival Cole wrote:

> Gimme old Melbourne, an' gimme me tart:
> An' then I am simply orl-right,
> Can any bloke point to a better old joint,
> Than Bourke Street on Saturdee night?

Tasmania. Before November 1855 Tasmania was known as *Van Diemen's Land*, and strictly speaking should be referred to as such when dealing with that period.

tautology. A *tautology* says the same thing twice but in different words. A friend of ours when in England wrote down a splendid tautology she heard on a BBC weather report: "Intermittent rain followed by occasional showers."

Tautologies, like **pleonasms**, are undesirable in writing and in speaking but are easily overlooked. At times, however, they are used for deliberate effect.

Examples of tautologies are:

> The hunter courageously dared to face the tiger. (Prefer *The hunter courageously faced the tiger* or *The hunter dared to face the tiger*.)
> The flasher, wearing no clothes, ran naked across the cricket field.
> He returned home to his own dwelling at midnight.
> He preceded his successor.
> I heard it with my own ears.
> Will this number be adequate enough?

tea/dinner/supper. See **dinner/lunch/supper/tea**.

tea-tree/ti-tree. In his journal of his second voyage Captain James Cook talks of the "tea plant", a name, he says, "obtained in my former voyage from our using it as tea then, as we also did now."

Cook's plant has been identified as *Leptospermum scoparium*. Early Australian settlers followed his practice, and the name *tea-tree* refers to any species of *Leptospermum* as well as to several species of the allied genus *Melaleuca*. *L. scoparium*, in fact, is one of the few plants common to Australia and to New Zealand, where it is known as *manuka*. The usage *tea-tree*, as above, is however common to both countries.

The spelling *ti-tree*, which is not uncommon, is therefore incorrect, which is no reason, however, why people should not use it if they want to. After all, the Rose Hill parrot has become the Rosella.

The proper ti-plant or ti-tree is the palmlike cabbage-tree of New Zealand, *Cordyline australis*. A relation, found on the eastern seaboard of Australia, is sometimes called *ti-plant*. In this case *ti* is a Polynesian word.

technobabble. The computer industry has been responsible for much of the present-day mangling of the English language. Clearly it is not enough to be skilled in the use of computers; that skill must be demonstrated through office jargon which creates a barrier between the elect and the non-elect. Thus *analysation* for *analysis, transportation* for *transport, where do you office?* for *where is your office?* and even *fruitation* for *fruition. Shippee-addresses* and *contact points* proliferate, *interfaces intercourse* with each other in various *modalities,* and *bottom lines* achieve a spurious dignity. *Project teams* orientate their goals and *report in a matrixly fashion.* We *input* our skills and *workshop* our differences.

Computers already correct spelling mistakes. May we hope, then, for a *software program* on *language malfunction*?

See also **jargon.**

technologist/technician/tradesman. Properly used, there are important distinctions between these words.

A *technologist* is an engineer or scientist who works in industry. Although the word is sometimes misused in the interests of status-seeking, it properly refers only to those who are qualified to be members of a professional institute (see **engineer**). As with *engineer*, the word *technologist* has no legal protection in Australia. In the United States the word has a slightly different meaning. There the technologist is understood to occupy the ground between the craftsman and the professional engineer, rather closer to the latter.

A *technician* is an engineer, laboratory worker etc. trained to 'certificate' or similar standard, performing skilled work usually in association with professional engineers, or scientists, but not a professional in the strict sense.

A *tradesman*, defined narrowly, is someone who has undergone apprenticeship training and is competent to handle skilled work of a 'hands-on' nature. More loosely, *tradesman* can apply to anyone recognised as competent in a given trade.

temporary/temporarily. *Temporary* may be pronounced *TEM-pry, TEM-prary* or as spelt.

Temporarily may be pronounced *TEM-prily, TEM-prarily* or *TEM-porarily.* With these generous alternatives there seems little call for the American pronunciation *tem-por-AIR-ily,* now creeping in on the Australian airwaves.

tendency/trend/trendy. Most authorities make no distinction between *tendency* and *trend,* holding them both to mean *the general drift or direction that something or someone is taking.*

Fowler, however, would like to preserve a distinction: *trend* for *a specific inclination or leaning, tendency* for *a trend that is continuous and consistent.* A *trend,* in other words, may develop into a *tendency.*

We do not think this worthy distinction is likely to be followed in practice.

Trend as a noun also has another, and modern meaning, *a passing fashion*. In this sense it is often used in a derogatory way, especially when transformed into *trendy*, which is a very trendy word.

tendentious has come to mean, in popular and journalistic use, *argumentative, quarrelsome, prejudiced*. Its correct meaning, however, which should not be lost, is *having a deliberate tendency, having controversial intent; arguable* rather than *argumentative* in a bad sense. For all that the word frequently, though not inevitably, conveys a sense of bias in an argument. Writers, for instance, who use the words *we* and *us* in their arguments in an attempt to draw the readers in as allies (*this does not add to our knowledge*) may well be accused of manipulative and *tendentious* writing.

tend/tender. A garden is *tended*. An account is *tendered*.

tense. The word *tense* comes from the Latin word meaning *time* and tells us *when things happened. I spelt* is *past tense. I spell* is *present tense. I shall spell* is *future tense.*

That, at least, is what traditional grammarians would say. Modern grammarians (if they allow themselves to be called grammarians) tell us that the *tense* of a verb tells us about the *degree of completeness* of the relevant event. They also tell us that there are only two real tenses in English, the *is* and *was* tenses, and that the future is conveyed by fiddling about in various ways.

We may learn something by placing the definitions of the traditionalists and moderns together.

	Past	*Present*	*Future*
Traditional			
Simple action	I saw	I see	I shall see
Continuous action	I was seeing	I am seeing	I shall be seeing
Perfect or complete action	I had seen	I have seen	I shall have seen
Modern			
Events that simply happened	I saw	I see	I shall see
Events that were happening at a particular moment	I was seeing	I am seeing	I shall be seeing
Events that happen in a period of time leading up to a particular point	I had seen	I have seen	I shall have seen

1. The second and third tenses shown in the table may be combined: *I had been seeing, I have been seeing, I shall have been seeing.*
2. There is a tense called *the future in the past*: *I should see, I should be seeing, I should have seen.*
3. There is another tense called *the future in the present*: *I am seeing him tomorrow.*
4. There is another tense called *the present in the past*: as in a chapter heading (say): "I enter the jungle and I return safely." Or *Aristotle is the most interesting of the ancient Greek philosophers.* The *present in the past* is more commonly known as the *historic present.* This is a dangerous addiction among writers, used to attempt to give immediacy to a past event:

> If we glance at their journals, we find that the climbers are now approaching the most dangerous part of the ascent. Just at this moment, a whole cliff face breaks away, and one of them is suspended in mid-air.

The trouble about this way of writing about the past is that it is seductive, it gets tiresome, and it can be very hard to break back to the normal past tense.
5. Care has to be taken with a tense called the *perfect infinitive* (*to have seen, to have gone*) The catch here is that the *perfect infinitive* has to refer to a time previous to that of the main verb. So:

> I would like to have seen her. (*Correct*)
> I would have liked to see her. (*Correct*)
> I would have liked to have seen her. (*Incorrect*)

See also **participles; passive voice; (the) subjunctive: is it still alive?**

tenterhooks. "I am on tenterhooks," *not* "I am on tenderhooks," though the latter is what one usually hears. *Tenterhooks* are hooks used for stretching cloth after it has been woven. To say that you are on tenterhooks means that *you are 'stretched' with excitement, anxious to know the outcome of something.* The word is related to the word *tent*, i.e. stretched canvas.

terminus. The plural of *terminus* is *termini*.

Terra Australis. See **New Holland**.

thank you. See **please/thank you**.

than what. This is a usage much beloved of politicians, in such phrases as "Why should he have a bigger electoral allowance than what I do?". The *what* is not needed and should be avoided in both speech and writing. See **indicator words; (the) wandering what**.

that.
1. *They saw that the tree was surviving,* or *They saw the tree was surviving*?

Either. Use whichever sounds best to you. But: *Barbara said when the telephone rang she was going home.* Did she say this *when the telephone rang* or did she say it some time before? If she said it some time before, then there *must* be a *that* before *when*.

Similarly, *Barbara said on Monday the luggage would arrive.* Did she say it on Monday, or will the luggage arrive on Monday? If the latter, there has to be a *that* before *on*.

See also **that/which/who/whose**.

2. Avoid the use of *that* when *so* will do. Prefer *It's not so bad* to *It's not that bad*; prefer *It was not so important* to *It was not that important*. Many people would wince at the sentence *I was that sick I stayed at home.* Then why say *that bad*, *that important*?

that/which/who/whose.

Here we are talking about which of these words to use with *dependent* (or *subordinate*) clauses. In a sentence such as *We visited the people who lived on the island*, the words *who lived on the island* constitute a *dependent* clause because to make sense they *depend* on the words *we visited the people. We visited the people* is a *main clause* because it can, if necessary, stand alone and make sense — it is not dependent.

Dependent clauses may be linked with main clauses in various ways, most of which give little trouble. Here we are concerned, however, with the *relative pronouns* which perform this work. The main ones are *that/which/who/whose*.

1. A simple rule-of-thumb is to use *who* of people and *which* of things:

The flag-bearers, *who* were numerous, were loudly clapped.

The horses, *which* we brought with us, were hard to handle.

But you can also use *that* for both people and things. If you do so, it must sound right. *The flag-bearers, that were numerous* sounds graceless. One suggestion is to reserve *that*, when speaking of people, for those occasions when a *type*, rather than individuals, is being referred to: *The flag-bearer, who arrived late*, but *A flag-bearer that heads a procession should be smartly turned out.*

2. But now we enter slightly deeper waters. To keep our heads up we have to understand the difference between a *restrictive* and a *non-restrictive* dependent clause.

This is a restrictive clause:

Hospitals which care for old people are understaffed.

It says that *the hospitals which care for old people* are understaffed. Other hospitals may not be. The meaning is *restricted* to *some hospitals*.

This is a non-restrictive clause:

Hospitals, which care for old people, are understaffed.

This time we are being told that *all hospitals care for old people.* In fact we know this is not true, but it is what we are being told. It is a *non-restricted* statement.

395

Note what a difference two little commas make.

Now, the key question is this: *Is it only by the use of the two commas that we can tell the difference between these two ways of using precisely the same words?*

There is a strong and strengthening body of opinion which wants us to go further and make the differentiation even clearer. The proposal is that we use *that* for restrictive clauses, and *which* for non-restrictive clauses. In other words, that we should write:

> Hospitals that care for old people are understaffed.
>
> Hospitals, which care for old people, are understaffed.

To take another example, if someone says to you *Drive to the fourth farm which has a white gate* it is not quite clear whether they mean *Drive until you have passed three farms with white gates* or whether they mean *It is only the fourth farm you come to that has a white gate.*

So, if we wish to make our meaning clear, we should say either *Drive to the fourth farm that has a white gate* (*restricting* the meaning to *farms which have white gates*) or *Drive to the fourth farm, which has a white gate* (*unrestricted*, because you are not restricting the idea of farms only to those that have a white gate).

A quick way to distinguish is to ask youself if a comma can be placed before the *that* or *which*. If a comma can be inserted, then your word is *which.*

Having said all that, it is also necessary to say that not all those interested in this matter agree that the added precision of distinguishing between *that* and *which* is worth the loss of literary freedom, the freedom to use whichever word sounds best in a given context. Especially in speech. *Which* is harder to say than *that*, and people are not going to say *the car, which I bought* when *the car that I bought* is easier to say and sounds less affected, even if it is 'wrong'. Nor is *This is the house that Jack built* going to become, in the nursery or anywhere else, *This is the house, which Jack built.*

3. Use *that* instead of *who* and *which*:

(a) After superlatives: *This was the greatest pianist that ever played on this stage.*

(b) After ordinal numbers (first, second, third, etc.): *He's the third that came to grief.*

(c) After *some, any, something, everything, much, little, all* and *nothing*: *All that can be done has been done*; *there are some that are broken.*

(d) Where both a person and a thing are referred to (the one normally requiring *who* and the other *which*): *The jockeys and the horses that appeared on that day.*

(e) After using demonstrative pronouns such as *this, that, these* and *those* in sentences such as *Pass me those nails that are on the bench.*

4. *Whose*, to be consistent, should apply only to people: *The flagbearers, whose costumes were magnificent.* In theory the form for things should be *of which*: *The horses, of which the bridles were gleaming.* This, however, sounds silly, so

we use *whose* for animals and things as well as humans.

5. Note that we cannot use *whose* in a question, except when that question relates to people. We can say *Whose turn is next?* but we cannot say *Whose saddle is this?* if we're talking about a horse. The question has to be turned around to *Which horse does this saddle belong to?*

6. Do not confuse *whose* with *who's. Who's robbing this coach?* not *Whose robbing this coach?* Not, as an *Age* journalist had it, "an American photojournalist from who's book these pictures are taken," but "from whose book these pictures are taken."

See also **clauses; pronouns; who/whom.**

the.

1. *The* is pronounced quite strongly before a word starting with a vowel sound, so that we get the pronunciation *thee* with *apple, evening* and so on.

2. Otherwise the weak *the*, hardly more than *th'*, is used.

3. The *thee* pronunciation is also used before weak consonants such as the *h* in *history, hotel, habitual,* and of course it is used when there is a need to stress the *the*: "You are *the* Paul Hogan?"

the Australian accent. See pronunciation in Australia.

"The best-laid plans of mice and men / Gang aft a-gley." Well, they don't, not if you are trying to quote Robert Burns. The correct quotation is:

The best-laid schemes o' mice an' men
Gang aft a-gley.

the dash. See dashes.

the electronic media. See electronic media, the.

the Establishment. See Establishment, the.

thee/thine/thou. Let us take *thou* first. This is the old singular form of the plural personal pronoun *ye* or *you*. In early English this was the invariable form of address to *one* person: *thou ridest far, thou speak'st true.* If you were speaking to more than one person, you addressed them as *ye*, later as *you*.

How, then, did *thou ridest* become *you ride*? No doubt careers have been built on such a question. But the essence of the matter is that *thou*, like the present-day French *tu* and German *du*, was a sign of familiarity. It could be the familiarity of love, it could be the familiarity of the hater to the hated, but it expressed familiarity. What then if you were addressing a feared superior when he was in a bad mood? You could hardly *thou* him. So *ye*, and later *you*, were pressed into service as singular words, though they were originally plural, because the sense of familiarity did not cling to them.

Why do Quakers to this day cling to the *thou* usage? It was not a gratuitous attempt to be different. It was a strong statement to the world that (as Henry Lawson later put it) they raised their hats to no man. It took a great deal of courage, in the seventeenth century, to say *thou* and *thee* to *everyone*.

The great critic and philologist Richard Chevenix Trench said that we should regret the passing of *thou:* "that is, as the pledge of peculiar intimacy and special affection, as between husband and wife, parents and children, and such others as might be knit together by bands of more than common affection."

Thee is the *objective* or *accusative* form of *thou: Thou hast the letter* but *I gave thee the letter.* (In modern English we use *you* for both subject and object.) *Thine* is the genitive (or possessive) of *thou*, as in *Thine is the Kingdom* (in other words, *Of you is the kingdom*). The dative is again *thee*, as in *I gave it thee* (*I gave it to you*). We may set the matter out in a table.

Case	Singular	Plural
Nominative (subject)	thou	you
Accusative (object)	thee	you
Genitive (possessive)	thine	yours
Dative (indirect object)	thee	you

Thine appears again as a possessive adjective, this time in company with *thy*. *Thy* is used before a consonant, and *thine* before a vowel. Both mean *your*.

Thy will be done.   Thine apple is here.

See also **verbs: the old declensions; ye.**

the eve of. See eve of, the.

the geographical possessive. See **geographical possessive, the.**

the female critique. See **female critique, the.**

their. For the use of *their* to replace *him or her* — that is, to use a plural pronoun as the object of a singular verb — see **(the) female critique,** paragraph 4.

theirs. Not *their's*.

the late. See late, the.

thematic. *Thematic* is supposed to be the adjective from the noun *theme*, and nothing more than this. Thus its use should be confined to such settings as *The* *thematic treatment of this melody in the sonata was complex.*

Just as nouns change into verbs, so adjectives change into nouns, and certainly with less justification, because the noun is already there and is in fact the word the adjective comes from.

So to say, in the kind of phrase beloved of academics and intellectuals, *We now confront a familiar thematic in the work*, is no more than an inflated and pretentious way of saying *We now confront a familiar theme in the work.*

See also **problematic**.

the Mr/Mrs/Ms problem. See **Mr/Mrs/Ms problem, the**.

thence. A useful word, though a mite old-fashioned. It means *from there: You drive to Bathurst and thence it's fifteen miles to the farm.* Compare **thither**, meaning *to there*.

the possessive and the 's' sound. See **possessive and the 's' sound, the**.

the proverbial. See **proverbial, the**.

the reason why. See **reason**.

the reverends. See **reverends, the**.

the silent 'e'. See **silent 'e', the**.

the smallest room. See **smallest room, the**.

the subjunctive. See **subjunctive, the**.

the turn of the century. See **turn of the century, the**.

the way of the wise. See **way of the wise, the**.

the writing on the wall. One of the most terrible phrases in the Bible is *Mene, mene, tekel, upharsin*. During a feast King Belshazzar saw fingers writing this message on the wall of his banqueting room. We are told about it in chapter five of the book of Daniel. Daniel interpreted the mystic words to King Belshazzar, who succumbed to them. The message from God says, in part, "Thou art weighed in the balances, and found wanting."

We tend to say "It's the writing on the wall" when all we mean is that something seems destined to happen. That's certainly part of the message. But we should remember that the core of the text is that what is destined to happen is destined because of a man's own imperfections. In other words, if we're talking about ourselves, then the writing is on the wall because of our own sins. It's primarily about responsibility, not about inevitability.

they shall not grow old. Probably the line most frequently misquoted in Australia is Laurence Binyon's:

> They shall grow not old as we that are left grow old,

from his "For the Fallen" (1914). Spoken at thousands of military commemorative occasions each year, these words are usually given as *They shall not grow old, as we that are left grow old.*

Third World. *Third World* countries are countries of Africa, Asia, Latin America and the Pacific which are not politically aligned to either of the two major power blocs. Third World countries are usually (but not always) 'under-developed', a word of vague meaning but usually taken to mean that such countries lack an effective industrial base.

What then is the *First World*? And the *Second World*? Some seek to argue that the First World is the Old World of Europe, the Second World the New World of the Americas and the Pacific countries. Overwhelmingly, though, the First World is accepted as the advanced capitalist countries, normally in some form of alliance with the United States of America, and the Second World as the world of the communist countries, usually in some form of alliance with the Soviet Union.

The world of the stateless refugee has sometimes been defined as the *Fourth World.*

thither means *to there*, as in the sentence *You want to go to the Black Stump? It's a long way thither.* Compare **thence**, meaning *from there*.

though. See **although/though.**

throes. "We are in the throes of assessing the damage," says someone interviewed on television. *In the throes* does not mean *in the process of*, as it here appears to mean: it means *struggling with great effort. Throes* is a plural noun (there is no singular) and means *a condition of violent pain or convulsive effort.*

tides. Describing the action of the tides correctly is a little more complicated than is generally realised. Properly speaking, the action of the tide's coming in is called *flooding*, that of the tide's going out is called *ebbing* (*the tide is flooding, the tide is ebbing*). In this sense tides do not *rise* and *fall*, except when you are talking about a vertical measurement, as in *the tide has risen six feet.*

till/until. These words are normally interchangeable, and the prejudice against *till*, because it looks more colloquial, is unjustified.

Until is the more desirable at the beginning of sentences, and in more formal contexts. Some commentators suggest the use of *till* for a specific point of time (*She worked till seven o'clock*) and *until* for a period of time (*We shall have to stay here until the ship comes in*).

The speaker or writer should use which sounds best in a given context.

But *till* should never be written *'til*, as it often is by people frightened that they are committing a solecism in using *till*.

titles.
1. Underline book titles in manuscript — this shows they are to be set in italics.
2. Underline similarly names of ships.
3. Do not underline individual names of poems or chapters of books. These go in inverted commas: "To Daffodils", "Bullocky". See **quote/unquote**.
4. Names of newspapers and magazines will normally be underlined (that is, set in italics when printed), but the 'house style' of many publications is *not* to italicise in such cases.
5. The names of plays and films will normally be placed in inverted commas, not in italics, unless you are specifically referring to the book of the film or play.
6. The tendency these days is to write all book titles in **lower case** throughout: *For the term of his natural life* rather than *For the Term of his Natural Life*. This is in part because title-page typography is no longer standard, and where titles of books appear in **upper case** letters only, in transcription the use of capital letters for some words and small letters for others becomes a matter of individual choice. A standard agreement to quote all titles in lower-case letters throughout does at least have the virtue of consistency.
7. If words are to be given capital letters in titles, the words so capitalised should be the nouns, verbs and adjectives.
8. *Swanston Street*, *Swanston street* and *Swanston-street* are all acceptable. Whichever is chosen it should, of course, be used consistently within the one manuscript. House style, in the case of material written for publication, will determine which variant is actually adopted.
9. In mentioning the names of newspapers and magazines which start with *The*, the *The* is either omitted entirely or is given a lower-case initial and no italics:

See *Economic Record,* vol. 3, no. 4, p. 66.

She said that she read the *Age* every day.

See also **book titles; honorifics.**

tizzy. The word *tizzy* is given in *Collins Dictionary of the English Language* (1979) as a noun meaning *a state of confusion or anxiety*, with its origins in the nineteenth century.

The *Macquarie Dictionary* (1981) recognises it as a noun (*Don't get in a tizz,* or *tizzy*) and as an adjective, *tizzy*, meaning *gaudy*.

Neither refers to the word as a verb, though this usage was more familiar to the author of this book than any other, and was often used by parents and grandparents. *She tizzied herself up for the dance.* Is this, perhaps, a distinctive Australian usage?

to gerund or not to gerund? The issue of the gerund in English is a complex one and is best pursued, by those with the time and inclination, in Gowers' revision of Fowler's *Modern English Usage*.

However, the most common issue regarding the gerund frequently presents itself to all who speak or write, whether they know it or not.

Take, for instance, the following sentence from a published short story: "On their last visit there was a feeling of Australia's being a modern land of promise." The author had in fact written *of Australia being a modern land of promise*, but his editor changed *Australia* to *Australia's*. Why?

The basic argument is that, in such cases, *being a modern land of promise* is a kind of noun, and hence *Australia* should take the possessive just as "Australia's population" takes a possessive.

Another example is *I hope you don't mind me asking you.* The argument here is that *asking you* is in fact the name of something, in this case an action, even if it looks like some kind of verb. Since all names are nouns, this phrase demands a possessive and should read, not *me asking you*, but *my asking you*.

Similarly, *Wasn't there enough strife already without his stirring up more?* is preferred to *without him stirring up more*, and *Her being here is important* to *She being here is important*. Indeed one of the few things that can be said with some firmness about the gerund is that proper names and personal pronouns seem to require it. Few would prefer *She running the marathon was a good effort* to *Her running the marathon was a good effort*, or *Marjory running the marathon ...* to *Marjory's running the marathon ...*

Note the distinction between (a) *I watched John's running* and (b) *I watched John running*. In the first example it is the *running* that I watched, and the word becomes a gerund-noun which (in theory) needs a possessive. In the second example it is John whom I watched, and *running* is a verb-participle qualifying *John*. Useful though this distinction is, recognition of the gerund in cases such as this is becoming less common.

Desirable though the gerund is, it must be admitted that there are some contexts in which it appears absurdly forced. To insist that the sentence *It did so to avoid a constitutional change being forced upon it* should in fact read *It did so to avoid a constitutional change's being forced upon it* (which is, strictly speaking, correct) would be pedantic and, what is worse, make the sentence more difficult to comprehend.

In general, if in doubt about the gerund try to turn the sentence round so as to avoid it. If this is too awkward, then there almost certainly will be no confusion of meaning whichever way we put it. People of a more literary bent may feel uneasy if the possessive is not used and the gerund thereby recognised, while others may regard it as an unnecessary affectation. Yer pays yer penny and yer takes yer choice.

toilet. See **(the) smallest room**.

tomboy. Efforts are being made by some to establish that *tomboy* is yet another of those words designed to diminish the female. Many will disagree.

Including at least some women. The following from a television review by Richard Coleman in the *Sydney Morning Herald* (9 August 1986), relating to an interview by Susan Mitchell of Dawn Fraser:

> "You were described as a tomboy many times over the years," Susan began.
>
> "Oh yes, I was."
>
> "Does it offend you?"
>
> "No not at all. I was proud to be called a tomboy by my brothers. That was a statement of endearment. They were proud to speak of me as a tomboy. I wasn't a little girl. Little girls, when I was growing up, weren't ever included in little boys' games. So I thought that was lovely."
>
> Susan shifted in her seat but persevered:
>
> "Hmmm. But it's a strange term, isn't it? I mean just because a girl is active, athletic, energetic, got a bit of get up and go, she's somehow called a boy. Because clearly that's based on the notion that really girls are the opposite."
>
> "Hmmm," said Dawn, and recalled some successful litigation against a paper that had rashly questioned her sexuality.
>
> Susan was making no headway. What could she do with a woman who had dedicated her brilliant career to the memory of a dead brother, who didn't mind being thought of as a tomboy, who was allowed to tag along with her brothers as long as she carried their equipment and who acknowledged she'd been helped back on her feet by a male friend?

Tonga, the island-nation in the Pacific, is pronounced to rhyme with *gonger*, the *gong* as in the word *gong*.

tons/tonnes. The imperial measure of weight, the *ton*, is equal to 2240 pounds. It is sometimes called the *long ton*. The US *ton*, the *short ton*, is equivalent to 2000 pounds.

The imperial *ton*, which was in general use in Australia before metrication, is equivalent to 1016 kilograms.

The equivalent measure now in use in Australia is the metric *tonne* of 1000 kilograms.

The *tonne* has, since metrication, been pronounced in Australia to rhyme with the word *bon*, in order to distinguish it from the imperial *ton*. This does not seem to be necessary any longer, and a reversion to the traditional pronunciation, in other words *tonne* to be pronounced to rhyme with *bun*, is desirable. If the old imperial ton is referred to, it can be identified as the *imperial ton*.

There are also other kinds of *tons*. A *shipping ton* (also called *measurement ton* or *freight ton*) is a rough-and-ready measure for measuring shipping cargo, usually taken to equal 1 cubic metre, 40 cubic feet or 1000 kilograms. A *net, gross* or *deadweight* tonnage is a measure of capacity in cubic feet, divided by 100. *Displacement tonnage* represents the actual weight of a ship as measured by the volume of water displaced, and may be expressed in either *tons* or *tonnes*.

tortuous/torturous. The ABC tells us that the Russians are making a *torturous* withdrawal from Afghanistan. Elsewhere we are informed that the path to an agreement on nuclear weapons is also *torturous*.

If you are suffering from agonising pain you may properly call that pain *torturous*, the kind of pain you might have if you were being physically tortured.

If, however, you are thinking in terms of a "track winding back to an old-fashioned shack", and meditating on the twists and turns in the road, you are contemplating a *tortuous* path. *Tortuous* means *twisting or winding*.

You may have a *tortuous* mind — one that is *devious*. But if you have a *torturous* mind you like inflicting great pain on others.

totally. *Totally wrong, totally lost, totally absorbed, totally involved.* Most of the time this over-used word is redundant. The enthusiastic speaker or writer who imagines that the use of *totally* for emphasis in fact strengthens the point is usually quite wrong. The indiscriminate use of such a word as *totally* in fact indicates an insecurity in the writer.

If needed, there are preferable synonyms: *wholly, quite, entirely*, for instance.

The phrase *sum total* is tautologous — that is, it says the same thing twice.

toward/towards. *We are driving toward Sydney* or *We are driving towards Sydney*? Both are correct, but *towards* is more common and acceptable in Australia.

These words, together with the adjective *untoward*, meaning *unexpected, unwelcome, unpleasant* (*an untoward event*), were traditionally pronounced *tawd, tawds.* Increased emphasis on spelling has driven the pronunciation into agreement with the written form.

trades unions or trade unions? *Trade union* is a compound noun, and compound nouns in English may make their plural in three ways.

(a) by adding *-s* to the first word, where that is thought to be most significant: *sons-in-law, hangers-on, passers-by;*

(b) by adding *-s* to the second word, where that is held to be most significant: *poet-laureates, major-generals, spoonfuls;*

(c) by making both the first *and* second words plural: *men-servants.*

Strictly speaking there is a case for making the plural of *trade union trades unions*, in view of the fact that once you get more than one union you get more than one trade. *Trades unions* is certainly not wrong, but Australian usage leans strongly towards *trade unions*, which is the recommended form.

trait. A *trait* is a distinguishing characteristic, as in *His worst trait was his meanness.*

It may be pronounced as spelt, or in the French way, more or less, which is *tray*. *Tray* is probably still the preferred pronunciation.

See also **attribute/character/property/quality/trait.**

transfer follows normal rules (see **doubling up**) in making *transferred*, but is anomalous in making *transferable*.

transpire. In physiology *transpire* means *to breathe through the skin.* But the word is more commonly used in other ways. What is acceptable is the broader meaning that is clearly related to the scientific meaning: *to leak out*, and hence *to become known.*

> It transpired gradually that there had been a palace revolution and that the President was dead.
>
> Security was not good enough to prevent details transpiring.

It is, however, widely regarded as incorrect to use *transpire* as though it means *happen*. *It'll be interesting to see what transpires at the picnic* is regarded as something of an illiteracy.

transportation. *Transportation* has a penal meaning, of course, which is well known to Australians. It may also mean *a system, or the act, of transporting*, as in *The transportation of two hundred harrows creates many problems.*

The word, however, is best left alone. The simpler word *transport* can almost always be used in its place. *Transportation* has become a bureaucratic word because it sounds impressive. But *a transport system* is preferable to *a transportation system*. The Americans say: "You've got to have transportation in this town." Australians should say: "You've got to have transport in this town."

Transport and *transportation* are nouns and not adjectives. But how do we describe them when they are used, apparently as adjectives, in *a transport system, a transportation system*? It could be argued, simply, that here they *are* adjectives, whatever the dictionaries say. But those writing dictionaries today say that they are *modifiers*, in this case a noun modifying the meaning of another noun.

See **modifiers.**

trauma. This sadly abused word has only two dictionary meanings: (a) *a state of psychological shock which may have long-term effects,* or (b) *an actual injury or wound, and the physical effects following from it.*

Trauma does *not* mean *any kind of personal crisis.* The young woman who was overheard saying to a companion "She's going through a relationship trauma" was seeking both to dramatise the event she was describing and to inflate her own sophisticated image. See **bully words.**

trial is a noun and has a number of well-known meanings: *trial by jury, sheep-dog trial, trial and error.*

Trial is, however, and although the dictionaries don't recognise it, becoming a verb. Two examples from ABC television, within an hour of each other: *This vaccine is now being trialled for koala bears; Trialling is in full swing off Fremantle for the* America's *Cup defence.*

Regrettable, no doubt, especially since there is no difficulty in putting these sentences into more acceptable form. And perhaps especially regrettable in that the Australian Broadcasting Corporation might be expected to maintain some sensitivity to the use of words.

It may also be said, however, that it is a virtue of the English language that it is adaptable and innovative, and that if *trial* is becoming a verb then we had better relax and enjoy it. The argument against this is D. J. Enright's, that what we are witnessing today is not the orderly development and progression of the language, but a "series of jolts — imposition rather than selection by the test of time". To this process television, as instanced above, is the main encouragement.

trillion. See **billion.**

triumphal/triumphant. Something that is *triumphal* celebrates a triumph: *Collingwood had a triumphal celebration after winning the Grand Final. Triumphant* means *victorious: Collingwood was the triumphant team.*

Truganini. Truganini is generally considered to have been the last full-blood Tasmanian Aboriginal. She was born about 1812 and died in Hobart in 1876. Her name is variously spelt *Truggernanner, Trugernanna* and *Trucanini.* According to the Rev. H. B. Atkinson, of Evandale, Tasmania, who knew Truganini, she pronounced the name as *Truganini* with the *trug* as in *rug.* (Westlake Papers, Pitt Rivers Museum, Oxford.)

Other Tasmanians are believed to have survived Truganini, including Sukey, who died on Kangaroo Island in South Australia in 1888. Fanny Cochrane Smith, who died in Hobart in 1905, is also sometimes claimed as a full-blood, but this is very unlikely.

try and/try to. *You must try and do it* or *You must try to do it*? There is no doubt that *You must try and do it* is grammatically wrong, and is certainly not acceptable in written English. In spoken English in Australia it has, however, now acquired the status of an idiom. Nevertheless, it will be avoided by careful speakers.

tsar. See **czar/tsar**.

T-shirt. The approved ways of printing this word are *T-shirt* or *tee-shirt*, but not *t-shirt*. The derivation is presumably the appearance of the T-shirt laid out flat, in other words like a T.

-t-/-tt-. For the use of one or two *t's* in such words as *regrettable*, see **doubling up**.

turbid/turgid. *Turbid* means *muddy, discolored, cloudy* or *in confusion.* You may speak of *the turbid waters of a river in flood*, or even of *a turbid fog* or *a turbid crowd*.
  Turgid means *swollen, distended.* It is often used of a pompous speech.

the turn of the century. The phrase means the period around 1800, 1900, 2000 and so on. It does *not* mean the period around 1850, 1950 and so on.

typist. Not *typiste*.

U

Ulster. See **Britain**.

ultimate/penultimate/antepenultimate. The ABC's "Backchat" program discusses, among other issues, the misuse of words. In February 1987 the presenter of the program informed us that we were now to hear the "penultimate" — by which he meant the final — comment.

Penultimate does not mean *the last*, but *the second-last*, just as *antepenultimate* means *the third-last* and *ultimate the last*. Prefer, in any case, *third-last*, *second-last*, *last* or *final*.

unanimous. See **nem. con.; unique**.

unconscionable. King Charles II is said to have apologised for being "an unconscionable time a-dying." If the King did use these words (Macaulay is said to have made them up) he was using the word in one of its two meanings: *immoderate, excessive.*

The word comes from *conscionable*, which comes from an old form of the word *conscience*, and which means *acceptable to one's conscience*. *Unconscionable*, then, should mean *not acceptable to one's conscience.*

This is compatible with King Charles's use of the word. A stronger meaning, however, is *unscrupulous, unprincipled: an unconscionable rogue.*

What did the Leader of the Opposition, Mr Howard, mean when, on 6 May 1986, he claimed that the government had allowed the High Court to be involved in the affair of Mr Justice Murphy "in a most unconscionable way"? Presumably he meant that the government had acted in an *unprincipled* way.

The word is rather a difficult and ambiguous one. It is best avoided.

under way. The idea of 'greenways', or bush corridors for Australian animals, *is underway*, Vincent Serventy writes in the *Age* (7 December 1987). There is no such word as *underway*, which must be two words, *under way*. The phrase may mean either *in progress* or *in operation*.

under way/under weigh. The correct term is *under way*. It has nothing to do with weighing an anchor.

unexceptionable/unexceptional. Something that is *unexceptionable* is something that is *acceptable*, that is *not meriting criticism*: *I found her remarks,*

409

though hard-hitting, were unexceptionable. Something that is *unexceptional* is *ordinary, normal, run-of-the-mill: It was unexceptional for Bradman to score fifty runs in an innings.*

uninterested/disinterested. *Uninterested* and *disinterested* are not synonyms. They do not mean the same thing, although they are often used as though they do. There is of course an argument for saying "If that's the way they're used, then that's what they mean." We think it's still worth fighting for a distinction between these words.

Disinterested means *unbiased, able to view a matter objectively.* It does not mean that the person who is *disinterested* lacks interest. We would expect a judge to give *disinterested* advice to a jury in a trial. We would certainly not expect him to give *uninterested* advice.

Both these word are needed in the language, each with its separate meaning. It must, however, be admitted that we have other words to convey the 'proper' meaning of *disinterested*; that these include *unbiased, objective* and *impartial*; and that in the interest of avoiding confusion these words should normally be preferred.

Union Jack. The popular name for the flag of Great Britain and Northern Ireland, which also appears quartered on the Australian national flag and the New Zealand flag, and will also be found on other flags, such as those of South Africa and Hawaii.

Misnamed a 'jack' because it was originally flown at the jack-staffs of British ships, the proper name of the flag is the *Union Flag*, though only pedants would insist on this.

unique. "The Queensland Parliament is a rather unique Parliament," said the Minister for Primary Industry in the House of Representatives on 25 March 1985.

Unique means *the only one of its kind.* Can something, then, be *rather* unique? The answer is No, despite a contrary ruling in the first edition of this book.

There are a number of words expressing an absolute quality in the English language, among them *perfect, complete, total, identical, imperative, indispensable, minimal, full, unanimous, certain.* We have no difficulty, logically or otherwise, in saying *almost perfect, nearly full, almost unanimous, nearly complete, nearly identical, almost certain.*

The point is that we may comment on *degrees of approachability* to an absolute quality. The examples above are all expressing *approachability.* They are not doing injury to the intrinsic meaning of the word *unique* itself.

The situation changes when the qualifying word comments directly on the absolute quality of words like *unique.* It is nonsensical to talk of something's being *very unique*, or *absolutely unique*, in the same way that it is nonsensical to talk of a woman as *somewhat pregnant*, a jug being *very full*, of twins as *completely identical* or of an opinion as *very unanimous*. The words *pregnant*, *unique*, *full*, *identical*, *unanimous* admit of no direct qualifiers. There is nothing to qualify. They are absolute.

Now, as to *rather unique*. Our original view in this book was that *rather*, the dictionary definition of which is *fairly* or *somewhat*, was what we may term an *adverb of approachability*. We therefore argued that *rather unique* was grammatically the same as, say, *almost unique*. We now think this is wrong, and that *rather* attacks the absolute quality of uniqueness in the word *unique*, that it is as objectionable as *very unique* or *more unique*. The Minister for Primary Industry was therefore in error.

Which is not to say that in ordinary, everyday speech we do not say *quite identical* and *very complete* and even *rather unique* all the time. This is idiomatic, even if it is not logical, and talk would be poorer without such idioms. The writers of the Constitution of the United States of America commenced: "We, the people of the United States, in order to form a more perfect union . . . "

Even so, to say *very unique* is a solecism which it would be wise to avoid. People are conscious of it and it can make them wince.

We may reject the insidious argument which is heard every now and then that *unique* is used in Australia mainly to mean *most unusual* rather than *the only one of its kind*. Even if this were true, there need be no rush to surrender. *Unique* is a graphic and powerful word. Its sense of *the one and only* should be retained. The easiest and surest way to avoid compromising and depreciating the worth of this word is to avoid all qualifiers, even the legitimate ones, and to use it by itself alone.

unit is a little word to be approached with some care. It can mean many things. *an undivided whole, a part of a whole, a complete system* and so on.

When Joseph Furphy wrote *Australia is the unit, mind!* he meant that Australians had "no loyalty to share". We will not object to that. But when Australian educationists take to calling children in the schools *social units*, as they did in the early years of this century, we have proper cause to fear that something unpleasant is happening in social thought.

When flats are called *units* (see **apartment**) and even garbage disposal machines are called *units* we begin to feel some concern that laziness and convenience may lead to the word running wild. (Winston Churchill, in the House of Commons, once tried to sing "Accommodation Unit, Sweet Accommodation Unit" to the tune of "Home Sweet Home".) In addition, of course, this kind of debasement of language leads to a debasement of feeling and of thought. No doubt the Nazis thought of the Jews not as *people*, but as *units*.

United Kingdom. See **Britain**.

universally. "It is a truth universally acknowledged," says Jane Austen in one of the most famous opening lines in English literature, "that a single man in possession of a good fortune, must be in want of a wife."

To say that something is *universally acknowledged* is, when you come to think of it, quite a claim. It means that it is acknowledged not only within our solar system, and within our galaxy, but within all the other galaxies in the universe as well. It is a claim that should be made with some care.

For the correct address of Earth, see under **Earth**.

unlike. "American Jewry, unlike in Australia and even Israel, is predominantly liberal," says an article in the Melbourne *Age* of 3 October 1987, discussing the differences between the liberal and orthodox strands in Judaism today.

Unlike in Australia and even Israel? With *like* and *unlike* the next words *must name the person or thing which is like or unlike.* When using these words it is imperative that you should say to yourself, in writing them, *unlike* (or *like*) *who, what?* The sentence we have quoted from the *Age* should clearly read "American Jewry, unlike Jewry in Australia and even Israel, is predominantly liberal."

What the writer of the article is trying to do is to force *unlike* to act as an adverb instead of the preposition it is. If he wanted an adverb where he used *unlike* he would have to write something like *in contrast to the position.*

There is another catch with *unlike*:

> The University of Melbourne, unlike Monash University, is situated near the heart of the city. (Correct)
> The University of Melbourne does not, however — unlike Monash University — have a suburban campus. (Wrong)

What has happened is that we have introduced a negative into the second sentence, and this negative must cancel out the *un* in *unlike.* The sentence should thus read: *The University of Melbourne does not, however — like Monash University — have a suburban campus.*

See also **like**.

unthinkable, together with words like *inconceivable, unimaginable* and *incredible,* has become a lazy word used far too loosely to express disagreement and opposition.

While nothing within human consciousness is, presumably and by definition, *unthinkable,* the word is appropriate enough to mean *very painful to think about,* or to condemn some action that should not have been thought about in the first place.

But to use it to condemn the local council's extension of a car park, an increase in the price of beer or the creation of a new public holiday is to weaken and diminish not only the word but the language.

until. See **till/until**.

untoward. See **toward/towards**.

upcoming. "The upcoming talks on trade arrangements." This comes from a variety of the English language known as **Hawkespeak**:

Prime Minister Hawke clearly meant here *the talks on trade arrangements which are forthcoming or coming up*. Some would argue that, so long as his meaning is clear, it doesn't matter what words he uses.

Perhaps. Consider, however, the following possibilities foreshadowed by the shanghaiing of *coming up*:

> The downbacking position of the Leader of the Opposition is disgusting.
> The Shadow Minister has infallen to his own trap.
> In this matter we waygive to public feeling.

And a further example, recently heard on the airwaves:

> We don't know why it does outbreak.

To be fair to Mr Hawke, the process he is trying to accelerate with *upcoming* has happened to other words. *To grade up* has become *to upgrade, to go on* has given rise to *ongoing. Upcoming* will almost certainly become respectable too.

Although ABC announcers have been heard talking about "upcoming programs", the word is still not familiar enough to discourage people from trying to make fun of Mr Hawke for using the word.

upper case/lower case. These are printing terms, meaning *capital letters* and *small letters* respectively. Old-style hand compositors had two cases of type, the top case containing capital letters and the bottom one containing small letters.

See **capital letters**.

upper class. See **working class**.

upstanding. The injunction *Be upstanding*, heard at formal dinners and in courts of law, is a piece of institutional jargon that may well be dispensed with. *Please rise* is to be preferred.

Uranus, the planet, is pronounced, perhaps regrettably, as *your anus*. Since, in these liberated days, far more people are familiar with the word *anus* than in grandma's time, there is more sensitivity to this pronunciation, and an attempt to change it to *YOUR-annis*. Which pronunciation you favor will depend on your sense of humor.

Actually, there is a word already pronounced *YOUR-annis*. It is the word *uranous*, an adjective meaning *containing uranium*.

urban/urbane. *Urban* means *to do with a city*, as in *the urban population. Urbane* has the same origins — it means *citified rather than countrified* — but is used to describe *courteous and polished manners.*

urinal. Prefer the pronunciation *YOO-rin-al* to *yoo-RHYN-al.*

usable/useable. Either spelling is acceptable.

usage. This word may be pronounced either *YOU-sidge* or *YOU-zidge.*

utilise. Prefer the word *use.*

utility. In Australian English *a utility* (apart from being *something that is useful*) also means *a small tray truck with an enclosed cabin.* In other words this is the versatile *ute*, beloved of farmers and tradesmen.

Lew Bandt, a designer at the Ford works in Geelong, was approached by a farmer in the early 1930s and asked for a vehicle which would combine the comfort of a passenger car with the usefulness of a tray truck. The utility entered the market in May 1934, with a rival General Motors vehicle only months behind. Vehicles with similar characteristics had been known earlier than this, but the production of *a coupe truck with integral panels as a catalogued production-line model* was a 'first' for the industry. See *Age*, 19 and 27 March and 2 April 1987.

Lew Bandt died at the age of 80 in March 1987 as a result of a collision while driving his fully restored, original 1933 model ute for a television documentary.

V

vagary, meaning *a whim or eccentric notion,* may be stressed on either the first or second syllable. Prefer *VAG-ary,* the *vag* pronounced as the word *vague.*

valet. While there can surely be no more than half-a-dozen valets in Australia, the word does crop up in literary and other contexts. The 'up-market' pronunciation is *VAL-et,* the more common pronunciation *VAL-ay.*

valiant. Pronounce with the *val-* rhyming with *pal,* not with *vale.*

Van Diemen's Land. Those interested in historical accuracy should refer to Tasmania, before November 1855, as *Van Diemen's Land.* Van Diemen's Land was in fact part of New South Wales until June 1825. Note that the spelling *Van Dieman's Land* is incorrect.

Van Gogh. The name of the artist Van Gogh is, in English, pronounced to rhyme with the Scottish word *loch.* The pronunciation *Van Go,* often heard in Australia, was otherwise never heard on land or sea. Not even in his native land.

vantage point. A *vantage point* is not a place from which you get a good view. It is a position which gives you *a commanding advantage,* in warfare or, by extension, in any other situation.

various is an adjective and not a pronoun. Thus it is correct to say *They looked at various houses but found none suitable,* but incorrect to say *Various of the houses looked at were unsuitable.*
In other words, *various* must not be followed by *of.*

vase. Pronounce to rhyme with *parse.* Affected pronunciations such as *vawse* and *vayse* have no support.

vegetable. Pronounce *VEG'table,* not *VEG-e-table.*

vehicle. Sandy Stone, in one of Barry Humphries' sketches, is famous for his remark, "Had a bit of strife parking the vehicle."
The word *vehicle* is a useful one, especially when referring to a variety of motorised transport (*More than two hundred vehicles entered the enclosure*) but it should never be used as an inflated word for a motor-car.

venal/venial. *Venal* comes from the Latin *venum* (for sale), and means *corrupt, capable of being twisted, dishonest.*

Venial comes from the Latin *venia* (pardon) and means *pardonable*. It is applied to an act which is wrong but not of much consequence, which may be disregarded.

venue. *Venue* is a vogue word imported from the law. It is increasingly used as a puffed-up word for *meeting place* or *site*. We have even seen *The site of the venue is to be at* . . . Avoid this word if possible: better *The luncheon will be held at the Dorchester* than *The venue is the Dorchester.*

veranda/verandah. Prefer *veranda*. The final *-h* seems to have no justification in the history of this word.

verbal communication. To be in *verbal communication* is simply *to be in touch by means of words*. These words may be spoken, written or heard. The distinction is with communication by some form of signal.

verbs. Verbs are one of the eight **parts of speech** in traditional grammar.

The verb is the part of speech that expresses *action* or *existence*. In the sentence *He is the man who hit the runs, is* is a verb (expressing existence) and so is *hit* (expressing action).

A less traditional way of defining a verb is to say that it is *the word or words that comprise or introduce the* **predicate.** (The predicate is the part of a sentence that tells you about the subject of the sentence. In *The cattle ran madly down the hill*, the predicate is *ran madly down the hill.*)

Verbs may be described in various ways. The following are some.

TRANSITIVE VERBS

Transitive means *crossing over* in Latin. A transitive verb requires an object. In the sentence *The ball hit the window, the window* is the object of the transitive verb *to hit. To hit* is transitive because you cannot say *I hit* without saying what you hit.

INTRANSITIVE VERBS

These are verbs that do not require an object, such as the verb *to sneeze. I sneezed* will stand perfectly well as a sentence on its own.

Note that many verbs are both transitive and intransitive, according to meaning. The verb *to break*, for instance, is transitive when it means *to cause something to fall apart* (you can't just say *I broke:* you have to go on to say what you broke). On the other hand, when the verb means *to cease resisting*, it is intransitive. *The police interrogation was such that I broke.*

STRONG (OR IRREGULAR) AND WEAK (OR REGULAR) VERBS

Strong verbs are verbs that form the past tense by a variation within the word itself: *draw* becomes *drew, drive* becomes *drove, run* becomes *ran.* Weak verbs comprise the rest, the ones that form the past tense by adding -*d*, -*t* or -*ed*.

Note: there is disagreement as to whether the *meet/met* verbs and the *cast/cast* verbs are strong or weak.

COMPOUND VERBS, OR VERBAL PHRASES

These are verbs formed with the aid of other verbs, or of prepositions, such as *would have gone*, *to go out*.

FINITE VERBS

These are verbs that have a subject. In *He runs home*, *runs* is a finite verb and *He* is the subject. These verbs are *finite* because their form reveals a specific, limited (i.e. *finite*) meaning. In this example the word *runs*, for instance, tells us that the running was done by a he, she or it, and that there was only one of them, and that it is happening now.

NON-FINITE VERBS

These are verb-forms without a subject, such as *to swim*, *swimming*, *swam*.

See also **noun to verb: is change decay?; tense.**

verbs: the old declensions. "The mailman hath cometh again" was heard from the presenter of the self-congratulatory ABC television program "Backchat" (6 May 1986). The veteran political reporter Alan Ramsey told us in the *Sydney Morning Herald* (19 September 1987) that "Bob Hawke might holdeth, but the party factions both giveth and taketh."

These gentleman were trying to be arch but, in the course of so doing, tripped themselves up. The statements are grammatically nonsensical.

The old way of conjugating English verbs was as follows.

PRESENT TENSE

I am	I have	I hear
Thou art	Thou hast (*short for* havest)	Thou hearest
He/she/it is	He/she/it hath	He/she/it heareth
We are	We have	We hear
Ye are	Ye have	Ye hear
They are	They have	They hear

PAST TENSE

I was	I had	I heard
Thou wast *or* wert	Thou hadst	Thou heardest
He/she/it was	He/she/it had	He/she/it heard
We were	We had	We heard
Ye were	Ye had	Ye heard
They were	They had	They heard

In other words, the second person singular, present and past, was formed by adding -*st* or -*est*, and the third person singular present (normally, and in southern England) by adding -*th* or -*eth*. These forms are still found in some legal, poetic, religious and dialect usages.

One may say *The mailman cometh* or *The mailman hath come*, but one may not say *The mailman hath cometh*. Similarly, one may say *Bob Hawke heareth* or *Bob Hawke might have heard*, but not *Bob Hawke might heareth*. And, in old English, the party factions *hear*, not *heareth*, which is singular.

See also **thee/thine/thou**.

veterinary. Pronounce *VET-rin-ry* or *VET-rin-ery*, not *VET-nary*.

viable. *With the infusion of capital the operation was now viable. Viable* is one of a number of words taken over from the scientific world in the belief that to use them in general writing or conversation adds an air of authority which would otherwise be absent. It is a **bully word**.

In science *viable* means *capable of living*, and the word is best left to science. There are less pretentious words we can use to convey the same meaning. *The operation was now practicable*, for instance.

vice versa is a common phrase from (late) Latin which means *in reversed order, the other way round*, as in *Either we go to the pictures before we eat, or vice versa*.

The phrase is so very much a part of the English language that it does not require italics.

The approved Latin pronunciation would be *wicky wersa*. Ignore that. The dictionaries, or some of them, suggest it should be pronounced *vysee versa*. Ignore that, too. *Vice versa*, the *vice* pronounced as in the normal English word *vice*, will do perfectly well.

Victoria. Before July 1851 Victoria was properly known as the Port Phillip District of New South Wales, and strictly speaking should be referred to as such in writing of that period. It was also occasionally referred to as **Australia Felix**.

Victorian. In Australia, this may mean either (a) relating to the State (formerly the Colony) of Victoria; or (b) relating to the period of the reign of Queen Victoria, 1837–1901.

There are thus sometimes grounds for confusion, for instance in such a simple sentence as *Melbourne is a Victorian city*. It may be necessary to make clear the meaning intended.

Since the word *Victorian* can mean *old-fashioned, prudish*, some organisations in the State of Victoria drop the *n* at the end of the word: the *Victoria Institute of Colleges* (when it existed), the *Victoria Police*. By doing so, of course, they are trying to turn a noun into an adjective.

See **modifiers**.

victuals/victualler. *Victuals* are *food, provisions*. Appropriately, the word stems from the Latin *vivere, to live*. A *victualler* is someone who provides victuals. In

British and Australian English the word is better known in the term *licensed victualler*, which means *a merchant allowed by law to sell alcoholic drinks*.

The words are pronounced *vittles, vitteler* (or *vitler*). The pronunciation of these words as spelt is sometimes heard in Australia, because of their unfamiliarity and because of the pronounce-as-you-spell tendency noted elsewhere in this book. It has, however, no dictionary support.

Spell *victualling, victualled* in Australian English. Americans write *victualing, victualed.*

vide. See **referencing**.

vie. *To vie*, meaning *to contend for superiority or victory*, changes its spelling to *vying* in such a sentence as *He and I were vying for the championship.*

virtual/virtually. "His life was virtually over." "The race was virtually won." *Virtual* and *virtually* mean *in essence, or in effect, though not in fact*. The words should not be used to mean *veritable, bordering on* or *real*. To say *It was a virtual gale* is open to the objection that either it was a gale or it wasn't; say rather *a near gale. Virtual* and *virtually* can easily become slob words, shoved into a spoken or written sentence simply for purposes of inflation.

virtuosic. Lenore Nicklin, writing in the *Bulletin* (22 July 1986) of the artist Ann Thomson, comments that a reviewer had written of the painter as "one of the most virtuosic contemporary painters in Australia."

It is not clear whether the word *virtuosic* is Lenore Nicklin's or the original reviewer's, but in any case the word does not exist.

A *virtuoso* may be either *a master of some skill* or *a collector of works of art*. And you may say that someone *displays virtuosity*. Perhaps the word *virtuosic* should exist; perhaps one day it will exist; perhaps the person who used the word is trying to *make* it exist. If so, it is a courageous act. People who try to invent words, without making it plain that they *are* trying to invent them, are liable to be accused of not knowing what they are doing.

visa. A *visa*, of course, is an endorsement in a passport permitting the bearer to enter a foreign country.

The word comes from the French, and means *something seen, inspected, examined.*

Note: *two visas; my passport was visaed; she is visaing my passport.*

vis-a-vis is a French phrase which literally means *face to face*.

In English it is mainly used in the sense of *in relation to, regarding*, as in such a sentence as "*Vis-à-vis* the New Zealanders, French diplomacy was under strain following the terrorist attack on the *Rainbow Warrior*."

The phrase is pronounced *vee-zah-vee*. In writing, the phrase may be placed in italics (in which case it should take the French accent) or may be treated as an English phrase, in which case it will not be printed in italics and should not take the accent.

visual. See **aural/oral/visual**.

vitamin. This word may be pronounced with the *vit-* rhyming either with *bite* or with *hit*. The former is preferred, because of the relationship of *vitamin* to such words as *vital*.

vitiate. *To vitiate* is *to weaken, make faulty, destroy the force of. All their efforts to control the flood-waters were vitiated by the continuing rain.* Pronounce *VISH-iate*, not *VIT-iate*.

vocal cords. Not *vocal chords*, a common error. Presumably those who make this error confuse the human voice-box with a musical instrument.

voluntarily. Pronounce with the stress on the first syllable: *VOL-in-tre-lee*. The pronunciation *vol-in-TAIR-ily* is to be avoided.

vowels. Vowels are 'singable' sounds made by the human voice. You cannot sing the letter *t*, which is a consonant, and if you try to you will end up making an *ee* sound, which is a vowel sound. With vowels your breath, which vibrates the vocal cords, has a continuous and largely unobstructed passage through the vocal passages, including the mouth and lips. Sounds which are interrupted and shaped by the movement of tongue, mouth and lips are called *consonants*.

Vowels are important because it is largely through the manipulation of vowel sounds that everyone has an individual voice, and that pronunciation 'families' exist. While Australians and New Zealanders, for instance, appear to outsiders to speak similarly, they can often 'pick' each other through certain vowel sounds. Australians claim, no doubt with much exaggeration, that New Zealanders say *fush and chups*, *sax o'clock* and *up on the hull* (*up on the hill*).

The letters *a, e, i, o* and *u* are traditionally considered *vowels* in English. That may be all right so far as the alphabet is concerned, but a vowel is not an alphabetical term but a *phonetic* one. The vowel *o*, for instance, is pronounced differently in the words *not, note, woman* and *women*. Contrast, too, the sound of *u* in *cut* and *put*. To make matters worse, the same sound may be represented by different letters: *sun, son; park, clerk*. There are in fact fourteen vowel sounds in standard English, but only five letters to represent them. This is why there are phonetic symbols which are used in most dictionaries, and in specialised discussions on pronunciation, and why George Bernard Shaw left his fortune to the cause of devising a new English alphabet.

To make matters worse there are 'pure vowels' and 'impure vowels'. In the latter the sound actually changes in the process of being uttered, as a result of the movement of the tongue. Where there are two vowel sounds concerned, as in the words *cow*, *mice*, *boy* and *late*, the resulting sound is called a *diphthong*, and where there are three sounds (*shower*) it is called a *triphthong*. There are nine diphthongs and two triphthongs in English.

The slurred sound heard in the second syllable of words such as *cousin*, *mattock*, *reason*, *roses* is called an *indeterminate*, *neutral* or *obscure* vowel sound. It is said that Australians make more use of this sound than any other speakers of English.

The subject of phonetics is an enormous one. The best introduction is through Anthony Burgess's *Language Made Plain*, and there is a valuable essay by J. R. L. Bernard in the introductory pages of *The Macquarie Dictionary*.

vulnerable means *open to attack, injury or temptation*. Many Australians have great difficulty in pronouncing this word. It is not pronounced *vunerable*: the first *l* is fully sounded.

W

waistcoat. The pronunciation of *waistcoat* as *weskit* may be (and is) considered desirable by some of the British, but in Australia can only be regarded as an affectation.

wait. See **await/wait.**

waiter/waiting/waitress. A *waiter* in a restaurant is occupied (or should be occupied) in *waiting*, not *waitering*. Nor should a female waiter be *waitressing*. Opinions differ as to whether a female waiter should be called a *waitress*. On the one hand the word seems to convey no inferior status at first consideration. On the other hand, and on further thought, perhaps it does. We should work towards the unisex *waiter*. See **(the) female critique.**

waive/wave. You *wave* your handkerchief, but you *waive* your right to be heard.

waler/whaler. A *waler* is, or was, a horse bred in New South Wales, especially a remount purchased for the Indian army. During the century in which the Australian-Indian horse trade flourished (up to 1938), *waler* became a general name for Australian remounts supplied to India.

Whaler, apart from its common meaning of *someone who catches whales*, in Australian English means *an itinerant rural worker*, or *a swagman* or *sundowner*. "Murrumbidgee whaler," "whaling in the [river] bend," used to be common phrases. The term presumably derives from the attempts to catch fish to supplement a meagre diet.

"Waltzing Matilda". The following, we are assured by a leading Latin scholar, is an elegant rendering into Latin of the first verse and chorus of "Waltzing Matilda:"

> Olim sedebat prope ripam fluminis
> Solus grassator sub umbra fagi,
> Et cantabat homo dum aestuaret cortina:
> Veni saltemus Matilda veni.
> Veni Matilda, veni Matilda,
> Veni saltemus Matilda veni
> Et cantabat homo dum aestuaret cortina:
> Veni saltemus Matilda veni.

the wandering what. "He's as good as what I am" is an illiteracy. The *what* is not needed. The same problem comes up with such a phrase as "He's no better than what he should be." The intrusive *what* should be avoided, because it is unnecessary and awkward.

See also **indicator words**.

waterside worker. See **stevedore**.

wave. See **waive/wave**.

the way of the wise. The suffix *-wise*, as in *salarywise, countrywise, employmentwise, familywise, womenwise, departmentwise* and thousands of other examples, has been an unhappy development in spoken Australian English over the last ten or fifteen years.

It could be argued, of course, that it is simply a handy way of saying "in the manner of". Well, it is. As such, the usage will have its defenders. These defenders may well point out that the *-wise* ending is simply a form or corruption of the *-ways* ending, and that both endings have an honorable ancestry in the language: *sideways, lengthways, clockwise*.

So far so good. But the application of the *-wise* ending to thousands of innocent words which had been living quietly is frequently an offence to the ear, an example of the slovenly and lazy use of words, and a mark of the semi-literate. Of course it can also be funny when used in a mocking way, but it is well to reflect that it *is* mockable.

There is another, and perfectly respectable, use of the *-wise* ending, and this is where the suffix means, not *ways*, but the actual word *wise* itself. *Pennywise* in this case means someone careful about money; *weatherwise* someone knowledgeable about the weather; *streetwise* someone who knows how to survive on the streets.

weave. A fabric may be *woven* or *weaved*. And you may say *I wove the tapestry* or *I weaved the tapesty*.

weighed in the balance. Strictly, *weighed in the balances*. See **the writing on the wall**.

weight. See **mass/weight**.

well. Avoid the phrase *She's not a well person*. Since *good* does not convey the meaning intended, it is necessary here to re-phrase: *She's not well*, or *She's far from well*.

See also **good/well**.

Wesley. John Wesley (1703-1791) was the founder of the Methodist Church, and many institutions in Australia are named after him. The word is pronounced *wezley*, not *wessly*.

West Australia/Western Australia. The name of the State is *Western Australia*. The people are *West Australians* and the adjective is *West Australian*.

wet/dry. The political use of *wet*, in the sense of *he was one of the wets in Cabinet*, occurred in the United States as early as 1931. Today it is usually applied to the more liberal, leftish and non-ideological members of a conservative party or government. Writing in 1983 of British politics, the Melbourne *Age* defined the *wets* as "expansionist, protectionist and welfare-orientated," and the opposing *dries* as standing for "small government, economic rationality and individual responsibility."

The word surfaced in British politics around 1980 and was quickly adopted in Australia, especially in discussions of the federal Parliamentary Liberal Party. *Wets* and *dries* in this sense may be spelt with or without capital letters.

we/us.

> The cockroach population at my house has been wiped out; the same home in Balmain . . . where nocturnal creatures rampaged and terrorised we poor, helpless inhabitants.

Thus Carmel McCauley in the *Australian*, 22 April 1986.

The cockroaches did not terrorise *we* — they terrorised *us*. The subject of this clause is *creatures*, the object is (or should be) *us*. *We* is the subjective form of the personal pronoun, *us* the objective.

Would you say *He helped we*? No? Quite right! Then no more can you say *They terrorised we*.

wharf. The plural may be either *wharves* or *wharfs*.

what. Writers trying to poke fun at what they want to be seen as illiterate speech will often write the word *what* as *wot*.

The implication is that nice people will pronounce the *h* sound in the word.

If this were ever so, it is not so now. The *h* is silent in virtually all *wh* words. *wheat*, *whale*, *when*, *white* and so on.

To pronounce the *h* is not incorrect, nor may it yet be called an affectation. It is, however, in no way called for.

what is/what are. *What is needed here is/are three more bedrooms on the first floor.*

Which of the two forms *is/are* should be used in a case like this, where *What* is assumed to be singular and has a singular verb (*is*) following it, but where the next verb along the line relates to a plural noun (*rooms*)?

Sometimes the form of the sentence will dictate that in such a case the plural verb (*are*) has to be used, but unless this emerges naturally and without thinking about it the rule is that the singular verb attached to *What* wins in this contest.

The correct form is: *What is needed here is three more bedrooms on the first floor.*

whence. A somewhat affected way of saying *from where?* as in *Whence do you come?* Compare **whither**, meaning *to where.*

when Greek meets Greek. The correct quotation is: "When Greeks joined Greeks, then was the tug of war!" It is from Nathaniel Lee's seventeenth-century play "The Rival Queens."

whereabouts. The word *whereabouts* is always plural: *His whereabouts are unknown.*

wherefore art thou Romeo? Frequently misquoted. The correct form is
> O Romeo, Romeo! wherefore art thou Romeo?

There is no comma after *thou*, and the *wherefore* does not mean *where?* but *why?* — why does Romeo have to be a member of the enemy family?

whether. *I have no idea whether or not they will come.* Why *or not*? The word *whether* already conveys the sense of *or not.*

See also **if/whether.**

which. See **that/which/who/whose.**

whilst. American visitors comment that the use of the word *whilst* in the sense of *in spite of the fact of* (*Whilst this may happen, it won't affect us*) is a noticeable Australian habit. They would say *while.*

whinge makes *whinger, whingeing.*

whiskey/whisky. Irish and American *whiskey* but Scotch (not Scots or Scottish) *whisky.*

white elephant. The story is told of the King of Siam who would present a rare and precious white elephant to any courtier he wished to ruin. Strictly speaking, to be a white elephant your vacuum cleaner should not only be useless but also be ruinously expensive to run. Even better if it were given to you by a rich relation you dare not offend by throwing it out, and who makes a point of asking to see it on visits.

who. See **that/which/who/whose.**

whoever/who ever. Where the meaning is *any person who*, the word *whoever* appears as one word, as in.

Whoever comes along that pathway must be stopped.

(When *whoever* relates to the object of the sentence, it is not now considered desirable for it to become *whomever*.)

However, where the *ever* part of the word is simply used as a means of emphasising the *who* part of the word, in other words if *who* would do just as well by itself, *it should always remain separate*, as in.

Who ever has been sleeping in *my* bed?

whose. See **that/which/who/whose.**

who/whom. *Who? Whom?* was a famous statement by Lenin, needless to say in Russian, which reminds us of the way distinctions in language which many want to get rid of nevertheless add to its subtlety and power. Lenin meant *Who are those who oppress, and whom do the oppressors oppress?*

The word *whom* is under attack, and some popular newspapers try to avoid its use altogether. But it is still very much part of the language. *Who* is the *nominative* (or *subjective*) case, *whom* the *accusative* (or *objective*) case. Probably no pair of words in English is so misused, the one for the other.

And yet in theory the *who/whom* matter is a simple one. It depends simply and entirely on being able to distinguish what is the *subject* of a verb, and what is the *object* of that verb.

The *subject* of a verb is the *doer*, or *initiator*. The *object* is, as the word suggests, *the person or thing done to*.

She hit the man.

The subject is *she*, the verb *hit*, the object *man*.

Should we then ask *Who did she hit?* or *Whom did she hit?* The answer is *whom*, which in any case we have already identified as the object, but another and useful way of reaching the same conclusion is to use the *personal pronoun, he* or *him, she* or *her. She hit he* or *She hit him*? If the latter sounds correct, then it is the accusative we have for *him*, and the accusative (or objective case) we need in *whom*.

Try this with a more complicated sentence, such as this one from the London *Times*:

He was not the man whom the police think may be able to help them.

This is in fact wrong. *Whom* belongs to *the man, the man* is the subject of *may be*, and hence should take the subjective *who*. Another way of reaching this conclusion is by asking whether *the police think he may be able to help them*, or *the police think him may be able to help them*, is correct.

Whom, then, remains desirable in careful writing when used as a relative pronoun. Here is another example.

> The organiser of the event, whom they desired to interview, has disappeared.

They desired to interview he, or *they desired to interview him*? If *he*, then write *who*, if *him*, then write *whom* — which is correct.

Note also that *whom* is always necessary when it closely follows a preposition: *For whom the bell tolls; to whom did you speak?*

If all this sounds a bit complicated the reader may take heart from the fact that the greatest of English-language writers have used *who* where they should have used *whom*, and vice versa.

Comfort may also be taken from the fact that in some contexts, especially the start of questions, the use of *whom*, though formally correct, is now regarded as impossibly pedantic: *Who were you with last night?* is to be preferred to *Whom were you with last night?* for instance.

whither means *to where?* as we remember fom *Goosey, Goosey Gander, whither do you wander?* Compare **whence**, meaning *from where*.

will/shall. See **shall/will.**

-wise. For *-wise* as an ending, as in *employmentwise*, see **(the) way of the wise.**

within is a word with several meanings, but the one concerned with time means *before a stated period has elapsed*, as in *Within three weeks of the accident he was dead.*

The word *after* is not required with *within. Within three years after the end of the war* is saying the same thing twice. So, for *after* read *of: within three years of the end of the war.*

wont. The word *wont*, as in the somewhat arch sentence *I was wont to lie in the sun*, is pronounced to rhyme with *don't*, not with *want.*

working class.

> The working class can kiss my arse —
> I've got the boss's job at last.

So runs a couplet much quoted in the Labor movement.

What *is* the working class, and what *is* the middle class? And, for that matter, what is, if anything, the upper class?

There is one major problem with the term *working class*, as well as with the associated word *proletariat* (which can mean either *the working class* or *the section of the working class which works in industry*). That problem is best summed up by the conjugation:

I am a gentleman [or lady]
You are middle-class
He is working-class.

In other words, you and I can recognise that someone is working-class, but he or she doesn't see it that way.

This problem with the term *working class* was illustrated by a national survey carried out by Macquarie University in 1979. To the question "To what class would you say you belong?" 56 per cent of those interviewed said "middle class," 26 per cent said "working class" and 4 per cent said "lower class". (One per cent labelled themselves "upper," 4 per cent said "none," 3 per cent denied the existence of class and "other" accounted for 2 per cent.)

When asked what social class their families belonged to in their youth, 36 per cent of respondents said "middle class" and 63 per cent said "working class." This process of pulling oneself up by one's own bootstraps, so to speak, is a form of what is termed *embourgeoisement*.

Those of a Marxist persuasion have a simple answer to the question of what a member of the working class is. Working-class people are wage earners, in other words those workers whose only significant possession is their labor, in other words those who are 'ripped off' by employers who expropriate part of the value of the work performed by those workers as 'surplus value'.

The *middle class* is then those employers and their associates who exploit the working class, sometimes directly, by employing them, sometimes indirectly, by living on the proceeds of rents or investments themselves the product of the exploitation of the working class.

There are problems with this simplicity, especially in advanced capitalist economies. One problem, as we have seen, is that people placed by Marxist theory into these categories frequently do not accept that placement. Another is where this leaves such categories of workers as employees of agencies owned, at least in theory, by the 'people': public servants, for a start. And where does it leave the self-employed including, say, the wealthy farmer who runs his property single-handed?

The real problem, of course, is that there is no real agreement among Australians as to the meaning of the term *social class* either as it applies to themselves or as it applies to others. Then there is a (Marxist) *economic* definition, and a different meaning when these words are used as a *sociological* device. Sociologists, as distinct from Marxist economists, may use the terms *working class* and *middle class* not to measure people's positions in terms of the *relations of production* (as the Marxists do) but either (a) to describe people's perceptions of where they place themselves in society, or (b) to serve as broad

429

descriptions of *social status* or *social attitudes* ("middle-class values", "a working-class suburb"). This kind of use presumes, very often, a meaning beyond the merely economic.

Middle class in these broader terms may then come to mean something as simple as *professional and business people who are self-employed or who draw salaries (paid fortnightly or monthly) rather than wages (paid weekly)*. In journalism the terms used are often *blue-collar* (working-class) and *white-collar* (middle-class). Different value systems are often adduced, such as private schools, wine, conservative political opinions (middle-class), State Schools, beer, Labor voters (working class). While such tags are often wrong, that such clusters can be formulated indicates that there is social differentiation.

Beset with the problems of the use of the terms *working class* and *middle class*, some English writers are now preferring the terms *under class* and *over class*, or *majority class* and *minority class*. This stems from a growing feeling, expressed by Ralf Dahrendorf and others, that attempts to maintain a simple relationship between economic and social class on the one hand, and the political expression of those interests on the other, are breaking down in the face of all sorts of *publicly* based movements to which the dynamic of social change is being transferred from governments seemingly powerless in the face of such transformations as mass unemployment. In other words, the state is no longer seen as the agent of social change. This is clearly linked with the view, put forward by the historian E. P. Thompson and others, that class is to be seen as *process* rather than as *structure*, that class can no longer be adequately defined in terms of a simple relationship to the means of production, that classes are constructed in everyday life, coalescing as a result of changing social processes rather than a formal employer–employee relationship.

To sum up, many would hold that time and events have overtaken the traditional terms and that new terms and new definitions are needed to cope with the problems of the post-industrial era.

Upper class is a term we need hardly bother about in Australia. It has no validity for the Marxists, and little historical or sociological justification in this country. In some countries it may relate to the pretensions of the aristocracy, or the extremely wealthy and favored. These need not be purely capitalist phenomena. Martin Boyd writes, in *Day of My Delight*, that "They may have thought I was a Communist, as I believed in aristocratic government and the Divine Right of Kings."

See also **bourgeois; (the) Establishment; indicator words**.

worth while/worthwhile.
1. The traditional rule has been that *worthwhile* is used before a noun, *worth while* otherwise: *The worthwhile task is worth while.*
2. Today, however, *worth while* is increasingly becoming *worthwhile*.

3. Retain *worth while* at least when it has *well* before it: *The cost was well worth while.*

4. Do not use *worth while* or *worthwhile* if a verb in *-ing* follows. *The climb was worth making,* not *The climb was worthwhile making.*

5. Avoid *worthwhile* as an insipid way of expressing approval: *a worthwhile visit to the zoo.*

wrack. See **rack/wrack.**

wrap/wrapped. See **rap/rapt and wrap/wrapped.**

writhe. The author Howard Jacobson writes of a Brisbane publisher "writhing his hands" while talking to him. *To writhe* means *to twist,* or *squirm,* or *to feel acutely embarrassed.* you cannot *writhe* something, for it is an intransitive verb, and cannot take an object.

writing on the wall. See **the writing on the wall.**

wry. Note *wryly.*

X

x. The letter *x* is pronounced as *z* when it comes at the beginning of a word: pronounce *xylophone* as *zylophone*, *xerox* (a trademark name) as *zerox*.

Pronounce *x* as *gz* when it comes before a vowel on which the stress or accent in the word lies. It will thus be pronounced this way in words beginning with *ex-* where the second syllable of the word is stressed: pronounce *exact* as (approximately) *egzact*, *exorbitant* as *egzorbitant*, *exult* as *egzult*. (Note that the initial *e* will hardly be sounded in these words.)

There are a few exceptions to this (*exacerbate* is pronounced *eksacerbate*) but not many.

Otherwise *x* is pronounced as *ks*.

Xmas. The use of *Xmas* as a synonym for *Christmas* stems from the Greek letter *x*, in English *chi*, pronounced *kye*. This letter represents the first letters of the name of Christ and is often used as an abbreviation for *Christ*.

The abbreviation *Xmas* is frowned upon, except in the most informal usage, and should never be used in printed material. Nor should it ever be pronounced *x-mas*, but always as *Christmas*.

x-ray. Prefer *x-ray* to *X-ray*.

Y

Yankee. Strictly speaking, and in the United States, the word *Yankee* refers to an inhabitant of the New England States: Maine, New Hampshire, Vermont, Massachusetts, Rhode Island and Connecticut.

More broadly, and again in the United States, it will be used to describe those who come from the same areas as the 'northerners' or Union supporters in the American Civil War.

To the rest of the world the word simply designates an American.

The word is thought to have come from the derisive nickname Jan Kees (John Cheese), applied by early Dutch settlers in New York to English colonists in Connecticut.

ye.
1. The word *ye*, when used to mean *the*, as in *Ye Olde Tea Shoppe*, is simply an old-fashioned way of writing *the*. The *y* represents the old letter called *thorn*, which is now replaced by *th*.

Ye, then, when it means *the*, always was and must be pronounced *the*. Unless, of course, you are trying to be funny.
2. The word *ye* when it means *you*, as in *Ye of little faith*, is pronounced as it is spelt. Note that it means *you* in the *plural*. The old-fashioned word for *you* in the singular is *thou*.

See also **thee/thine/thou**.

Yiddish. See **Jew/Jewess**.

you. For the history of this word, see **thee/thine/thou**.

yours. Not *your's*.

yourself. As with the word **myself**, *yourself* should not be used, at least in formal situations, as a simple substitute for *you*. And *your good self* should never be used at all.

Such a sentence as *We are hoping to see your wife and yourself* is certainly common and is not incorrect. It is just that here *yourself* rather than *you* is unnecessary and rather distancing.

Yourself is best reserved for use *reflexively* (*You enrolled yourselves?*), for *emphatic* use (*You will come yourself?*), and to distinguish the singular *you* from the plural *you*: *You went there yourself?/You went there yourselves?*

435

yours faithfully/yours sincerely. *Yours faithfully* should be used at the end of letters where you are writing to some anonymous, unknown person. You would use it, for instance, if you were writing to the Deputy Commissioner of Taxation in your State over some taxation query, knowing full well that the letter will never be seen by the Deputy Commissioner but will pass into the hands of some subordinate. The words will be used, then, when *there is no personal knowledge of the person you are writing to on a formal, business matter.*

There are traps, though. Because *Yours faithfully* is a common way of ending business letters this does not mean that it is the only way. It will do where you are writing to someone by their official designation and not by their personal name, but it will not do where you are writing business letters to people whom you know perfectly well, either by reputation or personally, whom you are addressing by their personal name and who you expect will attend personally to your letter.

The rule, then, is that, *where there is an assumption of a personal relationship between the writer and the recipient,* Yours sincerely *should be used, even in a business letter.*

Not to do so is ungracious, and could even be considered rude. When in doubt, use *Yours sincerely.*

Yours sincerely should always be used (unless you have a more affectionate statement in mind) when writing directly to individuals in private life, whether you know them or not and whether it is a business letter or not. Unless, of course, you actually *want* to be stand-offish or rude, when by all means use *Yours faithfully.*

Note that, with typewritten letters where *Yours sincerely* will be used, a good impression may be made by writing the *Dear So-and-so* and the *Yours sincerely,* as well as your signature, in your own handwriting.

Letters will normally open *Dear Ms Allen, Dear Dr Brown,* and so on, unless of course one is using a first name. In the literary world in particular it is not uncommon to write to an author unfamiliar to you as *Dear Joseph Conrad,* and this may sometimes be done where you are seeking for a middle way between excessive formality and excessive intimacy. The usage, however, is to be handled with caution. Offence has been taken at the presumption.

Letters to editors, intended for publication, traditionally start *Sir:* or *Madam:* and end *Yours, etc.*

youse. "Youse — give me the spluttering —" was an entertaining piece of the Australian vernacular which the author of this book heard from a Footscray boy on entering the army in 1942.

Youse, sometimes spelt *yous,* is a useful Australian colloquialism for the second person plural, in other words *you* when it means more than one person.

It is a word the English language needs. It is never used by gently-born people unless (a) they are trying to pretend they are really very working-class, or (b) they are trying to be humorous. Perhaps it will gently intrude itself into the 'accepted' language.

It has been suggested that the word is derived from the Irish *yez*, but that is as may be. It is a fairly obvious innovation in any case.

It has also been suggested that it may be used to mean *you* in the singular. Perhaps sometimes; but we think more often than not, when examples of this appear, it is because middle-class people with a bad ear are trying to imitate working-class speech.

yum cha. See **dim sim/yum cha**.

yuppy. This American import may be welcomed, for Australia has yuppies too, as Mr Neville Wran made clear when he attacked those who opposed the Darling Harbor monorail in Sydney as "a bunch of yuppies who jump on every environmental band-wagon going" (*Australian*, 2 June 1986).

Yuppies are people who (according to Robert Chesshyre, correspondent for the London *Observer* in Washington) "would feel spiritually deprived if they were not within jogging distance of a *brie*-selling delicatessen." He adds that President Reagan's "supply-side economic theory dignifies their relentless acquisitiveness as something more noble than simple greed."

John Silverlight discusses the whole matter in the London *Observer* of 5 May 1985. A yuppy (or yuppie) is a *young urban professional:* the *u* stands for *urban* and not, as often assumed, for *upwardly mobile*. For these latter there is another word, *yumpie.*

A *yummy* is a *young, upwardly mobile Marxist. Yuppification* is taking over from *gentrification* as a word descriptive of *the process of moving into working-class areas and turning them into desirable places of abode for yuppies, yumpies and yummies.*

Z

z. In Australian English the letter *z* is pronounced *zed*. To pronounce it *zee* is to pretend to be an American, for reasons which lie between the offenders and their Maker. See **offensive intruders**.

zebra may be pronounced either *zeebra* or *zebra* (with a short *e*).

zoology. Pronounce *zoe-OL-ogy*, not *zoo-OL-ogy*.